The Ragged Road to Abolition

The
RAGGED ROAD
TO ABOLITION

Slavery and Freedom
in New Jersey, 1775–1865

JAMES J. GIGANTINO II

PENN

UNIVERSITY OF PENNSYLVANIA PRESS

PHILADELPHIA

Published by
University of Pennsylvania Press
Philadelphia, Pennsylvania 19104-4112
www.upenn.edu/pennpress

Printed in the United States of America
on acid-free paper
1 3 5 7 9 10 8 6 4 2

Library of Congress Cataloging-in-Publication Data
Gigantino, James J., II, 1983–
    The ragged road to abolition : slavery and freedom in New Jersey, 1775–1865 /
James J. Gigantino II. — 1st ed.
        p.   cm.
    Includes bibliographical references and index.
    ISBN 978-0-8122-4649-0 (hardcover : alk. paper)
    1. Slavery—New Jersey—History.   2. Slavery—New Jersey—Legal status of
slaves in free states—History.   3. Anti-slavery movements—New Jersey—
History.   4. New Jersey—History—1775–1865.   I. Title.
E445.N54G54   2014
306.3'620974903—dc23   2014012275

To my parents, Lois and Jim Gigantino,
who have helped make me the man I am today

CONTENTS

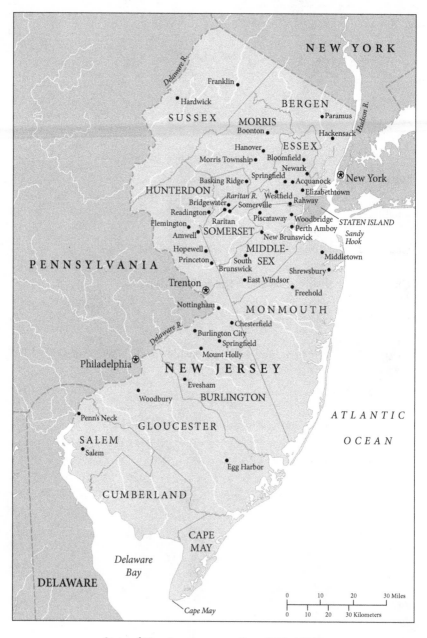

State of New Jersey, county lines 1753–1824.

Based on map created by R. Ryan Lash with information from Minnesota Population Center,
National Historical Geographic Information: Pre-release Version 0.1, 2004.

Introduction

This book is about the meaning of slavery and freedom in the United States. The setting, though unconventional, is central to American understandings of these two loaded terms. It follows the story of abolition in the North but reverses the usual narrative: slavery did not die after the Revolution, it sustained itself until the Civil War.

In 1789, Catherine was born a slave in Hunterdon County, New Jersey. Like thousands of other slaves in the state, she worked daily for her master, John Hagaman, on his hundred-acre farm in Amwell. Cate, as her master called her, forged relationships with other slaves and in 1811 at twenty-two bore her first child, a boy named Bob, though the boy's father remains unknown. Four years later, Catherine welcomed a daughter named Hannah. In 1840, Catherine moved with her master to neighboring Raritan without her children. Although the 1850 Census recorded her as a free woman, on February 16, 1856, Hagaman sold sixty-seven-year-old Catherine as a "slave for life" for twenty dollars to Charles Sutphin of Sommerville. After the sale, Hagaman, himself not much older than Catherine, moved with his son Dennis and daughter-in-law Mary to Joshua, Illinois, forty miles west of Peoria.[1]

Northern slaves like Catherine have usually been portrayed as peripheral to the overall development of the North and of the United States even though she experienced slavery decades after abolition's enactment and in the midst of national debates over abolition and slavery's westward expansion. Slavery in the North never attained the same position in the economy as it did in the Caribbean, the Chesapeake, or the Low Country since the North remained a society with slaves rather than a slave society. Indeed, early travel accounts describe New Jersey as both a place of few slaves and abundant opportunity. One visitor, Francisco de Miranda, the Spanish general, American ally, and future liberator of Venezuela, remarked during a 1783–1784 stay that he had not "encountered an individual who was ill clothed, hungry, sick, or idle." Out of all the places he visited in America, de Miranda had never "seen any other place in which the people appear happier and on more of an equality" than New Jersey. According to him, New Jersey was truly the "Garden of America."[2]

Just six years after de Miranda's visit, roughly 11,500 slaves lived in New Jersey. The "Garden of America" had more enslaved blacks than all of New England combined and almost the same slave to total population ratio as the much larger New York. Of course, the slave populations in most of the South easily outpaced New Jersey, though from 1790 to 1830 the state had more than twice as many slaves as Delaware. Additionally, some Jersey counties de Miranda likely visited heavily depended on slave labor. Bergen, for example, counted over 18 percent of its population as slaves at the time. Slaves likewise made up almost 15 percent of Somerset's population, while Middlesex and Monmouth had a slave population of just under 10 percent.[3]

While less than 1 percent of New England's population remained enslaved by 1790, about 6 percent of the population in New York and New Jersey were slaves. Historians have glossed over these differences to argue that, while abolition came later in these two states (1799 and 1804 respectively) because of the larger slave population, the end result was the same: abolition produced a free black North that contrasted sharply with an enslaved South. The idea that abolition crept inevitably across the North after the Revolution leaves out most of the story and indeed many of its best chapters. As one historian put it, "slavery died hard" in the North, but the way it died illuminates far more than the fact that it died at all.[4]

In this book I examine the long life of slavery in New Jersey and how whites and blacks adapted to the changes abolition brought. I see New Jersey and its gradual move toward abolition as part of a much wider web of interconnected relationships that crossed state and national borders as well as the Atlantic Ocean. By the end of the eighteenth century, freedom and slavery had been discussed from Boston to Barbados in the context of the Enlightenment and the American Revolution. New Jersey was part of this conversation by virtue of the trade, politics, and war conducted from its own ports, Burlington and Perth Amboy, and the nearby commercial hubs of New York and Philadelphia. New Jerseyans had a front row seat for imperial discussions over taxation, war, and abolition as the Delaware and Hudson Rivers became vehicles for the exchange of information, goods, culture, ideas, and people.[5]

New Jersey, therefore, is one of the best laboratories in which to test the meaning and influence of abolition in the United States because its prime location exposed it to issues and ideas of freedom from around the globe. The state was significant during the American Revolution, as British and Patriot armies engaged in more battles within its borders than in any other state, and its revolutionary experience made the call for liberty and freedom integral to the state's birth. Yet for all the patriotic fervor of the revolutionary generation, New Jersey delayed enactment of gradual abolition until 1804, later than any other northern state. This book explores why that delay occurred and how Jersey slaves experienced, or frequently did not experience, freedom after 1804.[6]

In the last twenty-five years, the memory of northern slavery has been revived as many northern states have created Amistad Commissions and mandated that the local history of slavery be taught in their classrooms. The 1991 discovery of the African Burial Ground in New York City likewise spurred debate over slavery's presence in the North.[7] Journalists shocked northern readers with stories of slaves living and working in the North, asserting that the North "helped create, strengthen, and prolong slavery in America."[8] Likewise, New Jersey's 2008 official legislative apology for its role in slavery forced residents to begin to integrate slavery into their local history and identity as northerners.[9] Of course, historians have understood that slavery existed in the North long before the discovery of the African Burial Ground. In the past forty years, they have explored the ways that slavery operated in almost every imaginable locale and time. Recently, the focus on transnational and Atlantic history has encouraged historians to reimagine how slavery in the United States compared to the experience of enslaved Indians in the Americas and the many forms of bondage operating in Africa, South America, the Caribbean, and Asia.[10]

Similarly, scholars in related fields have challenged the very definition of slavery. Sociologist Orlando Patterson's influential *Slavery and Social Death*, among other works, challenged the binary between slavery and freedom that formed the basis of American scholarship for decades. Patterson proposed that the foundational meaning of slavery differed based on individual societal definitions. Abraham Lincoln's clear dichotomy between slavery and freedom in his 1862 Emancipation Proclamation, that all slaves "shall be forever free," stood in sharp contrast to the experiences of slaves around the globe. Most slaves never experienced a clear division between freedom and slavery. Instead, as Patterson argues, each society had a very different understanding of what freedom meant and how that meaning shaped slavery. This nuanced understanding of slavery compelled historian Peter Kolchin to argue that people of African heritage across the Atlantic World experienced many different "slaveries" instead of one monolithic "slavery." Unpacking the meaning of slavery and freedom in this way has allowed historians to recast everything from indentured servitude in colonial Virginia to concubinage in twentieth-century Northern Nigeria as a form of slavery, mirroring chattel bondage in some ways but differing from it in others.[11]

This new scholarship has largely skirted the northern states, however, as the image of southern slavery has routinely colored understandings of what slavery *should* look like north of the Mason-Dixon Line. Northern slavery, especially in the Mid-Atlantic, was a flexible and varied institution that differed from the more regimented cash crop agriculture of the South. This flexibility has encouraged historians to argue that abolition was inevitable and easily accomplished in New Jersey. With the exception of a few notable works, the African American experience in the revolutionary and early national North continues to be one dominated not by the narrative of slavery but by the growth of freedom. Interposing New England for the North as a whole, using one state as fully representative of the region, or only teasing out minimal differences between the states has clouded understandings of the slow death of slavery and the incredibly convoluted legal and social relationships that it created for those who lived it and struggled to understand it on a daily basis.[12]

Indeed, the various ways that slavery ended in the North have confused historians for decades as few have really come to grips with the long-term impact of post-Revolutionary abolitionism. Slavery's end in Vermont used to be the easiest to understand since a constitutional amendment erased slavery before it really had a chance to develop. However, new work has shown that the 1777 constitution "did not end slavery or establish meaningful freedom for African Americans." Instead, abolition was "contested, contingent, complicated, and messy." Likewise, historians for decades used the Quok Walker decision in Massachusetts—in which the enslaved Walker sued for and won his freedom in 1781—to show how slavery quickly ended there by 1790, while New Hampshire's emancipation through brutal attrition over several decades continues to raise scholarly eyebrows. As with the Vermont case, new scholarship has called the Walker case into question, showing that contemporary accounts never claimed it had eliminated slavery—those developed only later in the nineteenth century. If Walker's legacy can be challenged, slavery's demise in the rest of the North certainly deserves greater scrutiny.[13]

From 1783 to 1804, Rhode Island, Connecticut, Pennsylvania, and New Jersey all agreed to the "gradual abolition of slavery," while New York approved "gradual manumission." In each case, these laws freed only the children born to slaves after a certain date and only after a period of service to their mother's master. Slaves in these states therefore never participated in a true *emancipation* or the decisive release from a system of control. Emancipation was the process by which an actual slave moved from a state of slavery to one of freedom. Instead, most of these states utilized the term *abolition*, meaning an end to slavery's existence by eliminating its perpetuation. It is no coincidence then that New Jersey's early abolitionists fully embraced the term *abolition* by supporting a program that mediated black freedom with white supervision, in this case by slaveholders. Throughout this volume, I therefore use the term abolitionist to describe the myriad types of men and women who pushed for a gradual end to slavery. Many of these New Jerseyans, like their contemporaries in New York and Pennsylvania, were routinely racist, believed that blacks could not live free without white tutelage, and, in some cases, still owned slaves or joined the American Colonization Society (ACS) to advance their own negrophobic agendas. However, they all fundamentally disagreed with the institution of slavery, though for different reasons, and hoped to see it end at some future point. Their practices and choices of wording were also motivated by realities on the ground—few slaveholders voluntarily wanted to free their slaves—thus, most Jersey abolitionists preferred that slavery's demise come through a prolonged ending rather than a quick transformation. Only in the late 1830s did a new breed of abolitionist come forward, one that believed in the immediate end to slavery and actively worked for emancipation both in their own organizations and with free blacks. They appropriated the term "abolitionist" for themselves and claimed the gradualists were actually not abolitionists. I believe both supported abolition, so I use the term to describe both groups. However, since almost all gradualists still operating in New Jersey after 1830 were colonizationists, references to abolitionists after that date refer exclusively to the second generation unless otherwise noted.[14]

The Ragged Road to Abolition examines this gradual end to slavery and highlights the integral role that black and white New Jerseyans played in defining slavery's place in their own state and within the larger nation in everything from the Revolution, to colonization, to the internal slave trade, to the sectional crisis. New Jersey was neither peripheral to slavery nor to

gradual abolition—it was central. As Daniel Richter has challenged historians to face east from the Indian perspective to better understand the colonial encounter, *The Ragged Road to Abolition* challenges scholars to stand
on the Mason-Dixon Line and look north to better understand the history
of abolition. By doing so, New Jersey appears far more dedicated to slavery
than if we look south. Reorienting our approach to slavery in this way helps
us to see that slaves like Catherine lived in a violent society with slaves.
Slaveholding remained at the heart of the white social imagination, determining how New Jerseyans interacted with African Americans until the
Civil War. Facing north also places New Jersey at the center of our understanding of what freedom meant in the nineteenth-century United States
and the larger Atlantic World. Slavery, as historian Edward Ayers argues,
"shaped everything it touched" and even in states like New Jersey, where
gradual abolition had begun to limit slavery's reach, slavery remained slavery to those who participated in it, worthy to be defended even into the
1840s and 1850s.[15]

This study examines the process of freedom in three parts. Chapters
1–3 look at the period 1770–1804 and ask why abolition became more
popular following the American Revolution. Instead of being motivated by
ideological strands of the Revolution as other historians have argued, gradual abolition began in 1804 for political purposes born in the partisan battle
between Federalists and Democratic Republicans. While it was rooted in
the revolutionary belief of individual freedom, the Revolution in New Jersey
did not heighten support for black liberty. On the contrary, the war reinforced slavery by highlighting the dangers white New Jerseyans would face
if they supported abolition. The economic destruction caused by the Revolution and fears of a black revolt in the aftermath of freedom calmed abolitionist calls. The two decades after the Revolution, therefore, saw the
growth of slavery in New Jersey, which helped keep pace with the world-
wide demand for New Jersey's foodstuffs, even as Pennsylvania, Massachusetts, Vermont, New Hampshire, Connecticut, and Rhode Island took steps
to eliminate the institution.[16]

Chapters 4–7 explore the early abolition period (1804–1830) in four
topical chapters and show how slavery became flexible after gradual abolition began. Instead of killing slavery, gradual abolition allowed it to survive
until the Civil War in myriad different forms, overturning the idea that
northern slavery's limited numbers sped its destruction. After all, at its core,
slavery was an economic institution, one that remained critical for many

Jersey whites. The abolition law provided for the freedom of children born to slaves after July 4, 1804, once they served a specified number of years (twenty-one or twenty-five) to their mother's master. These children, whom I call *slaves for a term*, were bought, sold, whipped, worked, and separated from their families just like slaves before them. Contemporary New Jersey sources remarked that these children were thought of and treated like slaves, though with the understanding that they would leave that status in the future. The presence of slaves for a term extended bondage in a different form to generations that came of age in the 1820s and 1830s so that in 1830 almost a quarter of the state's black population remained bound laborers.[17]

Of course, this extended servitude dramatically affected enslaved and free black life in New Jersey since each lived in a world where the line between slavery and freedom was thin. Thousands of Jersey slaves born before 1804 and therefore ineligible for gradual abolition negotiated intently for freedom; those who managed to break out of slavery argued for greater political and social rights within their newly formed community. This group failed to advance black rights primarily because of their limited numbers and a general apathy among whites for ensuring black freedom. Slaveholders likewise continually resisted abolition in order to profit from their bound laborers. Indeed, white New Jerseyans routinely sold their slaves and slaves for a term out of state to subvert gradual abolition and support slavery's overall national expansion. However, the most notorious slave trading ring, which operated in the late 1810s, significantly influenced how white New Jerseyans saw their state's slavery in a national perspective. With the crisis over the extension of slavery into Missouri coming on the heels of public concern over this slave trading ring, white New Jerseyans began to inculcate a proto-free soil ideology that opposed slavery's westward expansion into Missouri but supported its continuation in the South and New Jersey. This ideology, though antislavery, was not abolitionist and did little to alter the perceived link between the newly freed and the enslaved, which whites used to prevent their inclusion into the body politic. This was most readily apparent in the 1807 abrogation of voting rights for free black men and women, which began a systematic process of stripping legal and political rights from former slaves. The colonization movement sustained this link between "slavery" and "black" in law and custom. This perpetual tie between slavery and race limited opportunities for black independence and forced black families to live not as fully free people but in multiple gradations of freedom: some could be free, some slave, and some slave for a term. It created a hodgepodge of legal, economic, and social relationships that confused even the state's most learned jurists. These complex and frequently confusing relationships complicated how both whites and blacks functioned within, and sometimes outside, the boundaries of slavery. A stroke of a pen did not make anyone "forever free" but instead drew a blurry line of demarcation between slavery and freedom, one that whites and blacks struggled to constantly define and redefine.[18]

Chapters 8 and 9 examine the later abolition period (1830–1860) and place familiar nineteenth-century issues—race riots, abolitionism, fugitive slaves, and sectional antagonism—in the context of slavery's slow death. The 1830s represented a major shift in the freedom process and black life in New Jersey as that decade was a transitional one in which free blacks began to stay in New Jersey in larger numbers. Their numbers grew due to simple reproduction by those freed earlier and were joined by the first generation of slaves for a term who had just gained freedom. This demographic shift allowed blacks to more readily establish independent households, move out of white-controlled churches and schools, and develop their own institutions designed to fight persistent racism and its link to slavery. This decoupling of race and slavery also occurred in law when, in 1836, the New Jersey Supreme Court ruled that blacks were no longer prima facie slaves; freedom became the default legal category for African Americans. Of course, this development of an identity outside of slavery initiated reprisals from whites as they also felt, for the first time, threatened by the economic and social changes underway. Race riots rocked New Jersey in the 1830s and 1840s, when whites feared economic competition, racial amalgamation, and an increasingly smaller role for themselves in politics and society.[19]

The Ragged Road to Abolition closes by shifting focus back to the nation at large and examining how the uptick in fugitive slaves and the rise of the immediate abolition movement in the 1830s propelled New Jersey's slave system back into the spotlight. It shows how slavery's constant presence in New Jersey shaped the role, status, and history of African Americans in a way that historians have as yet failed to grasp. Slavery's survival in New Jersey confronted state, regional, and national politicians as the nation moved toward the Civil War since the state's border position allowed southern fugitive slaves to encounter a still functioning slave system. The constant interaction with fugitive slaves forced white and black New Jersey-ans to question how the state's legal and judicial system would deal with both Jersey-born slaves and southern fugitives. New Jerseyans never left slavery behind either in practice or in how it influenced their ideological identity. Their refusal to pass stronger personal liberty laws after the Supreme Court's 1842 *Prigg* decision, which allowed states to restrict their own courts from hearing federal fugitive slave cases, abolition's weak presence in the state, and the state legislature's wholesale rejection of black political rights were all influenced by New Jersey's past and continuing support of slavery. Even by 1846, when the state abolished the legal term "slave" and transformed its remaining slaves into "apprentices for life," yet another form of slavery, white actors consistently supported a gradual approach to abolition and resisted slavery's immediate end. Even in a society with slaves where gradual abolition was well underway, slavery proved resilient.

This consistent engagement with and appreciation of the state's past and current slave system stands in stark contrast to portrayals of New Englanders at the same moment in time. New England's prominent role in the abolition movement allowed abolitionists there to disown slavery from their own history and reinterpret it as a minor institution that resembled apprenticeship far more than chattel bondage. They used this New England identity to demarcate the entire North and define the two regions as in mortal combat over slavery.[20] New Jersey's embrace of slavery, not its disownment, has significant ramifications for historical understandings of the coming of the Civil War by showing how antebellum northern whites were influenced by their state's past and continuing relationship with slavery. Although white New Jerseyans repeatedly opposed slavery's expansion in the West, slavery's continuation forced a ready acknowledgement of the state's role in ensuring the return of fugitive slaves and in not interfering with the institution in the South. Indeed, Jersey politicians constantly reminded their northern and southern counterparts of their experience with slavery as they dealt with sectional tensions. Slavery's persistence therefore not only shatters the rather simplistic dichotomy between a slave South battling a free North but shows how those New Jerseyans who lived in a slave state used their slaveholding experience to create peace and order on the southern border over fugitive slaves, embraced a general anti-abolitionism and support for interstate comity to get that peace, and respected southern economic and social interests in keeping slavery more than their radical northern neighbors who opposed fugitive recoveries and courted southern distrust.

Several excellent works on slavery's demise in the North laid the groundwork for my understanding of slavery's place in nineteenth-century New Jersey. Gary Nash and Jean Soderlund's pioneering work on slavery's slow death in Pennsylvania showed that, like in New Jersey, masters "were more notable for shrewd calculations of how to extricate themselves at little cost from an involvement in owning fellow human beings than for a rise in their moral sensibilities."[21] Likewise, Shane White's expertly crafted *Somewhat More Independent,* which focuses on New York City, demonstrated slavery's growth there after the Revolution in the same way it grew in New Jersey. Graham Hodges's work is perhaps one that most emphasizes the role of African Americans in their own abolition and the growth of the free black community, which did much to move African Americans to center stage and advance northern slavery studies from its ideological and political foundation established by Arthur Zilversmit in the late 1960s.[22] Yet this resurrection of African American agency frequently directed the focus to a fully free black community and focused primarily on institutional life, not to the reality that gradual abolition created multiple gradations of freedom for blacks to inhabit daily in their work, family, religious, and social lives. Instead, my work here aligns more closely with Joanne Pope Melish's and shows how the gradual abolition process actually affected enslaved as well as free black and white lives on the ground.[23]

Focusing on the expansive reach of slavery does not mean an abandonment of African American agency. On the contrary, the enslaved remained key actors especially in the nineteenth century when they navigated a difficult terrain where slaves, slaves for a term, and free blacks all lived in overlapping layers of freedom. Jersey's enslaved did, as historian Ira Berlin has shown again and again, negotiate for better lives despite the fact that the institution's slow death "handicap[ed] the efforts of black people to secure households of their own" and "encouraged the notion that black free people were no more than slaves without masters." In this way, Berlin is correct in arguing that "slavery hardly behaved like a moribund institution" after gradual abolition began, remaining important in many areas of the North, most notably New Jersey. I build on Berlin's insights as I unpack the slow death of slavery to show how it shaped the state, nation, and New Jersey's nineteenth-century black communities.[24]

However, Jersey blacks did not only, as Berlin argues, "owe their liberty to the changes unleashed during the Age of Revolution," but instead to a much longer and convoluted process of freedom. It is within that longer freedom process that African American agency becomes somewhat limited. Jersey blacks faced insurmountable odds in the early nineteenth century, perhaps greater than anywhere else in the North. They had no white allies as the state abolition society quickly disbanded after gradual abolition began, lived under a legal system that was firmly controlled by slaveholders or those supportive of their interests, and saw most free blacks who could have assisted them leave for the larger black communities in New York or Philadelphia. For those reasons, the negotiations and interactions between the enslaved and white masters that resulted in freedom were fewer than in other northern locales. From the available sources, I show the integral role of Jersey blacks in gradual abolition, but far too often could not capture the extent of these negotiations, largely due to the rarity of sources recording Jersey slaves, especially after 1840.[25]

This book then is about a tug of war with a wide variety of protagonist voices. It engages the ideology of the Revolution, religious commitments to abolition, economic interests of slaveholders, familial bonds and community networks of slaves, the law's role in creating and sustaining slavery, and, most important, how whites and blacks dealt with the transition from slavery to freedom. It delves into a number of different historiographical arguments and pieces together how New Jerseyans and other northerners struggled with defining slavery's end. Above all, it shows that Catherine's 1856 sale was not a historical anachronism. Instead, her sale reflected the experience of slaves and slaves for a term in antebellum New Jersey. The "Garden of America" was a place of inequality and unfreedom, worked by slaves such as Catherine just like so many other gardens in the United States.

*   *   *

A study of slavery's slow demise in the nineteenth century needs first to be grounded in how the institution became an integral part of New Jersey society, since slavery's colonial beginnings had massive ramifications for how the institution sustained itself later on. Slavery's beginning in New Jersey cannot be divorced from its interaction with the Atlantic World and its relationship with neighboring New York. In 1626, the first African slaves arrived in New Netherland to work for the Dutch West India Company and soon became incredibly important since the new colony suffered chronic labor shortages as few white immigrants chose to settle there. This first generation of slaves quickly became integrated into society as the astute creoles understood that slavery was a form of clientage that they could use to their advantage. The paltry numbers of Europeans likewise gave slaves power as their labor became increasingly needed by the company in its bid to stabilize itself against Indian, Spanish, English, and Swedish threats. By 1630, Dutch and Walloon settlers had established themselves on the west bank of the Hudson River in present-day Bergen County and brought the first enslaved Africans to what would become New Jersey. However, continued Indian conflicts restricted how far the Dutch moved across the river and caused most Dutch settlements to be short-lived, such as Pavonia, which was destroyed by Indians, or founded in the last years of Dutch rule, as was Bergen after Indian threats had dissipated.[26]

Like in other colonies, New Jersey's charter generation lived in a society that had neither firmly delineated laws on slavery nor used race to determine enslaved status. Instead, freedom in New Netherland was flexible, with small free black neighborhoods growing in the 1630s, formed by blacks who managed to negotiate with the company or their individual masters for freedom. Some used religion to claim freedom since the Dutch Reformed Church mandated slave baptism and encouraged masters to establish pathways to freedom for their slaves. Others used the daily interactions they had working with whites to negotiate with masters to let them purchase or otherwise secure freedom. Yet, black labor remained at the core of New Netherland's labor force and the colony's growth did much to transform slavery into the main tool of agricultural expansion, especially in northeast New Jersey.[27]

Slaves in New Netherland were jacks-of-all-trades, feeding not only the agricultural base of the colony but performing artisan trades, building colonial infrastructure, and completing hundreds of other tasks to establish and maintain the colony. By 1664, one out of every eight white New Netherland residents owned slaves. At the same time, the enslaved also intertwined their creole and African roots with Dutch culture. Pinkster, a celebration of Pentecost, first was celebrated in 1628 and saw African music and dance come alive in the New World. This African influence was sustained by new slaves imported directly from Africa and from Spanish and Dutch Caribbean traders.[28]

After the Dutch surrender at New Amsterdam in 1664, Charles II's brother James, duke of York, gained title to the region and quickly granted New Jersey to two proprietors, George Carteret and John, Lord Berkeley. Unbeknownst to them, New York's military governor, Colonel Richard Nicolls, transferred large tracts of land to New England Puritans, Quakers, and Baptists who eagerly moved into the eastern part of New Jersey and established Elizabethtown, Newark, Piscataway, Woodbridge, Middletown, and Shrewsbury between 1664 and 1666. These overlapping land grants caused havoc in determining land ownership in early New Jersey and eventually led to a series of land riots and proprietary revolts in the seventeenth and eighteenth centuries. The proprietary period's conflicts also diminished the profits that Carteret and Berkeley reaped from New Jersey. After settlers in East Jersey established an independent assembly, ejected the proprietary governor, Carteret's cousin, and allied with the Dutch in the Second Anglo-Dutch War, the costs and headaches of colonial administration proved too much for the now bankrupt Berkeley. In 1674, he sold his share in the colony to a group of Quaker investors, including William Penn, who formed the West Society of Proprietors and established a separate colony called West Jersey. Carteret, left with East Jersey, sold to Quaker investors, who would eventually sell to Scottish businessmen, in 1682.[29]

Even though East and West Jersey operated as separate proprietary colonies for only twenty-eight years (1674–1702), the division had massive repercussions for the growth and eventual decline of slavery in New Jersey. West Jersey quickly became linked to Quaker dominated Pennsylvania and colonists swarmed into the region, picking up where the failed New Sweden colony had left off. Likewise, as the Caribbean embraced sugar, planters pushed out because of the sugar boom from Barbados in the 1660s and 1670s sought new homes in both Carolina and East Jersey. Barbadian planters, turned off by the harsher climate and disease around Charleston, saw New Jersey as a fertile and relatively untapped land ripe for settlement. They and their slaves came in droves to both East Jersey and New York so that by 1700 Barbadian immigrants owned the largest concentrations of slaves. They used them to work large estates granted by the proprietors since each settler received 150 acres and an additional 150 acres for each male slave and 75 for each female slave. These Barbadians quickly established towns such as New Barbados in northeastern New Jersey and made East Jersey a colony strongly attached to a slavery informed by years in the Caribbean. This experience also influenced non-Barbadians and led East

Jersey to quickly outlaw the harboring of fugitive slaves, trading with slaves, and prohibiting slaves from carrying guns. This East Jersey identity sharply contrasted to the Quaker dominated West. While colonial-era Quakers certainly utilized and relied on slave labor just as their East Jersey neighbors did, they never fully embraced it to the extent of their Caribbean neighbors. More important, though, the establishment of a separate Quaker colony in West Jersey ensured that almost all Jersey Friends gravitated there instead of to East Jersey for the remainder of the colonial period. Therefore, when the Society of Friends banned slaveholding immediately before the American Revolution, the colony and later state became bifurcated again, this time not by a political boundary but by slavery. West Jersey's Quaker majority freed its slaves and led that area to become mostly free by 1790, while a non-Quaker influenced East Jersey retained its slaves far longer.[30]

New Jersey's slaves during the proprietary period provided white settlers (Dutch, Puritan, Quaker, or Barbadian) with a labor supply to fulfill the growing demand for foodstuffs from New York, Philadelphia, and the Caribbean. Although no single crop came to dominate Jersey agriculture, the rotation of crops (grains, fruits, vegetables, and grasses) ensured that slaves could be used throughout the year on various agricultural projects. Additionally, if demand for slaves' services decreased, masters hired them out to artisans, shipbuilders, and tradesmen to produce additional revenue streams. Jersey slaves therefore continued to work alongside whites and became incredibly important to both the rural and urban economies in the Mid-Atlantic. Most slaveholders, however, owned few slaves—normally no more than two. Thus, those slaves' freedom of movement became incredibly important in sustaining their identity and community connections.[31]

The relative flexibility of the colony's charter generation began to wane in the early eighteenth century as the slave population grew and Barbadian planters from East Jersey increasingly influenced the colonial legal system. In 1702, East and West Jersey reunited as a Royal Colony and in 1704 passed its first omnibus slave code using the 1694 and 1695 East Jersey statutes as a model. This law began the transition from charter to plantation generation in New Jersey as it included provisions likely influenced by the Barbadians who had prompted similar legislation in South Carolina. The 1704 law mandated castration for slaves who fornicated with or raped a white woman or child, though this was later disallowed by the Privy Council in London. It also imposed restrictions against harboring fugitives, prohibited slaves and free blacks from owning property, disallowed baptism as grounds for freedom, and instituted harsher punishments for slaves convicted of theft. Since Pennsylvania passed a similar law in 1700 and New York in 1702, Mid-Atlantic whites likely had a "common awareness" that slavery was becoming an increasingly important part of their society and needed these restrictions to ensure order. In 1712, New Yorkers and New Jerseyans saw the true dangers that their reliance on slavery could cause when a slave revolt rocked New York City on the night of April 1. Eight whites were killed and twelve more wounded, likely a reaction by slaves to the new restrictions on black liberties.[32]

The firmer restrictions of the plantation generation took hold after the 1712 conspiracy with the passage of a new slave code in 1713–1714, which became the core of New Jersey's slave system and responded to the fears of many whites who saw the destructiveness of the revolt in New York. The new law reiterated the prohibition against free blacks owning property and, since legislators felt "free Negroes are an Idle Sloathful People and prove very often a charge to the Place where they are," owners who wanted to free their slaves had to pay a two hundred-pound bond to the colonial government and twenty pounds per year to each former slave. This requirement essentially ended manumissions, already depressed after 1664, and stripped slaves of almost any chance at becoming free in colonial New Jersey. The disappearance of black access to freedom had much to do with the Barbadians as their Caribbean experience influenced the legislative debate. Their most visible impact came in the form of a special court of justice for slaves accused of capital crimes, which replicated South Carolina's slave court that had been built to mirror Barbados'. The strong Barbadian lobby therefore not only wanted slavery but hoped to ground New Jersey firmly in an Atlantic system that relied on restricting black freedoms for white economic gain.[33]

The further tightening of legal and social restrictions against blacks came at the same time slavery became the "single most important source of labor in the North's most fertile agricultural areas." By the early 1720s, the shift to the plantation generation was complete as slaveholders realized that slaves "were no longer an adjunct to an agricultural economy" but central players. Between 1718 and 1738, the slave population of East Jersey doubled (now at 3,071) and by 1750 male slaves were more numerous than landless white males in most of the region. Hunterdon County, in West Jersey, likewise saw a massive increase in its slave population as it provided most of the wheat, barley, and corn to the Philadelphia market. Slaves therefore became key partners in ensuring that the North's breadbasket fed both Caribbean and northern markets, yet remained jacks-of-all-trades on small slaveholdings. Neither a gang nor a task system developed. However, the reliance on slave labor changed how slaves came to New Jersey. Originally purchased in small numbers on consignment or traded internally from other mainland colonies or, more likely, from the Caribbean, increased demand dictated that slaves needed to come directly from Africa. By mid-century, 70 percent of slaves arrived from Africa, a reversal from the first half of the century when only 30 percent did so. These new slaves became integral to the continued development of the Anglo-Atlantic World and, though they could be found disproportionally in agriculture, slaves living in New Jersey's cities worked in artisan shops, as sailors, or as ship-builders just as in New York or Philadelphia.[34]

As legislators in the plantation generation increasingly stripped rights away from enslaved and free blacks and racialized slavery became firmly set into New Jersey society, the enslaved in the plantation generation successfully negotiated for some freedoms within the institution. Just as in the charter generation, slaves in the 1730s and 1740s valued their freedom of movement since it was essential in establishing communities among small slaveholdings strewn across rural New Jersey. Slaves routinely congregated with other blacks in the woods or more likely in local taverns that flouted the prohibition against providing liquor to slaves to secure a new customer base. These taverns, however, bred not only community but also dissention and revolt. Two slave revolts rocked New Jersey in the first half of the eighteenth century and tested white resolve in keeping the institution. The first, in 1734, involved a plot to set fire to white homes in Somerset County, kill their masters, rape their wives, and escape to either Indian or French territory. Although the plot was discovered before its execution due to a slave's liquor lubricated lips, the apprehension of thirty conspirators fueled fears that revolt was a real danger. Likewise, the 1741 New York Conspiracy, also hatched in a tavern, was even more frightening as it involved an alliance between whites, most notably tavern keeper John Hughson, and the enslaved. The burning of New York's Fort George and its auxiliary fires in both New Jersey and Long Island reinforced the dangers of slave revolt. New Jersey convicted and burned several slaves at the stake in Hackensack and Newark for arsons thought to be part of the conspiracy.[35]

In response to the conspiracy, slaveholders cracked down on slave movement and the colonial legislature almost passed a duty on slaves imported from the Caribbean to dissuade bringing more blacks into New Jersey who were thought to be prone to rebellion. By 1751 the legislature prohibited slaves from meeting in groups larger than five but took no decisive steps to halt the colony's reliance on slavery. The institution had simply become too important to eliminate as it had become the primary labor supply across rural New Jersey. It had also begun to infiltrate other areas of the economy, including mining operations in Bergen County. The Schuyler mine, for instance, employed over two hundred slaves. With a colonial slave population of over 7 percent colony wide, the ratio was between 12 and 15 percent in some areas of East Jersey. On the eve of the American Revolution, despite fears of rebellion and an increasing number of fugitive slaves fighting against the system, New Jersey stood as a society with slaves that had fully embraced the institution and integrated it into their colony's economy and society.[36]

CHAPTER ONE

Debating Abolition in an Age of Revolution

In 1688, Germantown, Pennsylvania, Quakers released an antislavery petition that became the first in a series of discussions among Mid-Atlantic
Quakers on the morality of owning slaves. For the next hundred years, the
Philadelphia Yearly Meeting, with which most New Jersey Friends associated, debated the paradox of enslaving Africans while believing that all individuals were spiritually equal. The tension created by the paradox grew over
time and transformed Philadelphia and Western New Jersey into hotbeds
of abolitionist thought, protest, and activism that impacted how both non-
Quaker whites and African Americans debated abolition as slavery became
increasingly important in the late colonial period.[1]

The role of Quakerism in the growth of the eighteenth-century abolition movement is critical to the eventual enactment of gradual abolition
laws across the North. Quakers, although in most cases far from racial
egalitarians, became the first organized group to consistently advocate
against slavery. They successfully orchestrated slavery's end among their
own members and eventually moved their advocacy to a wider audience.
Quaker politicians and those elected from constituencies dominated by
Friends argued for statewide abolition while Quaker-authored pamphlets,
petitions, and newspaper articles circulated to members and nonmembers
alike. The debate over slaveholding within the Society of Friends therefore
influenced the statewide debate over slavery and fused together abolitionist
rhetoric, Patriot discussions of Britain's tyrannical enslavement of the colonies, and slaves' own calls for freedom. Abolitionists and slaves took advantage of the Patriots' similar rhetorical use of "freedom" and "slavery" to
make strong parallels between the imperial struggle over freedom from
Great Britain and the hypocrisy of continued African enslavement. The

Revolution therefore made the idea of freedom a right that transcended race and encompassed transatlantic affairs. This forced white New Jerseyans to debate slavery openly and decide if their fight for freedom from Great Britain should be seen as part of a wider freedom struggle.

As the eighteenth-century Quaker abolition movement developed, Jersey Quakers stimulated a debate on the morality of slavery that reached a far greater audience than that of their local meetings. These debates permeated revolutionary society and became part of much larger discussions about the role of freedom in the new United States. Quaker considerations of morality intertwined with the revolutionary drama unfolding around New Jerseyans and convinced some non-Quakers to join the debate about the future of slavery in New Jersey. Abolitionist ideology, its relationship to American freedom, and the ethical and moral implications of holding slaves during a war for freedom soon emanated regularly from multiple denominations' pulpits, print sources, and slaves' mouths.

However, despite New Jersey being a hotbed of early abolitionism, abolition remained a highly contentious and disputed proposition since slavery had been so deeply intertwined into colonial society. Despite debates over revolutionary freedom and its application to slaves, retorts of racial amalgamation, race war, racial inferiority, and potential economic losses limited that freedom's impact. In the heated ideological battle over slavery, Quakers, abolitionists, and slaves powerfully connected the Revolution and abolitionism to convince many New Jerseyans of abolition's importance, but this formidable weapon did not triumph over slaveholder and anti-abolitionist fear mongering and their systematic defense of the right to own slaves. The dangers of a radical restructuring of the state's racial order failed to win many converts to the abolitionist cause, especially in East Jersey where slavery had entrenched itself far more deeply. The failure of abolitionism to take hold allowed white New Jerseyans to strengthen the institution of slavery in the midst of the war and during its aftermath.

*　　*　　*

Although not the first Quaker abolitionist, Burlington County native John Woolman became one of the society's most ardent eighteenth-century pro-abolition voices. Woolman, an itinerant Quaker preacher, traveled from the Carolinas to New England to Europe advocating the freedom of both African slaves and Indians. Woolman went farther than Quaker leaders William

Edmundson and George Fox who expressed concern over the spiritual welfare of those Friends who owned slaves. Edmundson and Fox challenged
Quaker slaveholders in the Caribbean in the 1650s and 1660s to bring religion to their slaves and moderate their treatment. However, as Edmundson
and Fox did not attack the institution directly, they failed to change the
ownership patterns of any society members, although their actions influenced Woolman years later to take their ideas to the next level.[2]

After the 1688 Germantown Petition, Quakers in the Philadelphia area
began to question the morality of slavery. By 1713, the Chester, Pennsylvania, Monthly Meeting had called for the emancipation of slaves and in 1715
the Yearly Meeting requested that Friends treat their chattel with Christian
compassion.[3] With these debates as a backdrop, Woolman, while living
in Mount Holly, New Jersey, in 1742, "had a life-transforming attack of
conscience" when he authored a bill of sale for a black woman for his
employer. Woolman wrote extensively in his journal that "writing an
instrument of slavery for one of my fellow creatures felt uneasy," which
made him conclude "slavekeeping to be a practice inconsistent with the
Christian religion."[4] This inconsistency impelled him to embark on what
became his life's work: to convince Quakers to abandon slavery. Woolman,
unlike other Friends who had endorsed slavery as long as owners treated
slaves well, built his understanding of slavery from New Testament passages
that echoed the same Enlightenment ideals that would be utilized in the
future by Thomas Jefferson and Thomas Paine. Woolman argued that even
though Old Testament law accepted slavery, Friends must completely reinterpret their view of charity and morality to align with the Golden Rule.[5]

In 1754, Woolman, along with Anthony Benezet, authored an official
warning to Friends about slavery that reversed the Yearly Meeting's hesitant
stance on attacking slavery and "ushered in a new phase in the Quaker
fight against slavery." It had an "explosive impact" on Quakers in Greater
Philadelphia, and along with Woolman's own writings, declared slavery sinful and encouraged the society to fundamentally reform. Woolman argued
that the slave trade represented the root of slavery's evil since it separated
families and eliminated the ability of Africans to have a relationship with
God. He claimed that the Golden Rule alone dictated that slavery existed
in direct contradiction to Christianity.[6] The Philadelphia Yearly Meeting
took up Woolman's focus on the Golden Rule when it questioned its application to slavery that same year. The meeting asked "do we act consistent
with this noble principle" or have Quakers acted "so inconsistent with

ourselves to purchase such who are prisoners of war and thereby encourage this unchristian practice?" Answering in the negative, the meeting lamented the "dreadful scenes of murder and cruelty those barbarous ravages must occasion in these unhappy people's country" yet many Friends continued to support slavery since it had become so vital to the rural economy.[7]

Woolman's interaction with other major antislavery activists, including Anthony Benezet and Benjamin Franklin, produced a hotbed of Quaker abolitionist activity in 1750s Philadelphia. Benezet, on his own, went farther than Woolman in his belief in black equality, advocating that slaves lived as equals in the sight of God. Woolman and Benezet worked together to advance abolitionism within the Philadelphia meeting. Throughout the 1760s they discussed education reform for blacks, the lynchpin in Benezet's agenda, and created a transatlantic network of abolitionism that traded ideas, beliefs, and empirical evidence to assist abolitionists on both sides of the Atlantic.[8]

Woolman's death in 1772 did not silence the debate within the Philadelphia Yearly Meeting on slavery. Benezet, especially after his 1771 publication of *Some Historical Observations of Guinea*, which firmly advocated that Africans were equal to whites, forcefully supported a pro-abolition agenda in Philadelphia.[9] Along with Benezet, other Jersey Quaker abolitionists joined the discussion that Woolman had begun. In 1773, William Dillwyn of Burlington published a tract that he directed at both Quakers and political powerbrokers in the legislature. Dillwyn rightfully observed that although "many in these northern provinces" might admit the "injustice of the slave trade in general," they "may yet be unwilling to view it as a matter sufficiently important" for legislation.[10] Dillwyn argued that the issue of abolition must be addressed by making a comparison to the distressed situation between the American colonies and Great Britain, asking how can the colonies, "when so loudly complaining of (England's) attacks on our political liberty," tolerate "this violent invasion of natural liberty, subjecting the Africans . . . to the most abject state of perpetual personal slavery?"[11]

Other Jersey Quaker abolitionists picked up on the same linkage between the burgeoning abolition movement and the brewing discontent over British imperial policies and made that link a central focus of the revolutionary period. In 1774, Burlington Quaker Samuel Allinson wrote to Patrick Henry and claimed that the call for abolition had never been louder "than at a time when many or all the inhabitants of North America are groaning under unconstitutional impositions destructive of their liberty." Allinson further pondered if God would forgive Americans for their failure to treat African Americans humanely. Granville Sharp, one of Britain's leading antislavery advocates with whom Woolman and Benezet had corresponded, echoed Allinson's words when in 1774 he told Allinson that if the colonists "hope(d) to maintain their own natural rights and to have justice on their side . . . they ought not to deny the same rights to others by persisting in the practice of the most abominable and unchristian oppression."[12]

Faced with increasing pressure from multiple angles, Quaker meetings began to prohibit their members from owning slaves in 1774. By 1776, the Philadelphia Yearly Meeting banned members from slaveholding and placed pressure on those recalcitrant Quakers who refused to abandon it.[13] At this point, Quaker support for abolitionism was overwhelming compared to the tepid support that Woolman and Benezet first received when they authored the 1754 Epistle. The Yearly Meetings' instructions to abolish slavery set to work a manumission process that freed hundreds of Quaker-owned slaves. As the state had not yet developed a uniform system to record manumissions, Quaker meetings took responsibility for mediating slave freedom. In the Burlington Monthly Meeting, for example, Samuel Allinson dutifully kept a register of the forty-five manumissions completed by members from 1776 to 1781. This support paid dividends when in 1776 the Egg Harbor Monthly Meeting reported that it had freed all of its slaves, save one, and, in 1778, the Burlington Monthly Meeting claimed all but a few slaves under age twenty-one had been freed.[14]

Despite the large number of manumissions administered by Quaker Meetings, many within the society were reticent to free their slaves due to the substantial economic losses that freedom necessitated. Since 1713, the state required masters to post sizeable bonds to guarantee that former slaves would not become destitute and therefore dependent on poor relief, and many owners became understandably dissuaded from manumission. Many in Chesterfield slowed their support for abolition while the same lack of enthusiasm occurred at Salem in 1777 when that monthly meeting indicted Charles Fogg for selling "two girls . . . (and) render(ing) their case little better than slaves." Even though the meeting managed to buy back one of the two, Fogg's choice to sell rather than manumit illustrates the continuing power that economic incentives had over ideology. Similar incidents took place in Shrewsbury in 1772 when the freedom of two slaves dramatically divided the meeting. The Yearly Meeting stepped in to adjudicate the Shrewsbury dispute while in Chesterfield most members felt "discouraged from the apprehension of encumbrance which it might occasion to their outward estates and some few refuse at present" to liberate their chattel. Chesterfield continued to drag its feet on abolition, reporting in 1778 to the Quarterly Meeting that many members still did not wish to free their slaves.[15]

Fear of economic losses persuaded many Quakers to fulfill their abolitionist duty while maintaining the labor of their young slaves. As most Americans firmly believed in the indenture and unfreedom of minors, many Jersey Quakers granted provisional freedom to slaves under twenty-one but required them to complete a term of service before they could achieve legal freedom. Quaker meetings tacitly approved of this process as it ensured future freedom at adulthood. In one such case, Rachel Moore of Burlington manumitted her slave, seven-year-old Negro Jane, in 1771 by confirming her future freedom at age thirty, but first sold her to Thomas Gordon, a fellow Quaker from Philadelphia. Though Moore made it "clearly understood . . . that Negro Jane is hereby manumitted and made free," she first had to serve twenty-three years with Gordon.[16]

Even though some Quakers voluntarily left or were disowned by the society over slavery, a much larger percentage of Friends hoped to "erase the moral blot of slavekeeping" from their memory. Many Greater Philadelphia Quakers atoned for their lapse in moral judgment in owning slaves through a coordinated effort to assist their former chattel in their new role as freed people. In 1775, the Yearly Meeting remarked that abundant progress had been made in the promotion of abolition and "a considerable number (of blacks have) been restored to liberty." The overall success of the abolitionist movement within the Society of Friends led to a substantially freer West Jersey and a more concerted emphasis on the religious care of former slaves. Schools aimed at religious instruction, some led by Benezet, developed in the region along with the continued growth of abolitionism.[17]

Quaker attention to atoning for slavery in the late 1770s and early 1780s led Samuel Allinson and other Burlington Quakers to develop a system of religious and educational meetings for ex-slaves that met at rotating West Jersey meetinghouses in Burlington, Mount Holly, Crosswicks, and Mansfield to, in the words of the Burlington Quarterly Meeting, promote "their instruction in the principles of Christian religion and the pious education of their children."[18] Though the organizers of the meetings had a definite tone of moral superiority (they needed to "educate" their "uneducated" ex-slaves), these meetings soon became not only about religion but afforded free blacks badly needed educational opportunities. Indeed, they also promoted the formation of free black communities by bringing together a rural black population at regular intervals. These former slaves latched onto these meetings because of their usefulness—they endured the paternalistic rhetoric and embraced them to create alliances, bonds, and relationships that would help them survive in a society where blacks were still overwhelmingly enslaved. By 1783, Philadelphia Quakers formed a school dedicated to providing education to free black children while the Salem and Gloucester Quarterly Meeting began raising funds for its own school as early as 1780. However, the Salem Monthly Meeting had taken the initiative even earlier in 1778 when it built a school to educate both freed and enslaved blacks.[19]

*   *   *

As West Jersey Quakers pushed abolition in their own communities, they called for a much larger debate on slavery in New Jersey. Dillwyn's political tract against slavery echoed the intent of several petitions filed with the state legislature in the early 1770s. In 1773 and 1774, Jersey Quakers called for an end to slavery in the state and for an easing of manumission restrictions and limitations to the state's harsh slave code. In 1775, Chesterfield Quakers advocated for a gradual abolition program, claiming that they wished to "avert the judgments of God from our heads." The *Pennsylvania Gazette* replicated this use of religious ideology when it noted that several petitions had been filed with the legislature that advocated support for abolition as "we are Children of one common father." As the petitions from Chesterfield arrived in the legislature, Burlington and Cumberland County Quakers added their voices to the debate. They argued, in line with Allinson, Dillwyn, and Sharp, that Americans must "show to the World a conduct consistent with the principles of that liberty, which we claim as our birthright" especially in light of the ongoing debate over American liberty and freedom from Great Britain.[20]

As the imperial crisis heated debate over the idea of American freedom, New Jersey and Pennsylvania Quakers utilized the rhetoric of the crisis in their own fight against slavery. For example, in 1774, a Quaker petition to a Pennsylvania assemblyman made such a link by claiming that "at a time when the rights and liberties of the American subjects of the Crown" are at stake, the state must "take a strict view of our own conduct" and laws, which permit slavery to continue. The petitioners continued that "everything in our power should be done to establish impartial, universal liberty" for all slaves in Pennsylvania at the first opportunity.[21] This link between abolitionism and larger Atlantic issues continued to develop as men like Benezet interacted with French and British abolitionists. For instance, Granville Sharp argued in 1775 that while Africans possessed "a natural right to a free existence," landholders in the American colonies had a responsibility to "divide what lands they can spare into compact little farms, with a small wooden cottage to each." This land could be given to freed blacks so they would not revolt to gain economic standing after freedom.[22]

Benezet and Sharp no doubt hoped that these petitions would convince non-Quaker New Jerseyans and Pennsylvanians to see slavery in a new light. However, Benezet realistically understood that few even within the society agreed with him that blacks and whites were equal no less voluntarily would give land to them. In 1772, Benezet wrote to Allinson that Americans "would strenuously oppose the scheme of a total abolition of slavery" and instead, like the Chesterfield Friends, would support gradual abolition programs through which slaves could purchase their freedom. He believed that these modifications to slavery could help solve the economic complications that limited support for abolition.[23]

Calls for abolition provoked a firestorm of protest from New Jersey's non-Quaker population, mainly in East Jersey, who were even more dependent on slave labor than their West Jersey neighbors. In 1774, eighty-one angry Perth Amboy residents warned Governor William Franklin of the "dismal consequences" of abolition, especially the possibility of a revolt if whites could not use slavery to control the state's black population. They believed blacks were "the most barbarous in human matters" and that only slavery kept their barbarism in check. Without it, they would "invade the inhabitants and accomplish that unhuman design . . . to bring the white people into the same state that the Negroes are now in." They pleaded for Franklin to preserve "the liberty of the white people of this province" and not let the white population fall into bondage itself. Fifty-three residents of Middletown similarly voiced opposition to the Quaker abolition plan after they found their enslaved blacks "very troublesome by running about all times of night, stealing, and taking and riding people's horses and other mischief." Freedom would, according to the Middletown petitioners, dramatically increase the frequency of theft and mischief.[24]

On the eve of the Revolution, New Jersey slaveholders used the fear of insurrection and anxiety over the possibility of fighting hordes of barbarous blacks that sought to invade their homes and consort with their wives and daughters to effectively quell Quaker attempts at advancing abolitionism. The divisions between East and West Jersey exacerbated this tension as abolitionists from the West fought against eastern slaveholders. Slavery's strength and the lack of both abolitionism and Quakerism in East Jersey led slaveholders there to identify abolitionism as created by outsiders who, though in the same state, did not understand the true dynamics of living in a place where slaves made up a sizeable percentage of the population. The intense relationship East Jersey whites had with slavery before the Revolution prevented Quakers from convincing a large number of them to support black freedom, which effectively stymied any major abolitionist action as the colonies careened toward war.

*   *   *

Once the Revolution began, the rhetorical devices Patriots employed to rally support for the war moved discussions of freedom and abolitionism to center stage as Americans used language imbibed with the concepts of freedom and slavery to discuss their relationship with Great Britain. Slaveholding New Jerseyans positioned their own battle against the British as a crusade to free themselves from British bondage. For instance, in October 1776 the state's General Assembly, in describing the American relationship with Great Britain, called for "deliverance from the galling yoke of slavery, the unparalleled unanimity of the American states in refitting the encroachments of despotism." Even Thomas Paine's *Common Sense* used the image of slavery when he claimed that Americans had been "enslaved by the want of laws" and that the colonies had been "at last cheated into slavery." Bergen County slaveholders adopted this same rhetoric in 1783 when they argued that the United States would continue as a "vassal" of British slavery if the nation approved the Treaty of Paris. The binary between slavery and freedom gave Patriots a readily understood way to communicate that they believed the British impositions on the colonies were similar to the oppression of slaves by slaveholders.[25]

Abolitionists saw the widespread use of this antislavery rhetoric in the fight against Great Britain and increasingly employed it against slavery. For example, Allinson wrote to Governor William Livingston in 1778 claiming that the colonies went to war "to avoid what she called slavery and to preserve and transmit to posterity her right to possession of liberty" while at the same time they "confirmed laws that hold thousands of human beings, children of the same common Father . . . in ignoble and abject slavery." This emphasis on the hypocrisy of enslaving one race while fighting for freedom from the British, spread to other abolitionists and became a repetitive cry in abolitionist tracts.[26] Likewise, in neighboring Philadelphia, Benjamin Rush openly equated the American fight for freedom with the abolition movement. He argued that the Pennsylvania legislature needed to "excise the cancer of slavery from the American body politic" while Americans simultaneously fought for their own freedom from Great Britain. Paine joined Rush's attack on slavery by drawing on a natural rights argument related to the American Revolution. In response to Paine, a New Jerseyan wrote in the *New York Journal* that freedom was the birthright of all men regardless of color. Destiny, according to this author, dictated that freedom from the British would rid all who lived in America from future slavery. Accordingly, the *Journal* article claimed no man should be born a slave in a nation that fully supported freedom.[27]

Jacob Green, a Morris County Presbyterian minister, employed this same rhetoric in his church throughout the war to support the Patriots and address abolitionism. Green became heavily invested in the Patriot cause as a member of New Jersey's Provincial Congress and delegate to the state's 1776 Constitutional Convention. In a 1779 "Fast Day Sermon," also published in pamphlet form, Green preached that "supporting and encouraging slavery is one of the great and crying evils among us." He asked New Jerseyans, "Can it be believed that a people contending for liberty should, at the same time, be promoting and supporting slavery?" Green argued that slaves "never forfeited their right to freedom; 'tis as the Congress say, a natural right, and an unalienable one." With this sermon, Green entered into the debate on the paradoxical role of slavery in a nation founded on freedom. Like many others, Green's abolitionist belief came not from a firm sense of equality between blacks and whites but from the conviction that Americans' hypocritical actions were sinful.[28]

In 1780, the editor of the *New Jersey Journal*, Shepard Kollock, published a two-part letter of Green's under the penname "Eumenes," through which Green's call for liberty for slaves reached a wider audience and increased discussion on the slavery and freedom paradox as the Keystone State debated a gradual abolition law that same year. Green articulated that Americans fought so "that we may be a free people; that we may enjoy the natural rights of mankind, that we may not be reduced to a state of mean and abject slavery." He challenged New Jerseyans who believed in the natural rights of mankind, contending that those who fought against the British should "cast an eye of pity on the negro slaves among us" as they "are groaning under a bondage which we think worse than death."[29]

On March 1, 1780, the Pennsylvania legislature approved a legislative abolition program that angered proslavery advocates across the Mid-Atlantic and precipitated a newspaper war on the subject of abolition. In November, "Eliobo" wrote to the *New Jersey Journal* that the recent increase in abolitionist sentiment had no basis in any real need for freedom for slaves, since slaves lived "free from all anxiety, perplexing cares, troubles and disappointments." He rejected Green's link between the Revolution and abolition, claiming it inappropriate to equate the slavery Great Britain exerted on the colonies with African slavery as the two shared little in common.[30] A month later, Eliobo further advanced his proslavery argument by linking himself to the Perth Amboy petition six years earlier that had claimed that abolition would destroy white civilization. Eliobo argued that every "effort of the negroes" would be "to establish upon our ruin" and create a "kingdom of Cuffie." In an apocalyptic vision of destruction and death, the author predicted that freed slaves would form an alliance with the Indians who, as savage as blacks, would "sweep our land with sallies of murder and rapine. Then will the shrieks and cries of murdered children and the lamentation of assassinated friends weltering in gore" force Americans to realize that abolition produced destruction.[31]

"Marcus Aurelius," another author writing in response to Jacob Green and the Pennsylvania law in the *New Jersey Journal*, joined Eliobo in claiming that even the discussion of liberty for slaves could "stimulate servants to insurrection." Aurelius became even more enraged with the potential for revolt because he saw a clear difference between national freedom from the British and individual freedom of slaves. He argued that Green "in his heart knows they are measured upon two scales and have no connection with each other." He, along with others, attacked the very notion that American liberty could ever be construed as equivalent to black liberty because blacks existed in such an inferior state. Their racism not only informed their fear of a race war but also began the process that restricted how far revolutionary freedom could extend to African Americans.[32]

The proslavery voices that rose in protest were largely motivated by fears of slaves harnessing this abolitionist rhetoric for their own purposes. Like slaves in Massachusetts and New Hampshire, Jersey slaves knew about the debates flying around them in the state's newspapers and used them to negotiate with their masters. In Massachusetts, for example, slaves petitioned the legislature to demand an immediate end to their enslavement and used revolutionary ideas of freedom to do so. No formal petitions from slaves came to the New Jersey legislature, though rural slaveholders definitely believed that the Revolution's ideas of liberty had influenced their slaves. These rural slaves had let it be known that "it was not necessary (for them) to please their masters for they should not have their masters long." Revolutionary ideas therefore emboldened slaves to negotiate from a stronger vantage point by using language from the era that their masters knew, understood, and would cause a strong emotional reaction to.[33]

In the aftermath of Pennsylvania's passage of gradual abolition, abolitionist voices countered the proslavery opinions in the newspaper debates and again reiterated the powerful link between the American Revolution and abolition. In 1780, the *New Jersey Gazette*, the *Journal*'s rival paper, published a series of articles refuting the *Journal*'s proslavery pieces. John Cooper, a Quaker from Woodbury in Gloucester County who had repeatedly advocated for abolition as a member of the Legislative Council and Council of Safety, knew Green through their shared service in the provisional legislature and on the ten-person committee that wrote the state's 1776 constitution. Like Green, Cooper argued that the Revolution should force Americans to recognize African American freedom. Cooper believed "in our public and most solemn declarations we say we are resolved to die free—that slavery is worse than death. He who enslaves his fellow creature must be worse than he who takes his life." As he thought slavery a fate worse than death, Cooper advocated a much more radical agenda than other abolitionists: the immediate abolition of slavery.[34]

* * *

The Quaker-dominated abolition movement and the republican rhetoric it utilized attempted to transcend ideological and religious boundaries, thereby raising the potential for widespread acceptance of abolition during the Revolution. The revolutionary generation of American slavery brought significant potential for African American mobility and worked to change the way white New Jerseyans thought of slavery and how blacks negotiated for their freedom. The rhetoric of abolition had much to do with this potential and it brought the first real widespread discussions of black freedom to white New Jerseyans.[35]

Quakers had succeeded at ridding much of West Jersey of slavery but had been less adept at convincing a large number of their fellow white New Jerseyans to join the cause. Anti-abolition New Jerseyans stood steadfastly against black freedom and combated it by trying to break down the connections between the freedom white Americans fought for from Great Britain and the type of freedom abolitionists wanted to give slaves. A successful abolition movement failed to develop because of the fear of race war, raw racism, and the lack of support in slaveholding areas of East Jersey. These fears and lack of organizational support joined together with the economic devastation caused by the Revolution, explored in the next chapter, to stymie the movement even as Pennsylvanians and New Englanders supported gradual abolition. Therefore, by the end of the war, abolitionism in New Jersey remained the legacy of only the Society of Friends and a minority of non-Quakers.

CHAPTER TWO

Sustaining Slavery in an Age of Freedom

The slave Prime experienced a very different American Revolution from most other slaves. A Hunterdon County native, he understood the promise of freedom the American Revolution could bring, especially after Lord Dunmore's Proclamation and similar edicts from British commanders in New York. However, despite his best efforts, he could never capitalize on that promise as did other black Americans. Instead of ending the war as a freeman, Prime became a "slave of the State of New Jersey . . . liable to be sold as their property."[1]

Prime's master, Princeton physician Absalom Bainbridge, hid his loyalist sympathies until the British marched into his hometown at the end of 1776. On their arrival, Bainbridge volunteered his house as the headquarters of General William Howe and joined the king's army, in which he served until 1778. Bainbridge was stationed in New York until the British evacuation in 1783, when he moved to London. In his successful 1784 application to the Loyalist Claims Commission, established by Parliament in 1783 to hear cases of loyalists who suffered economic losses as a result of their loyalty, for damages totaling 6,000 pounds sterling, Bainbridge wrote that because of his early support for the king, New Jersey had declared him guilty of high treason and confiscated his property. In addition to his four hundred acre estate, Bainbridge listed numerous pieces of moveable property, including Prime. During the war, Bainbridge tried to remove Prime and his personal property to safety by sending his wife, Prime, and several wagons of household items to a relative's home in Princeton before moving them all to his father-in-law's in Monmouth. After Bainbridge left the army in 1778, he sent for his wife and Prime to join him on Long Island, though Prime took advantage of the confusion surrounding the war and successfully ran away to Somerset County.[2]

Jacob Bergen, the state official charged with the confiscation and sale of loyalist estates in Somerset, seized Prime and considered selling him as the state had done with Bainbridge's other property. Luckily for Prime, Bergen "humanely declined" to send him "to sale like a beast of the stall" and instead recommended he serve in the Continental Army to alleviate his owner's debt to the Patriot cause. Prime served for the duration of the war as a teamster and left Continental service in 1783 when he moved to Trenton and began a free life as a day laborer. Only a few months after the Revolution ended, a man named John Taylor appeared at Prime's home and claimed he had bought Prime from Bainbridge's wife. At the same time, attorneys representing the state affirmed their previous contention that Prime, as part of a confiscated loyalist estate, belonged to the people of New Jersey and any sale by Bainbridge or his family subsequent to that confiscation was void. As a slave either to Taylor or to the state, Prime would lose the freedom he had gained because of the Revolution. After months of legal wrangling and an appeal to the Supreme Court, in 1786 the state of New Jersey affirmed the legality of Prime's confiscation and the invalidity of Taylor's claims. A military veteran who honorably served the Patriot cause left the Supreme Court as confiscated property to be sold by the state to the highest bidder.[3]

Prime's transformation from free patriot veteran to confiscated property hits at the very heart of historical understandings of the Revolution. In contrast to arguments put forward by historians that the Revolution laid the groundwork for African American freedom, Prime's case represents the perpetuation of slavery because of the Revolution, not an extension of freedom supported by revolutionary ideology. Of course, Prime himself did not surrender his freedom and this ideology easily; he authored a petition to the legislature demanding his freedom based on his service to the nation. By 1786, the legislature had freed him and two other slaves caught in his same situation, illustrating that though this ideology had power in New Jersey, it helped only a limited number of slaves.[4]

Slavery survived the Revolution because of New Jersey's status as a hotly contested revolutionary battleground. British and American troops slogged through the mud of the well-worn road between New York and Philadelphia, trampled through the snow at Morristown, and fought on the plains of Monmouth, which caused state residents to feel the negative effects of war more than most. With almost three hundred separate military engagements and thousands of foraging expeditions by British and Americans, revolutionary New Jersey easily earned the name given to it by historian Leonard Lundin in the 1940s—"The Cockpit of the Revolution."[5]

The Revolution's destructive power and disruptive influence on the state's economy, coupled with the constant threat of British invasion, encouraged lawmakers and white citizens to decline to advance abolition even as it moved forward in Pennsylvania and New England. Opposition to black freedom had already been substantial as abolitionists failed to overcome fears of race war and social dislocation in the state's ongoing rhetorical battle over slavery. The fallout from the actual battles solidified this opposition to abolitionism and effectively ended the first moves toward abolition begun in the 1770s. Even as the war allowed thousands of blacks to escape to British lines and gain freedom, combat operations in this borderland at the crossroads of the Revolution inflicted a devastating economic toll as both armies routinely ravaged the state. The destructive reality of war overpowered abolitionism in New Jersey and suppressed any desire to free a valuable labor source from those grappling with wartime destruction and an uncertain future.

In addition to exacerbating economic losses, the absconding of hundreds of slaves to British lines and their return as loyalist soldiers created an even more powerful socially produced hysteria and anxiety over a potential statewide slave revolt. Reports of ex-slaves murdering, raping, and pillaging their former hometowns delayed serious discussions of abolition as many Jersey whites believed themselves under attack by a ruthless and uncontrollable enemy. The institution of slavery provided security and control over blacks in the insecurity of war, which encouraged lawmakers at the end of the Revolution to not free the vast majority of confiscated loyalist slaves like Prime. The state's role as a slave trader both during and after the Revolution reinforced its commitment to a slave system that would successfully defend itself for the next twenty years against a growing abolition movement in the North and the larger Atlantic World.

* * *

Anti-abolition activists responded forcefully in words and actions against the abolitionists' use of revolutionary rhetoric in support of slave freedom. The petitions that Quaker abolitionists had sent to the legislature and the newspaper debates they provoked helped anti-abolitionists drum up significant support in the state, motivated violence against abolitionists—

Jacob Green's church was sacked in protest—and allowed anti-abolitionists to clearly set out their reasons for opposing black freedom. This group primarily argued that slavery could not be abolished because the Revolution had devastated the state economically and a constant fear of future destruction remained. For instance, one abolitionist critic claimed that New Jersey could not follow its neighbors toward abolition because it had been "laid to waste and rendered desolate by the ravages" of the British army.[6]

Legislators repeatedly used this economic argument to halt abolitionism, believing it too radical a step to take in the midst of war. To the abolitionists, the moral stakes were high as Quaker activist Samuel Allinson wrote in 1778, the "eyes of the world have been and are upon America" in the matter of slavery.[7] Although Allinson thought the eyes looked specifically toward Pennsylvania and its battle to enact gradual abolition, he also lobbied Governor William Livingston to consider abolition in New Jersey. Livingston, a slaveholder himself, readily adopted Allinson's abolitionist ideology and freed his slaves. Through frequent exchanges with Allinson, Livingston not only embraced abolitionism but became more accepting of Quakerism, leading him to become Allinson's principal ally. At the same time, however, Livingston believed the legislature "thinking us rather in too critical a situation to enter on the consideration of it at that time, desired me in a private way to withdraw the message." Livingston thought that this "critical situation," the economic losses and fear of British attack, derailed the wartime abolitionist agenda.[8]

The reality of war in New Jersey hit the state's citizens from almost the very beginning when the British invasion of New York in 1776 forced Washington's army into a headlong retreat across New Jersey and into Pennsylvania. New Jersey became "a ragged borderline between the two Americas, Loyalist and Patriot," of which the "neutral zone of eastern and northern New Jersey, especially Monmouth and Bergen counties" was where "the violence was most brutal."[9] War in New Jersey became a long-standing foraging battle in which both armies scavenged for supplies, with major battles occasionally highlighting the daily struggle for food and influence. As Livingston had alluded, defending the state against British attack preoccupied the minds of most New Jerseyans and therefore limited the abolitionist influence.[10]

The relative brutality and cruelty that plagued New Jersey was made abundantly clear by legislators, soldiers, and citizens. In August 1776, Abraham Clark, a member of the Continental Congress, wrote that residents of

WILLIAM LIVINGSTON.
Nat 1723 — Ob 1790.

From the original painting in the possession of the Family.

Figure 1. William Livingston, governor of New Jersey, 1776–1790.
Courtesy of the New York Public Library.

his native Elizabethtown "are daily alarmed with news of an attack."[11] By the end of September, after British forces had actually invaded, patriots routinely discussed reports of British "savagery." American General Jedidiah Huntington recorded that with almost one-third of New York City in flames, "unheard of barbarities were committed by the Kings Troops . . . some, it's said, were thrown into the flames, others tied up by the legs and their throats cut," all done to "deter" further insurrection.[12]

After the British invasion of New Jersey in late 1776, dozens of state leaders and soldiers saw the devastation inflicted by the British, its devastating impact on state residents, and how it pervaded residents' focus throughout the war. For instance, Samuel Adams wrote to his wife Elizabeth about the "savage tragedies . . . without respect to age or sex" perpetrated by Hessian soldiers, which "have equaled the most barbarous" of all the "nations of the world." Adams reiterated his belief in the barbarity of the Hessian and British forces the following week to his cousin John, when he again claimed that they had "been most inhumanely used in their persons, without regard to sex or age, and plundered of all they had."[13] Echoing Adams, William Whipple wrote to his fellow New Hampshire delegate Josiah Bartlett of the "brutal vengeance of an abandoned soldiery . . . exercised on all without distinction." The "ravages committed by the enemy" in New Jersey were "really shocking to humanity." Whipple feared that if the British shifted their operations to New England, his constituents would suffer "greater cruelties than New Jersey has experienced."[14] These letters echoed reports from field commanders, such as Nathanael Greene, who wrote to his wife in early December 1776 that American soldiers from Maryland and Virginia had been dispatched to New Jersey to "stop the ravages of the enemy." Unlike other accounts of the campaign, Greene claimed both sides "take the clothes off of the peoples back. The distress they spread wherever they go exceeds all description."[15]

In early 1777, after a congressional committee began investigating British and Hessian conduct in New Jersey, delegates heard reports of numerous rapes and murders perpetrated by forces loyal to the king, further evidence of the war's destructive power. For instance, Virginian Thomas Nelson described how British soldiers "play the very devil with girls and even old women to satisfy their libidinous appetites . . . there is scarcely a virgin to be found."[16] In the same vein, Samuel Adams wrote to James Warren about the "shocking inhumanities shown to our countrymen in the Jerseys" as the British engaged in "plundering houses, cruelly beating old men, ravishing maids, murdering captives in cold blood, and systematically starving multitudes of prisoners."[17] John Adams and Richard Henry Lee both reiterated the "ravages in the Jersies" including "rapes, murders, and devastation . . . [which] would have disgraced the savages of the wilderness."[18] Likewise, New Jersey native Thomas McCarty recalled the brutal nature of the New Jersey-New York borderland during an engagement with a British foraging party in February 1777. McCarty reported that his unit "attacked the body and bullets flew like hail" causing significant casualties. In speaking of the American wounded, McCarty wrote that the British soldiers had "dashed out their brains those men wounded in the thigh or leg . . . with their muskets and run them through with their bayonets, made them like sieves. This was barbarity to the utmost."[19] Delegate Whipple believed that this wanton inhumanity inflicted by the British reflected the true state of "British humanity" and that "all America would have experienced" the same if they "submitted to the yoke of the tyrant."[20]

Reports of widespread destruction, rape, and murder from the initial 1776–1777 campaign fueled New Jerseyans' fears of future attacks by the British. This consistent fear made Newark leaders, in the spring of 1777, warn Governor Livingston of "the unhappy situation of this town being so contiguous to the Enemy who threatens us daily with an invasion."[21] These fears were never realized as the main British army quickly withdrew from New Jersey, but the campaign of 1777 brought renewed reports of attacks against American civilians. For example, while based in Perth Amboy, Hessian cavalry officer Baron Friedrich Adam Julius von Wangenheim wrote to his brother that "we will soon bring war to an area where no one is suspecting it" and "attack the enemy as on a hunt." He claimed that his men would "crawl on our bellies through the bushes and if one sees a rebel, one sneaks up to him and shoots him dead" and reiterated the orders of General Howe, who had decided that the army in this campaign needed "to be cruel, since he has seen that with kindness one does not accomplish anything with them—there will be burnings, hangings, and everything will be ruined."[22]

After the Patriot victory at Monmouth, New Jersey settled into a prolonged period of guerrilla warfare between patriots, loyalists, and British military units that sought food and supplies from the countryside, which further damaged the state's economy. A second cold winter at Morristown (1779–1780) made New Jersey no friend to Continental soldiers as harsh weather, lack of supplies, and poor living conditions affected both their health and discipline. Alexander Scammell, the army's adjutant general during the second encampment at Morristown, described that the complete lack of discipline rampant among American soldiers, especially thefts from other soldiers and the plundering of local residents' property, further exacerbated the already present civilian anxiety over their economic livelihood. In January 1780, for instance, Rubin Parker received one hundred lashes on the bare back for theft, while in February the Continental Army executed another soldier for the same crime. Similarly, Scammell recorded death sentences in May 1780 for four soldiers of the Pennsylvania line after they plundered the house of Cornelius Bogart near Paramus.[23] Plundering became so widespread that the General Orders issued on January 28, 1780, prohibited soldiers from leaving camp. Although some soldiers sought riches from plundering civilian homes, hunger motivated many more to search the countryside for food. Plundering continued after Morristown with Eliza Susan Quincy of Basking Ridge writing in her memoirs that in 1781 that a group of armed soldiers broke into her home searching for gold watches. The thieves stole thirty pounds worth of gold and silver before threatening to kill the home's inhabitants unless they turned over more loot. The robbers proceeded to ransack the house and took twelve ruffled linen shirts, all the plates, the tea and coffee service, and every piece of silver, threatening to burn down the house if the family reported the theft.[24]

Just as American troops did, British forces also routinely foraged for supplies and angered already economically vulnerable residents. In December 1776, for instance, General Howe reported from New Brunswick that so many solidiers plundered civilian property, it would "be absolutely impossible to prevail upon the inhabitants to bring provisions to market" where the army could legally buy them. Similar reports came from Middlebush in June 1777 when Howe ordered that anyone found guilty of "marauding or pulling down houses, barns or any irregularity" would be punished severely. Punishments for plundering happened with regularity as Howe reported that John Gibson had been sentenced to 1,000 lashes for robbery and Jacob Van Tessel faced death for the same crime.[25] Likewise, physician Martin McEvoy stood trial for illegally plundering a horse and cow in 1778, a charge of which the court-martial found him guilty and discharged him from the service. Lt. Boswell of the Maryland loyalists similarly stood trial in September 1778 for taking two horses. Boswell claimed that he only took them because he was "so very lame that he could hardly walk" and, after his unit left New Jersey, he sent the horses back to their owner. Even though the court found him not guilty, the actions he and others took affected not only the economic lives of New Jerseyans but their willingness to support the Continental Army.[26]

British forces quickly realized that foraging in New Jersey had turned many residents against their cause. As Howe had feared in New Brunswick in 1776, New York's British governor, James Robertson, wrote to Lord George Germain in 1780 after the Battle of Short Hills that the burning of several houses by area loyalists "deprived us of the reputation the general's intentions merited and gave too good foundation to the rebels to represent us as inimical to the country."[27] Benedict Arnold likewise argued in 1780 that "plundering the distressed inhabitants of New Jersey" would cause them to support the patriots.[28] British actions resulted in just that, as many New Jerseyans allied with Continental forces. By early 1777, Whipple reported that the "ravages committed by the enemy have had a most excellent effect on the people of Jersey" as "the militia now turn out with great spirit and harass the ravagers of their country in every quarter."[29] At the Battle of Monmouth in 1778, Hunterdon County militia officer Joseph Clark reiterated his men's support for the patriots when he wrote that the battle had "roused the militia . . . they turned out with such a spirit . . . never did the Jerseys appear more universally unanimous to oppose the enemy."[30]

The economic devastation caused by the Revolution became further exacerbated by the work of the slaves themselves since they capitalized on the war's destructive and disruptive power and struck out for freedom. For example, slaveholders in the most heavily slave populated county, Bergen, saw the loss of hundreds of slaves who joined British forces and no longer supported the county's agricultural base. One such Bergen resident, Richard Varick, bemoaned in 1778 that "in the beginning of the war, my father had two middle-aged negroes and wenches—he has lost the wench . . . one negro died and the last wench and one negro left with the enemy."[31] Varick's two escaped slaves joined hundreds more who heard the British promise of freedom. The fear that blacks could run away, disrupt New Jersey's slave system, and potentially serve in the king's army exacerbated the anxiety caused by the war and further damaged the economic viability of hundreds of slaveholders. The slaves themselves then, even as they sought freedom, inadvertently convinced many whites of the dangers of wartime abolition.[32]

British enthusiasm for offering slaves freedom and thereby economically hurting patriot masters began in 1775 when Lord Dunmore, the last
royal governor of Virginia, promised freedom to any slave who would fight
against the Americans. News of Dunmore's promise spread far from Virginia and soon slaves in New Jersey understood the British as a beacon of
freedom. British commanders across the colonies announced similar declarations. On June 7, 1779, David Jones, the British general in charge of New
York, declared that "all Negroes that fly from the Enemy's Country are Free
. . . no person whatever can claim a right to them." Jones's declaration
exceeded the limited scope of Dunmore's because he offered freedom to all
slaves who escaped to Tory lines, not just males that fought.[33]

New Jersey slaves quickly took advantage of the guarantee of freedom
by this powerful group of whites and ran away in large numbers. Lutheran
minister Henry Muhlenberg saw the support the British had among Jersey
slaves, writing that they wished "the British army might win, for then all
Negro slaves will gain their freedom." This belief, according to Muhlenberg,
was "universal among the Negroes in America."[34] For the most part, he was
right. Thousands of blacks ran toward British lines, covered by the disorder
of war, especially in the Mid-Atlantic. The fugitive slave population of Philadelphia doubled and nearly quadrupled in New York.[35] Runaway advertisements provide a rough estimate of the general characteristics and
quantity of slaves who fled New Jersey. From 1776 to 1783, New York and
New Jersey newspapers ran 314 runaway advertisements. As historian Billy
Smith found studying Philadelphia papers, the Revolution produced a significant uptick in runaways. Smith measured an annual average of 43 runaway advertisements per year from 1750 to 1775. During and immediately
after the Revolution, that number more than doubled to 102 annually.[36] In
New Jersey, these runaways remained, as would be expected, overwhelmingly male (79.6 percent), between sixteen and twenty-five (51.6 percent),
and therefore easily integrated into the British military. Of course, not all
slaves who ran away became soldiers. Phillis Sparrow, a twenty-eight year-
old woman who belonged to Charles Suydam of New Brunswick, left her
master in 1776 and fled to a free life in British-occupied New York. Similarly, in 1777, Richard Stevens's slave from Hunterdon County left his master and fled to Staten Island after coaxing by Jinlay Drake, who specifically
decried military service.[37]

The constant military maneuvering in the state transformed New Jersey
into a battleground not only over food but between slavery and freedom as

British lines within the state and the freedom they offered ebbed and flowed throughout the war. Fleeing slavery was easy in New Jersey, as few slaves needed to travel far from their masters' homes to find a British unit. As in other occupied areas, slaves could easily acquire protection from British troops and access freedom by "simply walking out of their master's homes."[38] Some did not have to walk far at all since passing British troops lured many slaves away with promises of freedom. A twenty-eight-year-old male slave owned by Joseph Holmes of Upper Freehold did just that when he fled to British troops that had marched onto his master's land.[39] Similarly, Ennis Graham claimed that a large body of Hessian soldiers carried off his slave Oliver on their way to the Battle of Trenton in December 1776, while Thomas Edgar of Woodbridge saw his thirty-five-year-old male slave flee to nearby British forces during the same campaign.[40]

Slaves ran away from their masters with the understanding that a chance at freedom with the British outweighed both the dangers of simply absconding and the realities of an unfree life in Patriot New Jersey. For example, in 1778 twenty-two-year-old Boston ran away after his owner, Ann Griffith, told him that he would be sent to serve with the Continental Army. In making his escape, perhaps Boston believed that military service with the British, who guaranteed freedom, was a better alternative than service with the Americans, who did not. Griffith, however, soon found Boston on the British schooner *Revenge*, commanded by Captain William Cook, who had just recently surrendered to American forces on the Delaware River. Griffith applied for Boston to be returned immediately. Cook, unlike other British mariners who interpreted Dunmore's Proclamation to free slaves who boarded British ships, met with a local man named Martin Delany and planned to sell Boston for up to 125 pounds. One witness overheard Cook plotting to sell Boston "to the first West Indian vessel that he met" and reap a huge profit. Griffith's case became even further complicated as an American Admiralty Court condemned Cook's ship and cargo, including Boston, as confiscated property liable for sale. In the end, Griffith regained custody of Boston, but many more who lost slaves to the British did not. In total, more than 150 Jersey masters filed claims with the state for slaves lost to British forces.[41]

The animosity caused by British foraging raids increased as New York became the epicenter of free black life in the United States, growing due to the surging numbers of Jersey runaways. A resident of New Barbadoes in Bergen County complained in May 1780 that "twenty-nine negroes of both sexes have deserted within two weeks past."[42] This represented a steady increase in absconding slaves and necessitated the expanded use of the militia to apprehend them. For example, in 1777, Major Samuel Hayes of the Essex County militia reported that he had seized two absconding slaves in Newark, bound for New York. That same year, Monmouth County militiamen captured slaves Joe and Scipio under suspicion that they intended to join the British.[43] In 1782, one slave arrested for attempted escape to New York was "tied . . . to the tail of a horse . . . his feet were fastened in the stocks and at night his hands also."[44] However, increased militia action barely scratched the surface of the runaway threat and did not effectively deter migration to New York.[45]

The foraging raids and the rising number of absconding slaves focused attention on the British and the perceived threat that a radical change in the state's racial structure could bring.[46] Thousands of New Jerseyans filed damage claims with the legislature in 1781 and 1782, showing how the British army, as Abraham Clark wrote, "one of which the most savage known among civilized nations" had "spread desolation through" New Jersey and precipitated an economic and social crisis.[47] However, Continental forces had also helped spur this crisis. Continental General Lord Sterling, for instance, ordered his quartermasters in December 1778 to seize American property and pay the "usual price" for it even though he found the whole process "extremely disagreeable . . . but necessary."[48] As inflation racked the economy, Sterling's paper money gave little comfort to Jersey families, leaving thousands upon thousands with limited resources for their own survival like William Dow, who had already petitioned the state legislature in 1779 for payment for property taken by patriots. Dow claimed that the military not only confiscated the ferry he operated on the Peapack River, but also twelve sheep, and that they severely damaged his house. Likewise, in Westfield, a small town in Essex County, 113 residents filed claims ranging from Susanna Halsey, who lost household furniture and clothing, to Daniel Connet who lost eight sheep, a horse, two hogs, thirty fowl, tea, wheat, corn, and three hives of bees.[49]

The damages inflicted by the war had a direct impact on slaveholders' unwillingness to support freedom for their chattel. Between 1775 and 1783, slaveholders in Newark, New Jersey's largest city, instructed the executors of their wills in the cases of nineteen different slaves to either transfer the slave to a family member or sell the slave and distribute the proceeds among their descendants. Statewide during the same period, 83 percent of slaves mentioned in wills were sold or bequeathed to a slaveholder's heirs, while only 17 percent gained their freedom. New York City slaveholders' wills similarly limited freedom; only 14 percent of slaveholders' wills from 1777–1783 provided it. Even as Quakers brought discussions of abolition to the forefront of regional consciousness, the revolutionary spirit did not infect the vast majority of New Jersey or New York slaveholders. This unwillingness among slaveholders to manumit their slaves had a direct correlation with the economic devastation. In East Jersey, the section of the state with more slaveholders and the most damage caused by the war, slaveholders likely felt they had spent enough to ensure the triumph of American freedom. A request from the state to grant freedom to their slaves and therefore lose more of their property would have been too much for them to muster.[50]

Pennsylvanians, on the other hand, had a much different war experience than did New Jerseyans, which made abolitionists there able to advance gradual abolition in the midst of conflict. The Pennsylvania state legislature had license to act on abolition in 1780 because the war had largely been confined to the state's sparsely populated western and northeastern frontiers after the patriots expelled the British from Philadelphia. With little interaction between the British and patriots in the last three years of the war, state legislators did not have, as New Jersey legislators did, a war-related reason to delay abolition.[51]

The Revolution, instead of forcing Jersey legislators to see the paradox between slavery and freedom and compel a radical societal shift from the colonial period, continued the status quo of slavery in New Jersey and only strengthened when ex-slaves began to use the Revolution to gain permanent freedom outside the United States at the end of the war. British General Guy Carleton, the commander at New York City, proclaimed that any slave who had joined the British before 1780 had the right to leave the colonies for a free life in Canada, Sierra Leone, or Britain itself. Carleton responded to Washington's complaints about the removal of former American slaves by claiming that he had "no right . . . to prevent their going to any part of the world they thought proper" as he had found many of them living free when he arrived in New York.[52] Therefore, any slave who had absconded to New York before Carleton had assumed command, and many more who had achieved freedom since then, could leave New York unimpeded. British Prime Minister Lord North affirmed Carleton's interpretation and extended that logic when he wrote in August 1783 that those blacks who had entered British lines before the "execution of the preliminaries of peace" should be able to leave as freed people, leading hundreds of former slaves to board British evacuation ships.[53]

The British decision to remove former slaves from New York, Charleston, and other British-controlled territory angered those New Jerseyans who had seen their property abscond to the British. American commissioners responsible for upholding the 1783 Paris Peace Treaty vehemently protested the decision as a violation of the treaty's seventh article, which prohibited the British from carrying away blacks from the United States. Three commissioners wrote to Carleton in June 1783 decrying the presence of fourteen ships bound for Nova Scotia that contained "upwards of one hundred negroes, seventy three of which appeared to be the property of American subjects."[54] The commissioners considered the sailing of these ships an infraction of the Paris Treaty, a point reiterated in a May 1783 meeting in Newark. The meeting of patriot slaveholders crafted several resolutions published in local newspapers and sent to Carleton, which claimed that since Great Britain had not complied with the treaty's provisions regarding slaves, the United States should not implement the fourth article, which mandated the full repayment of lawful debts owed to British creditors and the fifth article, which promised to restore confiscated loyalist estates.[55] Carleton linked the "circumstances of additional rage" that Americans had displayed by stripping loyalists of their lives and property with the increased discontent over treaty violations concerning slaves, one that he feared "will probably in the same narrow spirit be adopted by others."[56]

As Carleton predicted, arguments against removal surfaced in other meetings across New Jersey that questioned the commitment of both the British and American governments to the Paris Treaty with respect to slaves. In a second Essex County meeting, ninety residents claimed that the British had not done enough "to restore property found within their lines" and refused permission for Americans to attempt to secure ownership of their slaves individually. Many Jersey masters, without a system to recapture fugitives, saw their property leave New York for free lives elsewhere. One such Elizabethtown native, Sarah Haviland, complained to the American treaty commissioners that loyalists had forcibly taken her two male slaves, Jacob and Joe, to Staten Island. Both would soon leave the city bound for Nova Scotia as Haviland, a seventy-year-old widow, could not recapture them herself nor could she rely on any other means to assist her.[57]

Unfortunately for Haviland and other former masters, the British routinely defended escaped slaves who lived in New York. In one case, Constable Thomas Willis suffered fines and exile from the city for helping return escaped slave Caesar to Elizabethtown.[58] Dinah Archey, a runaway living in New York, hoped for a similar defense when her master, William Fancey, attempted to seize her in 1783. She requested protection from Carleton, claiming that she had answered Howe's Proclamation and entered New York five years earlier.[59] Likewise, New Yorkers Jacob Duyree, Adam Todd, and Fredrick Fighleman endured a British trial in June 1783 for trying to carry off Francis Griffin, a freed black under British protection. In this case, Duyree claimed that he had found Griffin, his former slave who had fled to New York City. Griffin had agreed to travel with Duyree up the Hudson River back to his home to help his former master transport flour to New York City and to reconnect with his wife, who remained Duyree's slave. Griffin secured a pass from the office of police, which, in his mind, allowed him to return unimpeded to New York because he had qualified for freedom under the British proclamation. Once close to the Hudson River, Duyree and his co-defendants forced Griffin into "a cart with a rope about his neck" and loaded him onto a sloop near Dean's Wharf. Luckily for Griffin, Hessian soldiers boarded his former master's ship, arrested Duyree, and freed him. After a lengthy trial, a court found Duyree guilty of trying to reenslave Griffin, fined him fifty guineas to be directed to "the poor and sick Negroes who have taken protection under the British government," and expelled him from British territory.[60]

The British, attuned to the unpopularity and potential ramifications of their decision to remove former American slaves from New York, agreed to record information on each African American who left on British ships in 1783. The Book of Negroes contains over three thousand names, including at least 175 ex-slaves from New Jersey. Of those, some like Joseph and Betsey Collins of Hackensack ran away together from their separate masters in 1779. Others like Polly of Burlington came to New York in 1776 in search of greater economic opportunities than she could have attained with the Patriots. In New York, Polly met her husband, Job Allen, a former slave from Maryland's Eastern Shore, and together they had two small children before leaving for a new life in Nova Scotia.[61]

This exodus of blacks to Canada, Britain, and eventually Sierra Leone represented a powerful step in the development of black freedom, raised significant ire among Jersey masters interested in sustaining slavery, and

proved important in delaying abolition. Although those who left represented a small percentage of New Jersey's total slave population, others
likely hid their identities as former slaves or possibly escaped via other ports
within the colonies. Detailed records remain for at least two of these men,
Anthony Smithers and John Baptist, both of whom filed claims for their
service with the Loyalist Claims Commission but do not appear in the Book
of Negroes. Smithers claimed that he lived as a free black man in Gloucester
County, where he owned fourteen acres of land and valued his property at
720 pounds. He reported that he had joined the British army during its
occupation of Philadelphia. Likewise, Baptist, also from Gloucester, testified
that he joined the British army in Philadelphia as a freeman. He had lived
with his sister on three acres of land and held an estate worth 675 pounds.[62]

The commission ruled both Baptist's and Smithers's claims invalid,
since they shared some key similarities, especially the certification of the
claim by the same two men, John Williams and Thomas Watkins. The
commission knew that Williams and Watkins lodged several blacks in London and helped them file claims. Dozens of former American slaves ended
their military careers starving in the city's streets. Both Baptist and Smithers
likely had participated in an elaborate fraud led by Williams and Watkins
in September 1783. All of the claims submitted by black men that month
had been certified by the duo and provided incredibly similar information
with little more than the name and some personal information altered.
These two claims, like those of other former American slaves, represent the
difficulties ex-slaves had even after they had gained freedom. These men
became destitute and desperate. Their condition led to an even greater dias-
pora of former American slaves as they left the difficult streets of London
for Sierra Leone or as criminals to the Botany Bay Colony in Australia.[63]

*   *   *

For white New Jerseyans, runaway slaves not only threatened wealth and
status, but more important, stoked preexisting fears of slave rebellion. After
the several slave conspiracies during the colonial period, Jersey whites had
highly regulated slave movement, deprived slaves of the ability to own
property or sell goods to whites, and prohibited slaves from frequenting
taverns, possessing liquor, carrying firearms, or congregating at night.
These new regulations, in full effect during the Revolution, resulted in
harsher punishments for slaves who committed crimes against whites and

further vigilance by whites trying to protect themselves. For example, in 1750 Perth Amboy authorities burned two slaves at the stake for murdering their mistress, which city leaders required that all Perth Amboy slaves attend as a warning against future transgressions.[64]

The anti-abolition petitions written before the Revolution had repeatedly warned of the death and destruction that would result from black savagery. These beliefs took on some basis in reality for many slave masters when fear of black revolt came alive in 1772 as, in the midst of abolitionist discussions, Somerset County slaveholders learned that their slaves had congregated in mass meetings at night to discuss freedom. Masters in Somerset had feared just such discontent as they had repeatedly observed their slaves disobeying the state's slave code. In 1771, for instance, Somerset County justice of the peace Jacob Van Noorstrand recorded the convictions of ten slaves for violating the nine o'clock curfew and for theft.[65] Similar occurrences of rebellious activity occurred in Middlesex County in 1771 when Isaac, a slave of Joseph Moore, stole from a neighbor's house, and continued throughout the Revolution, as George Ryerson of Bergen County found out when his slave Bet burned down his barn in 1780.[66]

Jersey slaves, absorbing the rhetoric of revolution from patriot sources, forced the issue of slave freedom even farther when, in 1774, slaveholders in Shrewsbury and Middletown complained that their slaves increasingly ignored the curfew regulations and, as in Somerset, met at night to create a plan to "cut the throats of their masters" and take over the state. In 1775, the Committee of Safety in Shrewsbury safeguarded against black revolt by banning all slave meetings. Any slave found off his master's property would be arrested immediately. Shrewsbury leaders ordered the militia to conduct nightly slave patrols and gave it authority to punish slaves with at least fifteen lashes for a variety of offenses.[67]

The fires that ravaged Baltimore, Philadelphia, Savannah, and New York in December 1776 further inflamed tensions among whites already anxious over the possibility of revolt. In 1797, Alexander Hamilton received a letter from Angelica Church, who still suffered from "terrors of fevers and Negro plots" that she traced back directly to the fires of December 1776. New York City newspaper reports claimed that "the minds of the citizens are in a state of agitation" because many believed rebellious slaves had set the fires.[68] The fears that kept Church awake at night had been realized for New Yorkers even before 1776. In 1775, whites in densely slave-populated Ulster and Queens Counties reported foiling two separate slave revolts. Ulster slaves had planned to set fire to their masters' houses and then attack the whites as they fled from the blazes. In Queens, white leaders reported that slaves for "many miles" had been involved in an abstract plot to "destroy the white people."[69] In 1778, masters discovered another such plot in Albany when an anonymous letter claimed that slaves had been ready to kill their masters and set fire to the town.[70] These fears were not confined to the New York area. South Carolina slaveholders were panicked by the "dread of instigated insurrections" when they thought that a sloop carrying the new royal governor, William Campbell, brought with it arms for slaves.[71] Likewise, Gervais Werch, writing from Charleston in 1775, believed South Carolinians were "threatened with insurrections from our slaves and invasions from our neighbors."[72] Even the Marquis de Lafayette's party chose, when sailing to Charleston, to "carry arms rather than clothing to defend . . . against marauding Negroes."[73]

As in New York and South Carolina, the danger of black revolt became more prevalent as British forces crisscrossed New Jersey and freedom for slaves became that much more tangible. In August 1776, Jonathan Dickinson Sergeant, a Princeton lawyer and member of the Second Continental Congress, wrote to John Adams that New Jersey had to call out its militia "in such numbers for the defense of our country" as the "slaves left at home excite an alarm for the safety of their families."[74] In 1779, Sergeant's fears became reality as local loyalists and British forces coaxed slaves near Elizabethtown to murder their masters. Even though Elizabethtown authorities discovered the plot in its planning stages and quickly suppressed it, that the plot existed at all highlights the important role that the British played as an outside agitator in stoking fears of rebellion. For these reasons, abolition became a far more problematic endeavor because whites believed slavery allowed them to maintain control over a potentially rebellious black population.[75]

British efforts at creating an atmosphere conducive to slave revolt caused owners to not only fear mass plots but individual slave action as well. Daniel Hart's murder by his slave Cuffee in Hopewell Township was representative of this fear among Jersey whites. In 1779, Cuffee stabbed his master with a penknife dozens of times before ultimately killing him with an ax. Local lore recorded that Cuffee fled the scene, pursued by Hart's neighbors. Cornered near a local stream, Cuffee hanged himself from a tree rather than be captured. A local writer quickly wrote a multiverse ballad about the murder, which claimed how "Hart's wicked negro did slay him

. . . the neighbors then for him did look . . . hung with a rope upon a limb
. . . the next day they did then prepare a fire to burn his body there . . . all
Negroes who have life and breath, take warning of his wretched death,
don't take an ax or use a knife to destroy your master's life." Of course, the
ballad served to make Cuffee's death an example to local blacks in order to
prevent similar violence in the tense revolutionary environment.[76]

Many Jersey masters saw British efforts to recruit blacks as particularly
dangerous because the British army provided a ready vehicle for ex-slaves
to spread destruction and death in retribution for past wrongs. In their
rhetoric about the Revolution, patriot authors frequently claimed that the
Crown had brought war upon itself through the agitation of the colonists'
enemies: Indians and slaves. For example, in 1775 Benjamin Franklin wrote
that William Draper's *Thoughts of a Traveler upon Our American Disputes*
had excited "the domestic slaves" and encouraged them to "cut their master's throats." Lord Dunmore's proclamation further fueled this desire and
excited a larger "insurrection among the blacks."[77] North Carolinian
Thomas Burke wrote in a similar vein in 1777, claiming that the British
had tried to entice the "savage Indians" to make war "on Western frontiers" and excite "insurrections . . . among the slaves." Even after the Revolution, George Mason remembered that slaves had been a "dangerous
instrument" in the hands of the enemy as the British had attempted to
"arm the servants and slaves" of both Maryland and Virginia.[78]

Of course, rhetoric turned into reality when British forces in New York,
inundated with runaway slaves, began to recruit them into the army. The
rate of recruitment increased significantly after Henry Clinton's 1779 guarantee of freedom to all slaves who deserted their masters, even though the
practice had been ongoing since 1777 and even had been discussed by the
colonial secretary, Lord Dartmouth, as early as May 1775. Indeed, in June
1775, General Thomas Gage believed that the "crisis" had become so dire
that "we must avail ourselves of every resource even to raise the Negroes in
our cause" as the American "rage and enthusiasm" for war had been shown
by this point. By July 1776, patriot leaders received reports of large numbers
of blacks mustering with British regiments.[79]

Black British troops plundering white-owned property first signaled the
elevation of black power in New Jersey and assaulted the state's racial hier-
archy since, for the first time, blacks had been empowered to take white
property and frequently did so in the king's service. In two cases adjudicated in Mount Holly in June 1778, British officials investigated former

slaves for plundering, even though foraging for supplies across the state had led to routine looting of private property. In one case, ex-slave Primus Cuffey captured and killed a pig, claiming in his defense that he did not know of the general order against plundering. The court still found him guilty and he received five hundred lashes. Unlike Cuffey, James Powers and Samuel Martin, accused of breaking into a civilian's home and stealing meat, convinced the court martial of their innocence.[80]

Direct action against patriots did more than property crimes to instill trepidations among white New Jerseyans, as black British regiments targeted patriots along the ragged borderland between American and British territory. Newark minister Alexander MacWhorter described the dangers of arming black men when he detailed the aftermath of a British attack on his city in 1777. The enemy force, which included black British troops, made the town "look more like a scene of ruin than a pleasant well cultivated village." Former slaves invaded and assaulted at least three men. One man was "cut and slashed" horribly while "three women were most horridly ravished by them, one of them an old woman near seventy years of age, whom they abused in a manner beyond description, another of them was a woman considerably advanced in her pregnancy, and the third was a young girl."[81]

The Newark raid reflected whites' most powerful fears, that ex-slaves would kill, rape, and pillage their former masters' homes and families. Even some British officers believed that marauding black troops were particularly dangerous because they "distress and maltreat the inhabitants infinitely more than the whole army at the same time that they engross, waste, and destroy."[82] The danger these blacks represented came into clearer focus in 1782 when the British court-martialed nine former slaves for the murder of Cornelius Nissee of Bergen County. The nine defendants all served as members of British militia units based in Bergen Neck. Major Thomas Grant, who commanded the Refugee Corps at Bergen Neck, testified that these soldiers operated independently of whites in certain circumstances. William Grant, one of the men on trial, confessed that a former slave named Sisco, whom they called Colonel, advocated that the group should "go out . . . to take a rebel." The nine left their camp, seized two Bergen residents and marched them a few miles before releasing one. Sisco ordered the group to shoot the other, Nissee, at which time Grant objected. Another prisoner, Caesar Totten, stepped in and shot him in the chest while a second shot came from Daniel Massis's gun. The group then took Nissee's money, clothing, and shoes, hid the body with branches and leaves, and traveled back to their camp.[83]

After further investigation, British officers discovered that one of the ex-slaves knew why the group selected Nissee to execute—he had been a fellow soldier's former owner. Harry Scobey, also accused of capital murder, had been Nissee's slave before he absconded to the British. According to the investigating officer, Scobey had been angry with Nissee because he had sold his wife out of New Jersey. For the British, the case hinged on if Scobey had been present at the killing or if he had motivated the men to search for his former master. In its decision, the court affirmed that Scobey and four other defendants either had not been at the scene of the crime or had not encouraged it. Four others, however, received death sentences for Nissee's murder. On a practical level, even though Scobey did not actively attempt to seek out his former master, it is of particular interest because the act of ex-slaves murdering slaveholders increased concern among Jersey whites that violence from blacks in British employ would affect slavery's operation.[84]

These vivid examples of former slaves conspiring to exert power over white New Jerseyans, especially their former masters, stoked white concerns across the state that the British were actively fomenting a race war. Colonel Tye, or Titus, a slave from Colts Neck in Monmouth County, became the prime example of these fears after he absconded from his master the day after Lord Dunmore promised freedom to Virginia slaves. Even though he did not yet know of Dunmore's Proclamation, Titus believed that the British would free him from slavery. Once the British occupied New York, Titus joined the British army like so many others who had fled their patriot masters. He returned to New Jersey as Colonel Tye and fought with British forces at the Battle of Monmouth. In 1778 and 1779, Tye led a band of mostly black guerrilla fighters who operated out of a base called Refugee-town on British controlled Sandy Hook. Tye and his men attacked wealthy slaveholding patriots, burned houses, seized guns, and foraged for food and supplies in order to disrupt patriot activities and maintain the British war machine. In one 1780 engagement, Tye led a biracial group of thirty blacks, twenty white loyalists, and thirty-two Queen's Rangers to capture leading Monmouth County patriot Barnes Smock. In addition to Smock, the party took twelve other Monmouth patriots prisoner, destroyed one cannon, captured two artillery horses, and burned several patriot homes. In his report of the raid to Governor Livingston, New Jersey militia officer David

Forman pleaded with him to take into "account of our other numerous distresses" and send additional troops to protect the region.[85]

Monmouth County residents decried the attacks by their former slaves and requested emergency assistance from Governor Livingston. The county had already been devastated by the early years of the war and was even more battered after the Battle of Monmouth. John Fell, a delegate to the Continental Congress, wrote to Robert Morris that Monmouth County had been ravaged by the war "as bad as Bergen," the county that bore much of the blunt of British raiding parties. Fell further relayed the story of a relative whose slave escaped from her Monmouth house. This slave, Fell claimed, "makes the fifth Negroe had gone to the enemy and has besides robbed the house."[86] After the attacks by Colonel Tye, the county residents claimed that "it is not possible . . . to prevent the frequent ravages of the enemy . . . they have been in Shrewsbury twice since" the last petition.[87]

In response to the distress caused by these former slaves, Livingston declared martial law and sent 210 men from Hunterdon and Burlington to Monmouth to defend against Tye.[88] However, during the summer of 1780, Tye continued to engage Monmouth County patriots and in September 1780 made his most dramatic attack, attempting to capture Monmouth militia officer Joshua Huddy. After a fierce two-hour battle in Toms River, he ultimately failed. Huddy escaped (though loyalists, including elements of Tye's unit, eventually captured and hanged him on a Monmouth County beach) and Tye and his soldiers returned to their base on Sandy Hook. Tye suffered a minor bullet wound to the wrist in the battle. Lacking appropriate medical treatment, the wound became infected and Tye died of lockjaw a few days after the failed raid.[89]

Tye, as leader of the Sandy Hook unit, had done much to bring fear and destruction to the county where he had toiled as a slave. His fellow ex-slaves continued to inspire fear after his death, where, led by ex-slave Colonel Stephen Blucke, they persisted in raiding patriot targets. In 1782, for example, forty whites and forty blacks under Blucke attacked the salt works at Forked River and raided nearby homes. These black troops continued operations until 1783 when the Black Brigade became the last British unit to evacuate New York.[90]

The attacks of Colonel Tye and the black guerrilla fighters from Refugeetown instilled genuine fear among white slaveholders throughout New Jersey and destabilized the racial order. They wondered that if Tye could be so destructive against his former owners, how their slaves would act if they gained freedom. While the destructive impact of the war definitely slowed the path toward abolition, the fear of black revolt and the images of black violence against whites caused many to question if abolitionism, making steady progress in Pennsylvania and New England, was right for New Jersey. Fear of the consequences of abolition, the violence MacWhorter saw in Newark, and the attacks Colonel Tye executed in Monmouth helped stymie efforts to extend the Revolution's rhetoric of freedom to those still held in bondage.

*   *   *

As opposed to the promises of the king's army, service with Continental forces never guaranteed freedom since Americans hoped to reinforce the institution, not destroy it by freeing too many slaves. New Jersey, like most states, did not allow slaves or freed blacks to join the militia, thereby reinforcing the state's existing racial boundaries. George Washington purged his army of all blacks only five days after Lord Dunmore's 1775 proclamation, fearing that the enlistment of blacks would "render slavery more irksome to those who remain in it" because black troops might lead an uncontrollable liberation movement. In a society that continually dreaded slave revolt, Washington's call for limitations on black enlistment seemed logical and comforting to many whites who feared armed slaves.[91]

By early 1776, however, Washington faced a manpower shortage and began to allow free blacks and slaves to serve, most notably in Rhode Island. Washington himself remained hesitant about their enlistment, especially in South Carolina and Georgia. The lack of strong support from Washington led both states to use slaves not as soldiers but as bounties. In the last four years of the war especially, South Carolinians used slaves as an enlistment bonus for white soldiers. However, South Carolina general and politician John Laurens believed that even this generous bounty would prove futile as most eligible men had already joined the military.[92] Instead, James Madison pondered if it would be more expedient "to liberate and make soldiers at once of the blacks themselves" since enlisting blacks would "certainly be more consonant to the principles of liberty which ought never to be lost sight of in a contest for liberty."[93]

In some commanders' minds, black troops had an important role to play in the American military: as foils against black British troops. In New Jersey, for example, Governor Livingston asked Washington in 1777 that if

nothing else could restrain the barbarity of the British who ravaged the
state the preceding year, "it may not be improper to let loose upon them a
few of General Stephen's tawny Yagers, the only Americans that can match
them in their bloody work." The men Livingston referred to, black soldiers
serving in Major General Adam Stephen's Virginia brigade, could, in Livingston's opinion, fight the black British troops on their own terms because
of their perceived inherent barbarity.[94] In the same way, General Anthony
Wayne advocated in 1782 that Georgia enlist black troops as "a matter of
necessity," since the British had actively recruited a black corps in Charleston and Savannah.[95] The British interest in recruiting blacks remained high
as Lord Dunmore, writing from South Carolina, believed that they would
be the "most efficacious, expeditious, cheapest, and certain means of reducing (the patriots) to a proper sense of their duty." Dunmore claimed that
blacks were better suited for service in the warmer southern climate and
many in the British ranks believed that using black troops would "strike at
the root of all property . . . making the wealth and riches of the enemy the
means of bringing them to obedience." These blacks, according to the
report, would "bring the most violent to their senses."[96]

In the midst of the British invasion of 1776, open discussion among
delegates to the Continental Congress ensued over the possibility of raising
a battalion of blacks in New Jersey to serve as a home guard. New Jersey's
Jonathan Dickinson Sergeant sent his plan to raise this regiment to John
Adams in August 1776 since he believed the militia could provide only a
limited defense. According to him, Congress could enlist blacks and pay
slaveholders fifty pounds per slave plus provide an exemption from militia
service for those who offered their slaves. Under Sergeant's plan, slaves'
monthly salary would repay the state for their purchase price. Once the
debt was extinguished, the slave would earn his freedom. Sergeant theorized
that any slave who committed a crime or engaged in misconduct while a
soldier would be returned to slavery, a punishment designed to stymie the
three objections he foresaw to his plan. The first, that slaves "generally are
cowards," would be answered easily by suggesting that the idea of "liberty
before their eyes as the reward of their valour" will motivate them. Second,
Sergeant claimed that his plan would negate the possibility of revolt because
the slaves, if they could gain freedom, would work toward that rather than
fomenting rebellion. Finally, Sergeant countered the fear many whites had
of the presence of large numbers of freed blacks in American society after
the war by arguing that ex-slaves could be resettled on western lands

because, in his opinion, "there is room enough on this continent for them and us too."[97] Adams responded to Sergeant a few days later that "your negro battalion will never do" because "South Carolina would run out of their wits at the least hint of such a measure." Adams then quietly dropped Sergeant's plan, fearful of South Carolina's response.[98]

Sergeant's plan, unpopular even among New Jerseyans who feared rebellion, was never adopted by state legislators, nor was any other regulated strategy for the enlistment of slaves or freed blacks. Instead, blacks in the New Jersey militia and Continental Line served in integrated units as teamsters, servants, and in some cases, ordinary enlisted men. Even though some used their Revolutionary experience to acquire freedom, land, or pensions, these men were atypical and did not represent the wider experience of Jersey blacks or any commitment to black freedom. Haphazardly executed, the enlistment of black troops mainly served white interests because slaves could serve as substitutes for their masters. Sketchy military service records reveal that at least twenty-nine blacks served with various New Jersey units, though it is likely that more remain unrecorded. Reports from Hessian soldiers indicate the wide use of black troops in New Jersey. Some, writing about their service in Springfield, remarked that "Negroes, in common with other cattle, are very prolific here." They claimed that "the negro is sometimes sent to war instead of his youthful owner" and therefore "there is scarcely a regiment in which you shall not find some well-built and hardy fellows" serving as substitutes for whites.[99]

One of these slaves, Samuel Sutphen of Somerset County, joined the Patriot cause as a substitute for his owner, Casper Berger. His original owner, Barbardus LaGrange, had declared his loyalty to Britain and fled to New York, leaving Sutphen to be confiscated as part of a forfeited loyalist estate. Berger bought Sutphen from the state and offered him freedom if he served as his substitute for the war's duration. Sutphen agreed and joined the Somerset County Militia and later served in a Cumberland County unit as well. In his 1832 pension application, Sutphen claimed that he fought at the Battle of Long Island and served on garrison duty at several locations in New Jersey that winter. In January 1777, he fought at Princeton with Washington, engaged in several skirmishes in summer and fall 1777 around the Millstone River, and, by 1778, marched to Monmouth where he narrowly missed the battle with the British. Sutphen then joined the expedition to Fort Stanwix, New York, where he and his unit pursued Britain's Indian allies as far north as Buffalo. On his return south, Hessians and

British Highlanders ambushed his company in Westchester County, where a bullet drove his pants button into his right leg just above the ankle. Waylaid because of his injury for almost three months, Sutphen returned to Readington and served until 1780. However, upon his discharge, Berger reneged on his promise of freedom and sold him to Peter Ten Eyck. Ten Eyck then sold him to John Duryea, who then sold him to Peter Sutphen. By 1805, Samuel Sutphen finally achieved legal freedom only by purchasing himself, not due to his revolutionary service.[100]

Sutphen, eighty-five when he applied for a federal pension, managed to secure numerous letters of support from prominent Somerset whites who believed, as supporter William Gaston claimed, that Sutphen was "highly meritorious of a pension" because he "ably and nobly performed" his duties as a soldier. The federal government, however, rejected his claim, explaining in an 1833 letter "that being a slave originally," Sutphen "was not bound to serve in the militia and the circumstances of each tour of actual service (were) not . . . stated as was required." In a continuing debate on the status of his claim, the Pension Office in 1834 and 1835 maintained that his service against the Indians remained "very doubtful" and that he most likely had not served a full six months as required by the pension law. In an unlikely show of support to a black veteran, the Frelinghuysen family, a powerful Jersey political dynasty, intervened and petitioned the state legislature to support Sutphen. In response, the state granted Sutphen a pension for the last five years of his life.[101]

Though rare, other New Jersey blacks managed to negotiate for freedom, pensions, and land in exchange for their participation in the Patriot cause. John Ceasar from Sussex County, for example, a private in the Fourth New Jersey, joined the army in December 1776 and served in multiple units before his discharge in May 1783. In a 1780 muster roll, his unit recorded that Ceasar had received a western land grant that he augmented in 1800 with another. Similarly, Oliver Cromwell of Burlington County joined the Second New Jersey Regiment in 1777 at age twenty-six. He served at the Battle of Short Hills among other engagements and was discharged in June 1783. For at least part of his service, Cromwell belonged to the same regiment as another young African American, Thomas Case, who served for nine months in Phillips' Company, Second New Jersey Regiment, from 1778 to 1779. For his service, Cromwell received a land grant in 1791 and successfully applied for a pension of ninety-six dollars a year in 1820 at age sixty-seven. In his application, Cromwell claimed that after his military service, he became a "common laborer . . . but from age" he could no longer "get a livelihood." He listed approximately ten dollars in property and reported that he needed to care for his twenty-five-year-old infirm daughter and two young sons, ages twelve and ten. Cromwell continued to collect that pension until he died in 1852, just two months short of his hundredth birthday.[102]

Unlike the cases of Sutphen and Cromwell, most records list only the most basic information about blacks who fought with the patriots. Negro Stephen, for example, joined the Second Regiment of Continental Dragoons in December 1781 as a private, while Negro Pomp, a teamster in charge of a four-horse wagon, served in Trenton in 1780. Negro Jack, Negro Cezar, Negro Dick, and Negro Will all did the same, but no additional information survives to tell more than their names and occupations within the army. With limited records available, it remains incredibly difficult to reconstruct the lives of these enslaved and formerly enslaved African Americans in Continental service. However, as New Jersey, like most other states, never actively recruited black soldiers or promised freedom in exchange for military service, it stands likely that most of these enslaved men returned, like Samuel Sutphen, to their masters as slaves.[103]

*   *   *

In addition to fears of slave revolt and economic devastation, anxiety over a sizeable loyalist population led the state to reinforce slavery by confiscating and selling loyalist property. The revolutionary government in Trenton demanded that residents take loyalty oaths to affirm their standing within the new American body politic. Those who refused became targets of both ridicule and violence, leading thousands of New Jerseyans to flee to British lines and thousands more to remain neutral or harbor secret loyalist sentiments. The anxiety created by the constant British attacks increased the intensity of anger and animosity toward Jersey loyalists and precipitated laws that punished the disloyal by confiscating their property to help finance the war effort. Loyalists Daniel and Henry Van Mater, for example, claimed in 1779 that Jersey loyalists "have been since obligated to quit their homes and property in a very precipitate manner," which had left many in severe financial straits after the state confiscated them. Guy Carleton similarly remarked that New Jersey patriots increasingly excluded the loyalists "with circumstances of additional rage," making their loyalty even more problematic for them.[104] Patriots regularly confiscated and sold loyalist estates, which included land, houses, horses, kitchenware, bedding, and, most important, slaves. The state-sponsored sales of slaves symbolized the state's reaffirmation that African Americans were equated with property, not freedom.[105]

Though the sale of loyalist-owned slaves reinforced the equation of slaves as property, it had more to do with the hatred of loyalists and the need to profit from them rather than a concerted proslavery effort. New Jersey's first state legislature, after it had deposed Royal Governor William Franklin, drafted new laws that imposed rigid guidelines on loyalty, which warned of the presence of persons "so wicked as to devise the destruction of good government or to aid or assist the enemies of the state." It declared those who remained loyal to the Crown guilty of high treason.[106] In 1778, the legislature enacted even more stringent regulations requiring the confiscation of property owned by those convicted of treason. The Commissioners of Forfeited Estates in each of New Jersey's thirteen counties began to depose witnesses and establish cases that called into question the loyalty of hundreds of New Jerseyans. The commissioners brought treason cases before sympathetic patriot juries that routinely found the accused guilty, which triggered the seizure and sale of the traitor's property.[107]

New Jersey patriots ecstatically supported the confiscation of loyalist estates and encouraged the state to enact harsher anti-Tory laws. In 1781, ninety-eight patriots in Morris County petitioned for a law to allow the confiscation of property belonging to "a number of evil minded villains and disaffected persons" who entered New Jersey "in a secret and clandestine manner for the purpose of plundering and taking away the . . . property of the (state's) good inhabitants." These patriots demanded compensation from them for their economic losses.[108] Similarly, Monmouth County residents applauded confiscation in 1779 and asked the legislature to use the money raised to reimburse them for damages caused by British raids, including those from Colonel Tye's unit.[109]

Patriotic fervor quickly turned to outrage and demands for greater state oversight when residents learned that the commissioners of the forfeited estates had abused their powers. Monmouth County patriots complained of the dishonorable conduct of the commissioners in manipulating sales so that friends, allies, and relatives could purchase estates at cut-rate prices. In Monmouth, as in other locales, the commissioners frequently published notices only one day before the sale, ignored higher bids in favor of their lower bidding friends, accepted bids after the auction had closed, sold estates as one cohesive package instead of in individual pieces, and prevented bidders from inspecting the property before the auction as required by law. These failures forced the legislature to enact even stricter sale regulations and required the legislative and executive branches to take an active and integrated role in the sales of loyalist property, including slaves.[110]

The state's role in slave sales had been ongoing since the early 1700s because British and later American admiralty courts routinely approved the sale of "Prize Negroes" captured from enemy ships. The eighteenth century especially saw hundreds of these captured black mariners sold into slavery since the colonies waged war almost continually since the 1730s in conflicts such as the War of Jenkins' Ear, King George's War, and the Seven Years' War. The war against Spain in the late 1730s and early 1740s brought hundreds of "dark-skinned Spanish sailors" into American ports, especially in New York and New Jersey, which served as colonial privateering centers. Mid-Atlantic admiralty courts frequently determined that "the mere darkness of the Spaniards' skin" enabled them to be sold as slaves even if they had been previously free. One such former Spanish sailor, George, a twenty-six-year-old slave from Burlington County, likely had been captured by privateers since records describe him in 1749 as a "Spanish mulatto fellow" who spoke "indifferent English" and had once "been a privateering."[111]

During the American Revolution, American admiralty courts continued the colonial practice of condemning captured black British mariners as slaves for sale. The prize system in the Mid-Atlantic both inflicted extensive damage to the British while enriching American seamen, ship owners, and government officials who regulated these sales. As historian Charles Foy contends, the prize system "extended the reach of American slavery beyond the shores of the Americas" and in turn reinforced slavery in the United States. Privateers, motivated more by profit than ideology, saw blacks as a profitable revenue source. These vulnerable individuals could be taken easily and sold as commodities in other ports, which led ship captains to actively seek out blacks on the high seas. Congressional laws on prizes allowed for considerable leeway in local admiralty court decisions about the status of blacks found on British ships. In New Jersey, especially along the Delaware River, courts operated from "the assumption that a black mariner was a slave" and could be sold as a prize along with any other goods found on the ships.[112] For instance, on June 26, 1782, James Esdall of Burlington adjudicated the sale of Obadiah Gale and Edward Cater, both of whom had served aboard a British privateer but who had not been slaves.[113] In the same year, John Bray, the captain and owner of the gunboat *Revenge*, attacked the British cutter *Alert* and forced the ship to run aground. Salvaging "a quantity of power, arms, a valuable chest of medicine," Bray reported to Governor Livingston that he sent the ship's crew to Elizabethtown for exchange but kept the eleven blacks he found on board because the admiralty court declared them captured goods instead of crew members. Bray, in June 1782, sold nine of these Prize Negroes in Trenton at auction.[114] The process played out the same way in October 1779 when American privateers captured the British ship *Triton* and six black mariners went to auction in Burlington.[115]

The state's experience in selling Prize Negroes informed its sales of loyalist-owned slaves. However, surviving records on these sales remain in short supply. Records of individual estate sales that contain inventories listing slaves exist for only a few counties and record only twenty-nine slaves sold by the state.[116] Records filed at the end of the Revolution with the Loyalist Claims Commission include evidence of at least 112 more.[117] Of course, the total of 141 slaves likely represents only part of the real total as extraneous sources refer to slaves not included in these records.[118]

A majority of the slaves confiscated from loyalists came from masters who had rejected the American cause very early on. For instance, Absalom Bainbridge, Prime's owner who began this chapter, joined the king's forces in 1776 and left Princeton with the British after their defeat in January 1777.[119] Like Bainbridge, fellow Princeton resident Richard Cochran joined the British as soon as General Howe entered the city in 1776. Cochran helped procure provisions for the army, served as a deputy commissary, and administered oaths to local civilians. He claimed that because of his loyalty, patriots had seized his property, sold it at auction, and, in his own words, threatened to "hang me up were I ever to return to that country." Due to poor health, he left military service and moved to London with his two sons in January 1778, leaving his wife and daughter in British-occupied New York. Cochran claimed an estate valued at just over 6,100 pounds, which included eight slaves (four men, two women, and two children), one of whom, his "Negro man named Mingo, was esteemed the most valuable Negro in New Jersey." The commission approved his claim but paid only 1912 pounds because they believed his new position as a clerk provided him a stable salary.[120]

While many loyalists fled the state with their families, others left their property in New Jersey to be protected by their wives. In July 1777, the state Council of Safety argued that these wives "obstruct(ed) the commissioners for seizing and disposing of the personal estate" by secretly and gradually moving property into New York. The council banished eighteen women to New York, "after their husbands," so that the commissioners could more easily confiscate their property.[121] Likewise, certain slave owners attempted to remove their slaves to New York so as not to let them fall into the hands of the patriots. Prime's owner Bainbridge attempted this, but because Prime ran away, he lost him to Patriot confiscation. However, some slaves did the opposite of Prime and resisted confiscation by running toward their loyalist masters. For example, the slave of loyalist John Ackerman escaped from the man who had bought him at auction, Andrew Hopper, in 1778. The slave, whose name remains unrecorded, fled to Ackerman's protection in New York.[122]

Like New Jersey, other states confiscated and sold slaves from loyalist estates and reinforced slavery within their borders. In Connecticut, Jeremiah Leaming joined the British along with his slave Pomp after loyalists burned Norwalk in 1779. Pomp ran away from his master but, as part of a traitor's estate, he belonged to the people of Connecticut. However, due to his perceived loyalty to the American cause, the legislature granted Pomp freedom.[123] Similarly, southern states like Georgia and South Carolina used confiscated slaves as teamsters, servants, and military laborers to build defensive fortifications. As discussed earlier, South Carolina offered a slave to every white man who joined the army and a slave to any soldier who could recruit twenty-five men, while Georgia awarded slaves to soldiers and sold them to finance the state government.[124]

The most important part of New Jersey's slave sales, however, rested in how the state dealt with its confiscated slaves at the end of the Revolution. In neighboring New York, the New York Manumission Society successfully lobbied that state's legislature to free all remaining confiscated slaves in 1786 instead of selling them, though most of the confiscated able-bodied slaves had already been sold. The society even obtained a guarantee of taxpayer support to care for the slaves in their old age.[125] In New Jersey, however, the legislature only agreed to free three confiscated slaves who had actively supported the Patriot cause. In 1784, the legislature freed Peter Williams, a slave of John Heard from Woodbridge who, in 1780, had joined the Continental Army after his master had enlisted in the British military.[126] Likewise, two years later, the legislature read the petition of Bainbridge's slave Prime, who had, like Williams, absconded from his loyalist master and joined the New Jersey militia. They granted Prime freedom in 1786. In 1789, Cato became the final slave to earn freedom due to military service, as he too had joined the Patriots after his master fled to the British.[127] With only three emancipation bills, the legislature made clear that it fully supported the sale of confiscated slaves and the continued bondage of those not under state control. That only three slaves gained freedom after the Revolution reinforced the unfree status of African Americans in New Jersey. These confiscated slaves would, in the mid-1780s, play a major role in convincing the legislature to delay gradual abolition.[128]

*   *   *

Prime's ability to negotiate for freedom due to his service in the Continental Army at one level places him among an incredibly small group of slaves who accessed a free life through service with the Americans. However, in a larger sense Prime is representative of the Revolution's impact on slaves. Some, like Prime, used the war to their advantage and seized freedom themselves but most understood that slavery remained an entrenched system in New Jersey.

The emergence of a strong post-revolutionary slave system owed much to New Jersey's position as a borderland between Patriot and Loyalist America. Abolitionists had championed the idea of black freedom but, with no organized state-level abolition society and the reality that British forces slept close by, legislative abolition stalled. The ravages of total war combined with the fears created by the actions of Colonel Tye and other ex-slaves who joined the British army convinced many whites that wartime abolition would result in further dislocation and lack of control. Of course, Jersey blacks used the Revolution to seek freedom on their own terms, yet these methods proved largely ineffective in overturning entrenched proslavery thought and practice for more than a small minority of slaves. Their exploits actually reinforced the state's racial boundaries, strengthened anti-abolition sentiment, and limited abolition's reach because absconding slaves helped exacerbate white anxieties of revolt.

In the end, the state's confiscation and sale of loyalist owned slaves represented the true meaning of the Revolution for African Americans in New Jersey: Revolutionary freedom would not extend to them. The Revolution reinforced the colonial slave system in the short run instead of convincing New Jerseyans to support gradual abolition laws, as had occurred in Pennsylvania, Connecticut, and Rhode Island. In New Jersey, it took twenty-one years after the Revolution's end to pass a gradual abolition statute. In that battle, the memory of the meaning of the Revolution, not the actual reality of its destructive power, became critical in convincing legislators to support abolitionism.

CHAPTER THREE

Abolishing Slavery in the New Nation

Julian Niemcewicz, the exiled Polish statesman and writer, moved to Eliza-bethtown in 1797 and married Susan Livingston Kean, the niece of former governor William Livingston. He bought an eighteen-acre farm and settled into his new life as a gentleman farmer. His wife had a close association with slavery, as her deceased husband, John Kean of South Carolina, owned over one hundred slaves. After Kean's death in 1795, Susan owned and traded those slaves, continuing to do so after her remarriage. Even though slavery was integral to the couple's household, Niemcewicz remained puzzled as to slavery's place in American society. After discovering that Elizabethtown's prison kept only "negro slaves who have deserted their masters," he wondered how Americans could support slavery in a "free and democratic Republic," especially after they had just fought a long and bloody revolution for that freedom.[1]

Niemcewicz recognized what historian Edmund Morgan eventually termed "the American Paradox," the growing interest in slavery in the aftermath of a revolution for freedom. While the American Revolution rep-resented a new birth of political freedom, most slaves remained in bondage after the guns fell silent. Economic imperatives allowed for slavery's growth in the Deep South while revolutionary ideology pressed for the institution's end in the Upper South and the North. This freedom paradox helped con-vince Massachusetts, Vermont, Pennsylvania, Connecticut, and Rhode Island to either abolish slavery or pass gradual abolition laws in the 1780s. Likewise, Virginians, Marylanders, and Delawareans questioned the institu-tion by forming abolition societies and loosening manumission restrictions. Though no Chesapeake states went as far as abolition, economic changes and rhetoric equating British tyranny to slavery's oppression slowly altered perceptions of the institution.[2]

However, New Jersey did not immediately follow the lead of Pennsylvania and New England. As opposed to Philadelphia physician Benjamin Rush, who believed the American Revolution was abolition's "seed," I maintain that the Revolution helped entrench slavery deeper in New Jersey and served as a bulwark against freedom. The years after the war likewise marked an increase in slavery's numerical pervasiveness and overall popularity. It took twenty years of abolitionist activity, protests from slaves, and a political realignment to force New Jersey to adopt gradual abolition in 1804.[3]

In this period of struggle, white and black New Jerseyans debated the ideas of freedom within the context of a growing economic and social interest in slavery. While slavery grew, Pennsylvania Abolition Society (PAS) members and Jersey Quakers founded the state's first abolitionist organization, the New Jersey Society for Promoting the Abolition of Slavery, in 1793. However, this largely West Jersey Quaker organization remained weak throughout its existence and actually aggravated racial tensions. By 1800, East and West Jersey had fractured on the slavery question. West Jersey had largely eliminated slavery, while in contrast, most East Jersey whites supported bound labor and saw the West's advocacy of abolition as an intrusion into their economic livelihood. Slavery became the divisive issue that inflamed a long history of disunity between the two regions that in turn delayed abolition.

Neither abolitionist rhetoric nor resistance from slaves alone tipped the state toward gradual abolition. Instead, the partisan debates between Federalists and Democratic Republicans in the 1790s dealt slavery's final blow. Unlike the movements in other states where abolitionism developed organically without strong political affiliations, Jersey Democratic Republicans advanced abolitionism to showcase their political suitability as adherents to the true spirit of 1776. They used abolition as a symbol of that revolutionary spirit, which united East and West Jersey interests and empowered the new party politically and morally.[4]

Gradual abolition was a consequence of this political wrangling and, as in other states, most white New Jerseyans supported it for self-serving reasons. Most abolitionists "dress[ed] it up as a gift" given from "the empowered possessors of freedom to the unfree and disempowered slave." Such motivations, though, should not mitigate the actions of slaves who advocated for their own freedom in the 1790s. Indeed, many achieved freedom or an amelioration of their condition in slavery and I explore their experiences as well, especially since they helped create the conditions that allowed legislative abolition occur. In the end though, New Jersey offered fewer avenues for slaves to negotiate than other northern states due to slavery's growth in the state. The lack of strong white support for abolition independent of politics allowed slaveholders eventually to exploit loopholes in the law, which forced most Jersey slaves to walk a complicated path toward freedom even after gradual abolition began in 1804.[5]

*   *   *

In 1784, Connecticut and Rhode Island followed Pennsylvania and passed gradual abolition laws while New Jersey abolitionists, supported by Governor Livingston, proposed that their state follow suit. Livingston strongly supported abolition, writing in 1786 that slavery was "an indelible blot . . . upon the character of those who have so strongly asserted the unalienable rights of mankind."[6] In 1785, Livingston and Quaker activist David Cooper had urged the legislature to ban slave importations and enact gradual abolition. Cooper himself readily believed that blacks and whites "are born equally free" and claimed that because the United States had just fought a war for freedom, Americans could not withhold that freedom from blacks. This revolutionary rhetoric fused religious ideology, morality, and Enlightenment ideals into the postwar abolition fight. Hunterdon County abolitionists, for instance, called for a restoration of the "reverence for liberty which is the vital principle of a republic."[7]

The 1785 abolition proposal failed because legislators still believed that stripping slaveholders of their property would push the state deeper into economic recession while continuing slavery could spur recovery. Even Pennsylvania, which enacted gradual abolition in 1780, grappled with abolition's economic consequences in the midst of war. Abolitionist William Rawle, remembering the 1780 decision years later, claimed that "a fear of inconveniences on account of the war then raging probably prevented the legislature from going further" to pass a stronger abolition law.[8] New Jersey, a battlefield for the entire war, registered significant economic losses, especially in the heavily slave-populated areas bordering New York. Whites there opposed a quick move toward abolition; Quaker-dominated West Jersey supported its speedy adoption. This sectional split furnished "some of the northern counties" who saw "too rapid a progress in the business . . . with an excuse to oppose it altogether." Livingston had hoped that abolition would "have gone farther," but economic distress and slaveholder's defense of property rights limited political opportunities to abolish slavery.[9]

Livingston also identified the state's decision to sell the remaining confiscated loyalist slaves at auction at the end of the war as the "fatal error" that doomed abolition in 1785. Their sale gave "a greater sanction to legitimate the abominable practice" and questioned the justice of mandating "the manumission of slaves, without compensation to the owners" while the state simultaneously "avail[ed] itself of the proceeds in cash of the sales of similar slaves." Livingston concluded that "it must be wrong in both cases or in neither of them." The decision to sell loyalist slaves therefore opened lawmakers to charges of hypocrisy if they forced abolition after profiting from the state's own slaves, resulting in few working to advance black freedom.[10]

After abolition's 1785 failure, slavery grew increasingly pervasive in both New Jersey and New York. In the 1790s alone, the slave population of New York City expanded by 22 percent and the number of slaveholders by a third. Few slaves were freed by manumission.[11] In New Jersey, the number of slaves increased by 9 percent though, as most of West Jersey was dismantling the institution, that figure clouds its growth in the East. In the 1790s, the slave population increased in seven of the state's thirteen counties. Essex had the highest growth rate (30 percent), while Bergen and Morris each saw a 22 percent increase. This growth of the slave population reflected the need to rebuild the devastated East Jersey economy, the growing demand for New Jersey's grain crops, and the dearth of available laborers. As young men migrated to larger cities after the war, immigration from Europe no longer filled the demand. In 1797, Niemcewicz complained that "hired hands are expensive and hard to get," while the owner of a Paterson textile mill reported "three-quarters of [the] machines lay idle because of lack of hands." Slave labor filled this gap in East Jersey especially as farmers hoped to profit from the increased value of wheat and flour that the nation had seen between 1780 and 1790. Prices had nearly doubled in that decade and increased throughout the 1790s as Europe descended into war. In comparison, West Jersey had "but few slaves and the number of these continually diminishing" according to the New Jersey Abolition Society in 1801, since

Table 1. Slave Population Growth and Decline by County, 1790–1800

County	Region	Slave population (1790)	Slave population (1800)	Percent increase or decrease
Bergen	East	2301	2825	+22%
Burlington	West	227	188	−17%
Cape May	West	141	98	−31%
Cumberland	West	120	75	−38%
Essex	East	1171	1521	+30%
Gloucester	West	191	61	−68%
Hunterdon	West	1301	1220	−6%
Middlesex	East	1318	1564	+19%
Monmouth	East	1596	1633	+2%
Morris	West	636	775	+22%
Salem	West	172	85	−51%
Somerset	East	1810	1863	+3%
Sussex	West	439	514	+17%

by that year, three-quarters of the state's 12,500 slaves lived in East Jersey's five counties.[12]

Far from a small cadre of older New Jerseyans who stubbornly kept their slaves against an increasing abolitionist spirit, New Jersey's slave system attracted new whites interested in slavery's benefits. Yearly tax records from Newark (in East Jersey) and Morris (in West Jersey) between 1783 and the early nineteenth century suggest little numerical change in the number of slaves held but reveal the popularity of slaveholding among whites. In Newark in 1783 and 1789, 88 different whites owned the city's approximately 60 slaves. Only 31 percent of Newark's 1783 slaveholders still owned slaves in 1789, yet few moved out of Newark. Of the 52 slaveholders on the 1789 list, 30 still appeared in 1796, but only 8 continued to hold slaves. Whites who had previously not owned slaves purchased them after the war even as other northern states had begun to abandon bound labor.[13]

Few slaveholders in Newark and Morris manumitted their chattel, further illustrating a continued interest in slavery. Between 1783 and 1804, Newark slaveholders provided freedom in 10 of 59 wills and probates. For example, Augustine Bayles of Morris County wanted slavery to continue in his family after his death. Bayles bought Quamini in 1780 and promised him freedom at his death if Quamini served him faithfully. On his deathbed in 1785, Bayles told Quamini that he had indeed "been a good and faithful boy," but one of Bayles's friends, Daniel Layten, argued that Bayles needed to provide for his wife after his death. Bayles rescinded his manumission offer and ordered Quamini to serve his wife until she remarried, at which time he would be freed. Bayles's widow, who eventually remarried, held Quamini in violation of Bayles's wishes. Although Quamini successfully sued for his freedom with the help of local abolitionists, most slaves in New Jersey never received such freedom after their owner's death.[14]

As expected, sales of Jersey slaves increased after the Revolution with Jersey slaveholders advertising 201 slaves for sale in newspapers from 1784 to 1804, forty of them children attached to their parents. Female slaves appeared most frequently (60 percent), as enslaved domestic servants became status symbols who could also reproduce if the state ever enacted gradual abolition. However, slaves used in agricultural or industrial production remained valuable commodities and represented a large proportion of these sales.[15] The use of slaves in nonagricultural occupations also became popular as slaveholders adapted bound labor to the new industrializing economy. For instance, the Andover Iron Works in Amwell and the Union Iron Works in Hunterdon County both used slave labor. Andover, for example, employed a slave, Negro Harry, in the late 1790s as a hammerman and allowed him to hire himself out to other forges when business slowed. Likewise, salt works in East Jersey also hired slave labor; one such business purchased Sampson in 1790 to cut wood and do other odd jobs.[16]

As the number of slaves increased, racism reinforced slavery's presence as an intense discussion of black distinctiveness and negative characteristics began in local print culture. Reprints of Edward Long's *History of Jamaica* (1774) showed Mid-Atlantic whites that blacks were a separate race and sensationalized their association with savagery and war. Almanacs picked up on these discussions and continually portrayed Africans as heathens or devilish apes. Depictions of blacks in literature as inferior and associated with evil followed. For instance, the author of a 1797 pamphlet titled *The Devil or the New Jersey Dance* described six young whites who hired a black fiddler for an evening. Instead of a single night of festivities, he kept the group for more than thirty days, leaving them "dancing on the stumps of their legs . . . their feet being worn off and the floor streaming with blood."[17]

Some New Jerseyans, like Dutch Reformed minster John Nelson Abeel, complained of the dangers of blacks and whites living in close proximity on equal footing and suggested how blacks' presence could destabilize the social order. Abeel offered that "those negroes who are as black as the devil and have noses as flat as baboons with great thick lips and wool on their heads," along with "the Indians who they say eat human flesh and burn men alive and the Hotentots who love stinking flesh," could prove dangerous if freed.[18] A 1792 newspaper reiterated this sentiment by claiming that blacks bore "the marks of stupidity . . . in the countenances composed of dull heavy eyes, flat noses, and blubber lips."[19] In New York, racist rhetoric derailed that state's abolition efforts in the 1780s, while in New Jersey it similarly worked to show blacks as unworthy of freedom.[20]

Slaveholders who embraced the institution in the 1790s convinced legislators that the institution needed continued regulation and in 1798 they passed a revised slave code that reaffirmed slavery's legality and confirmed the inclusion of any "Indian, Mulatto or Mestee" currently held as a slave in that category. The reaffirmation of Indian slavery resulted from a court case one year earlier in which Rose, "a North Carolina squaw," argued that her Indian status "furnishes at least prima facie evidence of her being free." Elisha Boudinot, a future Supreme Court Justice and abolitionist who assisted Rose, argued that Indian slavery had no basis in law or practice. The defense pointed to slave laws passed in 1713, 1768, and 1769 that made "no discrimination . . . between negroes and Indians." The court agreed and claimed Indian slaves "stand precisely upon the same footing . . . to be governed by the same rules as that of Africans." The 1797 court decision and the 1798 statutory reaffirmation of Indian slavery strengthened the differentiation between free whites and enslaved nonwhites and reinforced the place of bound labor in New Jersey.[21]

The 1798 law also regulated slave behavior, levying restrictions to strengthen the institution. It banned slaves from assembling in a "disorderly or tumultuous manner," prohibited their movement after 10 p.m., and affirmed longstanding prohibitions on slaves' ability to testify against free persons. The legislature continued to strengthen slavery in 1801 when it revised a law on slave punishment. That law, like those in the South,

allowed courts to sentence slaves convicted of arson, burglary, rape, highway robbery, attempted violent assault and battery, or attempted assault
and battery with intent to commit murder to sale outside of New Jersey.
Sale or transfer to the Deep South, discussed extensively in Chapter 6, further demonstrated the Revolution's failure to advance abolitionism.[22]

*   *   *

As slavery grew in East Jersey, Quakers and slaves worked to dismantle it
in West Jersey. The Society of Friends had been advocates for abolition
early on and therefore took the lead in advancing statewide abolition. By
1800, 80 percent of Burlington County blacks and 91 percent of Gloucester's lived free. In comparison, only 11 percent of Essex County blacks and
6 percent of Bergen's had gained freedom. This Quaker antislavery activity
further bifurcated New Jersey, leaving West Jersey to develop into a free
society even before the passage of a gradual abolition law while the institution remained entrenched in the East.[23]

However, even as Friends advanced abolition, few accepted free blacks
as members of their meetings with equal status. Race still proved a barrier
for Quakers, though they allowed black participation in certain religious
activities. For example, John Woolman officiated the marriage of William
Boen, a former Mount Holly slave, even as, the "way not opening in
Friends' minds, he was not received" by the meeting as a member. Instead,
he remained affiliated with them until 1814, when the meeting finally
granted him full membership.[24]

Like Boen, other Jersey blacks attended Quaker meetings in Burlington,
Gloucester, and Salem in what became a way for Friends to collectively
repay a debt owed for their participation in slavery. This Quaker "guilt,"
usually manifested as paternalistic assistance, helped the Society become
the largest (and only) lobbying group for black freedom in the state. The
Salem Monthly Meeting felt so passionately about these meetings that they
rearranged their regular worship schedule to allow blacks to use their meeting house at more convenient times. These meetings provided West Jersey
blacks with an organized structure to create networks of both white and
black allies, which they used to develop business ties, free family members,
and gain educational opportunities. In sum, many ex-slaves saw these meetings as an opportunity to develop the bonds needed to survive in a state
still ensnared in slavery.[25]

Calls for abolition routinely came directly from Quaker meetings as well as from those activists who had worked with Governor Livingston. In 1786, for instance, the Philadelphia Meeting for Sufferings, which included New Jersey, wrote to the state legislature to "restore this injured people to their natural right to freedom" and quickly enact gradual abolition. In 1788 they again called for abolition and stronger restrictions on the slave trade. Likewise, in 1792, the Meeting of Sufferings sent a delegation to Trenton to discuss ways to enact gradual abolition. That same year, Jersey Quakers joined those from Pennsylvania, Delaware, and Maryland to petition for the immediate abolition of slavery, citing the "oppressed condition of the African race" and their position as "solicitors on their behalf" following the "precept and injunction of Christ" to mitigate slaves' pain and suffering.[26] New Jersey Quakers again spoke in 1799 through the Philadelphia Yearly Meeting to the nation at large for the "spirit of meekness and wisdom in promoting" abolition.[27]

Quakers, especially abolitionist James Pemberton, also allied with Governor Livingston and worked to abolish the Atlantic slave trade. They sponsored a law that prohibited both the importation of slaves from Africa and of slaves from other states who entered the country after 1776, which tied the measure directly to the Revolution. However, as opposed to New Englanders who organized against the widely unpopular and sinful slave trade at the expense of local slaves, Livingston and his coalition fused the abolition of the slave trade with abolition at home. Despite the renewed push for gradual abolition in New Jersey, Livingston eventually abandoned the combined plan, believing that trying for both ran "the risk of obtaining nothing," especially since gradual abolition had failed the previous year. Therefore, he claimed it was "then prudence not to insist upon it but to get what we can and which obtained paves the way for procuring the rest."[28]

The attack on the slave trade tied Jersey Quakers to a much larger national coalition against the "barbarous custom" of slave trading. By the 1760s, both northerners and southerners, including New Jerseyans, had limited access to the slave trade by levying prohibitive duties. Although the Crown repudiated most of these duties, the Second Continental Congress enacted a ban on slave trading that lasted until 1783. Afterward, activists in individual states who opposed the trade worked to ban it and by 1790, as one newspaper article claimed, "the citizens of the United States [were] so generally united" in the belief of the trade's barbarity that it made it an easy abolitionist target.[29] Even though Georgia imported slaves until 1798 and South Carolina reopened the slave trade in 1803, most Americans opposed it. Closing the slave trade simultaneously helped fulfill the idea of revolutionary freedom, increased the value of those currently enslaved, and, as many thought, limited the potential for future slave rebellions. In New Jersey, Livingston's coalition found common ground with slaveholders and banned the slave trade in 1786. However, the victory did little to weaken slavery's hold in New Jersey because few slaves had been imported since the 1760s.[30]

Although unable to abolish slavery in New Jersey, Quakers and their allies petitioned the legislature relentlessly to make voluntary manumission of slaves easier, arguing that the colonial law requiring slaveholders to post manumission bonds dissuaded owners otherwise inclined to free their chattel. The same 1786 law that banned the slave trade allowed masters to manumit slaves age twenty-one to thirty-five without bond after an examination by two overseers of the poor and two justices of the peace who would certify the slave would not become destitute. It also required owners to support former slaves if they ever required poor relief. Following this law, Robert Armstrong of New Brunswick brought his slave Tony for examination before two overseers and two justices of the peace in 1790. However, when Tony fell into poverty six years later, Armstrong claimed he had released any and all claims on Tony "to all intents and purposes as if he has never been my slave," to escape paying for his care. Of course, the law prevented this very action and Armstrong had to support his indigent former slave.[31]

The continued efforts of abolitionists in the 1790s to expand the availability of manumission helped many slaves negotiate freedom for themselves. In 1792, for instance, Burlington and Hunterdon County abolitionists petitioned the legislature to expand the manumission criteria by permitting masters to manumit slaves under twenty-one if the ex-slave was then indentured until twenty-eight. This proposal mimicked Pennsylvania's gradual abolition law and encouraged slaveholders to sign away their future rights to children after a period of service. Although nothing came of the petition, it shows their desire to emulate a graduated system of abolition, one that extracted labor in exchange for freedom. This became the blueprint for the abolition plan enacted in 1804. In a larger sense though, the expansion of manumission was critical to hundreds of West Jersey blacks who used this viable legal avenue of freedom to achieve what they had strived for since the Revolution.[32]

The 1786 law also levied fines against masters who abused their slaves, further supporting Quaker amelioration efforts. This requirement led Henry Wansey, an English traveler who toured New Jersey in 1794, to observe that "many regulations have been made to moderate [slavery's] severity."[33] The law responded to a number of abuse cases, including one involving Monmouth County slaveholder Arthur Barcalow, who whipped his slave Betty for failing to follow his direction to return home. Despite acceding to her master's will, Barcalow continued to beat Betty. A neighbor testified that Betty "was dead . . . [her] arm bloody and appeared to have been cut with a whip." The coroner concluded that Betty died of blunt force trauma caused by the broom stick Barcalow wielded, which led a local jury to convict Barcalow of murder. Abolitionists made sure that all mistreatment, not just Barcalow's extreme example, would be punished under the law. This section of the 1786 law, while spearheaded by abolitionists, helped slaveholders defend slavery as they claimed that their slaves lived as a protected class of servants. Slavery therefore acted as a positive benevolent institution, worthy of support.[34]

A regulation that mandated masters teach their young slaves to read, also part of the 1786 law, further bolstered a paternalistic defense of slavery and reflected the abolitionist desire to educate young slaves with skills to prepare them for possible future freedom. No record of any slaveholder being fined under this law remains but evidence suggests that some slaveholders, like Aaron Malick, did send their slaves to school, which likely helped some achieve freedom in the future. However, slaveholders before the 1820s viewed reading "as a tool that was entirely compatible with the institution of slavery." Writing, in contrast, represented an "intrinsically dangerous" skill that slaveholders worked diligently to limit. As abolitionists never forced the issue of writing, the promotion of slave reading seemingly fits into the larger campaign to quell Quaker guilt.[35]

Quaker efforts to ease manumission requirements and temper slave treatment accentuated the differences between East and West Jersey. Slavery in West Jersey, due to Quaker influence, declined quickly due to manumissions. In Burlington County, for example, the county clerk recorded seventy-five manumissions between 1786 and 1800, which helped shrink the county's slave population by 17 percent. Similarly, between 1790 and 1800, Gloucester's slave population declined by 68 percent and Cumberland's by 38, while those in East Jersey grew by 20 to 30 percent. These ex-slaves added to the already burgeoning free black community that had formed as a result of earlier Quaker manumission efforts.[36]

Both Quaker advocacy of abolition on a personal level and individual slaves negotiating with masters to gain their freedom worked simultaneously to destabilize the institution. For instance, John Hunt, a member of Burlington County's Evesham Meeting, recorded his extensive efforts to convince recalcitrant Quaker slaveholders to abandon slavery. These Quakers put pressure on slaveholders to manumit at the same time slaves themselves pressured them for freedom from within. In July 1787, Hunt visited the home of Joseph and Mary Garwood, fellow Evesham Friends, to discuss manumission plans. Joseph purposely avoided meeting with Hunt, which led Hunt to instead "press things closest home upon" Mary. Ten days later, Hunt revisited the Garwoods with fellow Quakers Samuel Allinson and Elizabeth Collins. Mary again stopped the trio from seeing her husband, claiming he was "indisposed with bad fits." Hunt suspected that Garwood had feigned illness to avoid a confrontation. In this case, Garwood's slaves and their white allies failed in their negotiations for freedom as Garwood sold them to stave off potential economic losses.[37]

On the other hand, Hunt and Allinson convinced John Cox to manumit his slaves in 1787, though they failed to accomplish the same with Jacob Brown the following year. Likewise, Hunt visited the home of Micajah Wills and his wife several times between 1787 and 1794, but ultimately failed to convince Wills to manumit his chattel, though he kept in close contact with Wills' slaves. In 1794 Hunt attended a funeral for one of them, where he remarked that while the slaves "behaved very sober," the whites in attendance failed to keep quiet throughout the service, a jab at the demeanor of those who refused abolition.[38] Other Quakers, including Allinson's son William, continually toured New Jersey trying to convince individuals to free their slaves. In 1804, for instance, William "set out on a tour into Sussex" on a mission to secure the freedom of two black families, though in 1803 he recorded his displeasure at the task, writing that he had engaged in the "irksome" task of "abolition business most of the afternoon."[39]

In addition to individual meetings, Hunt attended religious services held by Burlington Friends for free blacks where they participated in both religious conversations and discussed the latest abolition news, which made them part of the abolition process and gave them power to take action to ensure freedom for themselves and their families. At one 1796 meeting, for instance, the organizers read information on the state of abolition in the

North from the PAS, which the blacks in attendance discussed. Hunt remarked that one black attendee, Hannah Burros, took center stage and explained New Jersey's complicated relationship with slavery to the others. Hunt seemed to think very highly of Burros, visiting her seven months later after she fell ill. Hunt wrote that she was "quite deranged and [had] lost her reason" and that he became emotional at her "sorrowful condition," praying for her recovery.[40]

These local Quaker meetings also sought to help educate West Jersey's free black population to show whites that blacks could learn and were worthy of freedom. In a 1790 letter to Quaker abolitionist William Dillwyn, Susana Emlen claimed that several night schools that taught "the Negroes reading, writing, and arithmetic" had recently opened in Burlington as a way "to atone in some measure for the wrong they have suffered."[41] The schools, opened between 1789 and 1791 by the Burlington Quarterly Meeting, joined those already operated by the Upper Springfield Monthly Meeting. Similarly, Salem Quarterly Meeting in 1790 solicited donations of funds to create integrated schools for both poor white and black children. By 1793, the funds raised by those Quarterlies funded the creation of three schools in southwest New Jersey, with another opening in 1794, all controlled by Quaker educators who taught an integrated student population.[42] Likewise, Philadelphia's Free Black School assisted Trenton Quakers form a larger school to teach reading, writing, and arithmetic in evening classes year round to the city's black adults. It copied the structure of the Burlington School Society for the Free Instruction of the Black People, formed in 1790, with both struggling against negative perceptions of their students by local whites. For example, in 1793, the Burlington school's leadership complained that it had encountered many who thought blacks too ignorant and unworthy to educate.[43]

The Quaker interest in manumission and education led hundreds of slaves to escape slavery but also gave ex-slaves allies to help develop their lives in freedom. Even though some Quaker efforts were undoubtedly paternalistic, freed slaves took advantage of them to create independent households and thriving businesses. One such ex-slave, Cyrus Bustill of Burlington, owned a profitable bakery that sold flour, cakes, bread, and biscuits to local residents and those who travelled on the Delaware. Eventually, Bustill and his family moved to Philadelphia, where he attended Quaker meetings, belonged to the Free African Society, and taught in a school for freed slaves before his death in 1806. Like Bustill, Samson

Adams, an ex-slave from Trenton, sold soap, which enabled him to buy a house in town and employ a housekeeper. Surviving records indicate that he had made a number of alliances with whites; almost fifty Trenton residents donated labor, supplies, or money to help him complete his home. The records reveal that Adams traded soap, food, and other goods with blacks and whites throughout the region. At his death in 1792, Sampson had accumulated a substantial personal estate that he divided among his family, with two white customers serving as his executors.[44]

*   *   *

Jersey Quakers had quickly realized that they needed an organization to coordinate their abolitionist activities and therefore latched onto the PAS, the most prominent abolitionist group in the United States. Sixteen of the original PAS members lived in New Jersey, many of whom prosecuted cases on behalf of the society. For example, Richard Waln, an affluent Monmouth County Quaker, communicated frequently with PAS leadership in Philadelphia and, as one of its founding members, helped free numerous blacks unlawfully held in bondage. In 1788, for instance, Waln intervened in the case of a Jersey child held as a slave even though his mother had been freed before his birth. Waln and the PAS, like most gradualists, believed litigation was the best avenue to defeat slavery. However, by early 1793 even Waln cited the lack of interest in abolition and the need for a more organized response to slavery in New Jersey. After Trenton PAS member Isaac Collins, who had done much legal work for slaves, ended his membership in the society, Waln lamented that a larger state network would be needed to fervently advance abolitionism.[45]

   Years of communicating with members like Waln had convinced the PAS that it needed to create an autonomous society in New Jersey. In January 1793, a committee formed to organize a New Jersey abolition society and by April they reported that they had founded the New Jersey Society for Promoting the Abolition of Slavery, headquartered in Burlington. The collaboration between the New Jersey society and the PAS continued as members from both organizations routinely exchanged information about specific cases.[46] The newly formed society used the Declaration of Independence's doctrine that "all men are created equal" to find fault with the state for withholding the principles of "justice . . . life, liberty, and the pursuit of happiness" from "an unfortunate and degraded class of our fellow citizens." This rhetoric, of course, had been used by other abolition groups throughout the Mid-Atlantic. For instance, Presbyterian minister Samuel Miller of the New York Manumission Society argued that "any civilized country . . . [should] oppose . . . slavery," especially in "this free country" where "the plains . . . are still stained with blood shed in the cause of liberty" and "the noble principle that 'all men are born free and equal'" reigns.[47]

Quakers joined the new society en mass and dominated membership in at least five county-level auxiliaries. In Burlington, for instance, Quakers made up 70 percent of the sixty-five total members, while in Gloucester they represented 40 percent of the membership. In proslavery East Jersey, all but four of the members of the Middlesex/Essex chapter came from the Society of Friends and the Hunterdon County chapter even met at the Friends' Meeting House. The society therefore became the arm of Quaker abolitionist outreach.[48]

The society continued to provide legal support for slaves and, led by former state attorney general Joseph Bloomfield, widely distributed previous New Jersey Supreme Court decisions to ensure their use as precedent in freedom cases. In one such case, Frank, a free black Middlesex County resident, had contracted with his wife Cloe's owner, Issac Anderson, in 1778 to purchase her for the sum of 180 pounds. Now both free, the couple had a child, Benjamin, but then separated. By 1803, medical issues prevented Cloe from supporting herself or her son. The local overseers of the poor followed state law and charged Issac Anderson for Cloe and Benjamin's care as her former owner. Less than a month later, Cloe died, which left Anderson supporting Benjamin. Because Anderson supported him, he believed Benjamin to be his slave. Applying precedent from previous cases, society lawyers sued Anderson and claimed that Benjamin, now twenty-one, had been born free because Cloe's owner had manumitted her before his birth. After an intense legal battle, Anderson finally agreed that he did not have the right to hold Benjamin but demanded $150 in payment for his expenses related to Benjamin's upbringing. After some negotiations, the society agreed to pay Anderson the $150 to ensure Benjamin's freedom.[49]

Abolitionist lawyers routinely faced staunch opposition from those who attempted to hold onto their slaves through duplicitous means. In the case that provided the legal precedent for Benjamin's freedom, Joseph Bloomfield argued in 1790 for the freedom of Silas, a child born after his mother,

Figure 2. This Membership Certificate of the New Jersey Society for Promoting the Abolition of Slavery illustrates how white society members saw themselves as bestowing liberty to the enslaved.

Courtesy of the Library Company of Philadelphia.

Betty, had been freed in her master's will but served that master's family under a fifteen-year indenture. The owner of the indenture, James Anderson (no relation to Issac Anderson above), claimed that since Betty had not yet been freed, her children should be considered slaves. Bloomfield countered that Betty gained her freedom at the moment of her master's death but remained under contract for fifteen years. He successfully argued that any child born during an indenture subsequent to manumission would be free from birth.[50]

The increased presence of abolitionists in New Jersey motivated slaves to take action themselves to press their freedom through the courts since they now had allies who could assist them. Cuff, a slave from Somerset County, had been promised freedom by his master, Gilbert Randolph, either at his own death or when his son, James, came of age. However, when James came of age, Randolph reneged on the agreement and demanded ten additional years of service. Cuff, likely hearing of the court cases proceeding across New Jersey, absconded from his master and eventually convinced abolitionist lawyers to take up his case, one that won him his freedom.[51]

Abolitionist lawyers also filed suit to protect free blacks from being kidnapped and sold south, thereby limiting the illegal slave trade that thrived along the coast from New Hampshire to Georgia. For instance, in May 1803 the society's lawyers litigated a case involving the sloop *Nancy*, owned by Ruben Pitcher, which had left Boston with four free blacks shackled in its hold. All had been held for debts, some as small as six dollars, in the Boston jail. Pitcher paid their debts and arranged for them to work off that debt on his farm on Martha's Vineyard. A few days later, Pitcher loaded the four onto the *Nancy* and set sail for Savannah to sell them as slaves. Pitcher docked in Egg Harbor, New Jersey, for provisions, where the four blacks seized the opportunity to escape and fled to local abolitionists who arranged for the *Nancy's* confiscation and their freedom. In a similar case, William Griffith, the future president of the society, arranged for the purchase and manumission of Charlotte, a Monmouth County slave whose owner had planned to sell her illegally to the West Indies.[52]

Outside the courtroom, the society lobbied legislators and participated in abolition conventions designed to address black freedom on a national level. In 1794, the society sent Joseph Bloomfield to a Philadelphia abolitionist convention, which elected him president. The convention called on Congress to halt the slave trade, arguing that its end must occur in order to "vindicate the honor of the United States, the rights of man, and the dignity of human nature."[53] Upon returning to New Jersey, Bloomfield and the society used these ideas of universal justice to argue that New Jersey needed to enact an abolition plan to fulfill the nation's revolutionary promise. Society members told the state legislature that "natural feelings of the human heart . . . acknowledged by Americans in their act of Independence, as among the most undeniable rights of man" demanded that the state assist in freeing enslaved blacks.[54]

Bloomfield used this tie between revolutionary freedom and abolition as the main vehicle to support black freedom. Under his leadership, abolitionists gathered dozens of petitions to show that whites wanted abolition. These petitions, signed mainly by society members and Quakers, called for an end to "heredity human bondage" in the state by using the "great principles of justice and truth" from the Revolution. This Enlightenment rhetoric and revolutionary ideology would ensure that "common rights and happiness" be granted to all New Jerseyans.[55] On a personal level, Bloomfield firmly believed in this logic, arguing in a 1795 letter to Philadelphia merchant Samuel Coates that in a state whose laws "proclaim liberty and happiness to all her citizens," slavery could never survive.[56]

Like gradual abolitionists in other states, few society members believed in black equality; racism still dominated New Jersey's abolitionist discourse and limited actions that alleviated the social and economic rift between free blacks and whites. In some cases, the society even opposed funding programs that supported free black education and instead focused their attention solely on slavery's destruction. For example, in 1796 the society forced its Gloucester chapter to recall funds earmarked to educate black children. Even in the society's pleas to the legislature, it targeted only the legal institution of slavery instead of improving free black life. The society claimed its members could be "consoled with the reflection that in a course of years, slavery would cease with the lives of those who *now* endure it," but few tried to advocate for either immediate abolition or for a wholesale change in the way that whites saw blacks. Indeed, on the eve of gradual abolition, society president Griffith claimed that the phrase "in New Jersey, no man is born a slave" should be the mantra of abolitionists. The society's primary goal remained gradual legal abolition.[57]

Overall, the society was largely ineffective at advancing abolition statewide. In 1798, it tabled action on several petitions and court cases due to the "the scattered situation of the Society and the extreme difficulty of forming efficient cooperation in those parts of the state where the necessity is the greatest." Three years later, in 1801, the lack of abolitionist support forced Bloomfield to report to the National Convention of Abolition Societies that "the scattered situation of this Society occasions many embarrassments and difficulties . . . [as] members . . . are often so far apart as to render it impracticable for them" to work together. Thus, the society was never as powerful as societies in Pennsylvania or New York. Jersey abolitionists struggled to coordinate branches across the state without a large commercial center to organize around. The society also received little support from residents in East Jersey, where the majority of the slaves lived and legal cases were heard. The dearth of active East Jersey members and the overabundance of members who happily talked of abolition in counties with few slaves caused difficulty in actually ensuring that the society's efforts reached those who needed them the most.[58]

*   *   *

Though white abolitionists believed their efforts had made great strides, New Jersey's slaves and free blacks worked equally hard to negotiate for the liberties that they had heard about since the first dissent arose between Great Britain and the colonies. In the Mid-Atlantic, blacks published several freedom petitions, following the lead of New England blacks. For example, in 1800 Philadelphia free blacks wrote to congressional leaders to highlight the Revolutionary antecedents of abolition, claiming that abolition shared much in common with "our struggle with Great Britain for that natural independence to which we conceived ourselves entitled."[59] Similarly, three Connecticut slaves argued in 1797 that they were "in a much worse situation than we were in before the war," even though Americans had defeated "the tyrant king of Great Britain" who "assumed the right of depriving all the Americans of their liberty!"[60]

In New Jersey, Revolutionary ideas encouraged slaves to actively seek out freedom themselves, most commonly by running away. However, absconding declined from its high watermark during the Revolution since slavery's growth in East Jersey made community and family connections easier. In Bergen County, for example, the average distance between slaveholdings dropped from 3 to 1.5 miles by 1800, which allowed slaves to marry in greater numbers and create families that tied them to their local communities. As opportunity and desire declined, New Jersey newspapers printed 40 percent fewer runaway advertisements between 1784 and 1803 than during the Revolution, averaging 5.8 advertisements per year. Young male slaves continued to make up the majority of runaways, with a median age of twenty-five years. These fugitives deprived Jersey slaveholders of essential laborers to repair the state's economy after the Revolution. As expected, most runaways (86 percent) came from East Jersey, though even this number represents a fraction of the likely total number. Circumstantial evidence, including Niemcewicz's account of the Elizabethtown jail teaming with runaway slaves in a year in which only one fugitive advertisement appeared, indicates that runaways remained somewhat prevalent in the late eighteenth century.[61]

Though slower than during the Revolution, abolitionist activity in the 1790s encouraged slaves to abscond from their masters. One such slave, James Alford, left his master's Rahway farm in 1794 and headed toward Pennsylvania because, as he described years later, he had heard a divine voice that told him he would soon be free if he sought assistance from local Quakers. Sneaking off the farm to the local Quaker Meeting House, Alford met several abolitionists who taught him how to read and write. He discussed with them at length the divine voice he had heard. After his escape, Alford's master accused the local Quakers of encouraging him to flee.[62]

Abolitionism exacerbated the long-held white fear of slave rebellion, leading some masters to negotiate with their slaves to stave off revolt. Newspapers reported vivid firsthand accounts of the bloody rebellion in Saint-Domingue while refugees and their slaves simultaneously spread news of the revolt to American ports from Maine to Georgia. Jersey abolitionists claimed that Francophone settlers and their slaves had migrated to Philadelphia in droves, many of whom eventually settled in West Jersey and dramatically increased the region's slave population. In Nottingham, for instance, almost half of the city's forty-five slaves belonged to new French settlers.[63] Likewise Susanna Emlen, writing to William Dillwyn in 1792, reported on "a new class of inhabitants in Burlington—a number of those unfortunate Islanders whose slaves have risen and made so much disturbance and valuable effects." Emlen was surprised by both the large number of new slaves and that many of them had actually helped save their masters' lives during the rebellion. However, she believed few could "wonder [why] their slaves should demand and forcibly take what had so cruelly been withheld from them."[64]

The same almanacs and periodical literature that had encouraged white New Jerseyans to see blacks as inferior and animalistic now began to disparage the Saint-Domingue rebels. Bryan Edwards's *Historical Survey of the*

French Colony of St. Domingo pointedly accused abolitionists of starting the revolt. New Jerseyans, from their Atlantic connections, learned much from Edwards's book about the dangers of slavery. They sought to protect themselves from a similar rebellion. In 1794, even local abolitionists warned that a general insurrection much like that of Saint-Domingue could occur if abolition did not begin soon.[65]

To prevent rebellion, both New York and New Jersey further limited slave movement and communication, and curtailed activities conducted without white supervision. New York banned gambling and the use of lanterns to limit arson, while Newark prevented slaves from meeting together or leaving their masters' home after ten o'clock at night. Despite these regulations, the mid-1790s saw mysterious fires break out up and down the Atlantic coast, which exacerbated worries of slave revolt. In New Jersey, investigators believed that slaves in Newark and Elizabeth had planned to set fire to the two towns and launch a massive uprising. Other potential revolts, such as when Middlesex County executed three slaves for planning an uprising, upset already anxiety-ridden New Jerseyans.[66]

In addition to the threat of slave revolt, masters faced the possibility that their own slaves could injure them or damage their property. For example, Margaret, a mother of five, burned down her New Barbados master's barn, while Nance poisoned her Sussex County mistress's coffee with arsenic, and Sam, a slave owned by Newark's Caleb Hetfield, stood accused of raping Mary Russel in 1785.[67] Crimes like these led Bergen slaveholders to complain of the "many atrocities, acts of burglary, arson, robbery and larceny which have been committed by slaves in this County and this frequent running away from masters." They demanded state officials pass stricter laws to preserve slavery.[68]

However, the fear of revolt, running away, and the increased abolitionist activity encouraged whites to more readily negotiate with slaves for freedom and for better conditions within slavery. The growth of slave communities in East Jersey was certainly a result of successful negotiations between masters and slaves. Slaves took advantage of revolutionary rhetoric and abolitionist agitation to argue for their own benefit. In this way, the nature of slavery slowly began to change as masters understood the limits of slavery in the early republic. These changes cushioned gradual abolition's eventual blow as masters continually sought ways to sustain slavery within the institution's changing framework.[69]

*   *   *

By 1800, Jersey slavery had grown despite assaults from abolitionists, fears of slave rebellion, and the constant ring of revolutionary freedom. New Jersey stood alone as the only northern state without a gradual abolition law, separating white New Jerseyans from other northerners who had begun to think seriously about slavery's place in the developing nation. An 1803 pamphlet concerning the death of a slave from Saint-Domingue confirmed this difference as the author noted that New Jersey law "authorized his master to remove him as he would a piece of furniture" unlike the rest of the North.[70] New Englanders especially used slavery as a way to contrast a free "North" against a slave "South," with New Jersey fitting into neither region. As historian Matthew Mason claims, "the North was proud to denominate itself as the 'free states' in an ideological world that proscribed bondage as immoral." White New Englanders saw themselves as fundamentally superior to southerners; their identity was based on the embrace of revolutionary freedom which, in their minds, proved their superiority. As New Jersey had yet to abandon slavery, it could not join this imagined morally superior "free" community, nor did many in the state desire to. Slavery still remained an important institution.[71]

The fascination with a "free" North began at the Constitutional Convention when regional distrust and differences based on slavery became readily apparent. James Madison famously claimed that the states diverged on issues "not by their difference of size . . . but principally from the effects of their having or not having slaves." Madison believed the main problem in forming a new government lay not in a debate over large versus small states but "between the Northern and Southern" as the "institution of slavery and its consequences formed the line of discrimination" between the two regions. Of course, differences of scale had always existed between the South's slave societies and the North's societies with slaves. But since Massachusetts had outlawed slavery and Pennsylvania, Connecticut, and Rhode Island had all passed gradual abolition laws before the convention, the development of "free soil" led southerners to believe that New York and New Jersey would soon follow suit and the idea of a homogenous North opposed to slavery was born.[72]

Northerners at the convention did not make it difficult for southerners to see the North as a distinctively free region since northern delegates identified slavery as the root of the new nation's evil. Rufus King, an adamant Massachusetts abolitionist, claimed that "the people of the Northern States could never be reconciled to" the expansion of the transatlantic slave trade.

Pennsylvania's Gouverneur Morris made the comparison even starker when he claimed that slavery "was a nefarious institution . . . the curse of heaven on the states where it prevailed." Morris boldly challenged southerners to "compare the free regions of the Middle States, where a rich and noble cultivation marks the prosperity and happiness of the people with the misery and poverty which overspread the barren wastes of Virginia, Maryland, and the other States having slaves." Morris's language harkened back to the colonial ideal that the Middle Colonies, Pennsylvania in particular, had always been "the best poor man's country." There, "noble cultivation" and hard work could make everyone successful, in stark contrast to the South, where slavery had corrupted whites and divorced them from productive labor.[73]

Though Morris acknowledged, at least tacitly, the Mid-Atlantic's ties to slavery, he made sure to highlight that northern slavery was not as harsh as the southern institution. He claimed that when crossing into "New York, the effects of the institution become visible. Passing through the Jerseys and entering Pennsylvania every criterion of superior improvement witnesses the change. Proceed south and every step you take through the great region of slaves" extenuates the dissimilarities between North and South. Morris believed that southern slavery was "so nefarious a practice" that it could never be equivalent with the institution in the North.[74]

Connecticut delegate Roger Sherman likewise argued that slavery in the North was intrinsically different by highlighting that abolition had commenced and "that the good sense of the several States would probably by degrees complete it." Fellow Connecticut delegate Oliver Elsworth latched onto the idea of "good sense" and argued that "slavery in time will not be a speck in our country. Provision is already made in Connecticut for abolishing it and the abolition has already taken place in Massachusetts." Elsworth also believed that free labor would expand and replace slavery, further strengthening the North's economic strength and separating it from the South's dependence on slave labor.[75]

Even as northerners tried to separate themselves from southerners, both shared a common belief in black inferiority. New Jersey's William Paterson offered that he "could regard negro slaves in no light but as property. They are no free agents, have no personal liberty." Likewise, Morris contended that "the people of Pennsylvania would revolt at the idea of being put on a footing with slaves." These arguments, while underscoring the hypocrisy of making slaves both persons and property during the three-fifths compromise debate, represented the widespread view that blacks were not equal to whites.[76]

The combination of sectional differences in the convention and abolition's success in New England and Pennsylvania convinced many Jersey abolitionists that slavery's days in New Jersey were numbered. Joseph Bloomfield linked abolition to economic opportunity in an attempt to persuade New Jerseyans that slave labor actually hurt the economy. He claimed that New Englanders "by their enlightened" abolition policy and their employment of "the labor of freeman instead of slaves are daily obtaining advantages over the southern states." The South, in their maintenance of the "injustice and immobility of their citizens in the unnatural and cruel treatment of their fellow men," prevents them from an adequate "competition" with "the freeman."[77]

Bloomfield intended to show white New Jerseyans that free labor would always be superior to slave labor by arguing that abolition would move the state closer to the Revolution's ideals, a message that led the state's Jeffersonian Republican Party to victory in 1800. This argument helped heal the rift between East and West Jersey, one caused by the tense economic times faced by the state immediately after the Revolution. East Jersey agrarian debtors battled the economic depression of the 1780s by printing more paper money and honoring existing paper at par value. These easterners lost key elections to more conservative West Jersey interests who supported pro-creditor policies. This conservative ticket later matured into the Federalist Party while agrarian-debtors became Democratic Republicans. The division had become so problematic that Jonathan Dayton remarked in 1789 that the "present temper and spirit of the people" could increase "into a flame not easily to be extinguished" and "resolve itself into a violent contention and dispute between Eastern and Western New Jersey, thence producing animosities and divisions which never can be healed."[78]

The Alien and Sedition Acts, Hamilton's economic plans, the Quasi-War with France, and Jay's Treaty splintered the parties even farther, yet also provided issues on which Jeffersonians in East and West Jersey could agree. Like national Democratic Republicans, New Jersey's party abhorred Federalist support of Great Britain. As a Republican orator claimed at an 1809 meeting, "such were the gloomy days of '97, '98, and '99" when "the sacred principles of our revolution were nearly prostrated at the shrine of aristocratical ambition." Jeffersonians believed that Federalist monarchical tendencies eroded revolutionary values and thought themselves the true defenders of American liberty. In this raucous political climate, the Democratic Republican emphasis on revolutionary ideology appealed to voters across New Jersey.[79]

These national partisan debates convinced many Americans that Jefferson's party truly represented a link to 1776 and indeed, this was essential in New Jersey. Jeffersonians "vindicated their own patriotism and called into question their opponents'" by using ideology in a way Federalists never did.[80] Starting with the passage of the Virginia and Kentucky Resolutions, Jeffersonians offered themselves as liberty's defenders. New Jersey Republican Thomas Wills, in 1809, claimed that Jefferson had "resist[ed] the torrent of aristocracy by the strong constitutional voice of elective franchise," saved the republic, and helped "the principles of liberty" to rise again. Bloomfield likewise linked the party to the revolutionary ideal by arguing that "in Republican men alone can our glorious independence be established and perpetuated," while Silas Dickerson, the first Jeffersonian Speaker of the General Assembly, prayed that the "rays of the sun of Liberty" would "dissolve that stubborn clay from" New Jerseyans, put there "by the hands of the oppressive Potter," the Federalists.[81]

Abolition allowed Jersey Jeffersonians to build a political consensus against Federalists and highlight their relationship to the Revolution's ideals in both East and West Jersey. As a political tool, abolition proved useful because it tied Jeffersonians and abolitionists together. Both equated the Revolution with political and moral action and led abolitionists to become early supporters of Jefferson. Joseph Bloomfield, while Abolition Society president, organized extensively for Jefferson and became the state's first Jeffersonian governor in 1800. With Bloomfield and at least six other Jeffersonian Abolition Society members in the legislature, the Democratic Republican Party and abolitionists united to defend revolutionary idealism. Jersey Jeffersonians took pride in that, by the end of the decade, they had ensured the "rapid civilization of our Indian tribes" and provided for "a glorious amelioration of the wretched state of our African fellow creatures" in addition to the "total abolition of that infamous and inhuman traffic," the slave trade.[82]

Jeffersonian campaign literature defended both revolutionary freedom and abolition, shielding them from Federalist attempts to link the party to Jefferson's slaveholding and a southern identity. In one such advertisement,

Gridley Sc.

JOSEPH BLOOMFIELD, ESQ.

Governor of New-Jersey.

Figure 3. Joseph Bloomfield was the first president of the New Jersey Society for Promoting the Abolition of Slavery and the first Democratic-Republican governor of New Jersey.

Courtesy of the New York Public Library.

Jeffersonians admitted that Federalists condemned Jefferson and other national Democratic Republicans for their slaveholding but pointed out that George Washington had "upwards of three hundred" slaves, many more than Jefferson himself.[83] In another, Jeffersonians used a fictional conversation between two slaves to target a Federalist candidate:

> Quacko: Oh no! Oh no! Sambo you right. I hear massa Parson sem-blyman too—is he?
> Sambo: Oh yes, massa Parson assemblyman, an I wonder at dat, very much indeed-indeed indeed.
> Sambo: Cleber man, indeed, no, he no cleber man, he keep negro slave and he tief too[84]

The stylized dialect argued that the Federalist candidate's slaveholding should bar him from representing Burlington County. This claim was particularly important for Jeffersonians to make since Burlington Quakers did not readily respond to the party's revolutionary references. Using this pro-abolition message in a Federalist stronghold allowed Republicans to embrace both abolitionism and racism as political weapons, though in the end the Federalists kept their hold on the county.[85]

Jersey Jeffersonians supported antislavery legislation after their victory in 1800 with state legislators joining local Democratic Republican Associations to organize grassroots abolitionism. For example, the Gloucester County's association petitioned the legislature to end slavery in 1803. It coordinated its appeal with one authored by local free blacks who petitioned the legislature on the same day. The association believed so forcefully in abolition that it helped elect Joseph Cooper to the General Assembly that same year. Cooper, a staunch Jeffersonian, also belonged to the county's chapter of the New Jersey Abolition Society, and, along with other abolitionist legislators, provided a conduit for antislavery activism to reach Trenton.[86]

The key to Jeffersonian ascendancy rested in convincing supporters in East Jersey to see abolition as a viable political weapon. However, slavery's entrenchment in East Jersey represented a sizeable roadblock; even discussions of gradual abolition aroused dissent. Bergen County slaveholders, for instance, complained that abolition of any kind would be "unconstitutional, impolitic, and unjustly severe in as much as we are entitled under our laws to protection of property."[87] Of course, the Bergen County slave-holders reflected a much wider anti-abolition sentiment and desire to pro-tect property embraced by thousands of Americans, including even George Washington. In 1791, Washington's private secretary, Tobias Lear, alerted him that his slaves residing in Philadelphia, the federal capital, soon would gain freedom because Pennsylvania's gradual abolition law exempted visit-ing slaves from abolition for only six months. Washington told Lear to send the slaves back to Virginia, but after consulting attorney general Edmund Randolph, Lear sent them to Trenton. The act of crossing a state boundary, according to Randolph and Lear, restarted the abolition clock. As long as Washington's slaves entered New Jersey at least twice a year, he could cir-cumvent Pennsylvania law.[88]

Jersey abolitionists and Jeffersonians remained sensitive to slaveholder fears over property losses since the defense of property became the main rallying cry against abolition. The sentiment became so powerful that one British contributor to the New Brunswick *Political Intelligencer* wrote that he was "sensible that this is a work which they [abolitionists] cannot accomplish at once. The emancipation of Negroes must, I suppose, be left in some measure to be the effect of time and manners" because any devia-tion in current property holdings would rile slaveholders. Jeffersonians responded by showing that gradual abolition would not deprive slavehold-ers of their existing slaves, only their future ones.[89]

A second anti-abolition argument came from slaveholders who ques-tioned the status of the children born under a gradual abolition program as many did not want to care for their slaves' progeny if they would eventu-ally lose their labor. To placate slaveholders and release them from respon-sibility for these children, the legislature created the abandonment system. Modeled after New York's abolition law, the abandonment system allowed slaveholders to surrender children born to their slaves to the local overseers of the poor before age one. These children would be bound out like poor white children until adulthood. This calmed slaveholders' concerns about caring for these children and showed that the state would protect slave-holder interests. From the slaves' perspective, however, the system necessi-tated the separation of children from their parents and weakened slave families.[90]

The slaveholder defense of property joined the persistent racism in New Jersey to mold the abolition system into its final form. Some whites hoped

gradual abolition might eliminate blacks from society entirely. Most abolitionists assumed racial inequality and many still owned slaves. Griffith, a
slaveholding abolitionist, spoke out against black voting rights and argued
that blacks could never be equal to whites. Abolitionists and Jeffersonians
supported gradualism because they believed to set slaves free without
teaching them how to "be free" would be both inhumane and dangerous.
They feared that blacks would become a drain on society and supported
continued white supervision through gradual abolition. Just as Quakers
had developed schools and religious instruction for freed blacks, these
abolitionists hoped to educate blacks about the meaning of freedom and
successfully integrate them into white society. They remonstrated that
blacks needed to attend worship services regularly, "read the Holy Scrip-
tures . . . be diligent in your respective callings . . . refrain from the use
of spirituous liquors . . . [and] avoid frolicking and amusements that lead
to expense and idleness." Abolitionists therefore formed committees to
"place children and young people in the hands of suitable" whites to
learn a trade and "superintend the morals, general conduct, and ordinary
situation" of these free blacks.[91]

Both the defense of property rights and racist-infused beliefs allowed
abolition to take shape in New Jersey on the grounds of practicality. Connecticut abolitionist Theodore Dwight believed the same had been at work
in his state, writing in 1794 that the "question of total abolition . . . has
met with steady opposition and has hitherto miscarried on the ground of
political expediency." Legislators used gradual abolition, as opposed to
immediate, to placate slaveholders and assert white control over abolition.
Children born to slaves would be free but had to serve their mother's master for twenty-five years if male and twenty-one years if female, exchanging
labor for freedom. The legislature approved the state's Act for the Gradual
Abolition of Slavery with only four dissenting votes in the General Assembly and one in the Legislative Council. The law's effective date, July 4, 1804,
allowed Jeffersonians and abolitionists to show that freedom was a gift from
those who had won it during the Revolution. July 4, 1776, had granted
freedom to white Americans and July 4, 1804, would grant it to blacks. In
this way, abolitionists emphasized the moment of emancipation and their
benevolent gift to blacks rather than abolition's long-term impact on the
lives of Jersey slaves.[92]

New Jersey's 1804 Act for the Gradual Abolition of Slavery could not
have passed the legislature without the support of Democratic Republicans

and Governor Bloomfield. Jeffersonian abolitionists worked for legislative abolition and even pressured West Jersey Federalists, including almost the entire Burlington County delegation, to support it. However, abolition was helped more by the Democratic Republican caucus system that united eastern and western interests. Like the national caucus system, the state caucus forced representatives from counties that still had a viable slave system (Essex, for example) to support the legislation by appealing to party unity based on the concept of individual honor. This system, a product of the partisan battles of the 1790s, allowed abolitionism to move forward despite disagreements over slavery.[93] The system proved so efficient that abolitionists used it between 1805 and 1811 to produce party line votes on three additional antislavery bills, uniting East and West Jersey in spite of their long antagonism.[94]

*   *   *

Quakers, the New Jersey Abolition Society, slaves, and the Democratic Republican Party all helped pass the 1804 gradual abolition law, even as whites conceded that slaves could never quite reach the intellectual or moral capacity of whites. The use of July 4, 1804, allowed abolitionists and Jeffersonians to link abolition to revolutionary freedom but at the same time treat abolition as a political proxy for a larger ideological battle. Abolition's gradual nature and the lack of strong support for it independent of politics mollified slaveholders by permitting unfreedom to persist after 1804. Slavery did not end. It merely began to function in a different way, just as the Revolution and 1790s had previously changed it.[95]

Abolition leaders believed that they had accomplished a herculean task by spreading the blessings of revolutionary freedom to African Americans, but they celebrated their own role in the freedom process more than its impact on Jersey blacks. In a letter to Dickerson after the act passed, Bloomfield wrote that "your feelings respecting the abolition of slavery accord with the cordial gratification I experienced when I signed the abolition bill, the most important act ever passed or which can ever be passed by the legislature of New Jersey . . . may the genuine influence of philanthropy and liberty eradiate every heart and be as extensive as the human races!" Bloomfield's letter emphasizes liberty and philanthropy, but, like most gradualists, he could not overcome a belief in black inferiority. Most had

supported a gradual end to slavery to ensure a role for whites in the freedom process. Indeed, Bloomfield's remark that the law was "the most
important act ever passed or which can ever be passed," indicates that few
would have supported a stronger abolition law.[96]

This "horrible gift of freedom" privileged slaveholders and gave them
power in arbitrating black freedom because few whites actively defended
blacks. Like other such laws, New Jersey's failed to free any slave immediately; those New Jersey slaves born before July 4, 1804, continued to live in
the same manner as they always had, bound for life. It did not, as a newspaper reported, wipe "off the foul stain of slavery from the character of the
state." Instead, the law changed the nature of slavery by introducing a new
category of bound laborer, children born to slaves after July 4, 1804, who
would be owned by their mother's master for upward of twenty-five years.
These children served slaveholder interests and provided them the tools
they needed to defend the continuation of the institution. The slaveholder,
now supposedly in the role of educator and arbiter of the freedom process,
used his power to limit black access to freedom. Over the next four decades,
Jersey slaves and their freeborn children struggled to achieve real freedom
and a place in American society.[97]

CHAPTER FOUR

Not Quite Free

In 1824, after crossing the Delaware River into Pennsylvania, Peter Chandler scribbled in his diary: "Today left the land of slavery, New Jersey. The blacks are permitted to be held in bondage. Almost every farmer has from one to half a dozen slaves." Chandler's assessment of the state of slavery after his seven-week tour of New Jersey stands in stark contrast to the historical memory of slavery fifty years later. In 1878, local historian Joseph Atkinson published his *History of Newark*, in which he boldly stated that "slavery was abolished in New Jersey in 1820 to the everlasting credit of Newark, and to the imperishable honor and glory of its local press." Atkinson believed that New Jersey opposed slavery and was a "land of liberty."[1] To Chandler's amazement, New Jerseyans still held over seven thousand slaves twenty years after lawmakers had slated the institution for destruction. Atkinson, meanwhile, argued that slavery was dead four years before Chandler ever set foot in New Jersey. Where did all the slaves in Chandler's journal come from? Where did all the slaves in Atkinson's account go?

Neither Chandler nor Atkinson grasped the whole truth of slavery's demise north of the Mason Dixon because no clear line separated freedom from slavery. February 15, 1804, the day the New Jersey legislature approved gradual abolition, did little to change slave's lives. Neither did July 4, 1804, the day the law took effect. Newspapers still advertised slaves for sale, slaves still farmed their masters' land, and "Negro" still meant the same thing as "slave" to white New Jerseyans. However, the law did force New Jersey into a period of transition, the abolition period, stretching from 1804 to 1846, when whites and blacks struggled to define slavery's end.[2]

Gradual abolition in New Jersey illustrates the complex ways in which Americans demarcated slavery and freedom in the early republic. Gradual abolition, far from emancipating slaves, confused the meaning of freedom and allowed white owners to exploit both slaves and their freeborn children. The law promised freedom to all black children born after 1804, but rather than joining the ranks of free citizens, these children entered another gradation of unfreedom. Apprentices, indentured servants, redemptioneers, slaves, free blacks, poor whites, and women all lived in gradations of unfreedom in the late eighteenth and early nineteenth centuries. Like these other groups, post-1804 black children "believed themselves denied [the] full liberty" promised by the Revolution.[3] Just as people of African heritage across the Atlantic World experienced many "slaveries" instead of one monolithic "slavery," children born to slaves after 1804 inhabited a new form of bondage that was neither a foil to slavery nor slavery itself.[4]

Gradual abolition opened a fluid boundary between slavery and freedom that slaveholders exploited to form this new type of bondage. Through judicial decisions and common practice, slaveholders treated these children like slaves bound for a limited period of time. They consistently attempted to separate them from white apprentices by legally categorizing them as similar to slaves. New Jerseyans, however, were markedly different from New Englanders. Those men and women created new racial categories (Negro, black, and colored) to delineate legal and social differences to begin the process of disowning their slave past. White New Jerseyans expressed little interest in crafting new societal roles for these post-1804 children. Not seeking to disown but rather to extend slavery into the nineteenth century, Jersey masters negotiated and engaged with these children as they had done with their parents and grandparents before them. Indeed, a pamphlet published in 1811 detailed New Jersey and New York slave laws, showing that the public understood slavery's continued role in both states. Instead of starting from a presumption of freedom, masters, slaves, free blacks, post-1804 children, and the law itself understood that anyone born to a slave after 1804 was a *slave for a term*.[5]

The process of defining slaves for a term was drawn out, lasting from 1804 until the 1830s, and the vagueness of the abolition law allowed slaveholders greater flexibility to maintain the institution. Demeaned by elites as part of the "lower sort," slaves for a term became part of a much larger discussion of how a society comprising free blacks, slaves for life, and slaves for a term defined social, cultural, legal, and political boundaries. As opposed to New England and Pennsylvania, with their much smaller slave populations and earlier enactment of gradual abolition, New Jersey's experience forced the peculiarities of a functioning slave system into nineteenth-century historical debates that had previously assumed the presence of a wholly free black population.[6]

*   *   *

In February 1804, no private parties, public celebrations, or fanfare marked the state legislature's passage of gradual abolition. Sandwiched between a debate on the construction of a statewide turnpike road and a petition advocating an additional tax on dogs, the upper house of New Jersey's legislature informed the General Assembly that it agreed slavery must end in a graduated fashion.[7] New Jersey's Act for the Gradual Abolition of Slavery declared a freedom of the womb by granting freedom to any child born to a slave after July 4, 1804, but required these children to serve their mother's owner until age twenty-five if male and twenty-one if female. This service requirement for slaves for a term, like the requirements in other northern states, respected the property rights of the slaveholder by shifting the financial burden of abolition away from the slaveholder to the slaves for a term, making them repay the cost of freedom.[8]

Of course, slaveholder fears over property rights were not unfounded as they suffered capital losses since the law stripped them of the profit they could garner from children born into perpetual bondage. The "breakeven age" in the abolition period, the age at which the value of the work done by a slave equaled the value of the master's investment, was roughly twenty-six years. Therefore, if a master kept a slave until age twenty-six, he suffered no loss but made no profit. If the state forced abolition before twenty-six, owners lost money. Since New Jersey law set freedom below the breakeven age, owners suffered an estimated loss of 4.7 percent.[9] Slaveholders recognized this and argued even after the law passed that they should be able to keep their slaves for a term at least until the breakeven age. For example, Benjamin Covenhoven fought a habeas corpus petition filed in support of his slave for a term Agnus. Citing his economic loss, Covenhoven claimed that if he had freed Angus at twenty-one as the law dictated, she would have failed "to make full satisfaction for [her] bringing up."[10]

The state's interest in providing slaveholders some compensation for abolition worked in tandem with abolitionist goals to use the abolition period to civilize and educate African Americans. William Griffith, president of

the state abolition society, pledged in 1804 that his society would immediately set out to "establish a fund for educating a certain number of young
men or boys of color" in order to make the transition from slavery to
freedom a smooth process. Just as masters sought a supervisory role in slave
families in the antebellum South, Jersey reformers desired to mediate the
freedom process.[11]

Griffith and other Jersey abolitionists, like those in other northern
states, held the patently racist belief that blacks could not survive without
white oversight. Gradual abolition calmed white New Jerseyans' fears that
unbridled former slaves "would overrun their communities with thievery,
idleness, and debauchery, destroying civil life."[12] Few whites believed that
blacks could live up to proper notions of citizenship in the new republic;
blacks needed to be controlled for civil society to survive. Even the most
active Pennsylvania abolitionists believed that slavery had so retarded black
intellectual growth that blacks had become generally "unacquainted . . .
with the art of self-government and destitute of the advantages of an education" and either needed to be removed to Africa or be guided by whites
toward freedom.[13] New Jersey colonizationists, such as Samuel Miller,
would later reiterate the same understandings of graduated freedom. Miller,
for instance, claimed in 1823 that slaves needed to be freed gradually since
a "gradual increase of intellectual and moral culture" would enable them
to exercise the "gradual extension of privilege" over time with supervision
and training. Just as historian Mary Niall Mitchell argued that children
remained central to understandings of freedom and acceptance in the post-
Civil War South, the economic and legal status of slaves for a term in the
abolition period dictated how whites understood blacks' eligibility to enter
nineteenth-century civil society. Gradual abolition became not only an economic process but a battleground where whites and blacks delineated social
and political status.[14]

*   *   *

As in other northern states, the appearance of slaves for a term challenged
Jersey whites and blacks to create new societal roles for these children. Few
saw differences between them and their parents, leaving slaveholders to
define these children based on their relationship to slavery instead of freedom. The courts followed suit and legally separated slaves for a term from
white apprentices and indentured servants in order to link them to their

slave ancestors. The case of Aaron, a slave for a term born in 1806, helped begin this process. Aaron stood trial for murder in Monmouth County in 1818, accused of killing his two-year-old white neighbor, Stephen Conelly, by throwing him down a nineteen-foot well in a cornfield near his home. Aaron originally proclaimed his innocence, but after an examination by the grand jury at the scene of the crime, he confessed that he indeed "took hold of his [Stephen's] legs and threw him over" the rim and into the well. John Hunt, a Burlington Quaker who followed the case, believed Aaron had killed Conelly for revenge (for what remains unclear). With a recorded confession, a jury found twelve-year-old Aaron guilty of capital murder. After his conviction, his lawyers (paid for by his owner, Levi Solomon) successfully appealed to the state Supreme Court.[15]

On appeal, the courts identified his case as *State v. Aaron, slave of L. Solomon*, which suggests they saw little difference between those born before and after the abolition law's passage. In the course of the appeal, however, the Supreme Court sought to clarify Aaron's ambiguous legal position as a slave for a term. Justices granted Aaron an appeal because the lower court refused to allow Solomon to testify because it believed he might purposely mitigate evidence to retain his slave. Associate Justice Samuel Southard, the future U.S. senator who helped draft the Missouri Compromise, argued that Solomon should have been allowed to testify because children born to slaves after July 4, 1804, "are placed in all respects in the situation of persons bound to service by the overseers of the poor. Levi Solomon was not then the absolute owner of Aaron. Aaron was not the absolute slave of Levi Solomon. They stood in the relation of master and apprentice." As a slaveholder himself, Southard understood how slavery worked in New Jersey; he continued to actively trade slaves throughout the 1810s. Southard therefore knew that Aaron legally differed from his own slaves and thus pushed him into the category of apprentice, something New Jerseyans could readily understand.[16]

In 1827, the court made a much firmer statement that placed slaves for a term into a new legal category, one different than apprentices and closer to slaves. In this case, Thomas Morrell purchased Betty, a slave for a term, and her parents, promising them freedom after seven years of faithful service. Instead of delivering that freedom, Morrell sold all three to Phineas Moore. Moore again promised that he would give Betty's parents freedom before they reached age forty but instead sold the family to Elihu Price in 1824. After this sale, Betty's parents still believed in the validity of Morrell's original manumission promise and left Price's household without his permission after the expiration of seven years. Price, not a party to Morrell's offer, filed a petition to regain his property and a Justice of the Peace ruled in his favor. Betty and her parents appealed and forced the Supreme Court to decide the validity of Morrell's manumission offer. If valid, her lawyers asked how could Betty serve her mother's master if her mother no longer had a master to serve?[17]

The justices thought the case hinged on the legality of Betty's assignability as property and ruled that the abolition law specifically stated that any child "born of a slave . . . shall remain the servant of the owner of his or her mother, and the executors, administrators, or assigns of such owner." Therefore, the "condition of service attached to the child from the circumstances of its birth . . . resulted from being born of a slave; it was separated at its birth from the fate and was no longer to follow the destiny of the mother." At the moment of birth then, the child existed as a separate legal entity from its mother, attached by kinship but not by law. In addition, since the law specified that executors, administrators, or assignees possessed the same rights as the mother's owner, the child could be sold or transferred regardless of the status or wishes of the mother. The justices compared sales of these children to the "very familiar" transfer of real estate with a long succession of property holders. In addition to solidifying the transfer of these children as property, Chief Justice Charles Ewing argued that slaves for a term bore "no analogy to that of an apprentice" and were to be governed under the regulations of the gradual abolition law only. Their assignability as property, owing to their close relation to slavery, made them fundamentally different from apprentices or paupers and therefore more closely related to slaves than any other legal status.[18]

The decision to treat slaves for a term like real estate in Betty's case confirmed the customary treatment of black children as more like slaves than indentured servants or apprentices. In an earlier case, Covenhoven, the owner who had argued that he should retain his slave for a term until her breakeven age, used this logic when he claimed that slaves for a term and apprenticed paupers were incommensurate. He stressed that the townships supported white paupers until age eight and then bound them out while slaves for a term received no such financial support. Likewise, Connecticut slave for a term James Mars believed he inhabited a separate legal status because apprenticed white children served only twenty-one years while the gradual abolition law required him to serve twenty-five.[19]

In 1836, the court reaffirmed the treatment of slaves for a term as different from apprentices in a case involving Ephraim, a "servant for a certain term of years," indentured to Edward Stille who ran away on July 15, 1833. Ephraim asked Captain William Jenkins, commanding the steamer *Thistle* on the Raritan River near New Brunswick, to give him passage to New York City. Jenkins agreed. Ultimately, Stille recaptured Ephraim and sued Captain Jenkins for $1,000 in damages for helping Ephraim escape. The court found for Stille and argued that since Jenkins knew Ephraim's status as a runaway, he was liable for the loss of Ephraim's time. However, Stille gained monetary compensation for the loss of Ephraim's labor instead of an additional period of service, the normal remedy for escaped servants, thereby showing a legal difference between slaves for a term and apprentices. Masters could only legally hold male slaves for a term until their twenty-fifth birthday, even if some of that time was lost through no fault of the master.[20]

The equation of slaves for a term with slavery and not apprenticeship led slaveholders to routinely sell them because their parents had no legal right to stop them, thereby replicating a major component of slavery that yielded high profits. These profits made Isaac Holmes, an Englishman who traveled across the United States in the 1820s, note that a Jersey farmer who fathered children with his three female slaves "could dispose of his own offspring . . . as he would have disposed of his hogs." Slaveholders carefully crafted sale advisements to denote the special status of slaves for a term. When he sold his "negro girl named Harriet" in March 1825, Ralph Smith of Hanover assigned the remaining twelve years of Harriet's "term of service" to Isaac Brittin of Chatham. Likewise, the estate of Vincent Boisaubin sold nine year old Mathusin on July 11, 1834, "until he arrives to the full age of twenty-five years," and another slaveholder advertised "an active black male child, nine months old" for sale in 1816. In contrast to these ads, one Newark owner inserted his male slave's birthday, May 16, 1804, to illustrate that he had extra value as a slave for life in an 1805 advertisement.[21]

Sales of slaves for a term represented 17 percent of all bound black laborers advertised for sale in New Jersey newspapers between 1804 and 1824.[22] Masters sold their slaves for a term individually (38 percent) or more commonly with their parents (62 percent). For example, Thomas Morrell, who had promised Betty and her parents their freedom, advertised Plymouth, an "uncommonly industrious" carpenter, painter, butcher, and coachman, for sale for a term of two years before his freedom, seven or ten years of service from his "industrious and prudent" nineteen-year-old pregnant wife, Phillis, and their sixteen-month-old slave for a term son, Mat, in 1811. With three different family members serving for different lengths of time before freedom, gradual abolition produced a hodgepodge of labor arrangements. In this way, New Jersey looked not unlike areas of the Upper South, where "workforces were often patchwork affairs stitched together" with laborers "whose varied backgrounds and legal status defied or at least muddied the neat distinctions between slavery and freedom."[23] Plymouth, for example, had a very short term of service, while Mat, born on March 27, 1810, had to wait until March 27, 1835, for freedom. Making the family's legal status even more complicated, Phillis's unborn child became legally free at birth per a 1790 ruling guaranteeing freedom to any child born to a slave who had been promised future freedom.[24]

Sale separated many slaves for a term from their parents, which further demeaned their supposed free status. Sarah Brocaw, born in 1819, lived with her mother for four years before her owner, John Autun of Bridgewater, sold her to Margaret McCain. McCain also lived in Bridgewater so the sale did not separate them, but she soon sold Sarah to Bergen Brocaw of Franklin Township, miles away from her mother. Similarly, Elizabeth Haines of Middlesex County forcibly separated mother and son in a dispute between herself and the child's master, Henry Force. Force had hired out his twenty-nine-year-old slave Minner to Haines for four years, during which time Minner had a male child whom Haines financially supported. After the initial term, Minner continued to work for Haines for another four years, but since no second contract had been negotiated, Haines and Force disputed payment for the pair's services, which ultimately led to Minner's ejection from Haines's home. Haines sued Force in 1836 for $2,000 for caring for Minner and her son, even though both had labored for Haines during that period. Haines told Force that she would keep Minner's son because she felt that he "would be better without his mother," who had "an ugly disposition." This was similar to arguments used by overseers of the poor to judge the suitability of free black parents.[25]

Jersey courts also began to treat slaves for a term as human chattel in debt suits, thereby expanding the ways these children could be separated from parents and further blurring their freeborn status. In December 1817, Middlesex County resident John Debow lost his slave, David, as well as Peter, a slave for a term, in a debt case brought by David Abeel. Similarly,

Moses Scott "seized . . . one black woman, Susan, and child, cow, and horse" from Nicholas VanBrant, also of Middlesex. Both cases affirmed in practice the Supreme Court's decision years later: slaves for a term were moveable property.[26]

The advertising and treatment of slaves for a term as market commodities mimicked the status of white indentured servants in the eighteenth century, but marked differences existed in the establishment of those labor agreements. For example, in 1782 the *New Jersey Gazette* advertised Nicholas Low's sale of "a number of male and female servants hired for one or more years." Similarly, an auction at the Taunton Iron Works in Evesham attempted to sell the "times of a number of indented Irish servants" in 1785.[27] Although on the surface the status of New Jersey's slaves for a term reminded residents (and future historians) of these eighteenth-century indentured servants, the 1804 gradual abolition act and the subsequent case law stemming from it distinguished slaves for a term and apprentices as legally different. Indentured whites were governed under contracts that clearly stated the conditions of their service. For apprentices, this included the skills the master would teach the child, the food or clothing provided, and any payment distributed at the end of the contract. The amount of money or goods payable to white indentured children varied. Those who lived in the vicinity of Connecticut slave for a term James Mars frequently told him that they received one hundred dollars, a Bible, and two sets of clothes, while Mars received nothing from his master. In addition to differences in freedom dues, parents, guardians, relatives, or friends helped craft these indentures. In some cases, they negotiated multiple points of the agreements, ranging from specific skills to be taught to quantities of money provided at termination. In contrast, parents of slaves for a term had no legal standing to direct their children's future nor did slaves for a term have contracts because the gradual abolition law wholly governed their existence.[28]

Although New Jersey's slaves for a term legally differed from apprentices, the ideology of their placement under white care was similar. Abolition Society president Griffith argued that black children needed to be taught freedom under white tutelage before they could truly function in society. In the same way that apprentices left their families to learn, the state hoped that a "proper family" could teach slaves for a term to become meaningful contributors to society. The abolition system considered slaveholders and government officials more suitable parents and gave them patriarchal control over slaves for a term. Conceptions of race and appropriate conduct then guided ownership decisions along with economic need. For whites, gradual abolition ideally functioned to mitigate black misconduct, prepare young blacks for their future legally free status, and economically maintain slavery.[29]

However, treatment of slaves for a term in early nineteenth-century New Jersey rested on both racial conceptions and conventions about child labor that were in flux. Although child labor had been a critical part of the colonial labor force, the increase in adult wage laborers after the Revolution drove down the price of labor and caused employers to shift away from apprentices and unskilled bound child labor. This shift had much to do with the appearance of slaves for a term. For example, a 1793 Pennsylvania Supreme Court case held that "no parent under any circumstances can make his child a servant" because there existed a clear and significant difference between binding a child for an apprenticeship to learn a skill and "bound labor pure and simple." The court argued that indentures without any educational component were "no longer deemed a sufficient education for a citizen" because these children would be "in a very degraded situation, a species of property holding a middle rank between slaves and freemen." Pennsylvania's thirteen-year experience with slaves for a term explicitly informed this prohibition for white children. Although not applicable to New Jersey, the Pennsylvania case illustrated that black and white children labored in related but separate spheres. More important, though, Pennsylvania slaves for a term had been demarcated as unfit for inclusion within civil society because they lived "in a very degraded situation, a species of property," which mirrored slavery more than freedom.[30]

In contrast to the New Jersey Supreme Court's idea that black children would "no longer follow the destiny of the mother," the everyday practice of holding slaves for a term made sure that their existence did not differ dramatically from that of their parents, at least for their first years of life. The perception that slaves for a term were equivalent to slaves spread far beyond slaveholders. For instance, William Dillwyn, an early Jersey abolitionist, had by 1814 become distressed that "black children are not getting freedom" in New Jersey. Ninety years after the gradual abolition law passed, a New Jersey clergyman even remembered these children as "temporary slaves."[31]

African Americans themselves also saw slaves for a term as closely related to slaves. Mars, for example, wrote that age twenty-five was "as long

Figure 4. Jude (left), a slave for a term owned by the Denman family of Elizabethtown, was born in 1812. Even though the 1804 gradual abolition law guaranteed her freedom in 1833, she and her daughter Sarah (right) continued to live with and work for the Denmans. Jude died in 1854 and was buried with the Denman family in Westfield.

Courtesy of the Cranford Historical Society.

as the law of Connecticut" allowed masters to "hold slaves." Making no differentiation between his freeborn status and the slave status of his parents, his narrative itself titled *A Slave Born and Sold in Connecticut*, showed how slaves for a term were ripped from their families, forced to labor for the benefit of their masters, and whipped and punished as their masters saw fit just as slaves were.[32] Likewise, a group of Paterson blacks argued to the state legislature in 1841 that slaves for a term existed as one of many variations of slavery in the Atlantic World. They believed the service requirement created by the 1804 law "should be entirely abolished" because they saw that the law held slaves for a term to a different standard than white apprenticed children in both the age at freedom and the lack of a requirement to teach them a trade. They therefore "look[ed] upon the servants for years . . . as slaves so long as they remain under age, slaves to all intents and purposes."[33]

*   *   *

To enforce this new limited bondage, the legislature mandated a registration system in each of New Jersey's thirteen counties. Within nine months
after a slave bore a child, the mother's owner had to register the name, age,
and sex of that child with the county clerk. Of course, since the child existed
as legally separate from his or her mother, the law did not require the
mother's or father's name to be listed, though most registrations listed at
least the mother. This registration, recorded by county clerks in a "Black
Birth Book," served as proof of the child's date of birth, which would accurately calculate his or her eventual date of freedom.[34]

Registration was important for slaveholders because it allowed the state
to administer the third section of the abolition law: the abandonment
clause. This clause required slaveholders to care for their slaves' children
until they reached one year of age. After that, if the owner had registered
the birth, he or she could abandon the child to the overseers of the poor.
Those children, considered paupers, would be bound out to anyone who
chose to accept their indenture. Most important, the law allowed the county
overseers to draw three dollars a month for their maintenance from the
state treasury. With these payments, the state took the lead in financing and
mediating the abolition process and continued its role as a slave broker.[35]

The abandonment system underscored the unfreedom of slaves for a
term since the notice of each abandoned child, sorted by age and sex, was
published beside newspaper advertisements for the sale of other slaves and
slaves for a term.[36] Although historian Lois Horton refers to abandonment
as an "economic safeguard" for whites and blacks, controversy surrounded
the system as soon as it became law since slaveholders quickly abused the
system rather than using or seeing it as a safeguard.[37] At first, the legislature
instructed county overseers to give preference to "the owner or owners of
the parent or parents of such abandoned children" if they agreed to support
the child. This followed Pennsylvania's practice; Tobias Lear, secretary to
George Washington, claimed that Pennsylvania officials "made it a point to
bind the young slaves to their original masters unless there should be some
special reason against it."[38] Many New Jerseyans who did not own slaves felt
that this abused the system's intent because overseers bound the abandoned
children to their former owners plus paid them the monthly stipend. Discontent over this practice spread like wildfire. Residents from around the
state pleaded with legislators to come to their senses for fear that the care

of black children would, as residents of Upper Saddle River claimed, bring "the intolerable burden of accumulating taxes." Calls of foul play and fraud echoed through the halls of the state capital, as many felt the abandonment system acted as a "thinly disguised scheme for compensated abolition" in which masters who had no intention of surrendering their slaves for a term only did so to secure payments.[39]

Support for the abandonment system waned as the bills began to pile up in the treasurer's office. In 1806, bowing to public pressure, the state legislature repealed the program for children born after 1806 but kept it intact for those already abandoned. That year, the state spent a little over $1,500 on these children ($39.5 million in 2012 dollars), which represented just over 3 percent of the state's total yearly expenditures. The following year, the payments amounted to 17.5 percent of state expenditures. By 1809, 27.1 percent of state outlays went to abandoned black children. With such a drain on the state budget, these large sums "caused suspicions" among state officials since their number should have remained stable. They believed that local overseers of the poor had "misconstrued the law and thereby obtained drafts on the Treasury which are not strictly just and according to the letter and spirit thereof." To stop the practice of paying slaveholders, in 1808 the legislature instructed overseers of the poor to bind out the abandoned children to those who would accept them at no charge. However, the law's execution fell to local overseers who held almost complete control over their charges. Therefore, local leaders, especially in areas with large slave populations, could provide payments to slaveholders in far more flexible ways than state leaders wished.[40]

Abandonment left many nonslaveholders with a sour taste in their mouths for financing such a large welfare program for slave owners. The legislature suspected the large sums "must have arisen from some misconduct of the law" and accused local overseers of participating in an unsanctioned covert compensated abolition plan. To combat these abuses, the state suspended payments "in doubted cases" yet continued to spend another $9,300 between 1810 and 1811 ($197 million in 2012 dollars). Recognizing its failure to halt the abuse, the legislature finally ceased payments for all abandoned black children in 1811, noting that "in some instances the money drawn for their maintenance amount[ed] to more than they would have brought if sold for life."[41]

The end of abandonment signaled an unwillingness of nonslaveholders to support a compensated end to slavery, which forced owners to exert

Table 2. Slave for a Term Registrations by County

County	Total registrations	Total late registrations	Total on-time (%)	Total before 1811	Late before 1811	Late before 1811 (%)	Total after 1811	Late after 1811	Late after 1811 (%)
Bergen	989	478	48.3	429	84	19.6	560	394	70.4
Essex	274	111	40.5	143	32	22.4	131	79	60.3
Sussex	205	84	41.0	64	25	39.1	141	59	41.8
Morris	195	90	46.2	67	17	25.4	128	73	57.0
Middlesex	407	215	52.8	161	39	24.2	246	176	71.5
Monmouth	639	247	38.7	227	29	12.8	412	218	52.9
Somerset	834	344	41.2	315	72	22.9	519	272	52.4

Bergen, Essex, Sussex, and Somerset County Black Birth Books, NJSA; *Middlesex Birth Book*, RUASC; Mitros, *Slave Records of Morris County*; George Moss. Jr., ed, *Black Birth Book of Monmouth County, New Jersey* (Freehold, N.J.: Office of the County Clerk, 1989), Monmouth County Library and Archives.

greater control over slaves for a term in order to stave off financial losses. While the abandonment system functioned, slaveholders generally supported abolition and frequently registered their slaves for a term with the county clerk. All seven counties with available records show similar high rates of on-time registration (within nine months of birth). After the abandonment system ended in 1811, a sharp decline in on-time registrations resulted. Bergen, the largest slaveholding county in the state, had the second lowest on-time registration rate after 1811 (70 percent late) while Middlesex saw the highest (71 percent late). Overall, no county after 1811 had more than half its slaves for a term registered on time, a marked decline in slaveholder support for gradual abolition.

The registration system's breakdown stymied the only legal mechanism that ensured slaves for a term differed from their parents. As no state officials actively enforced the law and the law itself penalized only owners who registered late, not those who did not register at all, slaveholders could hold slaves for a term in bondage with no verifiable way to determine their future date of legal freedom. For example, Middlesex County slaveholder Seth Dunn admitted that Peter, the seven-year-old slave for a term he had just purchased in 1816, had not been registered by his previous owner.

Without Peter's sale, the state would not have known to enforce the change in Peter's status when he turned twenty-five. In this manner, the state pushed the responsibility for enforcing freedom onto the slaveholder and the slaves for a term themselves, which could involve a tense negotiated relationship in which owners might not recognize their slave for a term's legal rights. Owners could therefore extend service obligations with little outside interference.[42]

Slaveholder resistance to freeing slaves for a term became an increasing concern since they continued to view gradual abolition as a program that restricted property rights. Morris County slaveholders, for instance, complained that it was "unconstitutional insomuch as it takes from an individual, a considerable portion of their property, not for the support of government, without their will and consent," while Bergen slaveholders believed that "holders of such slaves [deserve] an equal right to the unlimited services of their issue or offspring and more especially as they protect, clothe, and support the parents." The petition was signed by 714 men in heavily slave populated Bergen, almost 12 percent of the adult white male population in 1800. This sizeable minority effectively wanted to bypass the law's registration provisions and ensure that their slaves for a term could be treated as the previous generation of slaves had been.[43]

The lack of support for the abolition law seen in Bergen manifested in other northern states too, effectively limiting access to freedom. In New England, slaveholders not only failed to register slaves for a term but also never properly informed them of their ages and dates of freedom. Many transient blacks stood ignorant of their actual birthdates as their masters attempted to extend their servitude. In New Jersey, birth records frequently contained large numbers of registrations at or near the deadline, suggesting owners had altered their slaves for a term's birthdates to adhere to the law, especially during the abandonment period, when they could benefit financially. John Wicoff's registration of his slave for a term Rachel one day before the nine-month deadline and John Van Nius's registration of Mary exactly nine months after her birth suggests that local officials failed to actively enforce penalties on late registration. Overall, that none of the approximately 4,000 registrations mention any late penalty likely indicates that as timely registrations dropped, no corresponding increase in enforcement appeared.[44]

Slaveholders' ability to treat slaves for a term like chattel property hinged on both New Jersey's lack of registration penalties and the dearth of executive enforcement. In contrast, Pennsylvania required registration of all slaves, not just slaves for a term, and actively enforced the law by freeing nonregistered slaves. For example, in 1789 Pennsylvania courts freed Samuel Moore's slaves since he did not register them, while Belinda gained freedom in 1817 because her owner did not specify her sex in her registration, a requirement of the law. The stronger Pennsylvania law and the actions of the Pennsylvania Abolition Society in encouraging enforcement made evasion harder. In many cases, abolitionists worked with county clerks to determine if certain slaves and slaves for a term had been registered. In one instance, William Lewis wrote to the Philadelphia County Clerk in 1789 to verify if Henry Reily had properly registered his slave Sarah. Lewis discovered that no registration had been filed and therefore pursued legal action to free Sarah. However, evasion still occurred in Pennsylvania. A 1789 court decision regarding registration claimed that if the master could obtain the consent of the parents of a slave for a term, he could treat the child as an apprentice and keep him or her without registration until age twenty-one. In this instance, masters who had run afoul of the law could pressure their slaves to bind their children as apprentices and continue to use their labor.[45]

The failure of the state to ensure a timely and painless movement from servitude to legal freedom allowed local officials to turn a blind eye to slaveholder actions or inactions. The general public that voiced opposition to supporting abolition through the abandonment system placed slaves for a term in an even more precarious position because the end of compensation led to the end of incentives to register. Unlike the Pennsylvania Abolition Society, New Jersey's incredibly weak abolitionist organization could do little to compel registration. With the state exhibiting little zeal to actively enforce the abolition process, masters effectively controlled abolition individually and attempted to extend the servitude of their freeborn slaves for a term.

*   *   *

The ambiguity inherent in gradual abolition forced African Americans to build communities in which members lived in various gradations of legal freedom, either as slaves, slaves for a term, or recently freed blacks. The very law created to end slavery therefore helped perpetuate slavery's bonds and foiled the creation of fully free communities in the 1810s and

1820s. Therefore, blacks in New Jersey established their own households at a slower rate than in Connecticut, Rhode Island, or Massachusetts. Of the free African Americans living in Newark, 35 percent (229 of 656) lived in 126 white-controlled households. In comparison, blacks in Boston, Providence, and New Haven crossed the critical two-thirds threshold of independent households in 1790. As manumitted slaves gradually moved out of white houses, slaves for a term remained enslaved. In Newark, slaves for a term lived in 63 percent of the white households that contained blacks, which contributed to the slow pace of family and community formation.[46]

Primarily, the abolition law restricted labor opportunities and mobility for those who wished to maintain family cohesion. Ann and Rufus Johnson, owned by Hannah Thomson of Hardwick Township in Warren County, exemplified this problem. Thomson freed the couple in 1828, but they continued to serve in her household for wages, room, and board since she had not freed the couple's four children, George, Mary, David, and Matilda, born between 1819 and 1825. Under the abolition law, each child, regardless of the condition of his or her parents, owed additional years of service to Thomson. Mary, born in 1821, could gain her freedom in 1842, while David, born in 1823, could not have his until 1848. With their children bound to serve Thomson, Ann and Rufus remained with their former owner in order to keep their family together. The gradual abolition law therefore limited Ann and Rufus's ability to bargain for higher wages in the open market or join the larger legally free community in New York or Philadelphia.[47]

Similarly, the wedding of Sayers and Sarah Coe of Newark in 1796 created a household defined by multiple gradations of bound black labor. Sarah brought with her Massy, a twelve year-old slave, from her parents' residence in Bloomfield. Massy eventually married another of the couple's slaves and by the 1820s, they and their five children, all slaves for a term, outnumbered the household's white residents. Massey's children remained in service to the Coe family with Peter, the oldest son, working with Sayers Coe on the Newark and Springfield Turnpike in the late 1820s. Even after he gained legal freedom in 1831, Peter either could not or would not leave his family. In 1834, Coe's financial records show that Peter continued to work for him, a situation that Coe's granddaughter remarked on years later, claiming that Coe had "many men in his employment, most of them being colored, and living under his own roof."[48]

The gradations of slavery became even more complicated as some Bergen County slaveholders argued in 1806 that the gradual abolition law made no provision for owners to support the children of slaves for a term. Specifically, these slaveholders wondered about the legal status of these children, although they assumed that they would be free at birth. However, since the children lived in a household where the master utilized their mother as a slave in all but name, the child, once he or she was old enough, would also provide services to the master's household. For example, if a slave for a term had a child at age fourteen, her fully free offspring would live under her master's roof in the same manner as a slave for the next seven years. Alternatively, the master could surrender the child to the overseers of the poor, since he would never recoup the money spent on the child's upkeep before the mother's freedom, thereby further using gradual abolition to separate families.[49]

Pennsylvania slave masters had the same issues with caring for the children born to slaves for a term and routinely utilized these free children as bound laborers until their twenty-eighth birthday, the same age at which those born to slave mothers would gain freedom. Until an 1826 Pennsylvania Supreme Court case clarified that children of slaves for a term were born free, many masters kept those children in bondage in perpetuity. Since the abolition period in Pennsylvania had begun over twenty years before New Jersey's, children of Pennsylvania's slaves for a term lived without the protection of any law that ensured their freedom. Just as in New Jersey, servitude continued beyond the first generation of free blacks.[50]

Unlike the Johnsons' children or those living in the Coe household, many slaves for a term lived apart from their families due to their parents' subsequent manumission or their own sale to new owners. Rachel Van Dyke, an active young white diarist from New Brunswick, described how her grandfather had purchased Edward as an infant in the early 1800s. Van Dyke claimed that her grandfather had "always been more like a father to him than a master," because Edward never had any relationship with his own parents.[51] Likewise, Mary and Judith, two slaves for a term who belonged to Robert Rutgers, lived without their mother after Rutgers manumitted her in 1822. After two years apart, Rutgers died and their mother, Nancy, petitioned his estate for custody of her two daughters. With business plans disrupted due to the untimely death, the family agreed to transfer the children if Nancy signed an agreement exonerating the Rutgers estate from any further responsibility for their care.[52]

Circumstances like Nancy's allowed slave parents to use the same types of negotiated relationships that marked American slavery from the beginning to regain control over their children's lives. Jersey slaves used their own power to negotiate to keep their families together but too often they had to yield to slaveholder demands.[53] Dinah, a slave owned by Michael Van Veight, succeeded in this regard by working for other local whites to save money to purchase her daughter after Van Veight sold her in 1804. Two years later, she convinced Van Veight to allow her daughter to reenter the household.[54] Though purchase remained out of reach for many Jersey slaves, others pressured whites to sell their children to them for small sums, playing on their humanity and benevolence. For example, Phyllis Bodley saw her son, Charles of Salem County, sold as a slave for a term to Robert Johnson to serve until 1852. Bodley, however, convinced Johnson to sell her Charles for one dollar in 1829. Robert Ogden, on the other hand, sought to end his relationship to slavery. He freed his two slaves, Leonard and Abigail, in 1812 and transferred custody of their daughter Julia to them at the same time. Similarly, Joseph Scudder of Monmouth County, master of Catharine Benham, born in 1821, sold her to her father, Henry, a free black man, for one dollar in 1822. On the same day, he manumitted Catharine's mother, Henry's wife, Rachel, thereby completing the family.[55]

Negotiation frequently pitted slaves for a term against their recalcitrant masters who would not yield to requests for greater freedom and led them to understand that the law neither guaranteed freedom nor brought about substantial changes in their lives. Some slaves for a term rebelled against their masters' authority and rejected the supposed freedom the gradual abolition law offered. In one such instance, Benjamin Anderson, a seventeen-year-old slave for a term, assaulted his master near Woodbury in Gloucester County in 1832. A jury convicted Anderson and sentenced him to three years at hard labor. Slaves for a term also ran away from their masters, just like slaves. In 1818, Tom, a thirteen-year-old slave for a term, absconded from his master, David Meeker of Elizabeth. Tillman, a fourteen-year-old slave for a term, owned by James Van Dyk of Newark, did the same the following year. This wholesale rejection of the abolition process allowed slaves for a term to determine their own relationship with freedom.[56]

Unfortunately for most slaves for a term, negotiations with their masters or rejection of their authority failed and they were forced to complete their years of service. For male slaves, this experience lasted until age twenty-five, a significant portion of their lives. If a slave for a term reached twenty-five, he could expect to survive for another thirty-five years. Therefore, these children lived an average of almost half their lives in a master-slave relationship. However, as high mortality rates killed 54 percent of all American slaves before they reached twenty-five, bound legal servitude represented the only status that most slaves for a term ever knew.[57]

*   *   *

The abolition law created a new class of Americans who, by legal judgments and common practice, came to be treated as slaves for a limited time as New Jersey slaveholders resisted emancipation and sought ways to keep slaves for a term in a subservient status. By harnessing the ambiguities inherent in the abolition law, apathy of state officials, and indifference of many nonslaveholding whites, slaveholders extended slavery well into the nineteenth century. Slaves and slaves for a term attempted to reconstruct their families, negotiate with their masters, and reject continued slavery. Through this negotiated process, the gradual abolition law complicated how African Americans created families as well as how they bargained for legal freedom.[58]

These slaves for a term challenge us to rethink what exactly the term *freedom* meant to early national Americans. Obviously, being freeborn did little to change a slave for a term's legal or social standing: freedom did not emanate from the law. Nor did freedom come from white masters, as this system demonstrated that white New Jerseyans lacked true commitment to abolition. For slaveholders, slaves, and slaves for a term, gradual abolition did not represent an end to slavery but instead provided another tool for slaves and masters to negotiate their future status by opening a dialogue between slaveholders, their slaves, and the law. Freedom therefore came from that negotiation, one made much more troubling since the same system that kept slaves for a term in bondage raised economic, political, or social barriers for them and others in the new nation. The treatment of slaves for a term informs the larger debate on how the lower sort functioned in early America and how the lines of freedom were demarcated.[59]

With this in mind, Peter Chandler's pronouncement that every New Jersey farmer had slaves in 1824 came close to the truth. Slavery in the state did not exist only as the condition of the 7,557 slaves the 1820 Census recorded. In actuality, thousands more slaves for a term lived lives largely indistinguishable from those of their slave parents. Where did all the slaves go in New Jersey? Nowhere—Chandler accurately reported the widespread condition of unfreedom that marked many places in the early national North.

CHAPTER FIVE

Slavery, Freedom, and Citizenship
in the New Republic

In an 1851 memoir written by Quaker William Allinson, former slave Quamino Baccau described how his master, William Griffith, had offered him freedom in 1806 at age forty-four. Allinson, grandson of Samuel Allinson, an abolitionist in the 1770s, portrayed Quamino as "downtrodden, meek, and poor" and minimized Quamino's role in his own freedom by using his enslaved name, Baccau, instead of his freed name, Smock, to validate the role of whites as mediators of black freedom. In writing about Quamino's negotiation for freedom, Allinson claimed Griffith had asked him, "Would you like to be free?" to which he responded, "I don't know, Sir," to which Griffith stood, paused "a little while in silence," and then said "I've made up my mind to give you free." Quamino remembered that he replied, "You give me free, master! Oh, it all came on me so unexpected!"[1]

Although Griffith appears to have decided to manumit Quamino at that moment, possibly because of his position as president of the state abolition society, Quamino, at forty-four, did not qualify for freedom. State law restricted manumission to slaves between twenty-one and forty. As Quamino aged, perhaps Griffith understood that an extralegal manumission could rid him of the burden of caring for an elderly slave. Quamino knew his advanced age would prevent his freedom and, when he and Griffith appeared before two local judges to execute the manumission, Quamino claimed "Griffith probably kept [his exact age] purposely out of sight."[2]

As a *post nati* law, the gradual abolition act did not ensure freedom to those born before July 4, 1804; Quamino, like the just over 12,000 slaves who represented 6 percent of the state population, continued to navigate an enslaved world. His successful bid for freedom was not the usual path for Jersey slaves. Manumission presented limited opportunities for freedom. Surviving records indicate that 1,755 slaves achieved manumission during the abolition period, only 16 percent of the slave population in 1800. More likely than not, anyone born a slave in New Jersey would die a slave.[3] Racism and a desire to maintain the status quo helped minimize black freedom. As opposed to New York, where slaves saw gradual abolition's passage as a signal that whites had extended the umbrella of freedom across the color line, New Jersey slaves understood that in a society where slaveholders continued to sell their chattel and circumvent abolition, the 1804 law represented not a new birth of freedom but a continuation of unfreedom.[4]

As masters sought to continue slavery, however, new pressures in the abolition period forced the institution to evolve. With legislative emancipation unlikely, New Jersey's slaves born before July 4, 1804, knew that a transitional period had begun in which they could negotiate for greater freedoms within slavery and even for freedom itself. Slaves proved cunning negotiators as they helped define the porous relationship between slavery and freedom, even striking out on their own if those negotiations failed. Masters agreed to many different accommodations, such as permitting slaves to marry free blacks, joining black civic organizations, interacting with freed people, or hiring themselves out. All created increased flexibility within slavery and helped create stronger networks among blacks, enslaved and free.

Yet even within the agreements that some slaves managed to make, masters successfully preserved control over their bound laborers to create a complex labor and social system designed to maximize the extraction of capital. Owners used manumission to stabilize and extend Jersey slavery by, for example, routinely manumitting only older slaves who had outlived their economic usefulness. Jersey slavery thus functioned as the institution did in the Upper South, it strengthened itself through its coexistence with manumission. Though New Jersey's free black population grew consistently after 1804, that growth did not correlate to a rise in white antislavery sentiment. As in the Upper South, many Jersey whites continued to believe in slavery's importance and used manumission, in historian John Wood Sweet's words, "not as the antithesis of slavery but as part of its nature."[5]

The maintenance of slavery alongside manumission was helped in New Jersey because white allies who had supported abolition abandoned Jersey

blacks. The largest group, the New Jersey Society for Promoting the Abolition of Slavery, disbanded by the early 1810s and left the enslaved to negotiate individually for freedom. Likewise, the Society of Friends ended
abolitionist efforts in the Mid-Atlantic and instead focused on the South
and the Atlantic slave trade. Without strong white allies to help oppose
slavery's continuation, slaveholders successfully manipulated the abolition
law to maintain their slaves' services long into the nineteenth century.

Slavery's continuation made the institution a staple in New Jersey,
infecting the white imagination, and ensuring that whites continued to see
free blacks as connected to their enslaved past. The small but growing community of free blacks that had achieved legal freedom and established themselves in Newark, Trenton, and other smaller cities occupied another rung
on the ladder of unfreedom, above that of slaves and slaves for a term, yet
burdened with restrictions that placed them lower than whites. In neighboring Philadelphia, activist Cyrus Bustill claimed that even though he lived
free, he retained a strong bond with the enslaved. Like Bustill, most Jersey
blacks were former slaves or had family and friends who remained enslaved.
The geographic proximity and close relationships between free and slave in
shared households and neighborhoods compelled whites, such as Pennsylvania Abolition Society members, to warn freed blacks that they needed
not only to be virtuous and respectful, but also to tread lightly in "communication with those . . . who are slaves" to ensure masters would treat them
with "humane and gentle treatment."[6]

Whites who remade American society after the Revolution used race as
a powerful tool to appropriate power from free blacks, design specific social
spaces for them, and define their proper republican societal and gender
roles. As whites celebrated independence, slavery's persistence allowed the
rhetoric of gradualism that had infused the debates over abolition to persist
in the vocabulary of white reformers, anti-black agitators, and state lawmakers. The idea that blacks were dependent and could not enter civil society without a prolonged adjustment period, the main ideological reasoning
behind gradual abolition, became commonly accepted by white New Jerseyans and therefore limited free black participation in the new republic.[7]

*   *   *

In 1809, the major white organization that had allied with African Americans, the New Jersey Society for Promoting the Abolition of Slavery, held

its last meeting and dissolved due to multiple tidal waves of indecision, inaction, and inconclusive results. The society had consistently reported that abolition lacked general public support in New Jersey and, even by 1806, its representatives admitted to the National Convention for Promoting the Abolition of Slavery that it made no "considerable effort" to advance abolition in the past year. Three years later, as it decried that New Jersey's laws "regulating slaves and aiding their emancipation [were] in sundry points defective," it decided to disband.[8]

At the heart of the organization's collapse was the issue that had plagued it from its inception: the lack of a strong metropolitan center in which to organize. Especially in the last years of its life, the society's minutes abounded with irate complaints that members routinely failed to attend meetings and the few who did lacked the interest to truly make a difference. Organizational failures became routine as committees assigned to complete needed tasks broke down either because of gross inaction or because members lived too far away from each other to effectively support slaves in legal cases. For example, a committee appointed at the annual meeting in 1806 to appeal a manumission case reported at both the 1807 and 1808 meetings that it had done nothing because members could not find a convenient place to meet. Not until 1809 when the committee again reported that it had never filed an appeal did another member volunteer for the task. Despite continual admonishment of members for inaction and an attempt to reduce membership dues to attract more, the leadership decided in 1809 that little could be accomplished by continuing. In 1812, Joshua Newbold and Samuel Coleman, two of the state's most diehard abolitionists, traveled to Philadelphia for the American Convention for Promoting the Abolition of Slavery Annual Meeting and reported that "with some degree of sorrow and shame," the "zeal of the members of the different abolition societies of this state has so far abated." The still functioning Trenton Society for Promoting the Abolition of Slavery pledged to help prevent the removal of Jersey slaves to the South and advocate for a stronger gradual abolition law, but even they soon disbanded. They had warned that as many believed "the slaves in this state are clothed and fed decently and comfortably," there might be significant impediments in trying to further attack slavery.[9]

The society's other local auxiliaries fared little better than their mother institution. The Gloucester County Society for Promoting the Abolition of Slavery held its last meeting in May 1806, noting "nothing further worthy of notice" deserved "their attention since last Meeting." The Burlington

County branch, previously extremely active due to its large Quaker membership, held its last meeting in September 1809. There, members bemoaned the fact that since September 1808 the auxiliary had been bankrupt and could only attract a pitiful attendance at its meetings. In 1807, only five members bothered to attend the annual meeting, while three came to its last in 1809 to declare the organization dead.[10]

Jersey Quakers suffered the same declining interest in abolition, as most turned away from slavery in New Jersey. For instance, the little discussion the Philadelphia Meeting for Suffering recorded on African Americans involved free black kidnappings and the illegal removal of slaves to the South. In 1812, the meeting petitioned the legislature to support a law to make it more difficult to remove a slave from New Jersey, while in 1816 it asked Congress for safeguards against such kidnapping. In 1825 it sent pamphlets to several southern states advocating abolition and implored other Yearly Meetings to concentrate on areas "where slavery is tolerated and authorized." By not sending pamphlets to fellow Mid-Atlantic Quakers, the Yearly Meeting likely did not consider the region a place where it needed to devote attention. As late as 1839, the meeting published a Minute on Slavery where it again pledged to support abolition but made no mention of its own region where slaves and slaves for a term remained.[11]

Instead of the Mid-Atlantic, Philadelphia Yearly Meeting became far more interested in abolishing the Atlantic slave trade and assisting Quaker abolitionist efforts in the South. In 1824, a committee visited Washington to advocate for increased naval patrols while the following year they distributed pamphlets throughout New Jersey abhorring the continuing inhumanity the trade caused. In the South, Greater Philadelphia Quakers worked with Friends in North Carolina to manumit and resettle their former slaves. Since North Carolina prohibited manumissions, Carolina Quakers gave their slaves freedom but still legally owned them. As the state's racial climate worsened, they legally transferred their slaves to trustees who helped guide them to freedom in several treks to the Midwest, the Mid-Atlantic, and Liberia in the 1820s. Philadelphia area Friends provided almost $10,000 to relocate 202 Carolina blacks to the Mid-Atlantic and Liberia, assistance never offered to those who remained enslaved in New Jersey.[12]

The lack of white abolitionist interest in New Jersey stripped Jersey blacks of powerful legal and political advocates who could have supported their interests, ensured gradual abolition continued without pause, and

helped them access legal freedom. Instead, most whites saw gradual abolition as the only viable option to end slavery and saw no further need to
act. Both the New York and Pennsylvania societies recognized this dilemma.
In 1817, for instance, the Pennsylvania Abolition Society claimed that
"many of our aged brethren have retired from the contest." They complained that their membership had declined and among "our benevolent
fellow citizens, an apathy prevails . . . the more to be lamented as we fear it
is the result of a mistaken impression that work is nearly accomplished."
Even though members of the Pennsylvania Abolition Society and the New
York Manumission Society continued to help New Jersey slaves, those slaves
had to largely navigate the state's world of unfreedom without a dedicated
local group to assist them. This helped masters maintain their interest in
bound labor since no institutional force opposed them.[13]

Though a large part of this apathy came from the belief that gradual
abolition was working, the marked change in the nature of American slavery in the nineteenth century also made New Jerseyans unsure of the similarities between northern and southern slavery. The innovation of the
cotton gin and the expansion of slavery across the Deep South transformed
southern slavery into a remarkably different institution. Large southern cotton plantations contrasted sharply with the small wheat farms of northeastern New Jersey. The consistent northern claim that slavery could be "easily
eradicated" during the Missouri Crisis showed the inattention of many
northerners to the institution's meteoric growth.[14] Issac Hillard, a freelance
agent who worked to recover kidnapped slaves, argued that the slavery
remaining in the North drastically differed from slavery in the South. In
1797, Hillard believed that "Connecticut slavery was not really slavery at
all, because the statute gave existing slaves their freedom vicariously by
enabling them to enjoy their children's certainty of delayed freedom." The
gradual abolition law then "inaugurated a new state of freedom immediately enjoyable by slaves and freeborn alike," making Connecticut different
from other slave states. Southern travelers to the North especially relayed
the differences in Jersey slavery.[15] Even though one anonymous traveler
from Charleston, South Carolina, wrote after his 1810 trip that New Jersey
had "not yet followed the example of her neighbors Pennsylvania and New
York in emancipating the Negroes," he argued that "laws in Jersey are far
too lenient" in favor of the slaves. He offered that for "many crimes which
are punishable in most countries with death," including many slaveholding
Caribbean islands, "the negro [in New Jersey] only receives corporal

punishment."[16] The growing disparity in the treatment of slaves and the institution of slavery meant that northern slavery increasingly stood apart from its southern counterpart. This disparity helped to focus attention on the more violent institution in the South and stymie support for significant homegrown abolitionist activity in the 1810s and 1820s.

*   *   *

Even without abolitionist support, the ideology of freedom from the Revolution and the 1804 abolition law seized the imagination of many Jersey slaves as they sought ways to escape slavery or negotiate with their masters for future freedom. These hopes of freedom and the growth of free black communities in New York and Philadelphia created an even greater inducement for slaves unaffected by the 1804 law to strike out on their own. New York became such a popular destination for fugitives that the city's Municipal Almshouse records noted the presence of blacks from locations as disparate as New Jersey, Pennsylvania, South Carolina, Maryland, Virginia, Bermuda, the West Indies, and Africa. They could blend into the growing metropolis to hide from their masters and live independently.[17] This hope for freedom led twenty-eight-year-old Frank to run away to New York from his master's home in Orange in 1807. Leaving with a "brown cloth coattee, white dimity vest, and a common hat," Frank stole himself to join relatives in New York, thereby fulfilling the dual goal of securing freedom and reuniting with his family. In contrast, twenty-year-old farmer and blacksmith Jack left his Woodbridge home in 1814 in search of a new life in New York using the skills learned as a slave. With no family, Jack's road to freedom depended on his own ingenuity and assistance from black and white abolitionists.[18]

Aside from New York, many slaves fled to Philadelphia, Baltimore, or even other towns in New Jersey, including Newark. For instance, twenty-year-old Princeton native Lewis stole himself in 1811 and fled to Philadelphia or possibly Baltimore, while Bill, Newarker Israel Crane's slave, made it to Philadelphia along with a nineteen-year-old "Irish lad" in 1816. Likewise, Francis Cisco, Gary Wistenwell's slave from Hackensack, made his escape much later in the abolition period when he abandoned his master but was recaptured in New Haven, Connecticut, in 1845. Newark, with its growing free black population, served as an attractive destination for forty-year-old Sam when he left his Princeton master in 1811, as it did for Morristown native Elias Mills and Mt. Pleasant slave Jinney later that same year.

Family relations also dictated where slaves fled; Rachel left her Trenton mistress and fled to either Amwell or Sussex County because she had "connections" there.[19]

Runaways damaged northern slavery during the abolition period by robbing slaveholders of the institution's prime labor force, young men in their late teens and twenties. In New Jersey, almost 80 percent of runaway advertisements between 1804 and 1824 sought the return of male slaves. Pennsylvania had a similar figure, with young males making up two-thirds of the runaway population. In New Jersey, the median age of a runaway was twenty-two, meaning that these valuable and unattached males could prove a brutal blow to a slaveholder's economic livelihood.[20]

After running away, these fugitives frequently congregated with free blacks and exacerbated existing racial tensions, especially in Newark. Assembling at night, they caused so much trouble for white Newark residents that a citizens committee assigned two members to patrol each of the city's four districts to enforce laws against vagrancy and rioting in 1809. The committee apparently did not solve the problem because in 1811 an anonymous letter to the editor of the Centinel of Freedom decried the behavior of slaves on the Sabbath. The writer accused them of the "most scandalous" behavior, including "hovering around the Church doors yelling and whooping to the great disturbance of those" worshiping inside.[21]

A few months after the Centinel of Freedom letter, Jonathan Skinner, part of Newark's committee charged with quelling the "noisy and riotous" blacks, began to patrol his district on July 22, 1811, when several African Americans "knocked him down and left him senseless in the public highway." A group of white Newarkers assembled the next day to punish those responsible by making open war on the black community, destroying the home of one freedman and damaging another. In the melee of revenge, whites destroyed furniture and beds and looted several homes that contained large quantities of playing cards, proof, they claimed, that the July 22 commotion involved enslaved and free blacks who consorted together and engaged in games of ill repute.[22]

This racially charged atmosphere intensified in April 1812, when nine black men between eighteen and fifty orchestrated a jailbreak at the State Prison by piercing a hole in the south wing wall. In a story syndicated in newspapers as far south as Raleigh, North Carolina, the jailbreak exacerbated white fears of losing control of the black population. Similar fears continued after disturbances broke out on French Street in New Brunswick in 1815. In neighboring Pennsylvania, the borough of York warned residents in 1803 to keep all "negroes or people of colour . . . at home under strict discipline and watch so as they may be under your eye at all times," indicating that even twenty-three years after gradual abolition's enactment, York residents still feared disruptions by blacks.[23]

Slave assaults on masters and white property challenged white hegemony even more than did general disturbances. Local historian Andrew Mellick recorded one such event in Millstone, where Hendrick Bergen's slaves were routinely arrested for stealing from neighbors while Sam, the slave of the *Washington Whig* editor, burned his owner's barn to the ground with the help of fellow slave Chloe in 1816. Likewise, in 1813, thirteen-year-old Ann Hitchens of Hunterdon County poisoned her master and mistress. Whereas she only received seven years in prison due to her young age, the courts sentenced Sam and Chloe to transportation out of the state, which continued Jersey slavery in another jurisdiction.[24]

Perhaps the most sensational crime committed by an African American in New Jersey occurred in 1843, when fugitive Rosan Keen poisoned Enos Seeley and his wife. Keen was born in 1828 in Penn's Neck, Salem County. Her parents, fugitives from Virginia, lived in various locations in South Jersey before being sent to the poor house in Millville, where Keen was bound out to Enos Seeley. In her confession, Keen admits her "intention to confess frankly and fully every circumstance . . . for seeking to destroy the lives of Mr. and Mrs. Seeley." She claimed that she hoped to kill them both and "take what money and goods I could secrete and get my mother from the poor house." She attempted to poison the couple with a lizard and, when that failed, she put ratsbane in their coffee. The ratsbane only sickened the couple, so Keen tried fly poison next. On this third attempt, Enos Seeley died, but before his wife succumbed Keen's actions came to light. Arrested for murder, Keen attempted to escape from jail twice before she was hanged on April 29, 1844.[25]

Though the violent resistance in the above cases ultimately ended in jail time, death, or transportation out of state, fear of even the possibility of violence against them frightened many whites as they understood that slavery, although dying, was not quite dead yet. Ann Cox, part of an abolitionist West Jersey family, claimed that when a friend heard Cox had hired a black woman to work in her kitchen, she "looked a little disconcerted and asked if she had slept in her bed." The friend claimed she would have been scared the woman might try to kill her family. Indeed, Jersey masters repeatedly heard of rebellions and unruly slaves from the South and Caribbean. For instance, Philadelphia native Samuel Emlen noted in a letter to abolitionist William Dillwyn that in Barbados whites needed to routinely supervise food preparation because their slaves would poison them.[26]

The possibility of slaves stealing themselves or violently resisting slavery in the abolition period challenged masters and slaves to adapt the institution in order for it to survive. No longer could masters exert the same type of control over their chattel that they had used before gradual abolition began for fear that their slaves might kill them, disappear to Philadelphia or New York, and then contribute to society's general downfall had increased. This amelioration was apparent in the 1808 case of Cato, a slave of Abraham Cooper of Chester. He nearly died when Cooper severely beat him for an unknown infraction. Cooper stood trial and was found guilty of assaulting and "inhumanely treat[ing] and abus[ing] his said slave by branding the said Cato who was thereby grievously wounded and hurt." New Jersey courts and white slaveholders held Cooper accountable for his actions because they realized that the use of violence as the only tool to compel slave obedience was especially unsuited to the abolition period.[27]

Instead, some slaveholders met the reality of the period by using the promise of freedom to quell slaves' demands while maintaining control and reaping economic rewards from them. This alternative began after the Revolution, when the legislature removed the onerous 200-pound bond requirement in 1786 and allowed unrestricted manumissions for slaves aged twenty-one to thirty-five. The 1798 slave code further expanded manumission to slaves up to age forty. The relaxed regulations, still controlling in the nineteenth century, allowed negotiations for freedom between slaveholder and slave to accelerate as masters attempted to limit economic losses. Freedom gained through negotiated manumissions "represented a compromise or a second-best option" to slaves and slaveholders because it provided freedom while permitting owners to benefit from their slave's labor.[28]

These flexible agreements became a lifeline to slaveholders because few slaves forfeited guaranteed freedom for the mere possibility of it by running away. For example, on March 7, 1809 John Runk promised his slave Jack freedom if he served an additional eight years, seven months, and seven days, which Jack completed on October 14, 1817. Similarly, Benjamin Youmans of Sussex County bargained with his slave Daniel in 1805 for freedom in exchange for four additional years of faithful service.[29]

Slaves so valued these arrangements that they negotiated for them by promising to buy their freedom either by offering their life savings in one lump sum or by providing masters a string of smaller payments over time. However, since most slaves could not save enough money to purchase themselves, thus contracts for additional years of service remained more common. Some slaves did manage to accumulate enough wealth from hiring themselves out to buy freedom, a process that reflected a slave's dual status as both a person and property. For example, Sam, a slave of Bergen County's John Blauvelt, agreed to pay his master fifty dollars a year for four years for his freedom between 1809 and 1813, while Simon, Jeremiah Fisher's slave, paid a lump sum of two hundred dollars in 1831. These fairly low sums suggest that masters used self-purchase as an enhanced form of negotiation in which they ensured the continuation of their slave's services while gaining partial repayment of their capital loss. A total of fourteen manumissions mentioned self-purchase, but since New Jersey law did not require masters to report such contracts, the number could have been much higher.[30]

For those masters who did not agree to freedom, they recognized that they needed to provide greater flexibility in how slaves lived and interacted with the growing network of free blacks in the Mid-Atlantic so as not to encourage slaves to abscond to that free world themselves. Many freed people routinely communicated, socialized, and even lived with those still enslaved with the tacit approval of Jersey masters. For instance, in 1811 teenager Rachel Van Dyke saw both free and enslaved blacks intermingling and living together at Halfpenny Town, a shanty village along the Raritan River. The Catherine Market in New York City likewise saw significant interactions between enslaved New Jersey blacks and free New Yorkers on an almost daily basis. Many slaves sold their own wares alongside their masters' and established social and business contacts with whites and free blacks. These social relationships frequently manifested themselves in dance competitions after the market closed. One pitted Ned, the slave of Martin Ryerson of Tappan, against free blacks from across the region.[31]

Silvia Du Bois, a former Jersey slave who gained her freedom in the late 1790s, remembered that slaves and free blacks used General Training Day, the day when the local militia mustered, to "illustrate the ironies of governments that called upon their disenfranchised inhabitants for protection in time of need."[32] Du Bois traveled to Flemington to see the muster in 1805 and described Training Day as filled with dancing, laughter, music, and, most of all, rum. Freed men and women like her socialized with enslaved

Figure 5. Sylvia Du Bois (right), pictured here in 1882 alongside her daughter
Elizabeth Alexander, gained her freedom in Hunterdon County and operated her
own interracial tavern and liquor business during militia training days
in the early nineteenth century.

Courtesy of the Hunterdon County Historical Society.

blacks who attended the festivities. These days were particularly important
to black New Jerseyans because they united enslaved blacks, free blacks,
and whites in a common space where food, drink, ideas, and money
changed hands. However, not all masters agreed with this new flexible system. Du Bois claimed some slaves who returned home after drinking and
dancing would "get licked—good God, how they'd get licked! Why, they'd
tie 'em right up and lick'em to death—cut 'em into pieces—cut 'em all into
string."[33]

The African Association of New Brunswick was another place where
slaves interacted with ex-slaves and showed masters' willingness to grant

concessions and allow greater freedoms. Founded in 1817, the association primarily raised money for an African school sponsored by the Presbyterian Church. In its first year it boasted forty-five free and enslaved members. For the enslaved, the organization allowed a reduced membership fee but required their master's permission. These permission certificates, filed with the organization's charter and minute book, show the successful negotiation slaves undertook to achieve greater interaction with free blacks in exchange for continued labor.[34]

Many Jersey slaveholders also recognized the utility of allowing their slaves to marry free blacks because it would anchor the couple, decrease the chances of slaves absconding, and stabilize the institution. Some masters even organized formal marriage ceremonies officiated by white ministers, though these had no legal basis. Masters retained the power to sell their slaves and owned any children born to their female slaves, but the marriages did signify that slavery had become more flexible. For example, Morristown's Presbyterian Church and the Morris County Clerk recorded forty black marriages between 1804 and 1842. Nineteen involved two slaves marrying, twelve joined two free people, and the remaining nine wed a slave to a free person. The same phenomenon occurred in Bound Brook Presbyterian Church and Bergen County's Dutch Reformed churches.[35]

Without strong black churches in the early abolition period, enslaved and free blacks gravitated toward these white churches for important ceremonies, since in many churches black marriages and baptisms greatly exceeded the number of black members. For instance, Methodist minister Thomas Morrell married ten free black couples between 1816 and 1835 and baptized several more. Likewise, ministers at Trinity Cathedral, an Episcopal church in Newark, admitted, baptized, married, and buried hundreds of free and enslaved African Americans. Westfield's Presbyterian Church did the same and recorded twenty-four black members from 1804 to 1843, but its minister officiated at dozens of black marriages and baptisms of non-church members. Indeed, Westfield Presbyterian's records indicate that white and black congregants joined together for these important ceremonies. For example, the free black child of Prime and Hannah joined sixteen white children in a mass baptism on June 5, 1808. The abolition period therefore represented a mixture of segregation and integration depending on relationships with masters, former masters, and ministers.[36]

This hybridity, however, placed a burden on the freed person in the marriage or, in the case of a married enslaved couple belonging to two masters, on both of them to convince their masters to grant them simultaneous freedom. Betsey and Thomas Winner of Acquackanonk, both freed on the same day by the same owner, represented the very small number of couples who easily migrated together from slavery to freedom. Frequently, one spouse achieved freedom and then had to work to purchase the other. For instance, Sam Hall, a freedman in Somerset County, purchased his wife Read and their slave for a term daughter Sarah in 1824. Other slaves could not convince their spouse's master to manumit or raise enough money to purchase them before their partner reached forty and became ineligible for freedom under state law. Jane Berry lived with this particular dilemma as her husband, over forty when the couple raised enough money to purchase him, remained a slave owned by her.[37]

Interactions between free and enslaved blacks did, however, sometimes entice slaves to seek freedom since free blacks, either overtly or by their mere presence, encouraged runaways in the abolition period. Two Pompton slave masters, for instance, advertised for the return of Joe and Jack in 1807, whom they believed to be "at the Jersey races and supposed to have gone into New York or to Tappan near the North River" with free blacks from New York. Likewise, twenty-four-year-old Tom and seventeen-year-old James Roberts left their Newark masters in 1809, "seduced away by a stout black man named Sam Thomas who calls himself free." Finally, thirty-nine-year-old Robert Thompson fled his Elizabeth owner in 1814 along with a free black named Volantine. As a nest egg for his new life and perhaps to repay himself for his bondage, Thompson stole six hundred dollars from his master before he left.[38]

For masters, though, slavery remained important, as any agreement made with a slave provided greater flexibility in their effort to reap continued profits since they could sell them before their manumission date. The presence of these "term slaves" expanded the number of bound laborers available for sale, lowered their prices, and enlarged the pool of whites who participated in slavery. For instance, an 1809 advertisement featured a twenty-six-year-old male slave's service for seven years and six months, while an 1810 advertisement included a seventeen-year-old boy's service until he reached twenty-five. Jacob Plume of Newark bought one of these term slaves, five-and-a-half-year-old Jack, from Jabez Canfield in 1807. As a condition of the sale, Plume agreed to manumit Jack at twenty-five, which mirrored the gradual abolition law. Plume sold young Jack six years later to his brother Joseph, who then sold him to John Stewart, who then sold him to James Glass. Glass sold Jack yet again to Moses Condit in 1816. The value six different owners placed on Jack's labor and the labor of similar term slaves illustrates that slavery not only survived the 1804 abolition law but thrived.[39]

In the same vein as conditional manumission agreements, some masters promised freedom in their wills to compel obedience, though fewer than 11 percent of the state's manumissions occurred this way. For instance, David Johnson of Newark ordered his executors to manumit his slave Cuff within one month of his death in 1814. Similarly, Samuel Randolph of Piscataway manumitted his two slaves Sensor and Primus at his death in 1811.[40] Few wills communicated why their authors freed their slaves directly, though some cited morality or the idea of American liberty. Ezra Darby, for instance, wrote in his 1796 will, eight years before he voted for gradual abolition in the legislature, that he gave his slave Frank freedom because he considered "freedom . . . the birthright of all mankind" and would "think myself guilty to leave him in the detestable state of slavery." Even with these ideals, Darby set complicated conditions for freedom. If he died before Frank reached twenty-one, Frank would be sold until twenty-five. However, if he died after Frank turned twenty-one, Frank could be freed immediately. Darby died in 1809 when Frank had just turned twenty-five, so Frank gained freedom immediately and did not endure an additional sale.[41]

Unlike Darby, most slaveholders used their wills to extend their slaves' bondage in perpetuity. A survey of slaveholders' wills from the first twenty years of the abolition period (1804–1824) in two of New Jersey's largest cities, Newark and Morris Township, indicates that only two granted slaves freedom. Both, however, mandated future freedom in exchange for faithful service. For example, in 1805 Jeremiah Baldwin freed his slave Jack only when he reached thirty-one, while Aaron Malick ordered his executors to sell four of his eight slaves when they reached twenty-eight. The remaining slaveholder wills from Newark and Morris represented the more common experience, sale or transfer of a slave in perpetuity. Malick, although he provided for the freedom of half his slaves, ordered the remaining four sold and the profits distributed to his heirs. Likewise, Lydia Williamson of Elizabethtown ordered her slave Peter sold and the proceeds distributed to her son and grandchildren in 1814, while John Morris of Newark transferred his slave Bob to his wife and ordered his two remaining slaves and his slaves for a term sold for his wife's support in 1820.[42]

Table 3. Mean and Median Ages of Slaves at Manumission by County

County	Median age	Mean age	Total slaves with age data	Total slave population, 1810
Bergen	33	31.9	119	2180
Burlington	25.5	27.5	30	93
Essex	30	31.2	220	1129
Middlesex	30	30.1	130	1298
Monmouth	31	31	228	1504
Morris	31.3	31.1	26	856
Salem	22	24.2	29	29
Somerset	34	32.8	224	1968
Sussex	27	27.9	23	478

Data compiled from county manumission books. Cape May and Gloucester yielded too little information on ages to make comparisons; 1029 manumissions contained a slave's age.

Even if a slave achieved freedom, the age at that freedom indicates that many masters saw manumission as a tool to compel labor during a slave's prime years while relieving them of the burden of caring for aged slaves. Instead of a benevolent gift to slaves, many owners executed manumission agreements after their slaves had reached middle age and their productivity declined. Statewide, the average slave gained freedom at thirty. Slaveholders in East Jersey kept their slaves on average three years longer than the state average and eleven to twelve years more than slaveholders in most of West Jersey. Especially in East Jersey, slaves lived more than half their lives in bondage including their most productive.[43]

These owners believed that manumission served as "a carrot to hold out to slaves in order to motivate them to work" over long periods of dedicated service. In Pennsylvania, later in life manumissions had become commonplace; most manumissions after 1790 occurred after age thirty. Monmouth County slaveholders routinely kept the services of slaves aged fourteen to forty-five with manumissions from that age bracket "less acts of benevolence than calculated responses to changing legal conditions." These legal conditions reflect the much larger labor changes underway in the early nineteenth-century North and Upper South. The polyglot of bound laborers working together in these locales (slaves, slaves for a term, and term slaves) showed that masters believed slavery maintained an important place in the antebellum social and economic framework; delayed manumission allowed slavery to adapt into the workforce.[44]

This continuing popularity of bound laborers informs previous scholarship on the economic character of early America and the precise timing of its shift to a capitalistic system of exchange. To some historians, gradual abolition became central in the development of capitalism in the North because, as historian Allan Kulikoff has argued, it helped spur on the "process of proletarianization" and made free blacks a cheap labor force to fuel the growing manufacturing industry.[45] Peter Colt, superintendent of the Society for Establishing Useful Manufacturing in Paterson, reinforced this idea in several essays in 1792 that argued for the stimulation of manufacturing, since, as compared to "all the northern middle states," New Jersey had "an abundance of unemployed peoples or other people not fully employed" who could spur economic development.[46] Indeed, in 1809, the state legislature considered a lottery-financed plan that would have not only funded improvements to the Port of Perth Amboy, built manufacturing plants, roads, canals, and a state university, but provided compensation to emancipate slaves, suggesting that planners saw the benefits of developing the enslaved into a free labor force. However, the legislature's failure to adopt the lottery allowed bound labor to play an integral role in the state's nineteenth-century economy.[47]

In contrast, New Jersey's slaves and slaves for a term functioned not as a nineteenth-century anachronism but as part of a larger labor market that offered customers a choice of many different labor options. This situation muddied the divisions between slave and free labor but provided needed flexibility to meet varied labor needs. The flexibility was especially important as New Jersey became more intertwined in international trade markets for its agricultural products and began to grow an industrial base. Slaves, just as in the colonial period, remained jacks-of-all-trades after gradual abolition began and helped Jersey farmers feed the demand for wheat, corn, and other grains from both Europe and the Caribbean in the early nineteenth century. Slaves continued to work on New Jersey farms but, due to the country's continuing economic growth, they became even more valuable as they could be hired out in the agricultural off season to work in factories, build turnpikes and canals, or in any number of other occupations. This flexibility of the institution reinforces recent scholarship on slavery and capitalism that has suggested that slavery functioned not as the Marxian antithesis of capitalism but as part of a larger Atlantic economy where slaves became a key component of commerce, trade, and global capitalism. American capitalists therefore frequently hired slaves, indentured servants, term slaves, and apprenticed children and used them as interchangeable parts of the labor force.[48]

As a fully at-will labor market grew in the early national North, labor consumers valued the nonpecuniary means, such as violence and strict enforcement of legally binding labor contracts, by which labor could be controlled. Although pecuniary devices such as monetary penalties for sloppy or missed work could compel worker compliance, the continued popularity of slaves and slaves for a term indicates that employers enjoyed having the ability to legally or physically compel labor instead of solely being beholden to the variable labor market. The transition to capitalism thus was a gradual one, where slaveholders and those nonslaveholders who had lived with slavery understood the value of bound labor and never abandoned it. The capital invested in owning a bounded labor force helped stabilize the economy and grew slaveholders' influence, power, and personal wealth.[49]

This interest remained strong throughout the 1820s, but by the 1830s white New Jerseyans began to see not only larger numbers of freed blacks competing with whites for jobs but whites equated contract labor with slavery, the antithesis of the budding northern free soil ideology. This new generation understood blacks' association with slavery but believed bound labor was now less important to the state's economy. By the 1840s, only a small proportion of New Jerseyans steadfastly continued to see slaves as economically important, yet this group successfully advocated for its continuation in spite of the rapidly modernizing free labor marketplace.[50]

Finally, delayed manumissions had a significant gendered component because gradual abolition had made a slave woman's reproductive potential an even more important part of perpetuating slavery. Masters therefore held their female slaves longer to gain ownership over more slaves for a term while also retaining the benefits of that woman's labor. Female slaves then became increasingly common as domestics in early national New Jersey as they could not only serve families inside the home but also engage in agricultural labor as well. Rachel Van Dyke of New Brunswick wrote extensively on the presence of two female slaves, an older female slave born in Guinea, and a younger woman named Sylvia, a domestic in her parents'

Table 4. Slave Median Ages by Sex at Manumission by County

County	Median female age	Median male age	Total slaves with age data	Total slave population, 1810
Bergen	32	33	119	2180
Burlington	23	29.6	30	93
Essex	30	31.7	220	1129
Middlesex	30	30.2	130	1298
Monmouth	30	31.6	228	1504
Morris	26	33.2	26	856
Salem	21.5	25.6	29	29
Somerset	32	33.5	224	1968
Sussex	25	29.8	23	478

household. Like thousands of other slaves, this pair propagated slavery through both their domestic labor and reproductive potential.[51]

The favorability of female slaves meant that masters freed males in greater numbers. Fifty-eight percent of manumissions with the age listed freed males while 42 percent freed females. As for age at manumission, masters held their male slaves slightly longer than females. Bergen and Somerset masters kept their female slaves an average of thirty-two years, as opposed to thirty-three for males, while Essex, Middlesex, and Monmouth kept theirs an average of thirty, as opposed to almost thirty-two for males. Since in every county, slaveholders held females for less time than males, this possibly indicates that much of the profit from females, if they had already had several children who would remain slaves for a term and provide the master a profit, was bound in their reproductive potential and not, like men, in labor.[52]

With a higher proportion of female slaves of child-bearing age than males in the overall slave population, the majority of slave sale advertisements not surprisingly announced the sale of female slaves. Of 241 advertisements in 1804–1824 that advertised full transfer of title (not term slaves), 60 percent marketed women. Of these, the median age at sale was twenty-one, which could indicate that some of the enslaved women had already borne children but could still garner a prime price while in their childbearing years. The males advertised for sale had a slightly lower median age of nineteen years possibly because they retained their usefulness as laborers.[53]

*   *   *

Underlying the debate over manumission were concerns among whites that former slaves might become paupers; to many, poverty and dependence were blacks' normative state. Many ex-slaves had never even freed themselves from white supervision and continued to live as dependents, proof to many whites that blacks could never leave their former dependency behind. For example, Monmouth County farmers created a cottager system where sharecropping became the main way free blacks could access land. Samuel Wright, a sheep farmer in Upper Freehold, offered Isaac Vincent, a free black from Middlesex County, a job in 1809. As a wage laborer, Vincent toiled on Wright's farm during that year's growing season. Impressed with Vincent's work, Wright offered him an annual contract in 1810 that included a wage, a house on the property, and a small plot of land to grow his own food. In what historian Graham Hodges calls "mild slavery," Vincent's relationship with Wright marked a transition between slavery and true independence. Similar to Vincent's relationship to Wright, William Walters, a free black man from Hopewell Township, worked on Enoch Burgin's 160-acre farm in 1804 under an annual contract. These cottager relationships, used with whites as well, hid the reality that slavery had been slated for death and again illustrated blacks as subservient to whites.[54]

These cottager contracts shielded the government from caring for these seemingly dependent blacks, though when former slaves sought support from the overseers of the poor in increasing numbers when they failed to become economically viable after freedom, white concern grew. For example, in 1807–1816 Newark's overseers of the poor paid twenty-nine claims to blacks for food and housing expenses, funerals, and medical care. Because whites feared the ramifications of the government supporting anyone, overseers had few qualms about ejecting those blacks who did not legally live in Newark. Over this time period, authorities removed at least two impoverished free blacks to where they had lived as slaves, Springfield and New York. These ejections became routine across the North as whites sought to limit their economic exposure to abolition's products.[55]

The difficulties of life in the early abolition period led some ex-slaves to become so poverty stricken that the state's poor laws forced them to reenter slavery. In Cranbury, Thomas Truxton, owner of Phebe and her daughter, sold them to Boston, Phebe's free husband, for sixty-five pounds in 1796. Boston died after the turn of the century, causing Phebe and her daughter Elizabeth to fall on hard economic times. Phebe sought support from the Overseers of the Poor of West Windsor in 1813. After an investigation, the overseers decided that instead of a sale, the transaction between Truxton and Phebe's husband was tantamount to manumission. The overseers ordered Truxton to pay for Phebe's upkeep, as the law required a master to care for former slaves. Truxton, angered by the possibility of a prolonged series of payments to support Phebe, ignored her legal status and sold her as a slave to William Covenhoven. Instead of a clear differentiation between slavery and freedom, Phebe's status as an impoverished widow changed how the state defined her and her daughter's identity. Poverty in freedom meant suffering in the material sense as well as the possibility that, as in Phebe's case, government officials would not stop a return to slavery.[56]

Many white reformers set up private organizations to assist impoverished blacks and touted the same gradualist philosophies of white guardianship and black inferiority as the Abolition Society. One of the largest and longest operating, the Newark Female Charitable Society, began in 1803 and joined together the wives of prominent businessmen, legislators, and state officials to provide poor relief to both whites and blacks. The women divided the city into zones and a female manager took responsibility for relief distributed in each. Every manager visited applicants' homes to judge "their characters and circumstances," as any "immorality exclude [d] [the applicant] from the patronage of the society." These reformers, like others in the nineteenth century, tied the amelioration of poverty to an assessment of morality. In exchange for food and supplies, the managers forced applicants to accept certain conditions to bring them in line with the society's vision of proper moral conduct. Chief among these regulations required women to surrender their children to the overseers of the poor, who would bind them out to labor for a white family until majority. To free families, the separation of parent and child harkened back to slavery, yet without that separation they received no support. The imposition of moral ideals on blacks echoed the calls for the "civilizing" of blacks from the gradual abolition movement and limited the ability of blacks who sought to maintain family cohesion from receiving necessary support.[57]

Because of their experience with free black poverty, most whites felt that blacks, with their seemingly questionable work ethic and inherent inferiority, would be even more susceptible to poverty and loathed to care for them. Therefore, abolition era lawmakers and courts drafted laws that forced former slaveholders to provide monetary support for pauper ex-slaves. These regulations led many masters to decide against manumission if they doubted their slave's ability to survive economically. It also tied poor relief for ex-slaves to the town in which they gained freedom. From the former slave's perspective, this provided a constant reminder of their previous enslaved life because they could never establish a true residence outside of their identity as a former slave under the law. This marked them as different from other Americans and helped place them outside the boundaries of American democracy.[58]

In 1824, the New Jersey Supreme Court affirmed the responsibility of slaveholders to care for ex-slaves in a case regarding William, Samuel Canfield's former slave. The Overseers of the Poor of Chatham Township expended one dollar a week for William's care and sought to recoup some of that money from Canfield's heirs, his sons John and Benjamin. Canfield's will helped the township's case because it charged his sons to provide for William. With perhaps an air of clairvoyance, Canfield empowered his executors to sell any part of his estate if John or Benjamin "neglect[ed] or refuse[d] to comply." The Chatham Overseers argued that since Canfield had owned William, despite his subsequent manumission, Canfield's heirs and not the public bore responsibility for him. The court agreed and ruled that if previous ownership could be proven, the master or his heirs must accept responsibility because no slave or ex-slave should become a ward of the state.[59]

As in William's case, the court decided a month later that Jack should be cared for by his master, John Mount, and not his local township, affirming that former slaves could never truly escape their past—the bonds of unfreedom could drag them back to a former master or a town where they might not have lived for decades. Mount freed Jack when he moved from East Windsor to New York in 1802, while Jack moved to nearby South Brunswick where he became a pauper in 1823. South Brunswick's overseers contended that any manumitted slave assumed legal settlement where his master resided at the time of manumission. Therefore, they believed East Windsor had responsibility for Jack. After East Windsor sued to rid itself of Jack, who had already cost them $88.75, the court, in an interesting twist, ruled Jack's manumission invalid because Mount had never subjected him to an examination by the Overseers of the Poor to determine if he might become a pauper. As a slave, albeit one with a master who did not know it, he retained no tie to East Windsor. Instead, following the judgment in the Chatham case, South Brunswick had to care for Jack but could sue Mount to recover its expenses.[60]

Like New Jersey, other northern states drafted laws that limited the state's responsibility for caring for indigent slaves. In 1831, Flora, a slave of Elisha Pitkin of East Hartford, Connecticut, fell on the support of the local Overseers of the Poor after her master died and his executors refused to care for her. In the same way that New Jersey courts ruled that masters needed to care for slaves, the Connecticut judges argued that any "needy slave must be relieved by the town in which is his settlement" only if "both master and slave were paupers or a slave emancipated in accordance with the act of 1792 should become" a pauper. Unlike in New Jersey, slaves properly emancipated had no further tie to their masters. Jenny, a former slave who became a pauper in Colchester, for example, had to be supported by the township because she lived there as a free woman. However, since her master had manumitted her at fifty-six, above the legal limit of forty-five, her manumission was deemed invalid. As a slave, her former master had to provide support.[61]

In New Jersey, issues over responsibility for former slaves for a term eventually legally differentiated them from their enslaved parents. In 1820, the legislature made clear that indigent former slaves for a term should be considered residents of their birthplace unless they had lived in a new jurisdiction for seven years. This made their status different from ex-slaves since they could never establish a new legal domicile.[62] Sarah Brocaw, a former slave for a term, put the 1820 law to the test when she fell on hard times and moved into Franklin Township's poorhouse. Franklin sued Bridgewater, the location of Sarah's birth, to pay for her care because she had not been a free resident of Franklin for seven years. Bridgewater officials argued that Franklin had been the location of her transition to freedom, which controlled financial responsibility in cases of slaves. However, the Supreme Court ruled in 1846 that because Brocaw did not live as a free woman in Franklin for more than seven years, Bridgewater held responsibility for her care as her birth city. In the contest over Sarah's future, the abolition law linked Sarah back to her previous life as a slave for a term, although not as strictly as it did for slaves. Freeborn, she could establish a new residence and in the eyes of the law separate herself from her enslaved past.[63]

*   *   *

The flexibility that slavery provided in the first twenty-five years of the abolition period responded to the state's changing labor needs, though the increased concerns over black rioting, slave interaction with free blacks, and fears of black economic dependency after freedom also helped Americans define citizenship in the new nation. Slavery's continuation became part of that process since dependence became the antithesis to freedom, citizenship, and acceptance. Free white men pushed the most dependent Americans into a lower status because they believed dependents (free blacks, women, or slaves) could never have a truly full stake in the obligations of republican citizenship. This process of creating a unified nationalism frequently revolved around politicized rituals, those that historian David Waldstreicher argues created "citizenship as a national category." To this end, parades and other electoral celebrations became mechanisms to separate those deemed worthy or unworthy of that citizenship.[64]

Free African Americans across the North attempted to appropriate white political culture in order to seize power and portray themselves as true citizens. To them, this was "a matter of survival" as they realized that they needed to "establish their place among their white countrymen." Festivals such as Election Day in New England and Pinkster (or Pentecost) in New York and New Jersey gradually faded as freed blacks saw that they reinforced the white linkage between black and slave as they had been celebrated in slavery. Black elites replaced these older celebrations with parades in the first decades of freedom in the nineteenth century and believed they were integral in the battle for respect and rights, showing that they were "legally and politically vested" in the "full duties, rights, privileges, and pleasures of American life."[65] These parades celebrated major events, such as the ending of the Atlantic Slave Trade or emancipation in New York in 1827, and attempted to portray free blacks as respectable. By 1830, this need for respectability became even more powerful as black elites wanted to ensure any public celebration was, above all, orderly. In New Jersey, free blacks enacted this respectability by marching in an orderly procession to protest fugitive slave trials in 1837. However, this move to respectability was not universal; three years later, Newark's black elite grimaced when a large number of men "came in from the country, with a drum and fife" and proceeded to march through the streets of the city "in a manner deeply mortifying" to all respectable African Americans.[66]

As free blacks attempted to establish respectability, white abolitionists continually insisted that blacks needed white supervision and guardianship, especially through education. Jersey abolitionists had routinely worried over the country's future if masses of uneducated, illiterate, and unsavory free blacks entered American society. In 1809, they argued the need to educate slaves for a term and freed blacks, "both as it respects their present and future happiness and the harmony and interests of the community at large." These abolitionists, even though they couched education in terms of its benefit to whites, repeatedly reported that "very little has been done in this extensive and interesting field."[67] William Griffith and others had originally proposed to educate freed slaves in Sabbath Schools (also called Sunday schools or First Day schools). Classes met on Sundays after worship services and provided religious instruction where whites would teach blacks "sobriety, honesty, diligence . . . the practice of cleanliness, frugality, manners, and all the domestic virtues." With this mission, the abolitionists proposed to "civilize" the "uncivilized" newly freed population and make them into presentable and proper republican citizens.[68]

Some auxiliaries followed through on Griffith's recommendations and set out to fulfill their guardianship duties and "assist" in the education of black New Jerseyans. The society had ordered its auxiliaries to "encourage the admission of black children into schools of their respective neighborhoods, especially those who evince favorable dispositions and the promise of genius" and promote "private associations in compact neighborhoods in which the people of color abound" to help raise funds for Sabbath schools that would correct deficient morals and help them become civilized members of society. Five members of the Burlington County Abolition Society went into white homes where free blacks lived and encouraged those freed people to send their children to schools that taught "good manners, industry, economy, and cleanliness."[69] Although the auxiliaries had begun to educate newly freed African Americans, by 1812 the society warned that while "too many of the free people of color do not exhibit that industry, economy, and temperance that was expected by man." Overall, little had been done to create a network of abolitionist-sponsored schools to educate any of New Jersey's blacks.[70]

After the Abolition Society's collapse, Sabbath schools sponsored by churches and private donors took over black education and continued white paternalistic control over it. These schools were led by white teachers and administrators, focused primarily on reading, writing, and basic mathematics, and taught biblical reading knowledge and prayer to instill religious and moral lessons in their students. They gained popularity in the early nineteenth century among African Americans because they lacked alternatives. In Philadelphia, blacks represented over two-thirds of the Sabbath School population. In New Jersey, most Sabbath schools had nearly all black pupils, although several provided integrated classrooms such as the First Day School in Succasunna in Morris County, which opened in 1814. However, most Sabbath schools attracted more blacks than whites and therefore remained largely segregated. In some places in New Jersey, this segregation came through deliberate planning. Morristown, for example, had two schools simultaneously in session, one for whites and the other for blacks. Flemington saw the same thing when Presbyterians there started a Sabbath school in 1817. Whites became so strongly opposed to an integrated school that they created two segregated classrooms so that, even by 1850, almost all classes remained segregated. Aside from race, the two classrooms differed in that a wider spectrum of ages from youth to elderly sat ready to learn how to read and write in the segregated one.[71]

Private benevolent organizations enabled white control to continue over black education and supported the notion that blacks were in need of white guardianship before they were eligible for citizenship. The first, the Elizabethtown Free School Association, formed in 1815 with a mission to "afford instruction to the ignorant," originally targeting white pupils. Soon after its founding, a group of white teachers of a small independent black school asked to merge.[72] The association granted the request and the School for People of Color enrolled about eighty pupils of both sexes and all ages. The association included two other schools, a segregated School for the Instruction of White Female Children and another for white males. Teachers divided the pupils into classes based on their ability to read multisyllabic words and the New Testament, which taught both literacy and religious values. This model of a larger organization controlling segregated white and black schools was replicated in Newark by the Female Department of Colored School of the Newark Academy in the 1820s.[73]

With a very similar mission to the Elizabethtown Free School Association, the Female Department of the Colored School reiterated the common

assumption that blacks, even when offered education and "uplift," possessed values contradictory to the attainment of equality and full citizenship. For instance, the school reported in September 1821 that their "offers
of instruction are too much neglected and many . . . would rather spend
the Holy Sabbath in groups lounging about our streets in profanity and
idleness than . . . for the more excellent attainment of knowledge."[74] Two
months later, the superintendent of the Colored School again complained
that the "streets are overrun with ignorance and profanity" that make Sundays "a season of almost ungovernable excess of noise and confusion, especially the evening when boys of all descriptions and color . . . intrude upon
. . . peaceful abodes like the heathen manifest . . . of that decorum which
distinguishes a land of light from a land of heathenish darkness."[75] In this
report, the superintendent remarked on both the problem of African American education and how the education of "boys of all descriptions" could
cure the lack of morality and provide decorum to the city's streets. School
leaders saw unfreedom on both sides of the color line due to a lack of
education and believed that negative societal traits were characteristic of
the lower class, something that Quaker abolitionist Samuel Emlen firmly
understood. Emlen, while living in Burlington, observed in 1821 that free
black children grew up "without any advantage of school education." By
year's end, he had created a "little school designed for the benefit of the
colored children," though it had been difficult to convince black parents to
support the school since they needed their children's labor to survive and
could not, in Emlen's mind, see the long-term benefit of education. Therefore, in an attempt to "civilize" the unbridled masses that threatened to
destabilize society, these schools provided moral education in line with
privileged white assumptions of economic and racial inferiority instead of
acknowledging the true issues that affected New Jersey's young black
community.[76]

Blacks' lack of formal education certainly helped whites undermine
black calls for citizenship and push them back into dependency, though
slavery's continued existence in New Jersey provided an easy example of
that dependency for wide public consumption in print culture. Bobalition
broadsides, an attempt especially by New Englanders at justifying the continued marginalization of blacks, soon spread to the Mid-Atlantic.
Although New Jerseyans never created the same type of advertisements,
they certainly understood their power. Bobalition discussions first appeared

in Boston and ridiculed black celebrations of the end of the slave trade. These broadsides presented whites with anti-black caricatures and used crude racist humor to show that blacks could never become proper citizens. These advertisements permeated discussions of race in the North and reinforced the associations between black, inferiority, and slavery. By the 1820s and 1830s, these caricatures morphed into minstrel shows that satirized and demeaned free blacks and displayed white racial superiority. Minstrel shows worked as a "socially approved" mechanism for "institutional control" that, by "pretending that slavery was amusing, right, and natural," effectively excluded blacks from civil society in the same way Jersey courts had legally done.[77]

In New Jersey, the most active discussions over citizenship's boundaries concerned the right to vote. Unlike other states, New Jersey's 1776 constitution allowed any resident to vote as long as he or she possessed fifty pounds of property. Earlier historians interpreted this constitutional provision as merely an oversight. However, state officials repeatedly defended universal propertied suffrage, arguing that the law's "true intention" mandated that state officials "not refuse the vote of any widow or unmarried woman of full age, nor any person of color of full age" if they met the property requirements. Legislators also opposed new laws that specifically mandated suffrage for women and blacks because, as one legislator remarked, "our Constitution gives this right to maids or widows black or white" already.[78]

Suffrage debates highlighted white women's ability to vote decades before Seneca Falls and these "petticoat electors" joined not only white men at the polls, but free black men and women as well in the 1780s and 1790s. The small numbers of blacks initially did not challenge the racial boundaries of citizenship or white authority. In one famous case, future Governor William Pennington, who himself owned a slave and four slaves for a term, escorted a young free black woman to her polling station in Essex County where he voted alongside her.[79]

However, by the early nineteenth century the increased prevalence of white women and free blacks regularly voting led to calls for their disenfranchisement as Federalists and Democratic Republicans battled for legislative seats that often turned on the support of these two groups. Prejudice against African Americans and partisan politics combined to denigrate and eventually restrict black suffrage even as, over the previous two decades, election regulations had been liberalized so that the fifty-pound property

Figure 6. Life in Philadelphia. Grand Celebration ob de bobalition ob African slabery. Although never produced in New Jersey, broadsides like this mocked black celebrations of the end of the slave trade and abolition. They enabled whites to degrade free blacks' status as citizens and continue to associate them with slaves.
Courtesy of the Library Company of Philadelphia.

requirement could be met with paper money instead of land. This opened suffrage to almost 90 percent of white men by 1800 as well as most widows and many free blacks.[80]

Democratic Republicans feared that female and African American voters could thwart their plan to oust the ruling Federalist Party. The control of the statehouse and thus the governor's mansion (the legislature appointed the governor until 1844) hinged on only a few hundred votes around the state. In 1800, some of the bitterest political fighting emanated from Essex County, where Democratic Republicans lambasted Federalists for their dastardly un-American electioneering. Specifically, Democratic Republicans argued that "Federal corruption displayed itself some time since, in its blackest colors, at Elizabeth-Town, when they brought forward many free blacks as also the widows and maids of that place, and persuaded them to vote for the federal ticket."[81] In the same election, which coincidently propelled Democratic Republicans to power, they accused Federalists of "receiving among other votes known to be illegal those of negro wenches," as well as "votes of British officers on half pay, of Frenchman with no property, and pauper negro women." In 1802, Jeffersonians again claimed that in some towns, women (who overwhelmingly voted Federalist) made up a quarter of the electorate. With insults shuttling back and forth and the outcome of two competing political ideologies in the balance, Democratic Republicans challenged the electorate's openness and argued for stronger gender and racial boundaries to suffrage.[82]

As Americans redefined citizenship as a white male enterprise, New Jersey's Democratic Republican Party applied that logic to identify the votes of women and blacks as a corrupting influence on state residents, a task made much easier by slavery's enduring presence. Even though they had used abolition to show that they were the true inheritors of the Spirit of 1776, Democratic Republicans portrayed blacks voting for Federalist candidates as unfaithful and corrupt Americans, subverting the democratic process for their own political purposes at the expense of propertied white men. In the same way, women's presence at the polls corrupted the common virtue as republicanism informed early American men of women's inherent inferiority. Democratic Republicans utilized the rhetoric of black inferiority present in the gradual abolition debates to denigrate free black voters and solidify their own power. Instead of trying to convince free blacks to support the party that had helped pass gradual abolition, Democratic Republicans marginalized both widows and blacks because they feared Federalists would convince these dependent Americans to vote for them.[83]

Democratic Republicans continued to identify Federalist "corruption" by feeding newspapers reports of slaves coming to the polls with completed Federalist ballots to show that slaves and free blacks operated in the same way and that both were unworthy of political citizenship. In one article, a slave reportedly claimed "Massa be good, he gibbe my holiday. De tory again be de bes men of all he say, so de paper I tick in de box as he said, and I be no more slave, 'cause I vote for a fed" after an 1802 election.[84] Similarly, in 1807 a Democratic Republican legislator claimed that the 1802

Trenton city election should have been declared invalid because the "vote of a negro slave, the property of another negro slave" decided this tight race and resulted in an equal number of Federalists and Democratic Republicans in the assembly for the 1802–1803 session. This tie prevented either party from naming a governor and left New Jersey without a chief executive for that year. Federalists defended the election results by showing that the slave referred to was actually a free black woman who met the property qualifications. These messages that blacks and women were detrimental to the good order of American politics, regardless of their truthfulness, challenged white New Jerseyans to reconsider how far political freedoms should be extended across racial and gender lines.[85]

In 1806, the "corruption" involving women and blacks climaxed when Essex County residents voted on the location of their new county courthouse. Newark, in the county's northern half and the county seat, battled against Elizabethtown, the largest population center in the county's southern half. The competition for the courthouse led Elizabethtown voters, according to Democratic Republicans, to stuff their ballot boxes with votes favoring their city. Fearing rampant voter fraud, Newark sent officials to monitor the polls in Elizabethtown, where they reported that they saw women, blacks, and young boys voting en mass. These monitors warned that if Newark did not start stuffing their own ballot boxes, the election would inevitably be lost. To best their southern counterparts, Newarkers stuffed ballot boxes in earnest, bringing men, women, boys, and slaves together to vote at precincts around the city. Newark's white men even dressed as women in order to vote a second, third, or fourth time. In the end, municipalities like Acquackanonk, a community with about 350 voters, reported over 1,900 ballots cast, with a majority for Elizabethtown. Elizabethtown itself reported a voter turnout of 279 percent. Similar reports of widespread fraud flooded the state legislature.[86]

After hearing of the flagrant disregard for election laws, Lewis Condict, the same legislator who questioned the 1802 Trenton election, battled to restrict the vote to propertied white men. In 1807, Condict introduced a bill that eliminated voting rights for women and blacks, arguing that allowing these groups to vote in the past produced "striking evidence of the miserably defective system of New Jersey elections." Condict maintained that it was "highly necessary to the safety, quiet, good order, and dignity of the state" to restrict voting to propertied male citizens only. The presence of black men and women at the polls imperiled orderly society despite the fact that white men stuffed more ballot boxes than any other group.[87] Women and black men served as scapegoats for the lack of electioneering integrity displayed by all Essex residents. Jeffersonian political necessity aligned with ideological concerns over the meaning of citizenship and the creation of an American national identity to polarize politics against black and female participation. Although Jefferson's party spearheaded efforts at disenfranchisement, Federalists supported the plan and both crafted a united idea of citizenship. William Griffith, the Federalist Abolition Society president, argued against the "perfectly disgusting" practice of women's suffrage and for the disenfranchisement of "restless, ignorant, and vicious aliens, Negroes, and transients."[88] Both parties agreed that women and blacks had no place in the public political sphere and voted in 1807 to restrict suffrage to propertied white men to shore up the "proper" boundaries between the races and genders. This move early in the abolition period made it clear to the small but growing free black population that they would continue to be seen as dependents and not equal to whites.[89]

Disenfranchisement in New Jersey, however, was only the first step in a much larger process of restricting access to political power across the United States. Maryland and Connecticut both barred black voting by 1820. North Carolina and Pennsylvania followed in the 1830s, along with every other state that entered the Union after 1819. New York imposed such a high property requirement that it effectively ended suffrage there, using the logic that it should restrict the vote because New Jersey had done so earlier. Both states shared fears that suffrage would "invite among them a dangerous proportion of another race of men."[90] Only in Massachusetts, Rhode Island, Vermont, New Hampshire, and Maine could African Americans vote. In these states, where blacks represented 1 percent or less of the total population (save for Rhode Island's 3 percent), African American voting only minimally threatened citizenship.[91]

Whites in states that disenfranchised blacks made use of many of the same dependence arguments used by gradual abolitionists. Pennsylvania legislators went even farther, linking fears of "the ominous black aggressor" as a "threat to the security of white society and the preservation of the American republic" to voting. Using coded rhetoric, white Pennsylvania officials consistently argued against black voting, fearing it would result in equal rights for blacks. Even though disenfranchisement in Pennsylvania occurred three decades after New Jersey, a close election with disputed results provided the spark. Armed with fears of savage former slaves destroying America as well as the idea that blacks lived as dependents and could not truly become free, the Pennsylvania Supreme Court argued that blacks had been specifically exempted from the constitutional compact since the Revolution. Labeled not true citizens of the republic, Pennsylvania blacks suffered the same retrenchment into their slave past as those across the Delaware experienced decades earlier.[92]

*   *   *

The 1804 gradual abolition act did not signal a quick transition to freedom for slaves born before its enactment. As they did with slaves for a term, masters adapted slavery to continue in the abolition period. The promise of manumission remained a powerful tool to compel obedience and continued labor from their slaves. In most cases, however, slaves never actually gained that freedom. Instead, slaves born before 1804 typically lived out their lives as bound laborers, though with a greater flexibility in how they lived that life. Slaves chipped away at the institution to the point that they forced a new flexible system to develop where masters acknowledged their need for greater freedoms. More intense negotiations over issues ranging from marriage, to hiring out, to socializing with free blacks allowed slaves to develop stronger and more wide-reaching community networks to cope with slavery's slow and complicated death. Abolition's abandonment by whites, however, caused slavery's continuation to be debated individually between masters and slaves. Minimal white support led to a low manumission rate and an even greater chance that masters could pervert slavery to compel labor from their slaves in perpetuity.

Slavery's perseverance had dire consequences for those free blacks who lived in New Jersey and tried to exert their rights as free Americans in the early nineteenth century. The process of defining citizenship, ongoing after the American Revolution, became mired in the same notions of black inferiority that abolitionists and slaveholders had maintained since the 1770s. Blacks remained dependent, not only because of their inferior condition but because slavery's continuation easily allowed white New Jerseyans to judge that the race as a whole was not ready for full citizenship. Slavery's survival, not just simple racism, helped strip free blacks of political, social, and economic rights in the new republic.

CHAPTER SIX

Slavery in Motion

Jacob Van Wickle sat in his Middlesex County home in 1818 with money on his mind. He realized that New Jersey slaves sold at prices far below what Mississippi and Louisiana plantation owners paid for similar chattel. Van Wickle used this knowledge and a loophole embedded in state law to create the largest slave trading operation in New Jersey, selling dozens of "cheap" Jersey slaves to the New Orleans market. At the same time, dozens of Jersey slaveholders left the state with their slaves to take advantage of the growing economic opportunities available in the Old Southwest, specifically the states of Mississippi and Louisiana. For the first fifteen years of abolition in New Jersey, this interstate movement exploited the apathetic stance of most Jersey whites toward abolition and helped slaveholders stymie slavery's end by profiting from it. Simultaneously, kidnappers captured free blacks, especially children, from northern border areas like Pennsylvania and New Jersey and sold them into the same system. Many white northerners ignored the hundreds of victims abducted each year, allowing this profit-motivated system to thrive.[1]

Although kidnappings and the interstate movement of slaves represented a failure of gradual abolition, they allowed Jersey whites, for the first time, to see how their gradual abolition system fit into slavery's national development in the early nineteenth century. The raw commodity-driven economics of slavery drew suspicion from some who saw slave trading, the most distasteful part of slavery, as violating the law's intentions. By showcasing the real economic interests of slaveholders rather than the more paternalistic model that abolitionists had used to argue for gradual abolition, nonslaveholders began to look at slavery with a critical eye.

By 1820, this interstate traffic in slaves forced white New Jerseyans to reconcile their status as a slave state by believing that gradual abolition, while preserving the institution at home, rejected the expansion of slavery that the slave traded supported. Legislators therefore placed significant restrictions on the slave trade, especially the removal of slaves for a term, and cracked down on kidnappings. However, they firmly believed that anyone legally enslaved would continue in that status in perpetuity. In 1820, legislators passed a revised slave code that codified all existing laws and reaffirmed the guidelines for slavery's continuation as established in 1804.[2]

In a national context, white New Jerseyans living on slavery's border had become especially wary of the institution's growth into new regions and believed that they had to "man the dikes that kept slavery from overflowing," especially into the West. Since they most feared slavery's expansion and the resulting increased power it would give to the slave South, they hoped to apply their own gradualist philosophy to the Missouri controversy. Their adoption of a free soil ideology opposed to slavery's expansion mimicked New Jersey's gradualist abolition foundations—they did not oppose slavery as it existed but denounced its growth. This gradualist philosophy guided the state's position on slavery throughout the ongoing antebellum sectional conflict.[3]

*   *   *

In the abolition period's early years, abolitionists began to notice that Jersey slaveholders were increasingly moving to the South and decried the impact on those slaves who were removed from abolition's reach. Ann Cox of Burlington and other Jersey PAS members demanded that there needed to be an "effectual remedy" to "prevent the poor blacks from being taken and sold out of the state," which was increasing in frequency. Jersey lawmakers responded with an 1812 law that reiterated a 1788 law's mandate that a slave had to consent to be sold or transported to another state. The law required that two local officials, usually justices of the peace or inferior court judges, privately examine the slave to determine if he or she consented to leave. It extended this restriction to the newly created slaves for a term, allowed for parents of slaves for a term to provide (or withhold) consent for children under age twenty-one, and increased the penalty for violations to a $500–1,000 fine or two to four years at hard labor. This law theoretically acknowledged a slave's right to determine at least some direction in their lives but overwhelmingly relied on slaveholders to follow their slaves' wishes. Like many other abolition era laws, lax enforcement by state officials and slaveholder coercion resulted in the law frequently failing to protect slaves or slaves for a term.[4]

Slaves' status as chattel in the abolition period retained enormous weight and meaning, especially for those slaveholders who moved from New Jersey with their slaves to nearly every state and territory, especially to the Old Southwest. In what historian Adam Rothman refers to as the formation of the "slave country," new black and white residents helped this region become a hotbed of economic growth. Of the known removals from New Jersey, 41 percent were conducted by slaveholders who hoped to join the grand economic adventure in Alabama, Mississippi, and Louisiana.[5]

The examination of a slave's consent usually demonstrated coercion, not a protection from a journey to the South. Even though all slaves who moved to Louisiana, Mississippi, and Alabama "freely consented" to the trip, it is difficult to believe that any would agree to leave the wheat fields or urban environments of New Jersey for New Orleans, where the enslaved toiled endlessly on the sugar and cotton plantations amid dreadful heat and disease. By the end of the eighteenth century, northern slaves knew that slavery in the South was far more difficult and dangerous. Connecticut's James Mars, a slave for a term born in 1790, remembered that his father would have rather killed himself than go to Virginia with his master. Even after Mars's master offered freedom for Mars's father, mother, and sister in exchange for permission to take Mars and his brother to Virginia, the family still refused, and exerted their own power by hiding Mars until they arranged his sale to a local buyer.[6]

Mars's case illustrates that slaves could, and did, exert power within the interstate slave trade to stymie moving plans or influence them in more beneficial directions. Like in the antebellum South, slaves lived with the omnipresent threat of being taken out of state, though in New Jersey it was of course far less common than in the Upper South. Slaves still managed to develop strong communities among themselves and with free blacks that helped mitigate the dangers of transportation from New Jersey and maintain connections with family if those transfers went through. Manipulation of transportation plans helped slaves control at least some part of their lives. This occurred in the case of George and Esther, two slaves for a term owned by Carlisle, Pennsylvania, physician James Gustin. Gustin intended to relocate to Mississippi in 1817 and offered George and Esther freedom sooner than required by Pennsylvania law, one and two years respectively, as an inducement to leave. George's mother, Negro Mile, and the couple readily agreed, realizing that the move would give both freedom earlier and allow the couple to stay together. However, though a few slaves willingly left for the South because of familial ties, relationships they developed with their masters, or beneficial negotiated terms from their master, most slaves or slaves for a term left New Jersey because they had exhausted their limited resistance options and faced violent punishment if they refused to consent. Indeed, no record remains of any New Jersey slave or slave for a term who refused to travel out of state.[7]

Even when slaveholders followed the law, the actual transfer process hardly matched its letter, thereby reducing the effectiveness of a key abolition period protection. For example, in 1816, Abel Terrill of Elizabethtown brought thirteen-year-old Mulford in front of two judges to approve his transfer to New Orleans. Mulford, born in 1803 and therefore ineligible for freedom under the 1804 gradual abolition law, testified that he wished to travel with Terrill to reunite with his mother, who had already departed as a slave to New Orleans. In Mulford's case, his desire to join his mother likely outweighed an alternate life in New Jersey, though at thirteen he might not have understood his move's ramifications. The 1812 law foresaw this problem and required that the parent of any minor slave approve his or her transfer. However, with his mother absent and father unknown, the judges agreed to Terrill's travel without the necessary approvals. The lack of advocates for young slaves or slaves for a term in these proceedings stripped power from them and allowed owners' decisions to trump legal protections.[8]

Slaves for a term likewise did not reap any additional protections under the 1812 law and their moves south frustrated slavery's demise. For example, in September 1818 Willis Pope prepared to move his family, his fifteen-year-old-slave Wilson, and thirteen-year-old Sim, a slave for a term born in 1805, to Huntsville in the newly created Alabama Territory. Margaret, the boys' mother, approved their removal, but she stayed behind in New Jersey. Both Wilson and Sam could have felt the same about their sale as did Connecticut slave for a term James Mars about his. Mars clearly remembered that "it was a sad thought . . . being sold, not knowing whether I was ever to see my parents . . . I then felt for the first time that I was alone in the world, no home, no friends, and none to care for me."[9] Although it is uncertain if Pope owned Margaret as well, in light of the trauma her children's sale would have caused and the danger that Sim's future freedom could have been easily forgotten in Alabama, Margaret likely was not in a position to challenge Pope and therefore consented.[10]

Unlike those traveling south, Jersey slaves who moved with their masters to other northern states, especially New York and Pennsylvania, enjoyed some additional protections from those state's abolition laws and might have willingly went because of them. For example, Jane Carr of Sussex County successfully took her five-year-old slave for a term, Charlotte, to Bucks County, Pennsylvania, in 1815 with her parents' consent, where a Pennsylvania judge attested to her right to freedom due to her post-1804 birth.[11] As Nance and twelve-year-old Jude discovered after their master, Simon Hillyer, moved them to New York in June 1813, the Empire State actually provided a path to freedom unavailable in New Jersey. In 1817, New York enacted the only full legislative emancipation in the North, granting freedom to all slaves born before July 4, 1799 (including Nance), as of July 4, 1827. Similarly, an 1813 New York law extended New York's Gradual Manumission Law to slaves born after July 4, 1799, in another state. This gave Jude, born in 1801 and therefore ineligible for gradual abolition in New Jersey, freedom in New York at age twenty-five in 1826.[12]

In other northern states though, Jersey slaves found that their former slave status informed their new lives, as Phebe Ann Jacobs, a Morris County slave born in 1785, did when she traveled north to New Hampshire and then to Maine. Sold at a young age to the wife of John Wheelock, second president of New Hampshire's Dartmouth College, Jacobs became the personal servant of Wheelock's daughter Maria. Maria married William Allen, who in 1820 became president of Bowdoin College. Jacobs moved with the Allens to Maine, gained freedom, and lived there in service to both the college and the Allen family until her death. Like many free blacks, she continued to serve her former owners as a domestic servant since, while free, she faced racism and a lack of economic opportunities. Her former enslaved status therefore played a significant role in her Maine life, forming the background for both her historical legacy and her interactions with Bowdoin's famous alumni such as John Brown Russwurm and Joshua Lawrence Chamberlain. Her narrative, originally published as *Happy Phebe* after her death in 1850, hoped to reconcile Jacobs's irregularity in nineteenth-century Maine (a former slave in a whitewashed region) by showing that she easily integrated into the white world and was a model for black Christians because her "life evinces that she had clear and happy views of the way of salvation by Christ." Jacobs even influenced Harriet Beecher Stowe's *Uncle Tom's Cabin*, as Stowe reported that she had read "'a small religious tract' on the life of a 'coloured woman named Phebe,'" which literary scholar Theodore

Hovet argues proves that Jacobs provided Stowe with a template for her masterpiece.[13]

Unlike Phebe's journey to Maine that at least secured her legal freedom, Joseph Hagaman's move from Princeton to Cincinnati in 1812 continued the servitude of his two underage slaves, Mary and Bob, and one slave for a term, Anthony, and showed that flexible forms of slavery existed in other northern locales. Before they left New Jersey, Middlesex County judges examined both Bob and Anthony and authorized their removal without approval from their parents in violation of the 1812 consent law. However, Mary's mother, Tableak, manumitted a few years earlier, consented to the sale. Knowing that she might never see her daughter again, Tableak's actions suggest that even the free parent of a minor slave could do little to stop an impending removal.[14]

When the three children crossed the border into Ohio, the soil of the Buckeye State did not automatically free them. During the state's short life, Ohioans had battled over slavery and the meaning of Article VI of the Northwest Ordinance of 1787, which prohibited slavery and involuntary servitude. Dissatisfaction with the ordinance came from local proslavery advocates who wanted to ensure property rights and economic growth. They argued that the Northwest Ordinance violated the property rights of those slaveholders living in the Ohio Country before 1787 and believed prohibiting slavery handicapped Ohio's ability to attract new settlers and move toward statehood.[15]

Governor Arthur St. Clair used a 1788 congressional committee's interpretation of the Northwest Ordinance to permit the continuation of slavery that already existed but banned its future growth. This interpretation, never ratified by Congress, controlled slavery in the Old Northwest and allowed the institution to linger "so long . . . at least in part because the Ordinance itself was ambiguous, internally inconsistent, and written by men who were uncertain of their own objectives."[16] This interpretation encouraged Ohio's proslavery boosters to argue that Congress should officially overturn the ban on slavery and allow the children of those slaves already present to continue as such. Congress overwhelmingly rejected this request and the debate over slavery moved into the Ohio Constitutional Convention of 1802.[17]

Ultimately, the convention prohibited slavery but, by its careful wording, allowed involuntary servitude and apprenticeship to continue. Although apprentices gained some additional rights that slaves did not possess, Hagaman's agreements illustrate that the same flexibility and permeability between free, slave, and slave for a term in New Jersey existed in other places where slavery was gradually ending. That Hagaman understood he could legally bring his three black servants to Cincinnati meant that Ohio law readily (and perhaps commonly) allowed for alternate forms of slavery, just as New Jersey had. It also shows that he knew his new neighbors would readily accept this form of unfree labor, suggesting that many early Ohioans tolerated unfree labor to provide the maximum flexibility for their state's settlement.[18]

*   *   *

Though many slaveholders left the state with their slaves, the more common movement of Jersey slaves came from those who capitalized on the market's interconnectivity to begin an interstate slave trade. This led newspapers in Charlestown, Virginia, Charleston, South Carolina, Baltimore, and New Orleans to claim that New Jersey slaves perfectly complemented southern agriculture. This 1818 article advised that "Jersey negroes appear to be peculiarly adapted to this market . . . as it is understood that they afford the best opportunity for speculation."[19] Sales of slaves to the South made New Jersey a slave supply center just like the Upper South as slaveholders in both regions jumped at the opportunity to sell their slaves for high returns as slavery's long-term potential in both regions declined.[20]

Of course, the link between the South and New Jersey did not spring up overnight; like New England textile manufacturers, New Jersey farmers and businessman had long-standing relationships with southern consumers. Leather products, shoes, and clothing all moved south while southern money traveled north. Planters on buying expeditions frequented Archer Gifford's Hunters and the Hounds tavern in Newark, a well-known place for New Jerseyans to make deals with southerners. Shoemaker Moses Combs made a fortune selling his wares to the men who visited the Hunters and the Hounds, in one case making $9,000 on one shipment of sealskin shoes to Georgia. Advertisements in Newark's newspapers echoed this demand for Jersey shoes; one article advertised a buyer's intent to purchase five hundred pairs of "negro shoes of large sizes and good quality."[21] From these business dealings, New Jerseyans forged connections with southern slaveholders that eventually culminated in transfer of human cargo.[22]

Southern slave traders had long recognized that purchasing northern slaves brought them substantial profits. In 1788, four years after Rhode Island began gradual abolition, abolitionist Jonathan Edwards wrote to Moses Brown that since nothing in the law prevented the exportation of "slaves and of servants born since March 1, 1784 . . . the poor creatures will be carried out in shiploads" to the South as he heard had already begun.[23] In New Jersey, Quaker Joseph Shotwell reported in 1792 that New Orleans native Charles White had purchased several slaves and manipulated the legal system to gain the necessary removal permissions from Elizabethtown officials. Shotwell hoped that something could be done to stop White because he was "desirous of getting a number more" slaves before leaving.[24] Likewise, Henry Hunt of Baltimore wrote in 1809 to his nephew, College of New Jersey student Samuel Hunt, that he was pleased with the Jersey slaves Samuel and his father had already bought and asked him to quickly send them because "they are certainly great bargains at least fifty percent lower than they can be purchased for" in Natchez. Henry made clear that with "the cotton growing" it "will always enable a male to make 33 1/3 percent on his capital and much more at the prices of Negroes in Jersey." Since the trade from New Jersey remained relatively small, economic forces had not artificially increased prices like in Virginia. In the remainder of the letter, Henry detailed how to remove more slaves from New Jersey surreptitiously, telling Samuel's father to "set out before day from home" to ensure that they should "not be but one night in Pennsylvania." Henry argued that if Samuel brought his sisters with him on the trip to Baltimore, it would "have the appearance of moving," thus "the risk would be but little." The coffle also needed to "keep clear of the worst public roads, particularly the stage road, and to suffer no people to talk with his negroes nor stop at a house without having three all in a room." Samuel offered to meet the group outside Baltimore, where he would make the purchase and reiterated that Samuel's father should "bring every one he can . . . and if by waiting a day or two he can get two or three more, do so."[25]

The high demand for slaves in the Old Southwest had been ongoing since the cotton gin's invention and the Louisiana Purchase. In 1804, Daniel Clark, the first congressional delegate from the Orleans Territory, wrote to New Jersey Senator Jonathan Dayton and asked "if the prohibition of the African trade" would be repealed at Congress's next session because the demand for slaves in the new territory was so high.[26] Dayton had long expressed his "dissatisfaction" with the "impolitic and ill-judged regulations" of the United

States in prohibiting "the introduction of slaves from Africa" into Louisiana, arguing the regulation was "the most odious" and "injurious to their prosperity and [the] interests" of Louisianans.[27] Clark, who eventually began buying Virginia slaves to sell in Louisiana, believed that the interruption in the sugar supply caused by the Haitian Revolution gave Louisiana a perfect segue into this profitable enterprise if new slaves could be secured. Dayton readily agreed and, along with James Jackson of Georgia, argued in the Senate for reopening the slave trade to expand sugar production.[28]

South Carolina officials dealt with mounting pressure from their upcountry residents and the increased demand for slaves in the Lower Mississippi Valley by reopening the transatlantic slave trade to their ports in 1803. Slaveholders there realized the potential profit from the roughly 55,000 slaves who entered the United States between 1800 and 1810, most of them through the Palmetto State. The South Carolina trade and the debates in Louisiana set the background for New Jersey's participation in the growing interstate slave trade.[29]

The predominant plot to remove enslaved blacks from New Jersey and feed this growing market centered on Jacob Van Wickle and his brother-in-law, Charles Morgan, a Louisiana state legislator and plantation owner in Point Coupee Parish. In January 1818, he planned to buy slaves in Virginia but first detoured to New Jersey to visit his sister. Van Wickle, a former member of the Middlesex County Board of Chosen Freeholders, a justice of the peace, and Common Pleas judge, convinced Morgan that he could buy at least 150 slaves with his $45,000 since Jersey slaves in the late 1810s routinely sold for between $200 and $300; the highest in the abolition period, a nineteen-year-old "smart, active" male, had sold in May 1816 for $300. Traveler Isaac Holmes commented that the same slave could sell for upward of $800 in New Orleans. Sam Steer, a Van Wickle associate, likewise believed that since "fresh imported Guinia Negroes were lately sold in NOrleans at $1500," he could make a sizeable profit on the slaves he bought for an average of $300 each.[30]

Jersey slaveholders willingly sold their slaves to Morgan and other interstate slave traders since they understood that the payments they offered were far higher than what they could garner in abolition era New Jersey. Their buyers secured, the 1812 law that required a slave's consent to leave New Jersey became the main impediment to Van Wickle and Morgan's plan since the law entrusted the evaluation of a slave's consent to members of the judiciary who, according to the legislature, were above reproach. Above reproach Van Wickle was not; he used his power as a judge to falsify the consent of slaves and personally approved the removal of sixty slaves for life and thirteen slaves for a term in just six months. His connection to the slave trading ring was known far from New Jersey—the same newspapers that remarked how well Jersey slaves adapted to the South claimed that those "who bear the mark of Judge Van Wickle" were especially well suited for plantation life.[31]

Van Wickle routinely lied to slaves to gain their consent, promising them high wages in the South and a future return to New Jersey, or he simply ignored the law altogether. He only received parental consent to transport one of the seventeen slaves under twenty-one and only because the mother also "agreed" to leave. Van Wickle's blatant disregard for the law became most apparent when he certified that thirteen slaves for a term, ranging from six weeks of age to nine years, "as far as they could answer . . . declared their willingness" to travel to Louisiana. In taking the cries of a six-week-old slave for a term for approval of a life of unfreedom, Isaac Holmes referred to Van Wickle as an "outrage on humanity" who valued profit above all else.[32]

The potential profits were so enticing that Van Wickle cashed in on the enterprise himself by acting as both a judicial authority and, through his son Nicholas, as Morgan's purchasing agent. Nicholas easily bought slaves and kept them at the "South River Establishment," the name newspapers gave to Van Wickle's home. In New Jersey's own slave castle, Van Wickle examined his son's purchases, certified their consent, and confined them while they awaited transportation to Louisiana. After living under guard at the "garrison," another term used to describe Van Wickle's home, the slaves Nicholas bought, along with those purchased by Van Wickle allies Lewis Compton, Peter Hendry, and James Brown, boarded two ships near Perth Amboy, the *Mary Ann* and the *Thorn.* They carried a total of seventy-five enslaved men, women, and children.[33]

Loading the human cargo aboard the *Mary Ann* proved difficult because some local Quakers filed a complaint with customs officials that the ship's manifest invalidly reported the cargo onboard. After 1808, federal law required that every domestic slave ship file a manifest listing its slaves, so that officials at the voyage's end could ensure that no additional non-American slaves were imported illegally. Morgan bypassed the customs officials in Perth Amboy and completed all required paperwork with the New York customs house. The *Mary Ann* sailed from New York,

according to passenger James Elain, at 11 a.m. on March 10, 1818, but
soon anchored off Sandy Hook. A smaller vessel approached the *Mary
Ann*, which Elain identified as the Perth Amboy-based packet vessel
Thorn. It had thirty-six blacks onboard along with Morgan and William
Lee, who captained the *Mary Ann* to Louisiana. As the crew transferred
the slaves and their belongings to the *Mary Ann*, a lookout spotted a
revenue cutter headed toward them. Quickly, the crew hid the blacks
below deck since they were not listed on the original manifest. Elain cor-
rectly figured that the crew's quick actions and the hasty departure of the
Thorn signaled that they did not want the revenue cutter to know what
had just transpired.[34]

After the revenue cutter's crew boarded the *Mary Ann*, Elain remembered hearing the boarding officer accuse the captain of smuggling. However, an inspection of the ship's manifest satisfied him that the *Mary Ann*
was not engaged in illegal activity and the cutter released it to continue to
New Orleans. Luckily for the *Mary Ann*'s crew, the boarding party did not
find the twenty-nine slaves and seven slaves for a term from the *Thorn*
hidden below deck. Since Morgan had forced several on board, tying up
one slave himself while forcing another into the hold, he and his cohort
clearly realized that these men and women had certainly not consented to
leave New Jersey.[35]

Morgan and the *Thorn*, after she had dropped off the slaves to the *Mary
Ann*, continued to New Orleans with another thirty-nine slaves, where he
found the *Mary Ann* seized by officials for falsifications to its manifest.
Captain William Lee stood trial in New Orleans for sailing with false documents and lying about the ages of the slaves under his charge. Port officials
claimed that the exaggeration had been so extreme that there was no possible way the slaves matched their supposed ages and descriptions. Lee argued
that Van Wickle had signed off on each slave and therefore the transfers
had legal authority, but conceded that his crew had taken at least five by
force, a clear violation of their consent. Lee's confession differed from the
account given in a New Brunswick newspaper, which accused Van Wickle
of interviewing only roughly half those who left New Jersey. He probably
lied about or coerced the consent of the majority of the *Mary Ann*'s blacks.
However, regardless of the overwhelming evidence pointing to a shady ring
of collusion and deceit, a jury of sympathetic Louisiana slaveholders, eager
for more slaves to flow from the North and Upper South, found Lee not
guilty.[36]

Van Wickle maintained his innocence and published an open letter in the New Brunswick *Fredonian* to defend his reputation. He wrote that Charles Morgan had legally bought slaves in New Jersey, "paid a fair and full price," and intended to "remove [the] slaves and servants for years from this to other states" as permitted by state law. He extended "every reasonable liberty and indulgence" to the slaves and "they removed with perfect cheerfulness." Several local residents published affidavits in his defense, reiterating that "the colored people . . . appeared to me to be well satisfied," that they "appeared rejoiced that they were ready to go," and were not kept at "anything like a garrison . . . but the reverse, they all appeared to have their liberty and to be well satisfied." One even commented that "they all rejoiced all the way down to the vessel and there did not appear a dissenting voice among them" as they "hurried to get on board . . . the vessel."[37] Van Wickle's public relations maneuver seemed to work since no court ever indicted him—he actually appeared as a witness for the prosecution against Morgan and several other members of the slave trading ring who the state indicted for the removal of the slaves for a term too young to consent to their sale under the 1812 law.[38]

After Morgan's indictment, anti-slave trade supporters petitioned the legislature for a new law to prohibit the type of slave trading the Van Wickle cohort engaged in. They claimed that the legislature had intended gradual abolition to "abolish slavery in this state as fast as was practical and to prevent slaves and children thus born free (denoted servants for years) from being taken without their full and free consent out of the protection of these laws." The petitioners believed that the inflation of slave prices caused by the cotton boom and the closing of the Atlantic trade led New Jerseyans to disregard "the laws of God and Man" in service to their own "thirst for gain."[39] These petitioners singled out the trading of slaves for a term, not the continuing state of slavery, as the true moral violation. This reiterated their belief in gradualism and that slavery's survival was acceptable. In addition, they made a clear demarcation between the perceived benevolent system of northern slavery and the profit-motivated expansion-driven southern system that had begun to interact with the North.[40]

In these protests, white New Jerseyans directed their trepidation about slavery at the villainous slave trader and affirmed that slave trading, specifically the transfer of slaves for a term, was unacceptable in the abolition period. Yet, this attack against the slave trade did not lead to a simultaneous challenge of slavery itself. Whites remained mostly ambivalent toward ensuring African American freedom in New Jersey and instead embraced gradualism. Slave trading, however, riled their collective consciousness and brought them to action. As had happened in New England in the 1780s, the horrors of the Atlantic slave trade directed white eyes to the most vile and sinful image of slavery while allowing them to "make peace with slavery as an institution" at home.[41]

The legislature responded to this public outcry by passing a revised law on November 5, 1818, which, while it continued to depend on an individual slave's consent for removal, limited who could sell a slave out of state. The new law stipulated that a slaveholder had to live in New Jersey for five years before he could remove a slave and prohibited the sale of slaves to nonresident masters.[42] Legislators also asked New Jersey's U.S. senator James Wilson to introduce a bill to place a federal ban on the interstate trade in states where it was illegal. Wilson argued for the ban by claiming that the trade from New Jersey "had been carried on to considerable extent . . . [and] it was believed many free persons, or who were soon to become free, had been consigned to slavery for life." Wilson's bill passed the Senate but ultimately floundered in the House due to southern concerns over limiting potential sources of slaves. Mississippi senator George Poindexter argued that every slaveholder "had a right to remove his property from one State to another . . . if not prohibited" by state law and that the federal government had no right to interfere. Therefore, the House voted against Wilson's bill and any attempt to strengthen the federal government's ability to regulate the internal slave trade.[43]

The year after Wilson's bill failed, New Jerseyans entered a nationwide debate on slavery's westward expansion, which politicians used to carefully affirm the institution's continuation in New Jersey under the tenets of the 1804 gradual abolition act while arguing against expansion. The issue of slavery's expansion during the Missouri Controversy was of critical importance in New Jersey. It forced public debate and became essential in helping whites express gradualist views on a national stage. Missouri solidified white support for gradualism: slavery as it existed in New Jersey would be protected indefinitely but could not expand inside or outside the state. This would define the state's position on slavery for the next three decades.[44]

The remnants of the Federalist Party in the North began to mobilize popular support against slavery in Missouri and the growing slave power by gathering under the leadership of Elias Boudinot, a former president of the Continental Congress. Boudinot had long believed that political parties

had degraded politics and allowed slavery to thrive. He ecstatically organized against a pro-slave Missouri, helped by local activists who made sure
that the public knew the stakes of this impending decision. Indeed, Representative Ephraim Bateman believed it was "of the greatest magnitude to
the interest of humanity" ever debated by Congress and rallied his constituents against it. In a series of anti-expansionist meetings across the North,
Republicans and Federalists joined together to fight the Compromise of
1820. Even Mid-Atlantic Republican newspapers opposed their national
party and spoke out against slavery's spread. Federalists were only too
happy to rally against their Republican foe's Missouri plan; Burlington, still
a Federalist stronghold, became ground zero for the opposition. In New
Jersey, Samuel Emlen, a Burlington Quaker and son-in-law to abolitionist
William Dillwyn, organized several public meetings along with Boudinot
and William Griffith, Federalist former head of the state abolition society.
In one meeting at Trenton, the three allied with Jesse Upson, a Republican
from the state Legislative Council, and rallied hundreds of white New Jerseyans to prevent pro-slave Missouri from joining the Union. Participants
argued that introduction of slavery into new states had "a direct tendency
to perpetuate slavery . . . by extending the sphere of its influence and action
. . . and to promote and encourage the importation of slaves by providing
an extensive and growing market for them."[45]

The numerous meetings' messages reflected two ideas—that the slave
trade would grow the institution, an issue New Jerseyans had just dealt
with, and that slavery's expansion and not the system itself should be
stopped, a key tenet of gradualism. This antislavery feeling reflected northerners' fears that slavery's expansion would impact their future political
clout or ability to move west themselves. In New Jersey, this ideology was
very much alive as the state legislature approved a joint resolution that
opposed expansion specifically because it feared that Missouri's admission
as a slave state would embolden the slave power nationally and decrease the
power of nonslaveholding states or states that were in the process of abolishing slavery. However, anti-expansionism also reflected the gradual abolitionist philosophy pervasive at the time; these anti-expansionists essentially
argued for the same types of regulations in place in New Jersey. Many in
Congress had even wanted to institute a gradual abolition program in
Missouri modeled on the New York and New Jersey systems, which would
have allowed slavery's continuation but with explicit restrictions on its
expansion.[46]

Some directly linked the Missouri issue and slavery in the West to the institution's continuation in New Jersey, but mostly fell on deaf ears. In a letter to the editor of Newark's *Centinel of Freedom*, author "Fair Play" attacked New Jersey for its role in calling for strong restrictions on slavery's expansion into the Louisiana Territory while the state still recognized blacks as prima facie slaves and had been home to a massive slave trading ring only a year earlier. "Fair Play" claimed that New Jerseyans should first undo "the chains that bind their own slaves before they proceeded to resolve restrictions on Missouri."[47] However, the antipathy toward abolition among whites in the 1810s and the continued presence of a sizeable slave system—at this point the gradual abolition law had freed no one—led the legislature to not consider immediate abolition even though neighboring New York had enacted a full legislative emancipation in 1817. Instead, in 1820, legislators approved a revised slave code that affirmed the continued subjugation of slaves and slaves for a term and reinforced that slavery was acceptable in New Jersey.[48]

Though protests in favor of a free Missouri had been near-unanimous in denouncing the spread of slavery and the state legislature had overwhelmingly voted to oppose expansion, New Jersey's congressional delegates did not harbor the same sentiments and were punished by voters for it. In the Senate, Wilson, who had developed a severe drinking problem, resigned in the midst of debate over the Tallmadge Amendment and was replaced by Samuel Southard. Southard, the slaveholder and Supreme Court Justice who ruled that slaves for a term inhabited a new and separate legal category, discussed as late as the 1830s that slavery still operated in New Jersey and at least four other northern states. Southard supported slavery's expansion and worked with secretary of war John C. Calhoun to convince his father, Congressman Henry Southard, and at least three other New Jersey congressmen to vote in favor of a pro-slave Missouri. Bernard Smith, Charles Kinsey, and Joseph Bloomfield, the former governor and state abolition society president, all voted in favor of Missouri's admission with slavery and all lost reelection the following year.[49]

*   *   *

While the legislature debated the 1818 law, slaveholders still yearned to sell their slaves south and buyers hoped to buy cheap Jersey slaves, though they knew the task had become monumentally more difficult as public opinion turned against them. Slaveholders' profit motive did not change despite the growing rejection of slave trading. Rahway native John Marsh, for example, began buying Jersey slaves through his agents, William Compton and William Raburgh, as the legislature debated ending out-of-state sales. Marsh and his business partner, William Stone, imagined that they could stuff their pockets not with cotton but with much sweeter sugar in southern Louisiana, purchasing a plantation at Petite Anse, about 150 miles west of New Orleans in 1818.[50] In addition to the slaves, Marsh's agents secured the indentures of at least eleven free blacks from New York City for terms of three to five years.[51] Compton planned an overland expedition to Louisiana after he had his slave coffle "examined" by Judge Van Wickle. He left Perth Amboy on October 25 with four slaves while Marsh's two other agents traveled together with four of their own. The coffle crossed into Pennsylvania where authorities at Reading arrested them, suspecting, as the *New Jersey Journal* reported, "that these poor, innocent sons of Africa, whose only crime is that of being black, were purchased in New Jersey, with an intention of being conveyed to the south."[52]

The PAS had been working for years to stop men like Compton who transported slaves and free blacks to the South, while abolitionists in other states likewise warned the public to look for Jersey slaves illegally traveling south. In Leesburg, Virginia, the *Genius of Liberty* alerted readers that "human beings entitled by the laws of our country to their freedom" might soon come into the area, controlled by "monsters that infest society, called soul drivers," who would parade these free blacks "manacled and groaning under the chains of oppression." Similarly, Virginia's *Alexandria Gazette* told readers to closely "examine every drove of slaves passing through the state, and when this drove from New Jersey is discovered, effectual means will be taken to secure to them their rights, and to bring the villains who have kidnapped them to justice." These instances even led northern newspapers to become critical of the practice. For instance, the editor of the *New York Columbian* claimed that New Jersey's citizens should not have "permitted this shocking trade in their vicinity," while commending a group of Virginians that captured a group of kidnappers from the North.[53]

The increased movement of Jersey slaves resulted in neighboring states actively mediating New Jersey's abolition process since the interstate traffic brought the issue to their doorsteps. Compton, therefore, was convicted in Lebanon of violating the November 1818 law and all of his slaves were granted freedom, with two PAS members, William Wayne and Thomas Shipley, assigned to assist them. Unwilling to let go of his slave cargo, Compton traveled to Philadelphia to reclaim the slaves only to be arrested by authorities for false imprisonment. The PAS repatriated the now emancipated blacks to New Jersey, where Compton pursued and filed suit to reclaim them once again. Compton argued that since he had gained consent for the slaves' transfer out of New Jersey before the 1818 law went into effect, his cargo should not be subject to that law. Eventually Compton's persistence won out; New Jersey courts reenslaved the four blacks, who lived out their lives on Marsh's Louisiana plantation.[54]

Raburgh also worked with Van Wickle and Compton but participated in a separate trade to Alabama, buying Somerset County slaves right before the stricter 1818 law went into effect. Raburgh purchased ten slaves for life and one slave for a term from eight different owners and set out from Somerville for Alabama at the beginning of November 1818 on the same route Compton took through Pennsylvania.[55] As had happened to his fellow dealer, Pennsylvania authorities apprehended Raburgh near Reading, transported him and his slave coffle to Lebanon for trial, and granted all the slaves their freedom. Raburgh pursued his slaves back to New Jersey where the *Centinel of Freedom* warned that Raburgh, "the noted Alabama dealer in human flesh, has returned" and "seize[d] three of the poor blacks and confined them in jail at Somerville."[56] Raburgh, arrested in Somerville and held on $3,000 bail, successfully defended himself against a habeas corpus petition filed on behalf of at least two of the slaves, Walter Wilson and his wife Jane. He reclaimed four slaves lost in Pennsylvania and, as his overland expedition had failed, opted for sea travel instead, transporting all four on the sloop *Lydia* to New York in preparation for the voyage to Alabama.[57]

While in New York, one of his slaves, twenty-one-year-old Jane Wilson, sued Raburgh with the help of local abolitionists to gain her freedom. Wilson, born in 1797, lived with her master, William Skillman, in Hunterdon County before Bridgewater farmer Thomas Logan bought her. Logan agreed to sell Raburgh his three slaves (Jane, her thirty-three-year old husband Walter, and twenty-one-year-old Hannah) knowing that they would be resold in Alabama. After the group's arrival in New York, Raburgh realized he needed to establish cause for holding his chattel since their presence might be seen as illegal under New York's 1817 abolition law. U.S. Supreme Court Justice Henry Brockholst Livingston, riding circuit in New York, certified Raburgh's slaves as runaways, though for what reason is unclear since the New York Manumission Society knew that Livingston had realized Jane was not a fugitive and that her husband had already escaped.[58]

As in Pennsylvania, New York adjudicated New Jersey law as the movement of slaves forced gradual abolitionism to spill beyond the state's borders. The Manumission Society filed a habeas corpus petition to dispute Livingston's ruling and made sure the case appeared before Mayor Cadwallader David Colden, president of the Manumission Society, in the April 1819 session of New York's Court of Common Pleas, which the mayor presided over. Raburgh answered the writ by contending that Livingston's certification "was conclusive on the subject and ought to preclude all further inquiry." Additionally, he argued that even though he took Jane out of New Jersey on November 7, two days after the 1818 law's effective date, the 1812 law should still apply because he had acquired permission to remove her on November 2.[59]

Colden championed a rigorous habeas corpus process and attacked the very foundation of fugitive removals. He claimed that he could not fathom how Congress or the "principles of civil liberty" could leave to a single judge the decision "whether I may be dragged from my family and home upon the claim of one who may pretend a right to my services."[60] To Colden, no single magistrate had the right to decide issues related to slaves, especially when that decision resulted in a lifetime of bondage, even though Colden himself decided the case alone.[61] He made this point using an argument some abolitionists had been making for over a decade. Philadelphia Quaker Joseph Parrish, for instance, had argued in 1805 that it was ludicrous that "the evidence of a single person before a single magistrate" was enough to condemn a black person "to a tyrant of a master."[62]

Wilson's case perturbed proslavery advocates who feared that northern officials would not actively assist in recapturing fugitive slaves under the 1793 fugitive slave law. Foreshadowing the 1844 *Prigg* decision, Senator William Smith of South Carolina argued that the northern antislavery advocates' tactic of using habeas corpus petitions to give fugitive slaves a hearing before state courts circumvented the federal system's simpler summary judgment process. The contentious congressional debates infuriated even moderate antislavery advocates, Colden among them.[63]

In the end, Colden decided that the 1818 law controlled slave removals from New Jersey after the legislation's effective date and, since Jane Wilson had crossed the border after that date, she should be free because freedom was the appropriate legal remedy for illegal sales. He ordered her taken to "any place in the city where she thinks she will be secure" and gave her the ability to start a free life in New York. Thomas Shipley, the PAS treasurer who had assisted her in Reading, proclaimed his greatest "pleasure [in the news of] poor Jane and her children's triumph over such a base and villainous scoundrel."[64] The Manumission Society's advocacy ensured Wilson's freedom and distinguished her from the majority of Jersey blacks who did not have white allies. Colden continued to fight for fugitive slave rights after his election to Congress in 1821, claiming that the changes favored by slaveholders to more easily remove blacks from the North were "inconsistent with the principles of liberty" and promoted "the traffic which had been carried on to a great extent of seizing free blacks and selling them for slaves."[65]

Unlike the New Yorkers in Jane's case, New Jersey's defunct abolition society never intervened to prevent interstate slave sales and New Jersey courts denied slave freedom far more consistently than those in Pennsylvania or New York since slavery remained a staunchly protected system. No court ever convicted the members of the Van Wickle gang for any violation of the 1812 law because most lived out of justice's reach in Louisiana. Compton eventually stood trial for the removal of one slave by force, removal an infant slave for a term without consent, and removal of the four slaves to Pennsylvania. Prosecutors dropped charges in one case and a New Jersey jury found him not guilty on the remainder. Juries also found two other co-conspirators not guilty. An anonymous writer calling himself "Humanity" wrote in a letter to Senator Wilson, published in the Trenton *True American*, that the "vast profits they realize[d]" from the trade "enable[d] them to employ or retain the first counsels and attorneys in the state. By their money and through their connections, they can obtain" license to do what they please without fear of prosecution. Humanity complained that "such a combination of numbers, wealth, and influence" outstripped any effort to punish them for their crimes.[66]

∗   ∗   ∗

At the same time New Jerseyans participated in the internal slave trade, incidents of free black kidnappings in the Mid-Atlantic increased to fuel the Old Southwest's economic boom. To Mid-Atlantic blacks, Philadelphia mayor Joseph Watson was the greatest ally they had against kidnappers since he believed that the practice lay outside the acceptable boundaries of slavery in the abolition period. After all, kidnapping encouraged slavery's expansion in the South and West and violated a fundamental tenet of American freedom, one that whites routinely extended even to blacks. Watson had become especially interested in protecting free blacks after he had witnessed that "a great number of free colored children have . . . disappeared together with many grown up persons" in the first twenty years of the nineteenth century. He investigated this dramatic uptick in kidnappings and prosecuted numerous cases by encouraging citizens to help stop illegal kidnappings and offering rewards of up to $500 for information leading to perpetrators' arrests and convictions.[67]

Watson's primary nemesis in the battle over kidnapping was the Cannon-Johnson kidnapping syndicate, the largest slave trading operation in the Mid-Atlantic, run by Patty Cannon and Joseph Johnson from Cannon's tavern near the Nanticoke River on the Maryland-Delaware border. A frequent meeting place for slave traders, the tavern allowed the Cannon-Johnson family to liaise with traders and local sheriffs whom they frequently bribed to ignore their operation. In a two-year period in the 1820s, they kidnapped and sold over one hundred free blacks. The frequency with which the couple kidnapped them became so well known that in a complaint to Mayor Watson, a Maryland abolitionist claimed that fifteen of the seventeen blacks he had rescued had been "cajoled by Johnson's emissaries" from the network that extended "from Philadelphia to Accomack in Virginia."[68] In what historian Julie Winch calls "the other underground railroad," the Cannon-Johnson syndicate operated a network of safe houses, created false documents, and employed several black associates to coerce and capture Philadelphia blacks, especially children.[69]

In one such operation, John Purnell, a free black member of the Cannon-Johnson organization, found sixteen-year-old Samuel Scomp on the Market Street wharf hoping to earn some money unloading cargo in August 1825. Scomp, a slave for a term belonging to David Hill of Amwell, New Jersey, ran away to Philadelphia and drifted to the docks for work. Scomp agreed to help Purnell unload watermelons for a quarter, but once aboard, Joseph Johnson drew his dagger, bound his hands and legs in irons, and locked him in the ship's hold. After capturing a total of five young black boys this way, Johnson's brother Ebenezer took them to Alabama for sale.[70]

As in Scomp's case, an older black man kidnapped the young Peter Still while he played outside his New Jersey home. Pretending to take Still to see his mother at her church, Still's kidnapper instead took him to Kentucky, where he remained enslaved for forty years, until he purchased his freedom and returned to his native New Jersey. Unlike Still, however, Scomp's kidnappers tried to sell him to John Henderson, a native New Jerseyan who had settled in Mississippi. Scomp told Henderson that he was freeborn and described Philadelphia so vividly that Henderson wrote to Mayor Watson to inquire if Scomp could have been kidnapped. Watson sent High Constable Garrigues to Mississippi to retrieve Scomp and spent over $4,000 to secure his return, believing that the "public justice and dignity of this city" demanded the preservation of the "the rights of the inhabitants." Garrigues would likewise bring back fifteen-year-old James Dailley, a slave for a term from Woodbury, New Jersey, who had been illegally sold in Louisiana on the pretense that he was from Virginia.[71]

In 1827, Watson helped bring Scomp back to Philadelphia where it remains unclear if he, as a slave for a term, served the remaining ten years due his master. Watson communicated that New Jersey's chief justice, Charles Ewing, had declined to "affix the seal of his court to the deposition relative to Sam," perhaps since Ewing understood that Scomp, although freeborn, was still technically unfree.[72] Regardless, Philadelphia constables arrested Purnell, the free black man who had helped kidnap Scomp, in 1827. A court fined him $4,000 and sentenced him to forty-two years in prison, which he served in Eastern State Penitentiary after it opened in 1829. Philadelphia authorities also indicted Cannon, Joseph Johnson, and Ebenezer Johnson for murder after they discovered the bones of a Georgia slave trader and several African Americans on their property. Cannon admitted to her priest that she had killed eleven people and had been an accomplice in twelve other killings, including those of her husband and three-day-old child. She committed suicide in her jail cell before her trial. A Pennsylvania court convicted the Johnson brothers of murder in absentia and sentenced them to hang, though since they had already fled to Mississippi and Alabama, the sentence was never carried out.[73]

Of course, in the 1830s and 1840s, African Americans took on greater roles in protecting against kidnappings, though in the 1810s and 1820s, this was extremely difficult, especially in New Jersey with its small and relatively weak free black population. In New York, for instance, David Ruggles formed the New York Committee of Vigilance in 1835 to combat kidnappings, provide "disenfranchised blacks . . . a voice for their anger," and the kidnapped "a beacon of hope" for rescue. Like Watson and other white activists, Ruggles's organization would prove essential in forming a strong free black community in 1830s New Jersey.[74]

∗   ∗   ∗

The internal slave trade and the kidnappings associated with it greatly influenced the antebellum United States and makes New Jersey's experience as a supplier an important part of this American system. Historians have repeatedly investigated the extent of the state's participation to measure the impact of the trade on Jersey blacks. Robert Fogel and Stanley Engerman argued that since New Jersey's slave population decreased by 9,020 slaves, but the increase in the total black population amounted to only 8,670, a large number had to have been sold out of state.[75] Even accounting for ex-slaves who left New Jersey for surrounding states, a sizeable deficit of free blacks in the region as a whole existed. This suggests that many slaves did not gain freedom but instead were transported south. The same discrepancy appears in the next decade (1820–1830), when the slave population de-clined by 30 percent but the free population increased by only seven per-cent. Of course, it remains difficult to determine the trade's full extent, since only 121 removal petitions remain from 1810 to 1820. Many of these records either did not survive or more likely never existed because slave-holders removed their slaves without official license.[76]

Fogel and Engerman, however, relied on raw census figures that depended on cloudy assumptions of slavery and freedom as no clear rule existed for census enumerators on how to classify the freeborn slaves for a term. Between 1806 and 1820, the nine (of thirteen) counties with remain-ing records recorded the births of 2,294 slaves for a term, who should have been recorded in the 1820 census as free blacks under age fourteen. There-fore, since these children were not legally slaves, the census should have reported that no slaves under age fourteen lived in New Jersey in 1820. Yet, the census recorded 1,452 slaves and 6,421 free blacks of the same age. Therefore, the slaves Fogel and Engerman counted in their estimates using the raw census data may not have been slaves at all; many were slaves for a term. An example of this census irregularity appears in the records of Ann and Rufus Johnson's family. The 1830 census recorded Ann and Rufus as slaves two years after their master, Hannah Thomson, had granted them freedom. Census enumerators also listed two of their children, Mary and

Matilda, as slaves, while George and David appear as free blacks, even though all lived as slaves for a term with the earliest gaining freedom in 1842.[77]

Pennsylvanians recognized similar problems with categorizing the distinctions between free, enslaved, and slaves for a term in census records when in 1833 the legislature investigated a reported 83 percent increase in the state's slave population from 1820 to 1830. The legislators felt that, in light of other northern states becoming freer, it was an insult that the "land of Penn, which took the lead in emancipation . . . should exhibit an increase of slaves," especially since their presence had "excited considerable attention even beyond the limits of our own commonwealth." After an extensive investigation, they found that census enumerators had counted some slaves for a term and term slaves, those manumitted in Virginia, Maryland, or Delaware and brought to Pennsylvania as bound laborers, as slaves in twenty-seven counties. In reality, the enslaved population had actually declined from 211 in 1820 to 67 in 1830.[78]

The constant monitoring of abolition's progress, even into the 1840s, continued in New Jersey since despite the increased restrictions on slave trading, New Jerseyans still found ways to circumvent abolition and sell their chattel out of state. For example, in 1844 Thomas Russell of Pope County, Arkansas, bought Patsy, a slave for a term from Passaic, for use on his farm in west-central Arkansas. In the sale, completed without a written warrant, neither party attested to Patsy's status as a slave for a term. Three years later, Russell complained that Patsy was "unhealthy and subject to fits" and sold her to a local businessman (without any notation of her free status) in exchange for land near Russellville.[79] The same occurred when seventy-one-year-old Lorena Ward of Belleville sold Anaka, a seventy-year-old slave, and Mima, a four-year-old free girl, to Stephen Perry of Brazoria County, Texas, just south of Galveston, in February 1859. Perry owned Peach Point Plantation, a cotton plantation that had transitioned to sugar cultivation. The regionwide shift to sugar necessitated more labor, and by the mid-1840s slave traders in New Orleans had begun shipping large numbers of slaves to Galveston.[80]

Perry sought to expand his plantation with additional slaves in January 1857 and asked his commission merchant in New York, J.H. Brower and Company, for a $12,000 advance against the current year's sugar crop in order to "purchase nine or ten negroes . . . to make my force sufficiently strong to carry on my plantation successfully and make improvements."[81] John Brower, the owner of JH Brower and Company, had created an extensive commission business with Texans due to his previous position as the Republic of Texas' consul in New York. After Brower advanced Perry the loan, he spent $11,970 to purchase seventeen slaves from Charles Sayre, a local plantation owner with over six thousand acres. By 1858, however, Perry's plantation suffered from a poor sugar crop and a measles outbreak that killed five slaves. Drought and other financial setbacks stopped a planned land sale in summer 1857, which would have covered the $12,000 loan. Perry seemingly overcame these setbacks, buying Anaka and Mima only two years later, possibly with Brower brokering the sale. The pair joined the sixty-one other slaves who already lived on the plantation.[82]

Far different from the "voluntary" removals of slaves, New Jersey's criminal justice system also sentenced slaves to sale out of state, which allowed masters to profit from their convict chattel and frustrate abolition. In 1801, the legislature allowed state courts to sentence slaves to transportation if they committed arson, burglary, rape, highway robbery, or attempted murder. Catharine Mervit, one such slave, stood trial in 1810 for murder in New Brunswick, but a court convicted her on the lesser charge of manslaughter, and sentenced her to three years at hard labor. Hendrick Smock, Catharine's owner, pleaded with the legislature to pardon Catharine and allow him to sell her out of state to recoup his monetary loss due to her incarceration. Smock believed that his plan would "equally answer the end of justice and enable him to receive the same satisfaction for his property."[83] In the end, the legislature denied his request, citing the 1801 law that did not allow slaves convicted of manslaughter to be sold. Abolitionist John Parrish, writing about these judicial decisions, claimed that in "many instances . . . slaves have rather chosen death, than to remain in a state of bondage." Parrish cited the example of a Trenton slave who, after a magistrate ordered him sold to the West Indies in 1806, killed himself in Philadelphia before he was to board a ship bound for the Caribbean.[84]

*   *   *

Through the slave trade and a steady stream of kidnappings, New Jerseyans and other northerners fully participated in feeding the hungry southern labor market and helped solidify the United States as a "slave country." Both activities speak to the centrality of New Jersey slavery not only in the national conversation about the institution but also to the impact of gradual abolition in the North. Many slaveholders saw the growing southern demand for slaves as an easy way to reap huge profits from their chattel and did not believe that selling their slaves south interfered with either the letter or the spirit of gradual abolition.[85]

Even though Judge Van Wickle's exploits were originally made possible by the general apathy of whites toward black freedom, they forced white New Jerseyans to see themselves as part of a larger national slavery system. This led them to define kidnapping and slave trading, especially of slaves for a term, as unacceptable in the abolition period. The national conversation on whether or not Missouri would be a slave state likewise compelled political leaders to define New Jersey's position on slavery. Even though white New Jerseyans did not always follow the abolition law, legislators used it as a guidepost. The 1820 reissuing of the state's slave code ensured that slavery would continue in New Jersey under the 1804 guidelines; gradualism was still king. At the same time though, whites remained opposed to the institution's expansion, both at home and in the West. They used a free soil antislavery ideology to fight against the Missouri Compromise and the slave trade, punishing the politicians who voted for it. In the end, the dual acceptance of slavery's gradual death at home and antagonism toward its expansion gave Jersey politicians a roadmap for the antebellum sectional debates to come. For the next thirty years, they embraced the state's slave past and opposed the institution's growth across the nation.

CHAPTER SEVEN

Colonization and Gradualism's Persistence

Prime, who gained his freedom in 1786 from the New Jersey legislature for meritorious service in the Revolution, became part of the first generation of free blacks in nineteenth century New Jersey. In the early abolition period, he requested that the Hunterdon County Court of Common Pleas absolve him of fines levied for his failure to attend militia duty. Prime argued that since he did not possess "an equal right with white state subjects as I cannot hold land, serve on juries, nor be a witness, nor sue for debt," he should not be required to serve. Prime therefore experienced the intense social and economic restrictions that most former slaves in the early abolition period endured. As in the South, freed blacks in New Jersey became slaves without masters, legally free but denied basic rights as slavery continued around them. The American Colonization Society (ACS) became key in helping white New Jerseyans maintain this framework of slaves without masters and sustain the state's gradualist approach to abolition by linking free blacks with slavery.[1]

The ACS was able to sustain gradualism by positioning colonization as the natural successor to gradual abolition and by actively acknowledging New Jersey's slave past in its rhetoric. The collapse of New Jersey's abolition society left the state an open venue for colonization and allowed the ACS to rally former gradual abolitionists into their camp by arguing that, after abolition had freed slaves, removal to Africa was necessary to ensure their full freedom; they therefore continued the work of gradualism under a new name. Additionally, their racial beliefs mirrored many early nineteenth-century legal and political decisions, which all viewed blacks as inferior Americans who, because of their previous enslaved status, could never achieve true equality in the United States. These legal decisions helped reinforce colonization's popularity and mobilized free black New Jerseyans against the movement.

Colonization also allowed white New Jerseyans to further interpret the meaning of abolition and gradualism in the early abolition period. Jersey colonizationists readily embraced the state's slave past and reiterated gradualist rhetoric, including the persistent fear of black revolt and that freed slaves remained unfit to function in American society. Their embrace of slavery's continuation under the tenets of gradualism and colonization reinforced the institution's perpetuation in New Jersey and served as a clear break from New Englanders who used colonization to disown slavery and transform their region into a fully free one in opposition to the slave South. Colonization's popularity kept slavery alive in New Jersey and distanced the state from free labor New England. Even though white New Jerseyans still opposed slavery's expansion, colonization helped align them more with the Upper South than with their northern neighbors in the growing sectional divide.[2]

*   *   *

Bobalition broadsides, fears of racial amalgamation, and the consistent worry over slave revolt in the first twenty-five years of the abolition period led New Jersey's slaveholders to consistently apply the category of "slave" both to slaves for a term and freed blacks for far longer than New Englanders did. The persistence of slavery led to the perception of black inferiority among the general white population and precipitated a simplistic approach to defining race and status. Free blacks in the early abolition period suffered economically, politically, and socially from slavery's persistence and, despite their best efforts to navigate around it, found themselves still living in a society that equated "negro" with "slave."[3]

New Jersey's branch of the ACS trumpeted this connection between slavery and black color, claiming in 1824 that "color has become a signal of inferiority" and that New Jerseyans had connected "the idea of a slave with that of a dark skin." Across the Hudson River in New York, William Hamilton similarly argued that "no more shall the accursed name of slave be attached to us—no more shall *negro* and *slave* be synonymous" in a speech delivered before New York's African Zion Church celebrating the final abolition of slavery in that state in 1827. In both instances, blacks and whites understood that skin color tied all blacks to slavery. New Jersey's lack of immediate abolition maintained this link chronologically longer and in a more concerted manner than in New York.[4] With significant numbers of slaves and slaves for a term living among whites until the 1830s, racialized slavery made it quite easy for whites to identify color with servitude. As the *Colored American* explained in 1837, "where people of color most abound, as on Long Island and in New Jersey, there the progress of the cause of human rights has been the slowest and the prejudice is strongest." Race and white perceptions of what race meant wove the web of unfreedom that ensnared free blacks.[5]

These ACS positions reflected New Jersey law in the early abolition period; blacks were assumed to be slaves until proven otherwise. In 1821, the Court of Errors and Appeals, New Jersey's highest court, decided a case in which the defendant helped a slave abscond to New York on a steamer. The defendant claimed he did not know the black man's legal status and therefore should not be liable. However, the court affirmed that in New Jersey, "all black men were *prima facie* slaves" and therefore without proof of freedom, all blacks should be considered slaves. Despite the enactment of gradual abolition, the courts decided that New Jersey law denied African Americans the presumption of freedom—gradualism and slavery still very much controlled African American life. In many ways, this decision adhered to racial laws passed in the nineteenth century South and anticipated the U.S. Supreme Court decision in the Dred Scott case. As Chief Justice Roger Taney would do in 1857, New Jersey courts presumed that color dictated legal status, a reflection of the state's continued use of slavery.[6]

Five years later, the state Supreme Court affirmed the 1821 precedent in another case that reinforced connections between free blacks and slaves. In this fugitive slave case, the defendant was again accused of illegally helping a slave escape to New York. The Supreme Court reiterated the Court of Errors and Appeals previous ruling, contending that that "all black men in contemplation of the law are *prima facie* slaves . . . the color of the man was sufficient evidence that he was a slave until the contrary appeared." The firm basis the association between free blacks and slaves had in law no doubt helped the ACS make that connection among the white public.[7]

The ACS was the only organization concerned with African Americans in New Jersey after the abolition society's demise, thereby giving it a platform to discuss the connection between free blacks and slaves with little interference. Their task was made much easier since New Jersey and the ACS were linked from the very beginning. Robert Finley, a Presbyterian minister from Basking Ridge, helped found both the national organization and the state auxiliary. In his early tracts, Finley strongly asserted that blacks could not survive outside slavery in the United States and therefore needed to be removed to Africa to thrive on their own. He argued that as the northern free black population "increases greatly . . . their wretchedness . . . appears to me. Everything connected with their conditions, including their color is against them; nor is there much prospect that their state can ever be greatly ameliorated." Finley's idea that blacks would always be linked to their enslaved past became a key part of ACS ideology.[8]

Even though Finley died in 1817, Jersey colonizationists continued to recall his influence in creating the organization, crafting its key tenets, and ensuring the popularity enjoyed by the organization in the state. In 1838, for example, the Newark Colonization Society made clear to all that "a Jerseyman first proposed and powerfully urged" the ACS creation. A fellow "Jerseyman was his zealous coadjustor and first Secretary of the Society." Likewise, another "Jerseymen . . . successfully negotiated the first highly important treaty with the natives of Africa" while yet another Jerseyman first "superintended its location."[9] Articles in the *African Repository and Colonial Journal*, the national organization's propaganda publication, reiterated the state's close link with the ACS, claiming that New Jersey has "been styled the classic ground of the American Revolution" and "may, with equal propriety be called the classic ground of African Colonization."[10] Similarly, other articles asked members to "remember that to a Jerseyman" the ACS "owed its origin and from Jerseymen it has received much of its warmest support."[11] Reports from the state auxiliary reinforced New Jersey's strong support for the movement. In 1842, for instance, an article claimed that "New Jersey is one of the best States for the support of Colonization" because the movement's "friends there are firm . . . and the number of them is gradually increasing."[12]

Like many antebellum movements, colonization joined together three separate ideologies, all of which shared the goal of removing blacks from the United States and reinforced gradualism but for different reasons. The first advanced a humanitarian agenda, one that wanted to assist free blacks rise from their degraded condition. The second saw colonization as a way to continue gradual abolition and free those slaves unaffected by the 1804 law. The third used the ACS to channel their racism and remove a detested,

Figure 7. View of Bassa Cove in Liberia.
Courtesy of the Library Company of Philadelphia.

dangerous, and problematic population from the United States. All three
believed in Finley's idea that free blacks maintained a link to their enslaved
past and in his claim that because slavery had caused such an "injurious
effect on the morals" of the nation, free black habits of "indolence" and
"idleness" would be "unfavorable to" white "industry and morals." Echoing this concern for black industry, humanitarians in the ACS called for
greater support for blacks' miserable condition while racists highlighted the
need to remove a dreadful and socially dangerous population. These same
racists and humanitarians agreed that, if these freed persons could be
removed, it would "induce habits of industry and along with it a love of
order and religion" in them. ACS members believed that separating free
blacks from their former masters would allow the ex-slaves to "escape to a
land where their own race was sovereign and independent," while removal
would gradually "prepare the whites for the happy and progressive change"

slavery's end would bring, an idea that dovetailed nicely with gradual abolition's emphasis on its benefit to whites.[13]

The humanitarian quality of the ACS attracted many whites who believed in social uplift along with those who had supported abolition since providing needed assistance to a struggling race engaged white benefactors on a paternalistic and emotional level. Jersey colonizationists routinely bemoaned the "state of hopeless inferiority and degradation" inflicted upon free blacks "by their color . . . an inedible mark of their origin and former condition." This mark, as one Jersey colonizationist tract claimed, established "an impassable barrier between them and the whites . . . closed forever by our habits . . . our feelings . . . our prejudice."[14] Colonizationists of this brand saw freedom not as an opportunity for improvement but as an intractable status where "manumission [becomes] no blessing to the slave." The lack of ability to participate in white dominated society "pressed [him] down, till debasement becomes a habit." Only removal to Africa could rectify the situation.[15]

Of course, even humanitarians shared an anti-black bias and frequently understood that colonization would lead to the stronger operation of slavery and a better life for whites. These humanitarians often joined racists in the movement, recognizing that removing blacks to Africa would rid whites "of a population for the most part idle and useless and too often vicious and mischievous." Likewise, the slaves who remained in a New Jersey without freed blacks would be free of "temptations to vice and idleness" and become more "peaceful and moral" as they worked toward freedom.[16]

However, many humanitarians actually believed that colonization could solve the economic and social degradation free blacks suffered because of their consistent link to slavery. Samuel Doughty of New Brunswick argued in 1826, for instance, that colonization would remove the freed slave "from the land of his shame and degradation" where slavery had "worn from his soul all its nobleness, blotted out its ambition, and blasted all the lofty motives of its rational nature." According to Doughty, living where they had been slaves would never allow freed blacks to leave their enslaved past behind.[17] Similarly, the New Jersey Colonization Society hoped that same year "to offer to that unfortunate and degraded race of human beings an escape from their present condition" of unfreedom that slavery had caused.[18] Whites had been using this same rhetoric to petition the state legislature since 1816, when they decried the condition of thousands "who have been freed from slavery" that lived in a "degraded situation . . . [and] will probably remain" that way "while they continue among the whites" who had enslaved them.[19] Mid-Atlantic blacks even highlighted this condition when *Freedom's Journal* claimed that emancipation did not radically change an individual's life. Slavery's characteristic poverty and degradation continued even as blacks exited it.[20]

Although humanitarians certainly became one of the most vocal groups in the colonization movement, many Mid-Atlantic whites embraced colonization as a way to continue gradual abolition. The Pennsylvania Colonization Society, for instance, listed emancipation as one of its primary goals in its constitution and spent significant resources encouraging manumission. Since colonizationists argued that slaveholders refused to manumit their slaves due to fears of free blacks lingering in society, they believed that masters would manumit in greater numbers if removal was guaranteed. Members did not see a conflict between these two seemingly contradictory ideas; colonization therefore "reinforced racism [and] excused negrophobia" while advancing abolition.[21]

The New Jersey Colonization Society, like its Pennsylvania counterpart, listed abolition its "first and great object," portrayed colonization as a natural outgrowth of the gradual abolition movement, and understood that abolition and colonization worked in tandem. The state society argued that "emancipation alone will not" remove slavery from the state, noting that the 1820 census reflected an increased number of blacks in transition to freedom due to the 1804 gradual abolition law. It claimed that "at no distant period, the whole black population must be emancipated" and saw that although the mission of the abolition movement ended with legal freedom, the presence of a degraded number of free blacks in transition to freedom presented "a subject of vital importance to those who regard our future welfare."[22] The ACS believed that no amount of education or assistance would help these free blacks integrate into society and therefore advocated for their exclusion after freedom.

The idea that gradual abolition was somehow incomplete was repeated throughout New Jersey colonization tracts and helped the ACS reiterate its successor status to the gradual abolition movement. New Jersey colonizationists channeled these same graduated ideals to argue that blacks needed a gradual system of freedom to "learn" how to become free under white supervision. For example, in an 1825 discussion of black education and colonization, the authors of one tract claimed that by "the results of the manumission system, we are almost led to believe that to extend mere freedom to the slave is like the tender mercies of the wicked." In reference to slaves for a term, colonizationists argued that at the end of this freedom process, blacks were "set loose upon society . . . without qualifications . . . when to all the practical purposes of useful life he needs a guardianship more than infancy."[23] Jersey colonizationists placed themselves in the role of guardian and claimed that their guardianship would help blacks form a government in Liberia "by their own hands, offering all the rewards usual to industry and economy" that could not be achieved in the United States.[24]

Like in New Jersey, national voices firmly tied the ACS to the early gradualist abolitionist framework. For example, early ACS supporter Augustus Taylor claimed in 1825 that "the scheme of gradually eradicating the evil of slavery by colonizing the free blacks on the Coast of Africa" should be advanced because it stimulated some masters to free their slaves.[25] The American Convention for Promoting the Abolition of Slavery sanctioned this connection between gradual abolition and the removal of freed blacks to either Africa or Haiti in 1826. In doing so, the convention claimed the rapid increase in slavery and entrenchment of southern slavery mandated a new approach to abolition, one that was inherently gradualist in that it affirmed a voluntary movement away from slavery with colonizationists helping guide blacks toward Liberia.[26]

Above all, the colonization movement repeatedly affirmed its commitment to gradualism and rejected immediate abolition, fearing that its actions might be construed as opposing both northern and southern conservative viewpoints on slavery. This was especially important in the Upper South as slaveholders there feared any changes to slavery's hold on the country. In 1824, for example, the national meeting announced that the "scope of our design" can only be accomplished with wide ranging support, which necessitated a gradual removal "for if attempted suddenly, a void would be occasioned" and the movement would fail. To defend this point, ACS members routinely affirmed that colonization could only occur with the freed person's consent, a move which, as activist James Green claimed, would eliminate any "fear on the part of our Southern friends" that the organization supported forced abolition.[27] These same abolition caveats applied in New Jersey. For example, at the 1825 ACS national meeting, New Jersey's Robert Stockton argued that, unlike the "enthusiasts of the North,"

he "embark[s] not in the wild and destructive scheme which calls on the
South for immediate and universal emancipation," but instead on a graduated plan that encouraged manumission and maintained New Jersey's historic approach to abolition.[28]

Like other Jersey gradualists, colonizationists opposed the slave trade
since they believed it helped expand slavery in the United States and
abroad. Their opposition to illegal slave trading from Africa, which was
much smaller after the federal government categorized the Atlantic trade
as piracy and punishable by death, reinforced their gradualism and made
colonization incredibly popular among white New Jerseyans who had
opposed the state's own participation in the interstate slave trade. By 1824,
the ACS national office claimed that no "sufficient check to the trade by
American citizens on the coast of Africa, nor . . . any means of redeeming
and restoring to their country the unfortunate victims" existed. The New
Jersey Colonization Society likewise underscored the importance of the
antislave trade position in 1824, listing the suppression of the Atlantic trade
as its tertiary goal.[29] They went farther in 1831 when New Jersey's Theodore
Frelinghuysen claimed that the suppression of the slave trade was "our duty
as Christians and as men" since Christian settlements of former slaves along
the coast of Africa formed "a bulwark . . . against the slave trade more
effective than a thousand natives."[30] The state society's 1844 and 1846
annual reports likewise testified to the continued interest in suppressing the
trade. The 1844 report expressed outrage that in a six month period, American ships brought 18,000 slaves to Brazil, while the 1846 report expressed
encouragement as Liberia was no longer "the centre of the abominable
slave trade." Because of "diffusing knowledge, the useful arts, and Christianity," colonizationists believed that Africans had ended their relationship
with slavery.[31] However, the discovery of two Burlington County vessels,
the *Sooy* and *Pearl*, involved in the Brazilian trade shattered that belief and
caused antislave trading in the 1840s to remain a serious colonizationist
priority.[32]

Into the 1830s and 1840s, both New Jersey and national colonizationists
continued to meld antislave trading and gradualism together by using
Christianity to further solidify themselves among white New Jerseyans.
Christianity had always been a key ACS component, with Robert Finley
expressing that "the progress which the Colonization scheme has made is
to me plain indication that it is of God" before leaving New Jersey to
assume the presidency of the University of Georgia. He charged those left

to run the society should "devote to it your heart and soul . . . as the noblest means of servicing God and man that will ever be presented."[33] In the 1830s, spreading Christianity helped rally opposition to the slave trade since many humanitarian colonizationists thought that colonizing American blacks in Africa would simultaneously spread Christianity to Africans, build infrastructure, and combat slave trading. As historian Beverly Tomek argues, colonizationists "deluded themselves into believing that Liberia was helping them make up to Africa for the crimes committed by kidnappers and slave traders." Newark colonizationists, for instance, desperately hoped that "by colonization, the natives of Africa will become educated, civilized and Christianized," while the state society wrote that "the breaking forth of light from the lone start of Liberia" would fix "the wrongs of Africa at the hand of all other lands." Colonization's gradual abolitionism then morphed into a Christianizing and civilizing mission to benefit both freed blacks and Africans.[34]

To support the spread of Christianity, humanitarians and abolitionists in the movement launched a series of seminaries and schools designed to educate free black New Jerseyans and instill "proper" behavior in future ministers and public officials for Liberia who would help spread Christianity and end the slave trade. In 1816, the Presbyterians formed the African School at Parsippany, which New Jersey's ACS auxiliary soon took leadership of since many of its founding members were active colonizationists. Joseph Hornblower, for example, not only served as New Jersey's chief justice but also as treasurer of the African School and a key player in the ACS. The school, designed to prepare "teachers of their own race" for service in Liberia, believed that though "there will remain different orders in Society," Africa can enjoy the "blessings of Christianity and civilization" as preached to them by former American slaves. The school administrators argued that the West was culpable for the slave trade and became a "prison which has received all" of Africa's "captive sons." Hornblower reiterated this point, claiming that the school provided "the cause of Africa" with "extensive and liberal aid which her injured race have a right to demand of us." The success of the pupils confirmed that "Africans have capacity to learn as well as hearts to love our common Lord and Savior."[35]

Samuel Miller, a Presbyterian minister who preached in favor of the African School, argued that the school helped further gradual abolition in New Jersey by tying slaves' future freedom to Liberia. Miller had previously supported black integration in the United States as a member of the New

York Manumission Society.[36] Like many gradual abolitionists, he shifted to support colonization in the late 1810s and embraced the colonization society's gradual abolition agenda by offering that gradualism needed to continue because "the most serious obstacles to the immediate emancipation of slaves . . . is that they are not prepared for the enjoyment of freedom." This bridge to freedom through education would not only help those who removed to Africa but support ACS efforts at "abolish[ing] the slave trade [and] the gradual emancipation of slaves" domestically.[37]

The state colonization society reiterated Miller's arguments by claiming that the school's managers had embarked on an important mission that provided colonizationists with "a useful, intelligent, and respectable" group that would render the society great assistance in Liberia. Jersey colonizationists likewise advanced their mission to Liberia through the opening of a Kosciusko school, which they believed would improve the Parsippany seminary, an institution "of immense utility to Africa and the world." The Kosciusko Fund, a bequest from Polish-born Tadeusz Kosciusko administered with the assistance of Thomas Jefferson to benefit American blacks, debated helping construct additional schools in Newark. Sponsored by the ACS, these schools would have prepared "free colored children and youth for usefulness in Africa."[38]

Along with white colonization members, some Jersey blacks in the early abolition period supported the African School and the colonization movement since they saw it as the best option in a state that had largely rejected black freedom. The African American Association of New Brunswick, an organization founded in 1817 with both free and enslaved members, dedicated itself to raising funds to develop educational opportunities for young black men to become teachers and ministers, with the African School becoming the association's primary beneficiary. The African Society of Newark, another mixed slave and free black society, joined with the New Brunswick Association to support the African School. When Newark Presbyterian minister Edward Griffin preached to his white parishioners about the African School, he highlighted the integral role New Brunswick's black leadership played in the school's creation. Griffin's sermon contained shades of ACS paternalism as he described association president Peter Upshur as "forty-eight years of age with an intelligent eye, a large and prominent forehead, and a general physiognomy indicative of vigorous intellect" who is "much respected by the whites and exerts a benign influence over his colored brethren."[39] Indeed, Upshur's "benign influence" earned much praise from Griffin, who argued that the association set an example to all Jersey blacks.[40]

Students who attended the school, like Jeremiah Gloucester, firmly believed that colonization and education finally allowed African Americans to become "men of sound and culture" and take their place in a larger world order. Gloucester claimed that American blacks lived in ignorance and that only education from whites (and those trained by whites) could bring true power and respect. The empowerment Gloucester and others like him provided to the New Brunswick Association's ex-slaves helped them challenge the rest of the free black community that opposed colonization and shows how the gradualist rhetoric of education and empowerment influenced at least some Jersey blacks to see colonization as a viable option for their future lives as freedmen.[41]

*   *   *

The third group of colonizationists, those who participated in the movement solely to eliminate an unwanted and unequal population, made not only negrophobia an integral part of the movement but also introduced fears of race war as a reason to continue gradualism. These colonizationists saw blacks as potentially dangerous and hoped, like early colonization adopter Lucius Elmer, that the movement would free "the country from the living pestilence of a numerous black population."[42] Colonizationists like Elmer believed that black moral character was "far more debased than any part of the white population," which would lead them to turn to crime and the public purse for support. They would then create a dangerous and unstable society that might lead to race war, which white New Jerseyans had feared since the Revolution.[43]

Most of the fears over race war and societal instability came in the mid-1820s when white New Jerseyans worried that the increase in the free black population would create a future demographic imbalance and wrest control of the state away from whites. In 1824, for example, colonization leader James Green lamented the presence of "a mass of ignorance, misery, and depravity" that threatened "the whole with a mortal and political pestilence" after they discovered that the 1820 census had reported that the black population had increased to more than twenty thousand. Green asked his audience to look "at this domestic evil" and "feel the danger" that surrounded white New Jerseyans, especially since another twenty years of a growing black population, degraded and without political voice, would eventually have to "be resisted with arms" because this was a "natural process" in "all the evils of a civil and servile war." Green further claimed that these revolts could result in both the appointment of a black governor and in miscegenation between black men and white women, two arguments that provided colonizationists with powerful rhetorical weapons.[44] Samuel Doughty of New Brunswick likewise pulled on these same census figures in 1826 to argue that the dramatic increase in free blacks who were "shut out from all posts of honor and profit" could be "liable to many burdens" and will "at some future day be a fruitful source of trouble to our state."[45]

Colonization supporters played on white fears of an allegedly hostile black community that demanded increased power in the new republic to support their gradualist agenda since the same fears of releasing a criminal element in the North had been present ever since the debates over gradual abolition began. Pennsylvanians, for example, looked at the "tremendous consequences" of an increasingly dangerous black population in 1830 and projected that by 1929, the nation's black population could increase to sixteen million. They used Henry Clay's words to warn that immediate emancipation would bring an "aggregate of the evils" into society that "would be greater than all the evils of slavery."[46] The ACS in Washington reiterated the criminality and danger free blacks represented in several reports that described how blacks would disturb the public peace and tranquility if allowed to grow exponentially without white control.[47]

Colonization leaders used the persistent link between a degraded slave past and an uncertain future to depict blacks as intellectually deficient, prone to antisocial and criminal behaviors, and in need of white supervision. These fears of a dangerous free black population infected even the Pennsylvania Abolition Society, who warned in 1838 that Philadelphia's free blacks "have been brought up in poverty and ignorance" as a result of their previous lives as slaves or slaves for a term. Even though blacks had gained some status as property holders, many had been "debarred from the exercise of their moral and intellectual faculties" in slavery and might one day "indulge in vicious propensities and become the subject of criminal prosecution."[48]

Fears of an increased criminal element after a quick abolition without colonization combined with already present worries about racial amalgamation to create further hysteria and support for colonization's gradualist philosophy. In 1805, Thomas Branagan, an Irish immigrant in Pennsylvania, wrote two tracts that circulated extensively in the Mid-Atlantic and stressed that since slavery had destroyed black moral rectitude, blacks would attack the moral and economic prosperity of whites after freedom. Branagan saw amalgamation as particularly symbolic of morality's decline, a feeling that encouraged white Pennsylvanians to petition for laws prohibiting intermarriage. Although New Jersey legislators never passed an anti-miscegenation law, fears of white and black sexual engagements became rife in the state as a way of focusing white fears of a changing racial dynamic.[49]

Like miscegenation, fears of a combined free black and slave revolt because of blacks' lack of morality led many white New Jerseyans to flock to the colonization movement and embrace their gradualist ideology, especially in the 1820s. The belief that free blacks could destabilize the state's still functioning slave system had brought back an argument from the late eighteenth century gradual abolition movement but, as the free black population had swelled since then, it became far more pertinent. This fear ballooned when the ACS in 1820 published a post-apocalyptic vision of the future in which "the Negroes of this American Republic have overrun the better half of it from Florida to Pennsylvania" and enslaved their former masters. The ACS warned of "the dreadful massacre of a greater portion of the white population of St. Domingo" and claimed that the situation there was "one of the most solemn political lessons that history ever taught to a slaveholding nation." Ending slavery and fulfilling the movement's gradualist objectives, combined with removal of all blacks from the republic, would ensure that a rebellion similar to Haiti would never occur. In this sense, Mid-Atlantic colonizationists allied with southern whites in believing colonization could expel undesirables and limit threats to their safety.[50]

Others fueled fears of race war by referencing the Haitian Revolution and the dangers that a larger number of free blacks presented to white New Jerseyans, which only further strengthened colonization's appeal. Branagan, for instance, claimed that whites should question their safety in light of the rebellion in Saint-Domingue, a fear Newark preacher William Hamilton reiterated in an 1825 sermon, arguing that blacks would soon become the majority of the American population. Invoking the "insurrection and murder and flight and bloody retribution" on the "famed Hispaniola," Hamilton echoed New Jersey ACS concerns. In 1824, state leaders had warned that unless gradual abolition was mediated with colonization, "the bloody process of St. Domingo" would be reenacted in the United States. In 1827, Peter Vroom Junior, a state legislator and colonizationist whose father had supported gradual abolition in the legislature, complained that the presence of free blacks made whites imagine the possibility that "the carnage of St. Domingo" and "the piercing shriek of helpless innocence and then the shout of hellish satisfaction from the savage throng" could come to New Jersey. Colonization, according to Vroom, would "avert the impending blow" and "ensure their freedom and our safety."[51]

*   *   *

Amid the debates over the urgent need to eliminate freed black miscreants and vagrants, the colonization movement helped define how New Jerseyans understood slavery in the abolition period, continuing a process that had begun during the debates over the Missouri Compromise. New Englanders had used colonization to create an antebellum New England nationalism, one that excised slavery from its past and widened the rift between New England and the slave South. New England colonizationists minimized their former role as slaveholders and touted their region's free labor past, creating a "claim to a kind of historical whiteness" that questioned the "the anomalous nature of a resident black population and argued for a position of sectional superiority." To these ACS members, removing slaves to Africa became an integral component of removing slavery from their historical memory. However, New Jersey's colonizationists actively tied their movement to the state's slave past, which effectively reinforced slavery's presence in New Jersey in whites' collective imagination. They embraced the same gradualism that denounced slavery's expansion, via the slave trade, while acknowledging and supporting slavery's continued presence under the gradual abolition law. This made New Jerseyans far more sympathetic to southerners in the sectional conflict than their New England neighbors and displays the variety of northern opinions on slavery.[52]

Indeed, as discussed earlier, slavery's presence precipitated by New Jersey's slow abolition process became a key way that colonizationists argued for their cause as they saw New Jersey's gradual abolition system as a perfect complement to colonization. They could therefore uphold gradualist ideology and continue slavery's gradual eradication by advocating against slavery's quick death. For instance, Presbyterian preacher Phillip Hay claimed in 1826 that of the 15,000 blacks that had become "free under the act of

the Legislature of 1804," all still suffered "the same causes that have operated" under slavery "to degrade and deprave" them, which will "continue
to operate" unless colonization took hold.[53] Hay feared the growing black
population's proclivity for race war and miscegenation. Like other Jersey
colonizationists, he recommended against immediate abolition for the
state's remaining slaves, fearful of the disastrous consequences of unleash-
ing them without the white supervision that colonization could provide. To
the society, it would have been patently unfair to provide freedom without
first offering colonization as a way to educate and remove blacks from the
hazards of freedom.[54]

Additionally, Jersey colonization sermons, speeches, and pamphlets
directly referenced the state's continued interest in slavery and linked New
Jersey to the larger national sin of slavery, using the movement as a way for
residents to apologize for the institution. United States Senator Theodore
Frelinghuysen addressed the state auxiliary in 1824, asking the "citizens of
New Jersey" to "survey your cultivated fields, your comfortable habitations,
your children rising around you to bless you. Who, under Providence,
caused those hills to rejoice and those valleys to smile? Who ploughed those
fields and cleared these forests? Remember the toils and tears of black men,
and pay your debt to Africa." Frelinghuysen identified colonization as the
best way for whites to repay New Jersey's debt to its slaves for the state's
current economic prosperity. He also noted that while gradual abolition
had created a pathway to freedom, colonization would help blacks attain
true freedom in Liberia. This allowed whites to link gradualism and colonization, using the latter as a vehicle to atone for their part of the effort to
"enslave, degrade, and oppress a people through many generations."[55]

Six years later, Frelinghuysen again claimed that the North had an
intense relationship with slavery and had been just as guilty as southerners
in supporting the institution. State colonizationists, taking Frelinghuysen's
lead, continued to associate Jersey slavery and colonization. A "gentleman
from New Jersey," whose musings were printed in the *African Repository* in
1829, offered that colonization was a way to solve the "malpractices of an
age that has now happily passed away" while the Newark Colonization
Society wrote that "New Jersey was a participator in the wrong of slavery"
and needed to repay its debts by actively engaging in the colonization
movement in 1838. Colonization members in Elizabethtown in 1842 even
referred to colonization's link to New Jersey's past by specifically citing the
1804 abolition law and that slaves still lived in the state.[56]

∗   ∗   ∗

Most free blacks, unlike the state government and many white New Jerseyans, rejected colonization and labeled it a movement designed to further
prevent their acceptance into American society and prolong the race's association with slavery. African American ministers in Philadelphia, for
instance, loudly proclaimed their opposition to removal and especially to
the white-controlled colony of Liberia. However, blacks "stood virtually
alone in their public condemnation" of colonization. Particularly in the
1820s, Mid-Atlantic blacks expressed their sentiments against colonization
in large public meetings and disseminated their anticolonizationist ideas
through print culture, though with a small free population in New Jersey,
the epicenter of the opposition occurred outside the state.[57]

   Freedom's Journal championed the anticolonization movement in the
late 1820s and argued that it damaged freed people's ability to align with
the goals of the new nation since it considered blacks inherently inferior.
In a two-part 1827 editorial criticizing the sermon of a Newark procoloni-
zation minister, editors Samuel Cornish and John Brown Russwurm
attacked the idea that blacks could never be productive members of the
republic and affirmed that they deserved rights within the United States;
colonization to Africa was not a solution. They forcefully argued that ACS
characterizations of African Americans were "the most uncharitable and
inaccurate" version of the truth ever imagined.[58] *Freedom's Journal* showed
blacks on a weekly basis that colonization strengthened slavery while
degrading freed people's status. The newspaper rallied Mid-Atlantic blacks
against colonization, though not all joined the cause. About two hundred
left New Jersey for Liberia, including one of the movement's most outspo-
ken critics, Russwurm. Biographer Winston James argues that Russwurm's
embrace of colonization need not be interpreted as later abolitionists did;
he was not a traitor to his race. Instead, Russwurm and others made a
calculated choice from their experience with nineteenth century northern
racism. This choice made some sense, especially in New Jersey, where colonization enjoyed wide public support and the idea of black racial inferiority
subsumed white understandings of African Americans. Therefore, some
Jersey blacks no doubt believed it would be difficult if not impossible to
break through the racial barriers imposed by slavery and gradualism.[59]

   Even those Jersey blacks who opposed colonization understood that the
state's slave past made the movement difficult for whites to resist. In

numerous *Colored American* articles, for example, blacks highlighted that New Jersey had a unique dynamic and set of beliefs that prevented freed slaves from gaining status within the state. One article even went as far as to claim that the "hydra-headed colonization has fixed its strong hold in the hierto peaceful state of New Jersey" and has perpetuated the principles of black inferiority in order to engage in "unrelenting persecution of the colored people" of the state. The same author argued that the situation in New Jersey was so bad that Jersey blacks "are more persecuted and more brutally treated than the slaves" of the South while ministers from the Colored Presbyterian Churches in Newark and New York jointly argued that colonization helped slaveholders continue to subjugate free blacks and modeled itself after slavery.[60]

Anticolonization protests increased in the 1830s after black activists allied with white abolitionists and engaged the colonizationists in the context of the more radical abolition movement. This compelled the Pennsylvania ACS to respond in 1839 to the "direct and fierce attacks by societies exclusively northern in their origin and action to produce the immediate" freedom by reiterating that the movement only encouraged "slaveholders to emancipate their slaves" voluntarily and that they believed that slavery should be "left by the federal constitution under the exclusive control of the states in which it exists."[61] Trenton free blacks from Mount Zion Church, in 1831, responded by arguing that the ACS was "the most inveterate foe both to the free and slave man of color" and that they "are a positive libel on our general character." They warned that colonization's Christianizing mission was a front for the more sinister plot of removing blacks from the United States.[62]

White abolitionists involved in the second abolition movement also began to attack colonization in the 1830s and 1840s by hitting its core connection between gradualism and removal to illustrate its hypocrisy. For example, David Paul Brown delivered a speech before the Anti-Slavery Society in New York in 1834 in which he articulated that colonizationists, as opposed to abolitionists, joined "in the notion of natural inferiority on the part of the blacks and the impolicy of their liberation at home" unless they "consent to deportation." Similarly, Roberts Vaux, a noted Quaker philanthropist and social reformer, wrote in 1835 that the South advocated colonization only to compartmentalize abolition within a plan to remove free blacks in order to render slavery more secure. Likewise, abolitionist Samuel Emlen reiterated Vaux's complaints in 1837 and affirmed his own suspicion that colonization assisted slaveholders in reducing the number of free blacks to secure slavery.[63]

Abolitionist attacks on colonization challenged ACS supporters to advocate for their ideas in new ways since by the 1830s ACS auxiliaries displayed a marked decline in their efforts as compared to the bustling activity of the 1820s. In 1838, the New Jersey auxiliary distanced itself from its financially unstable parent, which revived the group's appeal and led to the movement's rebirth. The debt the national organization had accumulated similarly led the Pennsylvania and New York societies to separate from the leadership in Washington. These reorganizations led to increased home-grown colonization activity. Money raised by the state chapter became wholly controlled by New Jerseyans and was used to encourage more Jersey blacks to immigrate to Liberia. Traveling spokesmen Ezekiel Skinner, an ACS physician and agent who had lived in Liberia for two years, and dozens of other lecturers reinvigorated white New Jerseyans' commitment to colonization. Skinner's lecture tour alone raised significant sums and mobilized church congregations to actively support the cause. He spoke to numerous churches in Trenton, Newark, Newton, and Mount Holly and excited the "ladies of those congregations" to raise over two hundred dollars for the society. This campaign supported the July 1840 sailing of the *Saluda* to Liberia with over two thousand dollars in supplies.[64]

This reawakening of New Jersey colonizationists increased the frequency of black protests against the movement in the late 1830s and early 1840s when the growing free black population attacked the colonization society head-on despite the fact that resistance to black freedom remained strong among whites. For example, one 1838 article claimed that abolition had spread to "every part of our beloved country, save little Jersey" where "colonizationists and colonization efforts are swiveling up the souls and drying up the liberality, benevolence, and piety of Jerseymen." The following week, another article reported that "strenuous efforts are being made in New Jersey to persecute out, or to seduce our brethren to colonization inquiry," while a news report claimed that the "whining hypocrites" of New Jersey passed a law to secure a distinct colony in Liberia for the state's blacks. This article argued that to enact this law, the Jersey colonizationists had "all the apparatus of torture and blood which disgraced Papal Spain and Portugal in the barbarous bloody ages, to torture a single worthy and intelligent colored man from New Jersey to their African Golgotha." Since colonization had become so powerful in the state, one black author hoped that "abolitionists [would] . . . lose no time, nor spare any pains, in correct-ing public sentiment" in New Jersey. With an intense commitment to grad-ualism stemming from its relationship with slavery and the early abolition movement, most whites allied their gradualist ideals with the popular colonization movement as opposed to the infant immediate abolition movement. Jersey blacks realized that colonization not only continued gradualism but served as a bulwark against immediate abolition since "the minds of" white New Jerseyans "are already made up on the subject of African colonization."[65]

*   *   *

The colonization movement gave voice to much larger concerns among Jersey whites about black inferiority and their lack of ability to function in American society, while helping perpetuate New Jersey's gradual approach to abolition because it used the same reasoning that lay behind the 1804 gradual abolition law. Indeed, gradual abolition remained a main tenet of the ACS operation in New Jersey—the ACS hoped to end slavery by encouraging manumission, restricting the slave trade, and removing the free black population to quell white fears. State law in the early abolition period reflected the racial ideology and methods of the ACS, making this gradualist rhetoric reverberate in white imaginations and show that these freed slaves could never succeed in the United States because of their slave past.

The collapse of the state abolition society and colonization's resulting popularity made gradualism persistent in New Jersey and allowed whites to use the movement to interpret the role of slaves and free blacks in the abolition period. Nonslaveholding Jersey whites consistently recognized their state's continuing participation in slavery under the regulations set down in 1804. Colonization fit perfectly with slavery's continuation in its application of those gradualist principles. Therefore, instead of joining New Englanders to create an idealized free community, Jersey colonizationists reflected their state's continuing involvement with slavery and used it to inform their interactions with free blacks. However, free blacks vehemently opposed this connection and routinely spoke out against the movement. Since only about two hundred Jersey blacks left for Liberia, the movement was far more important in white interpretations of the abolition period rather than causing a dramatic decrease in the overall black population.

CHAPTER EIGHT

Creating a Free Life

Slavery's persistence in antebellum New Jersey worked to limit free African Americans' ability to succeed in the abolition period and placed them outside the body politic. Stripped of their right to vote, marginalized as slaves despite their free status, and declared "undesirable" by the colonization society, blacks tried to integrate into white political, economic, and social structures through a complex process of identity construction by which elite blacks challenged racial inequality through demonstrating their suitability for citizenship. Eventually they created their own communities to find respectability in a white-dominated republic. This fight for civil rights and the creation of free communities during slavery's slow death allowed free blacks to interact daily with the enslaved and forced them to battle against slavery's entrenched boundaries as they simultaneously fought to develop their own free lives. Slavery's shadow, therefore, hung over any attempt at advancement.[1]

The 1830s represented a turning point for African Americans in the abolition period since by then the gradual abolition law had produced a steady stream of free blacks who joined the children of the first generation of manumitted slaves to create a far larger and stronger free black community. In 1830, for example, roughly a quarter of Jersey blacks remained either slaves or slaves for a term with that number continuing to decline over the next two decades. Free blacks after 1830 more readily achieved economic success, lived independently, created their own schools and benevolent institutions, founded their own churches, and used all of them to combat white resistance to black equality. They simultaneously joined with the new radical abolition movement to reject the continuation of slavery and the continued graduated notions of abolition espoused by the colonization society.[2]

The growing influence of free blacks in New Jersey forced a legal change in their status, which made the 1830s a true tipping point toward freedom in the state. Although slavery still remained strong, the presence of a larger free black population caused the State Supreme Court to reverse itself in 1836. They found that blacks would no longer be considered prima facie slaves; freedom became African American's default legal category. The demographic and legal shift to freedom, however, exacerbated racial tensions and forced Jersey whites to draw even stronger lines of demarcation as white fears of black economic competition, miscegenation, and the general threat to the racial order culminated in a series of race riots that swept New Jersey and the rest of the North. Gradualism and a rejection of African American freedom, hallmarks of the abolition period's first twenty years, remained strong despite blacks' best efforts to establish their independence.

*   *   *

In the 1810s and 1820s, Newark's white residents became anxious over the growing presence of free blacks, a feeling that led them to use the state's 1798 Slave Code provision that prohibited free blacks from traveling across county lines without permission from at least two local judges to limit black population growth. Originally designed to enforce order in the state when the slave population had been near its height, Newark officials used it to adjudicate the black transition to freedom in the abolition period. For example, city officials called a meeting in 1812 "to adopt measures for the removal of free blacks not resident here and to prevent riots at night." This attempt by Newark's white leadership to slow the influx of blacks fed directly into gradual abolitionist and colonizationist beliefs that free blacks represented a clear and present societal danger. With both state and city officials restricting black community growth, many freed slaves either settled in sections of Newark away from its central core or left the state for New York or Philadelphia.[3]

By the 1830s, the regular demographic increase in population and the influx of thousands of new slaves for a term gaining freedom under the gradual abolition law tipped the scales, with their sheer numbers leading to the development of a much larger and stronger black community in Newark that whites could no longer restrict in the same ways. Jersey blacks had begun to form their own households and made a major leap forward in their transition to freedom. Instead of joining already established communities in New York or Philadelphia, free black communities grew in New Jersey, especially in Newark, the state's largest city. In 1830, roughly two-thirds of Newark's black population (427 freed persons) lived in 108 exclusively black households. With an average size of just under four members, these households became the bedrock of Newark's black community. Of course, as in New York City, the transition to free households came after a painful abolition process. After gradual abolition began in 1799, New York blacks increasingly moved from their former masters' homes to form their own households. By 1820, New York City achieved the ratio of free black households that it took New Jersey until 1830 to reach. New Jersey's slower pace was due in part to outward migration and delayed enactment of gradual abolition.[4]

These newly freed blacks, however, grouped their independent households in specific neighborhoods to solidify community bonds, create autonomous institutions such as churches and schools, and shelter themselves from prevalent white racism. The 1835 Newark City Directory indicates that most Newark black families (72 percent) lived in northeast Newark: north of Broad and east of Market; 16 percent lived north of Broad and west of Market (northwest quadrant) while the remaining 10 percent resided south of Broad. These neighborhoods were often tightly bounded; a group of fourteen families, for instance, lived in northeast Newark near the corner of High and Nesbit, while groups of two or three families remained standard throughout the city. Only six households stood isolated from at least one other black home. Though concentrated together, Jersey blacks, like those in New York and Philadelphia, lived in nonsegregated neighborhoods and routinely interacted with white neighbors. Most lived close to their houses of worship, which helped create social networks and space for blacks to communicate. The large concentration around the African Methodist Church at the corner of Academy and Plane Streets in northeast Newark bore close resemblance to Zion Methodist Church in New York's fifth ward. Twenty black households surrounded that Newark church and another nine encircled the Baptist Church on the corner of Academy and Halsey. As Newark grew over the next two decades, black households expanded beyond the northeast quadrant. By 1860, new clusters existed on the extreme east side, the southeast border along the Passaic River, and in northwest Newark.[5]

Those blacks who achieved independent living came by it through acquiring economic independence, something far more possible in the

1830s than before, and used it to attack the stereotype of black inferiority so prevalent among white colonizationists and other gradualists. Some who challenged the white hegemony of New Jersey's economy had assistance from their former owners. Benjamin Coe, for example, used his slave Cudjo as a substitute in the Revolution and afterward freed him and provided one acre of prime real estate in Newark. Men like Cudjo eventually controlled over seventy-five businesses in that city by the 1830s, including barber shops, carpentry businesses, and blacksmith workshops. These became stronger because their black customer base grew as more slaves achieved freedom, especially after 1830.[6]

Many more free blacks gained economic independence in the 1830s and used it to create vibrant communities around the state. For example, ex-slaves from across South Jersey migrated toward Middle Township in Cape May County to create a community of thirty-three black-headed households. Most of these (82 percent) held no land, likely living on rented land or as tenant farmers. However, six black households acquired rather large farms, averaging about seventy acres. Nero Amosen, the owner of a seventy-five-acre tract, even managed to pass it on to his descendants, and likely employed many of the nonlandowning blacks on his property.[7]

One of the most independent black settlements in the abolition period was on the Palisades just south of the New York border in Bergen County named Skunk Hollow. It was originally founded in 1806 to provide a "haven" for rural former enslaved field hands. At its height, Skunk Hollow had about seventy-five inhabitants, with the first lot owned by Jack Earnest who bought his freedom for a hundred dollars. According to Earnest, he gathered the money to buy the Skunk Hollow lot by "hard industry," which community members built on to create their own church, ministers, and economy that grew as more free blacks joined the settlement once the abolition period progressed. Similar South Jersey settlements, such as Timbuctoo and Gouldtown, allowed free blacks to develop apart from whites in the 1830s and became thriving centers of black life. However, Skunk Hollow existed primarily because of its ill-suited farmland; most was wooded and unproductive even when cleared. In this sense, "Skunk Hollow exemplifies a case of economically marginal land sold to socially marginal people." Even if Jersey blacks harnessed enough resources to buy land, it was usually located on the margins of acceptability. Like the nonlandowning farmers in Cape May, Skunk Hollow residents eked out a marginal existence unable to fully capitalize on their newfound legal freedom.[8]

Of course, economic prosperity ebbed and flowed for free blacks and even those who had used the skills gained or money accumulated in slavery to purchase real estate could quickly lose it through no fault of their own. One such New Jerseyan, Prince, the former slave of Joseph Hall of North Brunswick, gained his freedom in 1830 at age thirty-six and married Dinah, a former slave for a term, in 1834. Her mother, Flora, married Prince's father, Primus. The overlapping familial relationships motivated Prince to buy a house on Spring Street (adding an adjacent lot three years later) in New Brunswick, close to Halfpenny Town, a low-income racially mixed area near the Raritan River. Dinah died in 1838 and left her estate to her mother instead of Prince. Flora felt her daughter's will had granted her ownership of the house and, on her deathbed, she left it to her niece Theodosia who, with her husband, ejected Prince. Prince, lacking the resources to pursue legal action, an already difficult step in a white dominated judicial system, abandoned the house he had built after freedom. After years of neglect from Theodosia and her descendants, the house went into foreclosure in 1908. At that time, a judge ruled Flora's claim invalid and awarded the right to buy out the property to Prince. Since Prince had died in 1888, his daughter from his second marriage took ownership. Interestingly, the 1908 decision detailed Prince's wife Dinah's slave for a term status, claiming that her original owner "sold her as a slave" to a second owner until she came of age, which indicates that even in the twentieth century, New Jerseyans still believed that slaves for a term resembled slaves more than freed people.[9]

Although the black community in New Jersey boomed after 1830 in comparison to the 1810s and 1820s, not all blacks accumulated enough resources to create their own households and remained dependent to whites. A third of Newark's blacks in 1830 continued to live in white households, some to stay with their slave for a term children, while others used it as a transitional step toward freedom. Domestic service in Newark's white households helped blacks earn a living, though one that replicated their previous experience as slaves. Of Newark's white households that contained free blacks, 62 percent had only black women, which shows the centrality of domestic labor in a highly gendered postgradual abolition vision of free black life. White families routinely either hired these former slave women as live-in domestics or manumitted their slaves before hiring them to work in their households. For example, in 1870 the Wyckoff family of Readington mourned the death of 105-year-old Mat, their former slave who lived with them continuously since age six in 1771. Mat gain legal freedom but served her former master's family until her death after the Civil War. Black women therefore were more likely to fall under white jurisdiction, leaving them unable to fully participate in the creation of black communities and thereby slowing the creation of free black families, especially in the early abolition period.[10]

*   *   *

The larger free black population that developed by the 1830s complicated the legal link between color and slavery and forced a fundamental shift in state law; to balance the increased free population with the declining enslaved one, blacks were no longer to be considered prima facie slaves. In a case concerning slaves for a term, the state Supreme Court ruled that prima facie status "ought no longer to be admitted, both from the notorious fact that the generality of persons of this description in this State are not in truth held as slaves *now.*" The court recognized that African Americans lived in several gradations of unfreedom and that the law needed to delineate the sometimes confusing differences between them. The details of the case, however, illustrate that the court rejected prima facie status to protect whites who bought slaves for a term and slaves for life. The case involved an owner who did not clearly define his bound laborers' status at sale. The court contended that "the presumption that he [a fifteen-year-old black male] is subject to service till the age of twenty-five, is much stronger than that the aged man of color, is a slave." With this, the justices acknowledged that the various ages and legal statuses blacks held in New Jersey could complicate sales of bound laborers and mandated that owners of slaves for a term needed to, under "analogy to the law of chattels," specifically inform buyers of their laborers' exact legal status. The presumption of enslaved status based on skin color violated the "implied warranty" sellers needed to provide. In this particular case, the fifteen-year-old was, "in truth, an indented servant, bound to serve to the age of twenty-one years," while the buyer believed he had purchased "a special apprentice under our act of assembly," a slave for a term bound to age twenty-five.[11]

This 1836 decision began the process by which blacks became legally uncoupled from slavery, but recognized that slavery still played an important part in the later abolition period and affected how whites saw blacks. Even by 1840, Jersey whites remained slow to change their understanding of freedom and retained laws meant to regulate free blacks who lived in a still functioning slave system. In that year, antislavery advocate Thomas Booth criticized the legislature for failing to repeal the 1798 slave code that restricted slaves from testifying against whites, mandated a 10 p.m. curfew for free blacks, prohibited "disorderly" conduct by both slaves and free blacks, and barred free blacks from owning firearms and begging in public. Even though the 1836 decision acknowledged that the convoluted abolition process had clouded definitions of slavery and freedom, whites continued to see an equivalency between blacks and slavery through the 1840s.[12]

Blacks recognized that whites continued to associate them with slavery when, in 1837, the Colored American complained that New Jersey law "savors too much of the dark ages" and "degrade[d] her colored population to a level with the brutes" by requiring free blacks residing in or traveling through New Jersey to carry freedom papers. The Colored American's editors complained that New York blacks, "who were never in bondage," had no freedom papers to produce. As opposed to New York's more liberal laws regarding blacks, New Jersey's ex-slaves lived in a world where slavery largely remained the normative state of black residents.[13]

Despite the slow change in white perceptions of blacks, the formation of independent households, acquisition of property, and the achievement of at least some economic advancement allowed Jersey blacks to form their own institutions and fight for greater political, social, and economic rights in the face of colonization and slavery. Social spaces in which to communicate became incredibly important. By 1830, as northern whites expressed animosity toward Pinkster and Negro Militia Days because they believed the celebrations exhibited the "depraved nature" of blacks, elite blacks ended these festivals and instead used public celebrations and parades to tout blacks' suitability for citizenship. Likewise, blacks found new social spaces outside the public spotlight. Sylvia Du Bois, for example, opened the only black nightclub in Somerset County as a space for both free and enslaved blacks to congregate. Some whites also frequented the club, which became "an interracial milieu where cockfights, fox chases, prizefights, and prostitution took place."[14]

In addition to private spaces like Du Bois's nightclub and public parades, the church became the main focal point for ex-slaves' social, political, and economic lives. As in the South, where blacks and whites sought to make a world together, New Jerseyans used the church to establish their place in society. Whites and blacks attended the same churches in New Jersey but many declined to open their doors freely to ex-slaves or change their historic treatment of blacks. For example, between 1804 and 1818, New Jersey's Hanover Presbyterian Church admitted only three free blacks while it admitted three times as many enslaved members. Likewise, Stone House Plains Dutch Reformed Church admitted only three free blacks from 1804 to 1850. The free blacks and slaves who attended these white dominated churches suffered discrimination; sitting in segregated balconies and pews served as constant reminders of their inferior status. In Alexander Macwhorter's First Presbyterian Church of Newark, African Americans sat on the windowsills instead of the pews while blacks in Lamington Presbyterian Church in Bedminster used a segregated balcony and were buried in a separate cemetery.[15]

Even as the free black population grew in the 1820s, churches continued to group both free and enslaved in the same membership category. The Dutch Reformed Church in Rockaway admitted Martha, the slave of George Wyckoff, and several other local slaves to church membership along with several free blacks and recorded all on a separate mixed roster, as had Hanover Presbyterian. These hybrid communities grew over time as new members joined and slave members gained freedom. For example, at least four free blacks joined the Reformed Dutch Church in Middlebush in the 1830s after they had gained their freedom from church members but remained on a segregated church roll.[16]

A few churches bucked tradition and took integration further, adopting regulations that ensured that church justice operated equally across the color line, though this was certainly not common. Scotch Plains Baptist in Essex County routinely admitted black members and responded equitably toward claims against them. In 1816, for instance, a church committee investigated member Aaron Ball, Jr.'s suspected abusive treatment of his slave for a term, who attended church frequently, while in 1818 they gave a fair hearing to "our colored brother Thomas Ell in regard to some reports against him" and acquitted him of any misconduct. Similarly, an argument between two free black members, Peggy and Hannah, ended after church leaders helped them resolve their differences amicably.[17]

Active black engagement in many white churches waned in the 1820s and 1830s when the state's larger population of free blacks recognized that they no longer needed to worship as second-class members. Since most of these white dominated churches lacked black input and basic equality in services and church governance, former slaves created their own churches, which "symbolize[d] a new, more combative style of self-assertion" within the abolition period. As the *Colored American* illustrated, freed blacks starved "for the breadth of life . . . no one cares for their souls . . ." even in white churches because blacks "are not allowed equal privileges in the said to be, God's houses, nor at his table." In Morristown, for instance, "three hundred poor, outcast, oppressed colored people" could not "worship God in the houses that their sweat and blood has helped to build," a problem that motivated change.[18]

Beginning in the 1820s, Jersey free blacks formed their own churches and used them to serve their community's spiritual as well as temporal needs. In 1822, Christopher Rush, a black Methodist, created Newark's first black church on Academy Street. This church, the predecessor to St. John's Methodist and later Clinton Memorial African Methodist Episcopal Zion Church, drew free blacks away from white churches and by the 1830s had become a hotbed of antislavery activity.[19] On August 1, 1838, for instance, Samuel Ward, future agent for the Anti-Slavery Society of Canada, spoke to the congregation on the importance of celebrating abolition in the British Empire. A former slave who had fled to New Jersey from the South, he used the church to commemorate Emancipation Day in the British West Indies.[20] Rites of August celebrations applauded the enactment of abolition in the British Caribbean and spurred hope for a better future for enslaved blacks in New Jersey. These celebrations grew in the 1840s and 1850s in the Mid-Atlantic and New England and brought together Jersey blacks and white abolitionists. The interracial celebrations soon became a fixture each summer and by the eve of the Civil War had spread throughout the North. Black elites like Frederick Douglass used them to link free blacks in the North to discussions of slavery internationally. Rather than celebrate July 4, the day gradual abolition began, blacks in New Jersey chose to celebrate the end of slavery in the British Empire in their own churches in order to link themselves to a society that had embraced immediate abolition, something Jersey whites had consistently refused to do.[21]

The trend Rush began in the early 1820s continued so that by the early 1830s, other blacks who had worshipped in the balconies and windowsills rejected continued white control of their religious lives and created their own churches. Yearning for more active participation in services and a central role in the church itself, African American members withdrew from First Presbyterian of Newark in 1831 and established the African Presbyterian Church on Plane Street not far from Rush's church.[22] This black

exodus from white controlled churches mirrored the situation in Philadelphia, where Richard Allen and Absalom Jones led black congregants out of
St. George's Methodist Church when whites enforced segregated worship.
Allen's formation of his own church, Mother Bethel in 1794, began what
would become the African Methodist Episcopal (AME) Church. Allen officially formed the AME Church in 1816 with blacks from across the Mid-
Atlantic. Representatives from Salem, New Jersey, attended the first general
meeting on April 9, 1816, and began the process that spread it throughout
South Jersey and eventually into more heavily populated North Jersey. The
most well-known New Jersey AME member, Jarena Lee, became the
denomination's first female minister. Born in Cape May County, Lee began
her career as an itinerant preacher traveling throughout the North, just as
Allen had done early in his career. These black-controlled churches became
integral in the development of state's free communities and eventually
assisted escaped southern slaves transit through New Jersey.[23]

* * *

The growing numbers of free blacks necessitated the development of educational institutions to ensure their success in freedom and forced African
Americans to take control of their own education from paternalistic whites
who had organized it since abolition had begun. The state, seeing that white
churches and benevolent organizations had taken the lead in black education in the 1810s and 1820s, did little to advance it, even though some
legislators tried to promote the instruction of poor white and African
American children, a plan that failed when fiscal conservatives diverted the
earmarked funds in 1829. However, Newark had already begun to make
taxpayer funded contributions to schools for poor children. Educating
forty-five black and white children in 1813, the school on Market Street
provided education to only a handful of African Americans due to its limited size. Children competed against each other to gain a "charity scholar"
spot on the school's roster. But, when government-run common schools
opened in greater numbers in New Jersey in the 1830s, they refused admit-
tance to black students and caused dissention within the black community.
One writer to the *Colored American* decried how his thirteen-year-old son
could not attend public schools even though they were citizens of New
Jersey and paid taxes. In a similar vein, harkening back to the revolutionary
cry of "no taxation without representation," a Morristown free black man

who paid taxes on his house and eighteen acres of land in 1841 never had "been allowed to vote, nor even to send his children to the public school."[24] Without a strong government interest in financing black education, real change in the education system came only when African Americans gained control over their own schools and altered the tenor of education policy.[25]

The larger free black population allowed elite African Americans to grab the reigns of education, form their own schools, and transition away from a curriculum designed to "civilize." In 1828, one of the first black-controlled schools opened in Newark, surprisingly with some local taxpayer support. The use of public funds by a school with black administrators, however, created tension within the city. Newark's *Centinel of Freedom* reported that whites argued for continued control over black education by claiming that ex-slaves never took "a deep interest in the education of their children." Instead, "they are . . . very lax on the subject" and should attend schools "organized . . . by . . . a committee of white people."[26] Using this logic, whites shifted blame for the failure of African American education to the black community by underlining their "lax" demeanor. Free blacks did not heed this white advice and elected an all-black committee to oversee the school in 1830 who felt that "nothing was more essential to the well-being of their race than education." This shift signified the more active role that elite blacks took in providing education to fellow freed people in order to try to carve out a base of power in an otherwise white world. They rejected the proposition that blacks were either lax or needed morality driven education, believing that ex-slaves and young free blacks required a rigorous education to compete in the marketplace.[27]

Black-controlled schools opened not only in Newark but across the state with African American educators at the helm, though these new positions of authority caused class friction to develop with the community. Some started in basements, like the Colored School in the cellar of the African Presbyterian Church in Newark, while others followed the private school model and opened in New Brunswick, Princeton, and Perth Amboy. Likewise, a partially municipal supported black school administered by Elymas Rogers, the future pastor of the African Presbyterian Church in Newark, taught spelling, reading, writing, geography, and arithmetic to students in Trenton in the 1840s.[28] This school became embroiled in conflict when parishioners of Trenton's only black church, who had donated money to build the school, clashed with the larger black community who objected to the school's continued relationship with the church. They brought the matter to court and expended enough money "at law to have built a new school house and to have supported a well-trained and qualified teacher." Both a generational and class conflict developed between the older church-appointed elite board of trustees and the younger less affluent community members who objected to the status quo. The community infighting regressed some of the progress made in the previous twenty years and, as some Newark blacks wrote, relegated the community's children "to ignorance, to misery, to degradation" instead of an education. However, the infighting shows that Jersey blacks had created a community large and complex enough that class stratifications had developed, something never before seen in New Jersey.[29]

These social stratifications resulted from black economic success in the abolition period, due in part to education and their reliance on mutual aid societies to provide security for their members in an otherwise tumultuous economic environment. These organizations grew in the 1830s and allowed blacks to bargain collectively and pool resources to provide economic and technical assistance. The records of only two New Jersey black benevolent associations survive. The first, the Agricultural and Mechanic Association of Pennsylvania and New Jersey, formed in 1839, encouraged education and engagement with "useful trades" in Philadelphia, Trenton, and Burlington.[30] The second, the United Sons of Salem Benevolent Society of the Free Sons of Ethiopia, also formed in 1839, attracted elite blacks due to its high thirty-dollar specie initiation fee and primarily provided its members with disability and burial insurance. Sick or disabled members received $2.50 weekly and the society allowed a $12 funeral benefit, a $1 monthly stipend for widows, and paid clothing and education costs to children of deceased members for up to five months.[31]

These mutual aid societies, along with churches and schools, allowed black New Jerseyans to organize conventions designed to articulate demands for equal rights and equal access to state and national institutions in the 1830s and 1840s. New Jersey blacks took part in this first civil rights movement from its inception in 1831. Delegates from Pennsylvania, New York, Virginia, Maryland, and Delaware joined a New Jersey delegation in Philadelphia to overwhelmingly reject the "operations and misrepresentations of the American Colonization Society" and called on "Christians of every denomination firmly to resist" its mission. The convention argued that the ACS "perpetuate[d] slavery with all its unchristian like concomitants in this boasted land of freedom" and claimed they would rather "die at home" than travel to Africa.[32]

This 1831 convention took place in the context of a much wider move against African American political rights, especially in neighboring Pennsylvania. In 1832, a second convention meeting met in that city in response to the Pennsylvania constitutional convention's repeal of black voting rights. Convention delegates called on the memory of the Abolition Act of 1780 to argue that the "freeman" cited in the state constitution was the same as the "freeman" in the abolition act. Although this convention failed to stop the voting restriction, the idea that the convention movement would advocate for increased political freedoms, especially the right to vote, became ingrained in the minds of northern blacks. Additionally, the convention movement also stressed that freed blacks had a responsibility to work for abolition in New Jersey and the nation.[33]

This recognition by free blacks that they needed to battle against the continuing presence of slavery in New Jersey while advocating for free people's rights and the race's separation from its association with slavery led Paterson's black citizens to call attention to the "the disabilities, privations, and sufferings under which the colored population of our state labor" in 1841. These petitioners to the legislature believed that the 21,631 New Jersey blacks were "the number of human beings . . . who are deprived of those equal laws." They discussed the continuation of slavery at length and argued that "we cannot conceive of a reason either legal, moral, or physical, why young people of African descent should not be" free at birth. They decried gradual abolition because it provided no effective education to slaves for a term and continued their parents in bondage. However, they advocated for slavery's abolishment not solely because of the degradation it caused the enslaved, but because the institution influenced "the unjust prejudice which exists in the white population against" all blacks. Transitioning to a discussion of free black rights, the petitioners believed that the state did not follow the "watchword of our revolutionary fathers, 'no taxation without representation,'" because it routinely taxed black residents while barring them from voting. Furthermore, they complained that the 1798 slave law specifically prevented free blacks from traveling without passes in the state even in the 1840s, which further reminded free blacks of their former enslaved life.[34]

By the late 1830s, free black New Jerseyans fought for suffrage above all else, believing it would allow them to more easily advance on other fronts. An 1839 obituary for a prominent black revolutionary leader had decried how "in the Republican State of New Jersey" blacks "were oppressed and proscribed out of all their civil rights and privileges," which led to the creation of multiple committees designed to pressure whites for the vote.[35] Black leaders in Newark organized through the churches and in January 1841 petitioned the legislature to extend the right to vote to all African American men. These leaders worked with larger regional actors like Samuel Cornish, to better advocate for suffrage.[36] New York blacks even singled out "the brethren of Delaware and New Jersey" who argued that the leadership in those states had, through their inaction, "made themselves politically of as little consequence as the poor colored people . . . politicians fear and care as little about them."[37]

The convention movement in the 1840s reinvigorated the push for voting rights and provided an organized framework to fight for them. In an 1849 convention, for instance, they argued that a petition drive should be started with separate petitions for white and black citizens to show the legislature the overwhelming support from both races for the black vote. The petition itself argued that blacks possessed certain natural and inalienable rights, including the power to participate politically. Ending the petition, the delegates wrote, "we verily believe that the day is not far distant when New Jersey shall be hailed as the first consistent reformer of human rights in the Western World," a statement that challenged New Jersey to be something they had not been for the last fifty years, a haven for black freedom.[38]

A much longer version of the 1849 petition, published in the abolitionist newspaper the *North Star*, appeared in April that year and brought national attention to the issue. Convention organizers designed a lecture circuit through New Jersey to "stir up the state on the subject" and argued that blacks deserve the vote because they "are taxed in common and equally with other citizens" and "are native born citizens." They believed that it was not only unconstitutional to tax black citizens without representation but "contrary to the genius and prosperity of any republican country." In their rejection of what the ACS and other whites had espoused for the past three decades, the convention claimed that the race had made "rapid improvements in moral, intellectual, and political science" in comparison to other laboring New Jerseyans. These same points had been brought up before, by a delegation of black Newark residents organized by the AME church, who advocated suffrage in 1841. In both cases, the legislature refused to change the 1807 law that disenfranchised African American voters. Voting for black New Jerseyans would not be reinstated until 1870, when the Fifteenth Amendment allowed Perth Amboy resident and former slave Thomas Peterson-Mundy to vote in a special election in that city on March 31, 1870.[39]

*   *   *

The increase in black economic and social status, the legal uncoupling of free blacks from prima facie slavery, and their fight for increased political rights exacerbated racial tensions within the state as the growing number of free blacks angered white working-class New Jerseyans who saw unbound black workers as an economic threat. In the 1830s, this threat became much more real to whites as freed blacks took more unskilled jobs in urban areas like Newark. This fear grew across the Mid-Atlantic, most notably in Philadelphia where broadsides appeared depicting white laborers working under orders from black supervisors, the possible result of this economic competition. Racial animosities emanating from black workers' enslaved past separated whites and blacks from similar class backgrounds. These racial boundaries limited class alliances and increasingly created tension between them as blacks, through their own communities, fought for increased political and legal rights that further separated them from the white underclass.[40]

Distress over economic competition joined anxiety produced by the anti-abolition movement of the 1830s that played on white working-class fears of an uncontrolled black population. Nat Turner's rebellion in Virginia highlighted the dangers of uncontrolled blacks and excited rumors of how abolition would flood the North with southern fugitives. Negrophobia ran rampant as journalists spread tales of abolitionist support for racial amalgamation. The sexual intermixing of white and black also appeared more dangerous than it had earlier as New Jersey's black population became increasingly unconstrained by slavery. In addition, white New Jerseyans began to lose the ability to contrast themselves with the enslaved to measure their own relative freedom, precipitating an even more tension-ridden relationship between the races.[41]

The anxieties over increased black economic competition and status exploded in a series of race riots in the 1830s and 1840s across the North, with the largest in New Jersey occurring in Newark in the summer of 1834. Its spark came from the pastor of the Fourth Presbyterian Church of Newark who, on a Friday evening in July, announced he would deliver a sermon

Figure 8. "The Results of Abolitionism!" represented white anxiety over increased economic competition with the growing free black population in the 1830s. Across the Mid-Atlantic, race riots broke out because of this tension-ridden relationship between the races.

Courtesy of the Library Company of Philadelphia.

on "the Sin of Slavery." Fearful of a riot similar to one that had occurred in
New York earlier that year, several Newark citizens urged Reverend William
Weeks to cancel the service. Weeks rejected these calls and walked to the
pulpit the evening of the sermon in front of a large crowd of parishioners
and white residents, accompanied by an unidentified black man who took
a seat next to him on the altar. The presence of an African American sitting
in front of the church during an abolitionist sermon excited a number of
whites to charge the altar, seize the black man, and confine him in the town
jail for the evening.[42]

At the same time, a mob of between two and three thousand that had
assembled outside the church proceeded to smash its windows, destroy the
pulpit, and break the majority of the pews while Weeks and his wife narrowly escaped. The mob followed them to their home, but not finding him
there, returned to the church to destroy the last four windows and the
remaining pews. Violence quickly spread to other areas of Newark where
white mobs targeted free black businesses. For instance, the *New York
Gazette* reported that a mob forced its way into a black barber shop and
ransacked it before civil authorities dispersed them. The riot had been
motivated by, as Rev. Weeks would write the following week, the fear of
"the amalgamation of colors" produced by white fears stoked by the growing abolition movement and the simultaneous increase in the free black
population. Weeks, however, assured his fellow Newark residents that he
did not advocate amalgamation and instead believed "that God, in making
races of different colors, has sufficiently indicated the duty to us of keeping
them separate and of allowing no intermarriages between them."[43]

Mob action against amalgamation, abolition, and competition continued in the 1830s and 1840s in other parts of the Mid-Atlantic as concerns
over losing control of society to black domination increased white fears of
the expanding black population. For example, in South Jersey, Philadelphia
Presbyterian minister J. M. McKim, who also served as a reporter for a
Philadelphia abolitionist newspaper, reported being attacked by an angry
white mob. A similar mob overran a black camp meeting in Gloucester
County.[44] In neighboring Pennsylvania another riot rocked Philadelphia in
1834. Medical student Harry Horton reported that the mob "have shown
themselves most excellent at braking (sic) windows" and that "the coloured
people about the lower part of the city are at present in a dreadful fright."[45]
That same year in Columbia, Pennsylvania, just west of Lancaster, mobs
"collected in different parts of the town particularly in the vicinity of the

colored people." After an Irishman was assaulted, presumably by a black neighbor, white men "ran through the town crying the blacks had risen and murdered two white men," which then mobilized dozens more to rally with their guns to the town's black neighborhoods. After they destroyed several freed black homes, police dispersed the crowd, but the injured Irishman swore that he would "raise 500 of his countryman and destroy the blacks with their houses." Four years later, in 1838, the burning of Philadelphia's recently completed Pennsylvania Hall likewise illustrated the threat that discussions of slavery and civil rights had on white liberty. The white mob that burned the hall assumed that the immediate and gradual abolitionists who had built it supported racial equality and therefore wanted to silence such discussions before they began.[46]

The anxiety created by scenes like those in Philadelphia, Columbia, and Newark excited white New Jerseyans, encouraged them to see blacks as a dangerous group within society, and manifested pent-up fears and animosities. Although members of the mob likely engaged in violence for several reasons, fears of economic competition, the dangers of a wholly free society infused with radical abolitionist rhetoric, and frightening rumors of racial amalgamation all worked to give voice to whites who believed themselves disenfranchised at the expense of a free class of blacks. Therefore, despite the 1830s being a tipping point toward freedom, resistance among whites to that freedom remained strong.

*   *   *

Even amid a continuing racism in antebellum New Jersey, free blacks had by the 1830s created a community for themselves, which they used to fight for greater political and economic power. This free black community helped propel a transition in the 1830s. Freedom became blacks' normative legal status, independent black community organizations became dominant in African American life, and changing demographics allowed free blacks to distance themselves from slavery in a meaningful way for the first time. Slavery's slow death, however, delayed the transition to a fully free state; free blacks always lived in slavery's shadow. Many Jersey blacks could never move out of poverty because most had few marketable job skills and little to show for decades of work as slaves or as slaves for a term. Black communities therefore advocated for greater political rights and formed schools, churches, and benevolent organizations to help themselves.

The transition to independent housing and economies spurred increased white racism and violence, which manifested itself in the race riots of the 1830s and 1840s when abolitionist threats, fears of racial mixing, and the dangers of economic competition combined at the same moment large numbers of slaves for a term became free in New Jersey. This expression of anti-black feelings appealed to those whites who had never abandoned the gradualist philosophy in race relations. This gradualism continued to be promoted by the increasingly popular colonization movement, which articulated negative black stereotypes and ideologies across the state. In the end, the gradualism and accompanying racism present since the abolition movement in the early 1800s continued to restrict African American freedom and communicated white fears of black autonomy despite blacks' best efforts.

CHAPTER NINE

Debating Slavery's End

After gradual abolition's passage in 1804, former New Jersey abolition society member and Quaker William Newbold was one of the few whites who believed slavery remained a major issue in the state. Writing to his brother in 1823, he claimed that "slavery as it now exists amongst us, politically demands that something should be done. Morality and philanthropy echoes to the call and asks for an amelioration and final extinction." Newbold suggested that they "form an association . . . to embrace the willing minded" and engage in the "gradual and final emancipation of slaves . . . upon moderate and rational principles with the free consent of their holders." This association became a reality in the 1830s, with an important difference: it advanced immediate instead of gradual abolition. This renewed abolitionist spirit worked together with the more powerful and larger free black community in the 1830s to fundamentally change African American freedom in New Jersey. Alongside white allies again, the state's free black population warred against slavery's persistence and forced the larger white community to reconsider slavery's continued life in the state.[1]

Two issues in the later antebellum period forced Jersey whites to reconsider slavery's slow death: abolitionism and fugitive slaves. First, the rebirth of abolitionism in New Jersey (and its shift to immediacy) gave whites and blacks an organized way to advocate for black freedom, one missing since the first abolition movement folded in the early 1810s. New Jersey therefore saw a relatively clean break between the abolitionism of the 1790s and that of the 1830s in a way that other northern states did not. Second, and most important, New Jersey's geographic position on the South's northern border forced it to deal with a rising number of fugitive slaves in the 1830s and 1840s. This constant engagement with southern fugitives reignited the debate about slavery's continuation in New Jersey.[2]

The issues associated with fugitive slaves exacerbated white fears of the collapse of law and order—that southern slave catchers could violate their rights, invade their homes, and even kidnap their family members. This fear brought slavery to the forefront of statewide conversations, a place it had not occupied for decades. Jersey abolitionists latched onto these white fears and turned the conversation into one about the need to end slavery in their own state. Therefore, the actions of southern fugitives opened the door for two distinct conversations: one on fugitive protections and the other on the status of the approximately 3,000 Jersey slaves and slaves for a term living in the mid-1840s. Despite their best efforts, abolitionists never convinced the general public to support immediate freedom for New Jersey's bound blacks nor advanced significant protections for fugitive slaves. Nonetheless, the constant engagement with fugitives prevented New Jerseyans from forgetting their own domestic involvement with slavery and reinforced the state's measured approach to abolition. Jersey politicians routinely referred to their slave past in discussing southern fugitives, causing the state's own ongoing relationship with slavery to influence sectional issues.[3]

The slow legal recognition that all blacks were no longer prima facie slaves, the delineation of citizenship by race and sex, a weak personal liberty law, and a sustained trade in Jersey-born slaves and slaves for a term all contributed to the continued persistence of slavery in New Jersey. Indeed, Jersey slaveholders still found slavery and bound labor important as the sectional crisis unfolded. This made New Jerseyans markedly different from New Englanders, who hoped to disown their slave past and create an imagined North free of slavery in contrast to an enslaved South. New Jersey's border position with the South forced white New Jerseyans to constantly engage with the institution, making it difficult to forget. Additionally, New Jerseyans continued to see the institution in their own backyards since about one in ten African Americans remained slaves and roughly a quarter of the state's total black population were either slaves or slaves for a term in 1830. The failure to forget slavery, combined with a rather conservative and unpopular abolition movement, caused white New Jerseyans to express little interest in crafting new societal roles for antebellum blacks.[4]

The conversations brought about by southern fugitives and resulting debates inside and outside the courtroom, however, allowed white and black abolitionists to address slavery in New Jersey directly. It led legislators to finally abolish slavery in 1846, but influenced the course of that abolition;

gradualist approaches based on past experiences with abolitionism survived. Instead of freeing all bound blacks, the legislature abolished the legal
term "slave" and reclassified all former slaves as "apprentices for life." They
forced slaves for a term to continue serving their masters in order to maintain racial balance and secure slaveholder property rights. This outcome
challenges the rather simplistic notion that slavery was easily vanquished in
societies with slaves or those in transition to free societies. It also disputes
the contention that a monolithic "free" North stood in opposition to a
"slave" South and shows that northerners understood slavery and freedom
on a much more complicated continuum, rather than as polar opposites.[5]

*   *   *

In the late 1810s, the national debate on fugitive slaves' rights to jury trials
aroused the anger of many southerners since, as discussed in Chapter 6,
these debates forced the idea of personal liberty to the forefront of many
white northern minds. Northern states struggled with how to defend
against unwanted incursions into their territory while fulfilling their constitutional responsibility to return slave property to southern owners. Until
the 1820s, most states enforced the 1793 Federal Fugitive Slave Law, which
mandated that slave owners could bring fugitive slaves before a local judge
to gain permission to extradite them. Since all three Mid-Atlantic States
made various accommodations with their own slaveholders to protect
property rights through their gradual abolition programs, personal liberty
activists confronted a system that privileged the testimony of slaveholders
and minimized the ability of the enslaved to defend themselves. This debate
led to Pennsylvania's 1826 law, which increased oversight of slave catchers
and allowed suspected fugitives to defend themselves in court. New Jersey
passed a similar personal liberty law that same year, which required slave
catchers to apply for warrants from state judges for county sheriffs to arrest
alleged fugitives in New Jersey. The hope was that by involving the legal
system earlier, the 1826 New Jersey personal liberty law would provide
additional protections to Jersey blacks.[6]

The sustained demand for slaves in the Deep South increased the vigor
of the internal slave trade from the Upper South, enlarged the number of
runaways who fled to New Jersey to escape sale southward, and highlighted
the tensions over personal liberty on slavery's border. Whig representative
John Van Dyke of New Brunswick emphasized the state's border position

when he pontificated in an 1850 speech before the House that he was "not precisely certain whether I should class the State from which I come among the Northern or Southern. If that magic line, of which we hear so much, known as Mason and Dixon's line, should run straight through to the Atlantic, it will cut our state directly in two, leaving a part of it on each side of the line." Van Dyke claimed that South Jersey lay "on the same parallel with the District of Columbia" and that Maryland, a state that claimed "to be purely southern," was actually above that line.[7] Because of New Jersey's border position, the Underground Railroad grew as conductors shepherded fugitive slaves along almost exactly the same route as the modern day New Jersey Turnpike, from the southwest coast northeast toward New York City. This well-trodden road allowed Quakers and free blacks in South Jersey to interact frequently with escaping slaves. In addition to a large Quaker presence, the southwestern counties possessed a considerable free black population that had created several small independent communities, such as Gouldtown and Springtown in Cumberland County. AME churches in Springtown, Swedesboro, Gloucester, and Mount Zion all provided refuge to escapees while their congregations networked with AME Churches in Philadelphia and New York to find them other safe havens.[8]

Samuel Ringgold Ward, a fugitive from Maryland who made his escape through Springtown in the 1820s and later became an influential AME minister in New York, wrote in his 1855 narrative that he and his family knew that "New Jersey had not entirely ceased to be a slave state." Ward's family understood the dangers of moving to a place that still had slavery and might be hostile to African Americans, but crossed the Delaware River at Greenwich in Cumberland County where, as Greenwich native Bessie Ayres Andrews remembered, slaves frequently began their journey to New York. Andrews recalled that most slaves came to Greenwich from Dover, Delaware, while lookouts on "boats with colored lights" stood watch for slave patrols. Some escapees were taken to Swedesboro and Mount Holly while others "were hidden for days in the colored settlement at Springtown." In Springtown, Ward's family found a sizeable black population alongside friendly Quakers and no Jersey slaveholders.[9]

Unlike those who evaded slave catchers on the Underground Railroad, New Jersey routinely entertained southerners who successfully recaptured their slaves and found whites willing to assist them. For example, John Cooper of Queen Anne's County, Maryland, found his slave Nancy and her three children, all born in New Jersey, living with her free husband in

Figure 9. Many slaves crossed the Delaware Bay to southern New Jersey to begin
their escape to freedom. From William Still, *The Underground Railroad*.
Courtesy of the New York Public Library.

Burlington in 1835. She had run to New Jersey at age fifteen in 1824 and
managed to avoid recapture for eleven years before her master requested
her extradition. Cooper claimed that since Nancy had entered New Jersey
without his permission he retained ownership of all three of her children
even though they had been born under the tenets of the gradual abolition
law. The Burlington judge agreed with Cooper and sent Nancy and her
three children back to Maryland, declining to extend gradual abolition to
fugitives; Jersey whites would not allow their laws to alter the institution in
other states.[10] In the same manner, Gloucester County constable Isaiah Dill
brought Samuel and Louisa, alleged fugitives of Robert Hardcastle of Maryland, to judge John Cowperthwait in 1833. Hardcastle's son, Aaron, testified that he had known both since infancy, but they had escaped in the
spring of 1832. Samuel and Louisa's attorney introduced only one witness,
John Wood, who claimed that the pair worked for him but that he had no
knowledge of their legal status. With no additional avenues of defense,
Samuel and Louisa were declared slaves and sent south.[11]

Though most white New Jerseyans supported the rule of law and therefore the return of fugitive slaves to the South, they vehemently opposed any
attempt by slave catchers to circumvent the law, extend slavery, or enslave

those who were not fugitives. Severn Martin, born in Virginia in 1785, was one such former slave that New Jerseyans rallied around to prevent his former master from illegally taking him south. Martin had worked as a foreman on a tobacco plantation in Northampton County when his mistress died and willed him to her grandson, who promised Martin freedom at his death. When that master died, the estate's executors did not recognize that freedom and sold Martin to William Christian, another Northampton planter. Martin decided to escape after two years of the most abusive treatment of his life under Christian. After a brief stay in New York City, Martin moved to Slab Town, about five miles from Burlington, where he worked as a day laborer for a little over a year. He saved enough money to buy a one-acre plot with a house, married a free black woman from Burlington, and started a new life. That life was cut short in 1836 when the sheriff arrested Martin near his home after a free black co-worker exposed Martin's fugitive status for a fifty-dollar reward.[12]

Martin's fugitive trial provoked a massive uprising among local blacks and whites who, after a local judge ordered Martin's removal to Virginia, gathered to prevent him from being loaded onto a steamboat headed for Philadelphia. Remaining nonviolent, the 500+ person mob failed to stop Martin's transfer and dispersed after Burlington's mayor persuaded them to return to their homes. However, the protesters and Martin's Quaker neighbors supported him by raising eight hundred dollars to purchase his freedom. More important, though, they researched Martin's past and arranged for the legislature to pass a law in 1837 that confirmed his freedom. Martin had previously bought himself but due to an error that recorded his name as "Seborn Martin," his legal status remained in jeopardy. The law affirmed his freedom and showed that Jersey whites and blacks, even as they saw slavery continue in their own communities, actively opposed the work of villainous slave catchers who perverted the legal system to kidnap truly free blacks.[13]

Cases before Severn Martin's had encouraged white New Jerseyans to advocate for additional protections for blacks and by the mid-1830s, Mid-Atlantic whites increasingly demanded that states provide jury trials for alleged fugitives. New Jerseyans saw this debate unfold across the river in New York in 1834 when Elizur Wright published his *Chronicles of Kidnapping*, which challenged how the New York fugitive slave law operated and demanded greater oversight and accountability in fugitive slave cases. Three years later, Alvan Stewart, president of the New York Anti-Slavery Society, advocated that the Fifth Amendment required that fugitives be granted tri-als to ensure due process of law, an argument that precipitated a petition drive. Even the abolitionist standard, *The Emancipator*, demanded in 1838 that it was "IMPERATIVE that every question of personal freedom shall be settled by a JURY."[14]

In a shrewd propaganda move, abolitionists latched onto these argu-ments and the widespread anxiety over slave catchers' presence in the state, popularizing the notion that the Lower North was under attack. These abo-litionists used supposed southern disregard for state law to encourage what historian Stanley Harrold describes as "sectional antagonism," the frighten-ing of whites into thinking that slave catchers disrupted law and order. One newspaper article described how in December 1836 in Salem, "five or six men with drawn pistols but no search warrant" broke into a local Quaker's home in search of a suspected fugitive. It asked its readers if "a set of kidnapping marauders be suffered thus to trespass upon quiet unoffending citizens . . . or is our lot cast in a region where lawless freebooters and midnight prowlers are the sovereigns of the country who may violate the sanctity of our private dwellings to carry men and women into southern bondage?" Many Jersey whites, fearful of being assaulted, began to see the unregulated activities of slave catchers as dangerous and opposed to upholding order on slavery's border.[15]

Fugitives' presence reopened debates over personal liberty and culmi-nated in a landmark 1836 New Jersey Supreme Court case that mandated jury trials for suspected fugitives. Alexander Helmsly, also known as Nathan Mead, stood at the center of the case. He fled from Maryland to New Jersey, which he described, in contrast to Samuel Ward, as a place where the "peo-ple were free and nobody would disturb me" ensuring him "a state of liberty for the mind." He worked for about nine years in Evesham and Northampton where he married Nancy Helmsley and had three children. After a group of slave catchers discovered his status in October 1836, the sheriff arrested him. Pennsylvania Abolition Society lawyers defended him in front of Judge George Haywood, who Helmsly described as Virginia-born and "like the handle of a jug, all on one side and that side against me." Three whites and four blacks all testified that Helmsly lived free in Burlington County, although it is unclear if any of these witnesses knew that Helmsly was actually a fugitive, something he later admitted to in his own narrative. Their testimony allowed his defense team to rebut the four whites who affirmed his slave status.[16]

Despite the support of locals, Judge Haywood ruled against Helmsly and ordered him returned to Maryland. In some complicated legal maneuvering, Helmsly's lawyers appealed to the state Supreme Court where they argued against the constitutionality of New Jersey's 1826 personal liberty law on the basis that it did not ensure due process. Represented by William Halstead, former reporter for the New Jersey Supreme Court and current Newark mayor and former U.S. senator Theodore Frelinghuysen, chief justice Joseph Hornblower, a colonizationist who supported gradual abolition, heard the case in 1836. Hornblower ruled in *State v. The Sheriff of Burlington* that a single judge could not decide the question of a man's freedom alone. Hornblower linked Helmsly's case to the court's decision earlier that year that overturned the requirement that blacks must affirmatively prove their free status; blacks were no longer prima facie slaves. Hornblower argued that the state constitution guaranteed both Jersey born slaves and fugitives certain due process rights. As a question of fact, the identity of a fugitive slave and the decision to remove him or her into a state of slavery had to be decided by a jury, less a freeman be "separated forcibly and forever from his wife and children" or be "permitted to enjoy with them the liberty he inherited and the property he has earned."[17]

Although he was careful to not rule that the 1793 Federal Fugitive Slave Law was unconstitutional, the Hornblower decision remade the idea of personal liberty and, coupled with the rejection of African Americans' prima facie status that same year, indicated that the position of Jersey blacks was slowly changing. The growth of abolitionism and the increasing threat of attack from the South had challenged white New Jerseyans to see the necessity for state involvement in fugitive recoveries. This led to an 1837 law that authorized a three-judge panel to determine an alleged fugitive's status with provisions for either side to request a jury trial. The 1837 law placed New Jersey at the forefront of the battle over personal liberty laws in the North to ensure the proper adjudication of fugitive cases on slavery's border.[18]

In addition to legal protections, vigilance associations formed to protect African Americans from kidnappers and advocated "state pride and sovereignty" in defending New Jersey's right to regulate fugitive recoveries. In 1839, a white Camden resident, for example, claimed "we are tired of having our territory invaded by these myrmidons of the South. The day will come when the genius of liberty, planting her feet on Mason and Dixon's line will say to these savage hunters of men 'thus far shal lye go but no further'" after a group of slave catchers raided a small cabin near his home.[19]

Slave catchers easily caught the attention of vigilance associations and provided them with easy targets since, as many northerners had taken a hardline on slave trading since the late 1810s, slave catchers from the South who threatened law, order, and property did not garner much favor. One such Philadelphia based catcher, named Donahower, led a group of ten men in 1834 to recover two black families in Salem County early on a November morning during a heavy snowfall. Local resident John Mason and most other Market Street residents awoke to the commotion caused by two black men, two black women, and four black children walking in chains clad only in their shirts, led by the local constable and Donahower.[20] The early morning scene "excited" the community who opposed this type of spectacle in their town—dozens crowded the courtroom later that morning to hear the removal case. The judge ruled in favor of the alleged fugitives, to which Donahower waved a pistol in protest and claimed that he would hold the slaves by force if necessary. The local newspaper reported that the crowd in the courtroom yelled for officials to arrest Donahower. Disarmed by a local constable, the slave catcher drew a knife and threatened anyone who tried to apprehend him. In front of a crowd of angry New Jerseyans upset that he had made a mockery of their justice system, the sheriff successfully arrested Donahower for disturbing the peace.[21]

Although Donahower's breach of the peace in Salem did not provoke the formation of an antislavery mob, likely because the judge had ruled in favor of the alleged fugitives, the incident marked him as a danger to southwestern New Jerseyans. In December 1836, Donahower returned to New Jersey and tried to imprison a black family in a tavern's basement in Swedesboro. This time, his actions provoked the formation of a mob, which consisted of forty blacks armed with muskets, clubs, and stones. A journalist claimed that the incident was just one example of many where local free blacks fought back against slave catchers.[22] Indeed, violent reactions against slave catchers had erupted across South Jersey with Bessie Ayres Andrews remembering that all slave catchers who "came to Salem to recapture their slaves . . . were glad to escape with their lives." Likewise, Louisa Bryant, a black Springtown resident, claimed that "free people were always armed with their old flintlock muskets . . . in fact, Springtown had their watchmen and every strange white man had to give a good account of himself or leave."[23]

Mirroring the developments in New Jersey, the fugitive slave issue caused a massive outcry by whites in other northern states, especially after the U.S. Supreme Court ruled all state laws requiring jury trials for fugitives unconstitutional in *Prigg* v. *Pennsylvania* in 1842. Therefore, it enjoined New Jersey's 1837 personal liberty law. This caused other states to prohibit their officials from enforcing the 1793 Federal Fugitive Slave Law, an action heralded by abolitionists like William Rankin Duryee, who claimed in 1840 that "if the Pennsylvania laws uphold slavery then the people of Pennsylvania are in a moral aspect, themselves slaveholders." Samuel Wharton did the same, believing that Pennsylvania "commits a crime of the same stamp by directing in her laws" her judicial officers to "aid in forcing men, women, and children to go on to farms or plantations in other states there to be held as slaves."[24] On slavery's border, in south-central Pennsylvania, these cases led antislavery activity to focus intently on fugitive slaves. There, the conversation steered toward a political and legal defense of states' rights far more than wholesale abolitionism as it did farther north. Jersey abolitionists also hoped to defend their state's rights and likewise did not want it to lend "her magistracy, her police, and her prisons to the claimants of men as fugitives." They wished to remove any "connection with domestic slavery" by prohibiting slave catchers from using state jails or courts. Yet, the Anti-Slavery Society of Eastern Pennsylvania, New Jersey, and Delaware reported that public sentiment "was either not sufficiently matured or had not been sufficiently indicated itself to warrant" passage of such a regulation; New Jerseyans, excited about fugitives, desired the law to reinforce order on the border rather than exacerbate sectional tensions over slavery.[25]

Indeed, many white New Jerseyans actually believed that the real problem with fugitive slaves came from the fugitives themselves—they disrupted law and order more than the slave catchers did. One hundred and twenty-five residents called on the legislature "to prevent the disgracefulness of riot and bloodshed . . . and prevent the supremacy of the laws being trampled upon by lawless hoards of Negroes and runaway slaves."[26] New Jersey's congressional delegation voiced this anti-fugitive sentiment by painting New Jerseyans as uninterested in interfering with slavery and therefore distinct from other northerners. Whig congressman Van Dyke, who pondered whether New Jersey should be a northern or a southern state, claimed that in either case, "one thing is pretty certain, that neither she nor any of her representatives are very *fanatical* on the subject of slavery." Democrat Garnett Adrain of New Brunswick echoed Van Dyke in 1861, claiming that in the midst of the crumbling republic, "the whole North is not abolitionized," and that New Jersey had dealt fairly with the South. Senator Jacob

Miller, a Morris County Whig, went even further by claiming in 1850 that
the real "difficulty in New Jersey" had been "how to get rid of those worth-
less slaves [that] remain there to the annoyance of our people."[27]

New Jerseyans had actively encouraged the return of fugitives by providing easy access to courts, jails, and judicial officers. Similar to responses
in south-central Pennsylvania, fugitive slaves had excited New Jerseyans but
in a different way than New Englanders. Jersey whites developed a measured approach to abolition, one that stressed cooperation with southerners
to enforce law and order on the border. The presence of fugitives therefore
never compelled most white New Jerseyans to think deeply about abolition,
but instead allowed politicians to stress the state's allegiance to the Constitution, interstate comity, and anti-abolitionism. Indeed, Congressman
Adrain spoke extensively on how other "northern states have gone astray
in unwisely passing laws which obstruct and nullify" the return of fugitives,
yet New Jersey "has not followed their bad and prejudicial example" by
passing a restrictive personal liberty law. Instead, the state "adopted a fugitive slave law of her own" and "has gone still further to manifest a kind
and fraternal feeling toward her sister states of the South" by sustaining
sojourner laws.[28]

Most important, though, while other northerners had disowned their
former slave state status, New Jersey politicians consistently drew upon that
past to communicate solidarity with southerners, a desire for law and order
on the border, and for gradual approaches to abolition. For instance, in a
Senate debate in 1850, Jacob Miller claimed that southern charges that "the
North has committed certain high-handed acts of aggression on the constitutional rights of the South" were unfounded because New Jersey had consistently aided in the return of fugitive slaves. Miller claimed that "for my
own state, I am sure she is all unconscious of any aggressions on her part."
New Jersey differed from others, especially after *Prigg*, because she "was
once a slave state herself" and "experienced some of the difficulties in
recovering fugitive slaves." To that end, New Jersey had "thrown [no]
obstacles in the way of reclaiming fugitive slaves," especially since they
caused a "perfect nuisance."[29]

Likewise, future Republican vice presidential candidate Dayton, while
serving in the U.S. Senate, portrayed New Jersey as more aligned with
southern understandings of slavery than northern. In 1848, he claimed
"slavery . . . to be a positive institution" and made clear that white New
Jerseyans were "a constituency with nothing at all akin to political abolition

about them." Instead, they disclaimed "all identification with northern abolitionists of any kind or creed" and believed that the South should be left to deal with slavery in its own way.[30] He echoed this in an 1850 debate with senators Andrew Butler of South Carolina and George Badger of North Carolina. Dayton believed Badger's depiction of a monolithic North uninterested in returning fugitives created "an injustice . . . to New Jersey." He argued that his state had always fulfilled its constitutional obligations, even in Burlington where Quakers held "prevailing views and principles adverse to slavery." Dayton believed that New Jersey "has not now and never has had a law" like those crafted after *Prigg*. Instead, restrictions on removal of slaves from New Jersey "applied only to carrying, sending, or selling our own slaves," not the return of southern fugitives.[31]

The acknowledgment by Jersey politicians of the state's slave history encouraged them to continue the state's gradualist approach to abolition, charting a middle course on sectional issues. However, they were not mindless doughfaces. Instead, they argued that since New Jersey had made its own decision to gradually abolish slavery, it could not criticize other states for keeping it. In 1860, for instance, New Jersey's Senator John Ten Eyck claimed that New Jerseyans had chosen to excise the "cancerous malady," but admitted that "we had had the institution and I am not disposed to arraign or assail either the representatives or the people of other states who have not been so fortunate as we have been in getting rid of it." Policymakers therefore readily participated in the return of fugitive slaves but Jersey politicians from both parties opposed slavery's expansion in the West just as Jersey voters had wanted during the Missouri Crisis to prevent the slave power from becoming even more powerful. In 1847, legislators supported restrictions on slavery in the newly acquired Mexican Territories, a request that all of the state's senators and congressman acceded to. Again, in 1849, the legislature implored its delegation to prevent slavery's expansion into New Mexico and Utah. Most Whig representatives agreed though party loyalty led some Jersey Democrats to support popular sovereignty. This attraction to popular sovereignty rose again in the debate over Kansas when Democrat Garnett Adrain yet again invoked New Jersey's slave past, claiming that "the people of New Jersey exercised for themselves their rights respecting slavery . . . abolished it without the action of Congress" and asked that the nation give the same right to Kansas. Democratic congressman Jacob Wortendyke reiterated this approach in 1858 when he claimed that New Jersey's relationship with slavery "no doubt . . . is as odious to certain persons in other states as is this slave feature in the Constitution of Kansas," but that the federal government's meddling with it "is sheer imprudence . . . and usurpation upon states' rights." Therefore, Jersey politicians generally used their own state's experience with slavery to inform their anti-abolitionism, yet struggled between a wholesale free soil ideology and respect for popular sovereignty, due to party loyalty, as sectional tensions mounted.[32]

∗ ∗ ∗

Fugitive slaves' presence allowed white New Jerseyans to invoke past relationships with slavery to develop a measured antislavery response that defended law and order. Yet fugitive slaves also excited abolitionists who rejected both gradualism and colonization. These abolitionists founded the New Jersey Anti-Slavery Society in 1839 with a unique dual mandate, to end slavery in the South and in New Jersey. The society, in a momentous shift from gradualism, recognized that both slaves and slaves for a term needed to be freed. In addition, the society advocated for free blacks' political rights, seeing that battle as interconnected with abolition. In 1841, for example, the society made it clear that it hoped to "bring about an amelioration of the condition of the 21,000 colored persons in our own state." They believed that since "charity is said to begin at home," attention needed to be directed at slavery and servitude's persistence in New Jersey.[33]

The battle over fugitive slaves had piqued interest in the peculiarities of Jersey-born slaves when the New York Committee of Vigilance became involved in several cases where Jersey slaves were "hired from Jersey to a free state," an occurrence that the New Yorkers found "in a very many instances" in the 1830s. They claimed that Jersey masters routinely sold slaves and slaves for a term to the South and to New York, which led them to call "for the prompt and energetic exertions of the friends of abolition." In supporting Jersey slaves, the New Yorkers understood that the Hudson River, not the Mason-Dixon Line, divided slavery from freedom and made a direct link between the national fugitive slave issue and slavery's persistence in New Jersey.[34]

These whites joined black abolitionists who had already been fighting for abolition and civil rights. For example, black abolitionists in 1837 targeted the remnants of Jersey slavery, believing that a "horrible balance of oppression" existed for slaves for a term. They argued that "the progress of the cause of human rights has been the slowest and the prejudice the strongest" in East Jersey, where large numbers of slaves resided. Likewise, an 1840 article spoke to the moral bankruptcy that New Jerseyans exhibited by permitting slavery and allowing slaveholders to "carry on the trade when it best suits their convenience." In 1841, they pressed the idea that slavery's entrenchment supported restrictions on voting, economic growth, and education because, according to one traveler, when he "touched Jersey soil, SLAVERY gave me a knock." This link between slavery's continuation and the lack of black political rights led Newark's black leaders in 1841 to wonder how to pressure the legislature to overturn the "oppressive law" that disenfranchised "3000 free citizens merely from difference of complexion," the same complexion as the enslaved. Therefore, abolitionist discussions, black or white, routinely intertwined abolition with how "in the Republican State of New Jersey" free blacks "were oppressed and proscribed out of all their civil rights and privileges" since in their minds, one issue fed off the other.[35]

Meanwhile, white abolitionists rallied awareness of slavery's slow death by publishing articles using the Latin penname "Verus" and tried to convince white New Jerseyans that gradualism had failed. In 1840, Verus argued that "Mason and Dickson's (sic) line" was not "the northern boundary of slavery" but that "most of the northern states" retained slavery, leaving their "purification . . . from the stain of oppression to the tardy ministry of death." Verus used the 1830 census to show the presence of slaves under age twenty-six, impossible according to the gradual abolition law (in actuality they were incorrectly recorded slaves for a term). He, however, believed that southerners had infiltrated New Jersey with their chattel since they thought the state fully supported the institution. A second article a week later likewise raised alarm when Verus exposed how black New Jerseyans remained "the slaves of other men . . . liable to public whipping" and could be subjected "to a course of rigid discipline, as horse jockeys do with the subjects of their traffic." He exclaimed that a "glaring insult to human nature" occurred when a New Jerseyan had exchanged a slave for a dog, a transaction "perfectly right according to" state law. Verus questioned if New Jersey was indeed free, since "our own statute book sanctions" the same system in operation in the South.[36]

Many southerners had indeed taken advantage of northern states' lax regulations to bring their slaves to "free" states without any difficulty. In

1837, for instance, a Maryland woman had moved to Downington, Pennsylvania, and brought with her three slaves as "apprentices" and was indicted by her neighbors for "a most flagrant outrage not only upon justice and humanity but upon the spirit of our laws." Pennsylvanians argued that this was not an isolated incident, as "hundreds in the southern counties of the state are guilty of the same evasion of the law."[37] Verus claimed that New Jersey law also sanctioned these trespasses because the still operable 1798 slave code allowed any slaveholder who wished to move permanently to New Jersey to keep his slaves.[38]

In his third article, Verus turned his attempts at moral persuasion to political action and indicated that pressure could be used to influence a full and immediate abolition similar to that which had occurred in New York in 1827. Verus argued that in recent weeks the legislature had been "discovering the wrong they had committed" in relying on gradual abolition and no longer needed to pacify slaveholders by defending property rights. This political push worked in tandem with society efforts to use the voting booth to advocate, along with the Liberty Party, a political solution to slavery. One local auxiliary, the Essex County Anti-Slavery Society, argued that anyone who "either refuses or neglects to aid" abolition "at the ballot box . . . leaves the victim of oppression unrelieved and helpless in the hand of his oppression." In 1840, the society supported the Liberty Party, launched a campaign against President John Tyler's slaveholding record, and advocated that politics would be the way to finally end slavery in New Jersey.[39]

The society used the same arguments to highlight New Jersey's troublesome and ambiguous relationship with slavery in petitions to legislators. For example, an 1840 petition reiterated concerns over sojourner laws, branding the practice "insidious and unjust" because it helped "perpetuate slavery in New Jersey even after it shall have been abolished in all the other states of the Union." Likewise, in 1841 the society claimed that "the statute book of New Jersey is still disfigured with the laws of slavery" and accused the legislature of treating its previous petitions "with cold neglect . . . on account of the interests of a few dozen slaveholders among us" and "because of the unjust ascendency of the slave power in the national government." The abolitionists demanded "equal rights to ALL MEN," which to them included slaves and slaves for a term, and a redress for the "disabilities imposed on our twenty-thousand free people of color" in New Jersey without equal rights.[40]

These attempts at guilting legislators into supporting abolition filtered down to the grassroots level, where abolition society auxiliaries, especially in Boonton, the home of society president John Grimes, created their own petitions. Abolitionist Samuel Dorrance, for example, claimed that after lecturing on abolition in Boonton for four consecutive nights "to a full audience" in 1842, he could confidently say that "prejudice against the abolitionists is done for here" because many had joined the local move-ment.[41] In 1843, Boonton's citizens asked the legislature to repeal the requirement that blacks carry their freedom papers, seemingly unnecessary after state courts had ended prima facie slavery in 1836. The Boonton peti-tioners also recognized that slaves for a term needed "the opportunity of receiving a good common school education and of learning some useful mechanical art" instead of functioning as untrained agricultural or domes-tic laborers, which perpetuated their unfreedom.[42]

In October 1842, Grimes brought the abolitionist interest in freeing both slaves and slaves for a term to a larger audience by publishing the *New Jersey Citizen*, the state's first abolitionist newspaper. Grimes, a physician also active in temperance, believed that Jersey abolitionists had no ready means to communicate and hoped that the *Citizen*, as "a paper of our own," could "foster and enlarge the anti-slavery influence of the state." In the first issue, Grimes cited that the 1840 census counted 674 slaves in the state and remarked that the number of slaves for a term "must be very large." To him, their condition was "real slavery for the time being." He asked, "who will say that New Jersey is not a slave state" and wondered when "will New Jersey reach the standard of the age" and, "like that of most of the northern states," make its air "too pure for a slave to breath in."[43] The *Citizen* soon folded, but in June 1844 Grimes began publishing the *New Jersey Freeman* to show that slavery existed as "a grievous wrong, an outrage under every circumstance." He argued that Jersey abolitionists needed to maintain "the deep and unqualified sinfulness and impolicy of slavery and the obligation of immediate universal emancipation," by recog-nizing that the ballot box was an "instrument of great power for good or for evil."[44]

Though abolitionists had become more active during the debates over southern fugitive slaves, most whites supported law and order more than abolition as anxiety over economic competition, amalgamation, and racial tensions grew in tandem with the increased free black population. In 1840, the Anti-Slavery Society saw this anti-abolition sentiment when white Trentonians protested the society's annual meeting. The *Newark Daily Advertiser* reported that residents "hardly knew what to make of" the abolitionists since they had "not known that there was a single abolitionist in" the entire city. Henry Stanton and James Birney led the society's public afternoon session in Trenton, which resulted in both reporting that they were there "to hear as much as to be heard" since "the public began to bellow in the discordant tones of a many-headed monster," expressing many of the same racial views as those who participated in anti-abolition riots around the same time.[45]

One Trenton observer echoed the lack of abolitionist support in 1840 when he noted that abolition was "not a moving power among the people." An 1854 edition of the *Newark Advertiser* agreed, arguing that although "New Jersey has no love of slavery," most whites opposed the "reckless following out of abstract doctrines on human rights regardless of consequences" that abolitionists put forward. The *Trenton American*, on the eve of the Civil War, similarly claimed "we do not know that as yet there are a great many out and out abolitionists in New Jersey." The real numbers reinforce this lack of abolitionism as the state, in 1838, had fourteen abolition societies compared to Ohio's 251 and New York's 369.[46]

Grimes and the other Boonton abolitionists who began the *New Jersey Freeman* repeatedly reiterated that large portions remained wholly unsupportive of abolition either because of business connections with the South, antipathy, or the belief that New Jersey should not interfere with slavery in other states. In July 1844, for instance, the *Freeman* complained that "New Jersey is so far behind most of the free States in abolition sentiment," seen most readily through the lack of available meeting places for abolitionists. They claimed that less than 10 percent of New Jersey's towns would offer "even a school house" for an abolitionist meeting while a later article told that "churches, public halls, school houses, and all such places are in New Jersey . . . closed against those who feel it a duty to labor for the slave." Grimes lambasted churches that either opposed abolition or remained indifferent to it, believing that they brought the "dark spirit of Despotism" to New Jersey. In 1847 the tone became even more dire as the society could not find a location for its annual meeting in Trenton, leading the society to let it be "known to the world" that Trenton was "so deeply pro-slavery . . . the friends of liberty" could not meet "for the promotion of liberty."[47] This bleak picture of the movement's prospects was compounded by the lack of any antislavery organization in South Jersey and the "slowly progressing" movement of antislavery in East Jersey.[48]

Gradualism and antislavery, rather than immediate abolitionism, prevailed in New Jersey. Governor William Pennington, in 1840, reiterated this gradualist approach by arguing that under the state's abolition system, "slavery has become almost extinct." Pennington, like other gradualists, believed that "the condition of servitude [that remains] is of the most mitigated" form and immediate abolition was unnecessary. Likewise, few supported either the Liberty Party or the Free Soil Party with their vote and instead embraced gradualism. In the elections of 1840 and 1844 combined, only 200 supported the Liberty Party while in the election of 1848, 819 of 77,000 voters cast their ballots for free soiler Martin Van Buren. Four years later, the party fared even worse when only 359 of 83,000 supported John Hale.[49]

Pennington's lack of support and the widespread anti-abolition sentiment caused some abolitionists to wonder if slavery was still too strong to eliminate, especially as the 1844 Constitutional Convention neared. Activist Quaker Thomas Booth acknowledged in 1840 that "if slavery cannot be abolished without our territory at the present time," Jersey abolitionists should, as the gradualists had done before, work to improve conditions for those who remained enslaved. Booth specifically focused on the "odious and barbarous" 1798 slave law that still controlled the state's slave system and hoped that improved living conditions for slaves might be negotiated.[50] Abolitionists, however, were hopeful that the new constitution would change the state's slave-supporting legal system and deal a deathblow to the institution. Major players like Chief Justice Hornblower participated in debates specifically on slavery, with the judge's 1864 obituary remembering that he was "unwearied in his endeavors . . . to extinguish the last remnant of slavery which still lingered" in New Jersey. However, despite his support, no mention of slavery made it into the final constitution. Likewise, the convention took little notice of several petitions in favor of black voting rights, tabling the issue to instead engage in a lengthy debate on allowing nonresident students at The College of New Jersey and Rutgers College to vote. Slavery therefore remained imbedded in the state's 1844 constitution, with the society believing that it was "enough to make any liberal soul blush," as it is "so far behind the age," but representative of the state's "perfect apathy" to black freedom.[51]

With their petitions rebuffed and a constitution that "favor[ed] the maintenance and continuance of slavery," Jersey abolitionists decided their next best move rested in a legal attack against the institution and enlisted former New York Anti-Slavery Society president Alvan Stewart to assist. In choosing this course, they diverged from abolitionists in other states who used only moral persuasion or religion to advocate for abolition. Like their predecessors in the gradual abolition movement, they hoped the law would ensure black freedom. Abolitionists wrote extensively about the case, *State v. Post*, and placed the continuation of Jersey slavery in the context of abolitionism in Latin America, Asia, North Africa, and the British Empire. They claimed that it would hopefully render "many of the most abominable slave laws" that the state had "upon her Statute Book . . . null and void" while others hoped it would awaken "a more general interest in the subject." On the eve of the case, the *Freeman* reported that Stewart would "argue for the cause of Liberty" while the society declared, "let the people have LIGHT" and abolition.[52]

Stewart filed two writs of habeas corpus in defense of Mary Tebout, a nineteen-year-old slave for a term, and William, a sixty-year-old slave owned by John Post, to argue that slavery was unconstitutional under the 1844 New Jersey constitution. He claimed it was no different from the Massachusetts constitution, which he believed that its state justices used to eliminate slavery in the 1780s. Article I claimed that "all men are by nature free and independent and have certain natural and unalienable rights," language Stewart hoped would free the approximately 3,000 slaves and slaves for a term who remained in New Jersey. In an impassioned eleven-hour argument, he told justices that "we live in an abolition age, when the dungeons which have incarcerated suffering humanity are being broken in and unlocked in every corner of our benighted world." He begged them to "open this castle of slavery, New Jersey, with the key of the new constitution" and abolish slavery.[53]

The New Jersey Supreme Court, however, found that the constitution did not change the state's relationship with slavery and ruled that the institution had been accepted and supported after its ratification. Since it did not specifically contain an abolition clause, the broad ideas in Article I did not abolish slavery. Furthermore, since Virginia maintained slavery even though its constitution had a similar section, the judges concluded that Article I was a rhetorical device never intended to "interfere with . . . domestic relations." The negative decision shocked abolitionists, leading

the *Freeman* to "blush at our New Jersey Court" and report that the decision, "to the astonishment of almost all Jerseymen," left the "slave question
in our state" unsettled. They damned the court and believed that "New
Jersey is still, according to the last legal definition, a SLAVE STATE."[54]

However, the *Post* decision brought Jersey slavery into public debate
again, incidentally in the same year that the legislature conducted a review
of state laws to bring them in line with the 1844 constitution. A legislative
committee ordered further discussion by the full legislature for laws regarding fugitive slaves, apprentices, servants, and the 1798 omnibus slave code,
which the legislature extended its session to complete. This review also
coincided with national debates over the annexation of Texas, fears of the
encroaching slave power, and abolitionists' own efforts to "secure the freedom of the enslaved" in New Jersey and redeem it "from the stigma of
being in fact as it really is, *a slave state*." This perfect storm likewise collided
with the ever-present issue of fugitive slaves that reiterated a gradualist
mentality and a measured approach to abolition.[55]

When the legislature sat in 1846 to consider the "hypocrisy" of legalized
slavery in the North, the national discussions on slavery as well as the recent
State v. Post decision made slavery appear differently than during the early
nineteenth century abolition debates or the Missouri Crisis since it was a
much smaller institution. This legislative debate centered on northeast New
Jersey (Bergen, Passaic, and Hudson Counties) where the majority of slaves
lived. A populous slaveholding area since its settlement by the Dutch, slaveholding lineages passed these slaves down through the generations, resulting in slaves making up almost 20 percent of the population immediately
after the Revolution. This concentration of slaves, rivaling those in many
southern states, survived into the antebellum period where by the 1840s
they and their slave for a term children still actively worked as domestic
servants and farm laborers, feeding the fertile market of New York City.
This long history of slaveholding caused bound labor to remain an important labor choice even as the state moved closer to a free society. Wills and
probate records for Bergen County from 1804 to 1846 reveal that a sizeable
number of estates held slaves or slaves for a term throughout the abolition
period (17.3 percent of 1698 estates). Almost all slaveholders, even into the
1840s, did not free their bound property and instead transferred them to
willing buyers or family members. Only 9 of the 763 slaves and slaves for a
term mentioned in wills gained freedom and even these owners seemed
exceptional. Three of the six owners provided both freedom and financial

support. For example, Henry Spear freed Caesar and his wife Hannah, and left them forty acres of land, a house, oxen, a cow, sheep, and a plow in 1820 to ensure the couple's ability to support themselves. Spear also transferred the couple's two children, Leah and Harry, both slaves for a term, to their parents' guardianship, which essentially granted them freedom.[56]

Though slaveholders like Spear did exist, most slaves and slaves for a term in Bergen County wills remained bound to their masters' descendants or were sold in order to perpetuate slavery. Peter Merseles, at his death in 1832, for example, ordered that his four slaves for a term (Cate, Harry, Phebe, and Pegg) all be sold along with their parents, Susan and Dinah. Similarly, in 1833 John Hopper, by that point one of the larger slaveholders in the county, transferred his five slaves and five slaves for a term to his wife Maria and son Jacob. Although Hopper's will made clear distinctions between slaves and slaves for a term, specifically referencing the "five blacks who are born under the manumission act," his executors continued to view them as property, assigning them values ranging from $25 for Grace to $150 for Ant. Not surprisingly, his executors computed the value of his five slaves for a term at $95 more than his five aging slaves. The higher value of slaves for a term convinced slave owners like Hopper to oppose immediate abolition and continue the institution.[57]

Unsurprisingly then, senators Richard Paulison (Bergen), Cornelius Garrison (Passaic), and Richard Outwater (Hudson) systematically defended their constituents' property rights in a fiery debate in the state senate. Some of their passion likely came from their own relationships with slavery. Outwater's relatives had owned numerous slaves, while Paulison still owned a female slave and a slave for a term, Sam, who remained in his service until 1855. Thus, in 1846, Paulison had a clear understanding of how the abolition bill would impact both him and the slaveholders he represented.[58] The three specifically targeted the bill's section that granted black bound laborers the right to petition for a redress of their grievances against their masters. In a law passed earlier that session, the legislature created a procedure where, if a master had refused to provide provisions or cruelly mistreated a bound laborer, that laborer could file a complaint with a justice of the peace. Once a slave or slave for a term filed a complaint, three justices would convene and could, if they sustained the complaint, free them. Paulison feared that an abolitionist justice might release valuable slaves for a term and proposed an amendment that stripped this right from them. Failing in this regard, he attempted to alter the section a second time by eliminating the requirement that mandated masters financially support those freed by the redress procedure. Paulison failed yet again but introduced another alteration that changed the redress procedure so that justices could only levy a fine, not free the bound laborer if justices found the owner negligent. This last effort failed too, signaling a legislative shift to enhance the treatment of slaves and slaves for a term that remained in bondage.[59]

Unable to make any headway on the redress procedure, Paulison introduced an amendment that provided masters the right to move with their bound black laborers to other parts of the United States to preserve the portability of slave property. However, with a long history of legally restricting sales of slaves out of state, perhaps what many legislators thought might happen if abolition was enacted, Paulison's amendment failed. Surprisingly, the amendment that garnered the most support increased penalties for whites who assisted fugitives. Cornelius Garrison of Passaic wanted to increase the penalty from $100 (recoverable through a civil lawsuit) to a criminal misdemeanor, punishable by a $100–200 fine and one to two years at hard labor, for helping Jersey born slaves escape their masters. This amendment failed, yet its significant support showcases how many legislators at least tacitly approved protecting the operation of the still active slave system.[60]

Despite attempts to derail the abolition bill and disarm its key components, Jersey legislators approved abolition in 1846 because the fugitive slave issues that had excited abolitionists, white and black, helped them organize a renewed movement to force politicians to make a choice on abolition, one that they had deferred for decades. Succumbing to abolitionist charges of hypocrisy for slavery's continuation while they advocated for free soil in the West and the growing pressure exerted by the free black community, legislators sped up slavery's death but still relied on the same gradualism used by lawmakers in their past dealings with slavery. In many ways, the 1846 abolition law mimicked their response to the fugitive slave crisis by reinforcing the preservation of law and order, ensuring the maintenance of the state's delicate racial balance, and preventing whites from supporting hundreds of elderly ex-slaves. The law abolished slavery but reclassified slaves as *apprentices for life*. This convoluted legalese allowed for abolition with no impact to property rights, the hallmark of gradualism. Apprentices for life would be treated as slaves but with three important differences. First, apprentices could not be sold out of state. Second, they could file complaints for injurious service or working conditions. Third, they could be "released from service" (manumitted) if they could finan-cially support themselves. Masters would not be liable for their care if they became indigent, unlike slaves. This change likely encouraged masters to free apprentices, though no records survive to show its pervasiveness. Yet, despite some tangible legal differences, masters retained significant control over these apprentices. The law permitted their sale within the state, their temporary removal out of state, and sustained sojourner laws for non-residents.[61]

The law also did not free slaves for a term; they remained bound to their masters. Thus, Hannah, born on March 27, 1844, the last child regis-tered under the gradual abolition law, served her mother's master until March 27, 1865, less than two weeks before Robert E. Lee surrendered at Appomattox. The 1846 law did, however, mandate that children born to apprentices would be free at birth. Masters would maintain them until age six when the overseers of the poor would bind them out to age twenty-one. This might have happened to Alonzo, the son of Susan, an apprentice for life from Monmouth County, if Susan's free relatives had not volunteered to care for the boy to prevent this separation. Therefore, slavery's impact lingered as the legally mandated separation Alonzo might have experienced mimicked slavery's ability to rip apart families.[62]

April 18, 1846, became emancipation day in New Jersey, though like July 4, 1804, it was not marked by public festivities. Most apprentices for life continued to function as slaves. John Berdan, who died in Saddle River two months after the law passed, still owned two slaves and "the time of service" of five "persons of color born under the act for the gradual emanci-pation of slavery" whom his executors valued at between $10 and $50 each. The same occurred in September 1846 when Cornelius Van Buskirk of Hackensack left his "colored man slave named Charles" to his wife. Slavery also survived long into the apprenticeship period. Catherine, John Haga-man's sixty-seven-year-old "slave for life" who began this book, continued to live as a slave with Hagaman and was listed as such on her bill of sale to Charles Sutphin in 1856. Likewise, the executors of Jacob Demarest's estate in 1855 claimed that he owned the service of Jack, "an apprentice" valued at $15, while in May of that same year, the estate of Abraham Ackerman listed "a male colored servant" valued at $100.[63]

John Whitlock, of Marlboro Township in Monmouth County, did more than just use antiquated language; he successfully registered Sarah, the child of his slave for a term Phebe, with the county clerk in 1847. That the clerk allowed this registration and thereby acknowledged Whitlock's right to hold Phebe's fully free child illustrates that even government officials did not fully grasp the legal peculiarities that abolition had created. Indeed, twenty-three years later in 1870, Sarah and her children, Jane and Willie, lived with the Whitlock family as domestic servants. The *New Brunswick Daily Fredonian* likewise reported in 1868 that Bob, the last slave in Hunterdon County, continued to live and work near Sandy Ridge after his original owner, John Waterhouse of Rosemont, died. Two generations removed from slavery, the relationships slavery created endured after the Civil War.[64]

Abolitionists also saw their task as incomplete. In 1847, the *Freeman* argued that citizens still needed to "redeem their own state from the condition, the crime, and disgrace of a slaveholding state." The paper explained that "New Jersey is called a free state" but had "several hundred slaves, most of whom are likely to die slaves," that still needed to be freed. An article later that year compared the state to its slaveholding neighbor, Delaware, stating that "there is more genuine active antislavery spirit" there than in New Jersey. Decrying the limited antislavery sentiment, the authors recommended that Jersey abolitionists "cry out to the people of Delaware to come over and help" because the abolitionist situation remained more abysmal in New Jersey than in a southern state. This distress continued when in April 1848 the society decried that "in this age when even the Turks are abolishing slavery," New Jersey remained a slaveholding republic.[65]

Questions over New Jersey's slave past and slavery's peculiar false end continued to crop up after 1846 and sustained slavery's memory. For example, in 1855 Samuel How, a slaveholding Reformed Protestant Dutch minister who trained ministers and teachers through the ACS and African Association of New Brunswick, spoke in favor of admitting a North Carolina German Reformed Church in his Synod even though others had argued that they "ought not to hold communion with slaveholders" and that "slaveholding is a sin." This debate led New York minister Theodore Cuyler to fear that admitting "the handful of slaveholders from Carolina" would "rend my own church into fragments" because his congregation had "many New England people and many who are firmly opposed to slavery." Rev. How, however, argued that slaveholding was without sin and revealed that Jersey church members had held slaves. How distrusted abolitionists, who he believed had either willfully or through extreme negligence painted a mistaken image of slavery to northerners. In this extensive published argument, How claimed that the South had helped the North abolish slavery because "she was always ready to receive the slaves which . . . Northern owners found it profitable or convenient to dispose of."[66]

In response to How, Congressman John Van Dyke used New Jersey's slavery experience to attack the idea that slavery was not sinful. He argued that there might be some slaveholders who held slaves without sin especially "in New Jersey where old and worn out slaves are cast by the law of the land upon their master or his estate for maintenance and support." Van Dyke argued that "the owner could not sever the relationship" because the freedom process itself would be inhumane. He thought the South had a more vicious slavery after he personally saw how at "the auction block . . . parents and children sold like other beasts of burden to the highest bidder . . . to be subjected without restraint to whatever hardship and cruelty by his whim or malice might suggest or invent." Van Dyke was determined to show that although certain instances of slavery could be humane, such as that which continued in New Jersey, the institution in the South remained morally problematic.[67]

How's son Henry defended his father against Van Dyke's attacks and yet again showcased Jersey slavery in contrast to other northern states. Henry had already held "strong feelings of attachment to the South" and believed "that the interference of the northern abolitionists . . . is wholly unauthorized." Yet, he understood that "the sentiment of the mass of the people in New Jersey" opposed "to break our Union and trample on our Constitution because of slavery."[68] Henry reiterated many of his father's arguments to remind Van Dyke of "a fact well known to every well informed man;" the "Dutch Church both in New Jersey and the State of New York held slaves" and slaves remained "held by communicants belonging to the Dutch Church." Henry, however, asked Van Dyke to apply his same idea of "the old and the worn out slaves" to slavery in North Carolina since, "unless New Jersey is out of the world as well as the United States," the institution in the state was similar to slavery elsewhere.[69]

This constant engagement with New Jersey's slave past and how it affected life in the late antebellum period was likewise encountered by New Jersey officials who sought answers on how to integrate apprentices for life into society. In 1857, for instance, the New Jersey Supreme Court issued an advisory opinion to the Bergen County Board of Chosen Freeholders who wanted to know if apprentices for life discharged from their masters' service should be considered paupers and subject to poor laws usually imposed on whites or if previous decisions of the court that held owners responsible for the care of manumitted slaves be applied. The Supreme Court directed the Freeholders to section seven of the 1846 abolition law, which declared that the township where the apprentice was discharged had to provide poor relief. In certain circumstances though, masters retained the same responsibility toward their former apprentices as they had with their manumitted slaves. Just as many slaveholders considered apprentices for life to still be slaves, justices argued that "the master . . . may be sued for the support of his slave." Using the word "slave" demonstrated that even the state's highest court saw that slavery was still very much alive in New Jersey even after abolition in 1846.[70]

*   *   *

New Jersey's abolition period had introduced its residents to myriad forms of unfreedom and its end became as complicated as its beginning. After two decades marked by a pervasive apathy toward slavery, the 1830s represented a pivotal moment: slavery had been inserted back into public debate through the presence of fugitive slaves, which reenergized abolitionists who endorsed the immediacy of slave freedom. Fugitive slaves, sectional tensions, and abolitionist activity convinced legislators to address slavery in 1846, but they declined to dramatically alter slavery's slow death despite calls of hypocrisy from abolitionists. Instead, white New Jerseyans continued to resist abolition by using their past association with slavery to define their place in the increasingly divided nation. The New England paradigm of a wholesale disownment of slavery did not apply on slavery's border. There, the constant rush of fugitive slaves and concerns over maintaining law and order did not allow slavery's memory to die and instead motivated different approaches to the institution.

At one level then, New Jersey's experience with slavery shows that the institution survived far longer and more powerfully in the North than previously imagined. In a larger sense, it illustrates that the North was not monolithic—New Jerseyans did not rush to abolition. Indeed, slavery was extremely difficult to destroy into the 1840s, showcasing the vitality of the institution even in marginal locales. Most important, slavery's slow northern death demonstrates that the institution had a tangible impact on the sectional crisis. New Jersey and southern politicians shared an understanding of slavery and an astute knowledge of the various forms of unfreedom associated with it. This not only informed policy decisions but impacted the lives of those Jersey blacks who remained unfree until the Thirteenth Amendment finally abolished slavery and servitude in 1865.

Conclusion

Historian William Gillette cautions others not to "concentrate on the infinitesimal minority of eighteen quasi-slaves" recorded in the 1860 New Jersey census but on "the state's 25,318 free African Americans."[1] He shows that the presence of these slaves encouraged past historians to assert that New Jersey was a hotbed of Copperhead sentiment and made the state appear "separated only by an accident of geography from the rebellious South."[2] Of course, New Jersey's southern sympathizing had some electoral proof to it. New Jerseyans voted against Abraham Lincoln in both 1860 and 1864 and voted for Democrats to occupy the governor's mansion from 1869 to 1896, even electing George McClellan governor in 1877. On the face of it, New Jersey did not appear to be a vibrant Union supporter. However, despite its geographic oddity of being partly below the Mason-Dixon Line, New Jersey was not the fourteenth member of the Confederacy.[3]

The presence of those eighteen apprentices for life, and probably hundreds of slaves for a term and apprentices not properly recorded in the census, serve as a bookend to slavery's slow death in New Jersey; the institution successfully sustained itself, though incredibly weakened after decades of gradual abolition, until the Civil War. Along with those apprentices for life, free blacks who had for so long been prima facie slaves still lived tainted by their history with the institution. The apprentices for life then represent the thousands of enslaved New Jerseyans who had stamped an enduring legacy on the state and allowed slavery's memory to remain an important part of how white New Jerseyans understood African Americans.

Like those before them, New Jersey politicians debating the sectional crisis continued to use their state's prior relationship with slavery to inform their opinions and actions. The presence of fugitive slaves and the increasing tensions over slavery nationally forced New Jerseyans to continually revisit the issue and make connections between slavery's westward expansion and their own slaveholding experience. Democratic governor Rodman

Price, for example, charted a "position of just and honorable conservatism" for New Jersey in 1856 by pledging that the state would support any constitutional law that protected slavery and the return of fugitives.[4] Likewise, in 1858 a special committee of the General Assembly argued that "slavery existed at the time of the adoption of the constitution in all the States of the confederacy" and that New Jersey "had made ample provision by her own statue" to protect "the rights of the slaveholder" in returning fugitive slaves.[5]

Despite Jersey politicians' strong understanding of the state's slave past, other northerners consistently misinterpreted certain fundamental aspects of the abolition law. In 1856, for example, a presidential campaign advertisement for free soiler John C. Fremont used a map to show the Missouri Compromise line and the free and slave states. The map's key contained 1850 census data with an asterisk next to New Jersey's figures, claiming that the "census erroneously reports 236 persons in New Jersey under the caption of 'slaves.' In that state slavery was provisionally abolished in 1784; all children born of a slave after 1804 were free in 1820."[6] No 1784 law affected slavery and the meaning of the 1820 omnibus slave law certainly confused others as well. The 1820 law reaffirmed and continued many of the 1804 law's regulations, yet local historians like Joseph Atkinson in 1878, among others, believed that New Jersey abolished slavery in 1820.[7]

Atkinson retells a much more triumphal story of slavery's decline in New Jersey than actually occurred, one that by the time of the Civil War had begun to be openly debated among state residents; the outbreak of war heightened the memory of slavery and its meaning. That memory was tested when Jefferson Davis argued before the Confederate Congress in 1861 that the North had brought war to the nation by creating a "persistent and organized system of hostile measures against the rights of owners of slaves." He claimed that northern states, because their "climate and soil . . . soon proved unpropitious to the continuance of slave labor, consulted their own interests by selling their slaves to the South and prohibiting slavery within their limits."[8] Davis's accusation energized New Jerseyans to reconsider their past role with the institution. In 1861 the *New York Evangelist* investigated Davis's claim and reaffirmed slavery's importance, showing that while all states originally had the institution, New Jersey was "even more a slave state than New York and she was even more tardy in freeing herself from its presence." However, the article indicated that even though more than 2,000 slaves lived in New Jersey in 1830, state law had banned

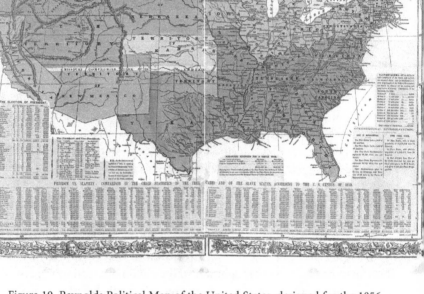

Figure 10. Reynolds Political Map of the United States, designed for the 1856 presidential election, shows the free and slave states as well as the status of slaveholding in western territories. It also displays 1850 census figures and incorrectly indicates that New Jersey abolished slavery in 1784.

Courtesy of the Library of Congress.

the "deportation of that class of persons" to the South, making Davis's statement "illogical in its conclusions as it is untrue in its premises" and New Jersey slavery seemingly more palatable to those who would soon fight for the Union.[9]

Once the war began, white New Jerseyans used the memory of slavery to again inform their actions on national sectional issues. Slavery's memory became a weapon politicians deployed for their own particular aims. For example, Democratic governor Joel Parker reconfirmed the state's slave past and its conservative stance on abolition, announcing in his inaugural address that if emancipation came to the United States, it should come as it "did in New Jersey, by the voluntary action of the people of the States where the institution exists, peacefully and gradually" and without federal interference. Parker's words had much to do with the state's slave past, yet even more with the role of Copperheads in Jersey politics. Parker won a landslide victory in late 1862, riding a tidal wave of anti-Lincoln sentiment after the draft, military defeats, the suspension of habeas corpus, and the announcement of the Emancipation Proclamation galvanized the state's Democratic Party. Parker used New Jersey's slave past as an integral part of his rhetoric, since it contrasted the state's conservative stance on slavery with the Republicans' perceived dangerous and radical abolitionism. Though a War Democrat, Parker argued that slavery's "introduction was not the work of one section alone." He and other Democrats feared that Lincoln's "project of emancipation . . . will prolong the war" and "have the effect of placing an obstacle in the way of the restoration of the Union." The following year, Parker reiterated his opposition to emancipation in his annual legislative message, claiming it not only "unwise" but "a great mistake to assume that the emancipation policy has contributed to our military successes during the past year." Parker believed that "slavery was introduced by our forefathers and incorporated in the institutions of both sections" and followed the same line that Jersey politicians had walked for the last two decades, arguing that since the North, "without interference from the other section, declared for its gradual abolishment," the South should be given the same opportunity.[10]

Race-baiting became quite common in wartime Democratic politics in New Jersey as Parker and other Democrats not only used the state's slave past to argue against Lincoln's radical Emancipation Proclamation but drummed up intense fears of how these newly freed slaves would overrun New Jersey. Jersey Democrats believed that emancipation would increase the status of blacks, intensify job competition, and thereby lower white wages as those newly freed blacks came to New Jersey to live. The prolifera-tion of free blacks would "constitute a public nuisance and a tax burden . . . endanger the property, prosperity, even the physical safety of whites" and might spur on amalgamation. Fears of economic competition, amal-gamation, and the burden of caring for paupers encouraged Democrats in 1862 to propose a prohibition on black immigration to New Jersey, just as many Midwestern states had previously done. Eleven petitions from white New Jerseyans demanded lawmakers take action on this issue and, by a vote of 33–20, the General Assembly prohibited blacks from entering New Jersey. Those caught living in the state for more than ten days would be transported to Liberia, continuing the legislature's support for colonization, it having appropriated funds for the state society in 1852 and 1855. The law failed to gain traction in the Senate, yet its passage illustrates that white New Jerseyans continued to embrace a conservative abolitionist platform, one that supported colonization and opposed radical changes in the struc-ture of American society.[11]

At the height of Democratic Copperhead influence in early 1864, mem-ory of the state's slave past became part of a much larger conversation about how New Jersey fit into slavery's role in causing the Civil War. In April 1864, the *Friends' Intelligencer* published a series of articles on slavery and the Civil War in which Jersey Friends reexamined their slave past and showed that Davis's 1861 statement was actually accurate. One article claimed that Quakers had been at the forefront of the early abolition move-ment and that if the country had followed their path and abolished slavery, there would have been no Civil War—an argument that probably resonated with Peace Democrats and even War Democrats who opposed Lincoln's handling of the war and chaffed at the laundry list of casualties that arrived daily from the front.[12] Another article did, however, admit that "a brisk traffic in slaves was conducted between New Jersey and the southern states and it was even published in a southern paper that slaves from New Jersey bearing the marks of a certain Judge (no doubt burnt in by a hot iron) were in high repute among slave-buyers in that locality." This statement, refer-ring to Judge Van Wickle's Middlesex slave trading ring in the late 1810s, provided a connection to the state's past. An understanding of how the state's relationship to slavery and freedom fit into a larger national picture existed during the war, one that revealed to the public that New Jersey had fed demand for slaves and perhaps impacted how the war began.[13]

By early 1864, anti-Lincoln sentiment in the state Democratic Party was strong as Governor Parker and others pitted Lincoln's emancipation policies, draft regulations, and the unpopular suspension of habeas corpus against a much more conservative stance on abolition and an interest in removing the Union from a war it still might lose. After a series of Union victories in the summer and fall of 1864, however, Copperhead popularity plummeted as Peace Democrats began to be perceived as traitors, causing McClellan's 1864 presidential bid to receive support from only three slaveholding states: Kentucky, Delaware, and New Jersey. Likewise, Republicans won a super-majority in the Thirty-Ninth Congress. Even though New Jersey Democratic representative George Middleton lost reelection to Republican William Newell in 1864, Democratic influence in the state remained strong because the 1864 elections for the state legislature hinged much more on racial tensions than the course of the war. Democrats continued to use race as a lightning rod, introducing a bill that banned intermarriage between whites and blacks, which newspapers used to feed "on racial fears by spreading the notion of Republicans as 'nigger-worshippers' bent on imposing social equality for blacks." Democrats in their 1864 state party platform likewise condemned equality for blacks and campaigned against Lincoln by arguing that "whites died pointlessly for the welfare and equality of three million idle, shiftless, thriftless negroes."[14] Republicans, rightly sensing race as key in the 1864 election, supported the anti-miscegenation legislation and the Assembly unanimously passed it to deprive the Democrats from using it as a divisive campaign issue, though the Senate declined to pass it. The race-baiting, however, worked as Democrats retained a majority in the Senate, yet Republicans picked up ten seats in the assembly by winning three-quarters of that year's competitive districts, causing a 20–20 tie. Therefore, even as the national Democratic Party was crumbling and the Confederacy looked on the verge of defeat, Jersey Democrats rallied a strong and somewhat successful opposition to the Republican ascendancy.[15]

In January 1865, when the new divided legislature took their seats, Jersey Democrats still believed that full emancipation was too radical a power-grab by the Republican Party while the Democratic South lay vulnerable and unrepresented. On a national level, Democratic representative Andrew Rogers delivered a stirring speech on the House floor damning the Republicans, the federal government, and the other northern states that had no interest in slavery for making a decision that affected millions of disenfranchised southerners. Their actions would deprive these southern "men whose fathers fought side by side with men of New York and New Jersey" against the British in the American Revolution of their slave property without due process in a supposedly republican government. Rogers reminded the House that "slavery existed in every state save one at the adoption of the Constitution" and that New Jersey, "which has clung to the Constitution . . . as a ligament of the Union . . . has never yet cast her vote in favor of the wild fanaticism of abolition which has run riot all over this land." He squarely laid blame for the war not on slavery but on the "acts of the abolitionists of the North" that were "responsible for all this bloodshed which is now wetting American soil" and now interfered with what Jersey politicians had championed for decades—interstate comity.[16]

Rogers's sentiments were echoed two months later when the Camden Democratic Association adopted a resolution that argued that New Jersey had always, unlike the rest of the North, followed constitutional principles in supporting slavery and applauded Democratic legislators for "rejecting the pernicious act of the Black Republican party." They likewise damned Lincoln and the Republicans for destroying "every vestige of State rights" and endangered "the last hope of a restoration of our once cherished union" by supporting an amendment "designed to abolish Negro slavery." The Camden Association's anti-abolitionism had more to do with being anti-Lincoln than with the preservation of slavery in New Jersey, but it does show continuity with the state's long-standing conservative approach to abolition.[17]

The legislative debates on the amendment were exhaustive, with Republicans arguing that the destruction of slavery was a necessity and that a formal emancipation would safeguard the peace by confirming what Union troops had already done in the field. Democrats, on the other hand, opposed the Thirteenth Amendment, believing as Democratic legislator James Goble claimed, that northerners had been "so misled on this subject of slavery that they are blind, deaf, and dumb to the rights of the slaveholding states." Men like Goble feared that immediate abolition would unleash a torrent of uneducated and uncontrolled former slaves who would wreak havoc on American society and "bring disaster to both races." Goble, for instance, believed that if abolition were to come, blacks "soon will be not only equal but superior to the white race," objecting to abolitionist attempts at stopping the white race from being "uncontaminated in general." They likewise opposed the seizure of private property without southern consent or compensation, especially in the loyal border states of

Delaware and Kentucky. Just as Jersey politicians had done before, legislator Leon Abbett claimed that the state "abolished [slavery] by state legislation" and has "always upheld and asserted the rights of states to control local matters to suit themselves, without national interference." Likewise, William Iliff reiterated that New Jerseyans had decided to abolish slavery themselves and "then, as now, considered slavery a local institution." Since the South had "conceded the right" to abolish slavery to New Jersey, Iliff asked "should we not then act in the same spirit to them?" Therefore, Democrats in the legislature firmly believed that ratification would signal the end of state power, a retrenchment of federalism, and would be "a roadblock to reunion" instead of a way to secure the peace. Thus, they continued to favor gradual abolition as a solution to slavery even in late 1865 when many slaves in the Confederacy had already been freed.[18]

Above all, however, the debate over the Thirteenth Amendment was a partisan one. Conservative Democratic newspaper editors rallied the party together by warning moderate Democrats who favored emancipation of the dangers of supporting Lincoln's amendment. Fearful of challenges from their own party in subsequent elections, moderate Democrats joined conservatives in defeating ratification of the Thirteenth Amendment in 1865 along a strictly party line vote.[19]

Democratic opposition to the Thirteenth Amendment gave Republicans a major issue to campaign on in statewide elections in 1865. Jersey voters, swayed by Republicans who reminded them that Democrats had opposed the war, called for an armistice, and could easily be considered treasonous for their opposition, expelled Democrats both from the governor's mansion and from control of the legislature. At least 5 percent of Jersey voters who had supported the Democrats in 1864 voted Republican and were joined by the large numbers of returning soldiers, previously barred from voting while stationed outside the state, who supported the Republicans in overwhelming numbers. The new Republican controlled government spearheaded the ratification of the Thirteenth Amendment in 1866, though it had already gone into effect the previous December, to restore the "good reputation of the state." However, despite its easy path to ratification, New Jersey's past slaveholding cropped up in the letter that Charles Perrin Smith, clerk of the New Jersey Supreme Court, sent to President Andrew Johnson announcing the ratification. Smith cited the amendment as the state's chance to "vindicate her ancient shame" and "at last stand redeemed from the reproach of abetting human slavery," thereby resuming "her proper position among the faithful sisters of the republic." Slavery's place in the state's history, therefore, was very much alive, especially since the Thirteenth Amendment had just freed the last apprentices for life and slaves for a term.[20]

After the Civil War, the memory of slavery's longevity in New Jersey reappeared several times, but like had happened in New England in the antebellum period, the state's slave past had become cloudy. In 1892, for instance, the *Christian Advocate* published an article that announced the death of New Jersey's last slave, 106-year-old Jinny. The article claimed that Jinny was "New Jersey's last slave by law" and stated that had she been under forty-five when the Emancipation Act took effect in 1821, she would have been freed. By the late nineteenth century, the reality of slavery's slow death in New Jersey had begun to fade—there was no Emancipation Act of 1821 and no slaves had ever been freed. As Jinny was older, the "family have always kept her," thereby not only highlighting the paternalistic role of the slaveholder but the beginnings of a reinvention of slavery's end and a masking of slavery's more violent and exploitive features. Likewise, in 1898, the *New York Genealogical and Biographical Record* published an extensive look at slavery in colonial New York and New Jersey, erroneously claiming that "slavery was slowly disappearing . . . and the unfriendly sentiment against it was steadily increasing." This, the article claimed, led to the 1804 abolition law and complete abolition in 1820. Thus began the common misperception that the ideology of freedom emanating from the Revolution had destroyed slavery in the North, one that is patently false. White New Jerseyans never opposed slavery in large numbers nor was the institution in decline after the Revolution.[21]

Even though white New Jerseyans began to reinterpret and question their past associations with slavery in the late nineteenth century, professional historians began to revive the institution's real history in the state. Though incomplete and often simplistic in their approaches, there remained at least some who understood slavery's true meaning for New Jerseyans. Henry Cooley's 1896 Johns Hopkins dissertation, "A Study of Slavery in New Jersey," the first academic work to examine the institution in the state, corrected some of these falsehoods by arguing that "slavery was very evidently an institution in New Jersey life" and that the 1846 abolition law "simply substituted apprenticeship in the place of slavery which allowed the institution to survive."[22] Cooley's work found few readers in New Jersey though it remained foundational for historians studying slavery in the North. Until now, it has been the only statewide study of slavery and abolition in New Jersey and therefore has informed hundreds of scholars since its publication. At least some did understand what Cooley knew about New Jersey's slave past, evidenced from a 1915 article detailing women's suffrage. These suffragists claimed that the legislature's failure even to consider women's suffrage reminded them of how New Jersey would only follow other states on important social issues, as it did "when it abolished slavery," after every other northern state had already done so.[23]

Although the present volume has been very much a New Jersey story, the same issues of freedom and unfreedom pervaded the nineteenth-century North. Pennsylvania, Rhode Island, Connecticut, and New York all enacted gradual abolition laws and had sustained interests in slavery into the 1810s and 1820s. While New Jersey's transition to a freer state occurred in the 1830s when free blacks had established communities and institutions of their own, later than in other northern states, the same issues were at play. New York, of course, remains an outlier, as it was the only state that legislatively completely abolished slavery in 1827, which sped its transformation to a predominantly free society. The jubilee that ensued from Washington Square Park to the Battery celebrated the freedom unattainable to slaves elsewhere in the North. However, beneath the excitement of that day, the 1817 law that began emancipation in 1827 failed to grant freedom to any slave for a term. Instead, it merely decreased the service requirement for children born after 1817 to twenty-one years (from twenty-eight for males or twenty-five for females). Therefore, a male child born to a slave on January 1, 1827, would serve his mother's master until 1848.[24]

The complicated relationships that these slaves for a term experienced as they moved toward freedom are central to the story of slavery and freedom in the North. The laws passed in the late eighteenth and early nineteenth centuries created a new status for these children, neither fully slave nor fully free. It became one of the many "slaveries" in the Atlantic World. Most white and black New Jerseyans saw them as slaves for a limited time and disputed their freedom throughout the abolition period. This contested relationship informed a much larger debate on the meaning of freedom in the early national North, impacted the lives of free blacks, and pervaded discussions of everything from slavery's westward expansion to the status of fugitive slaves.[25]

To return to Catherine's 1856 sale to Charles Sutphin that began this book, William Gillette might see her case as exceptional because by that year very few slaves for a term remained and even fewer apprentices for life still called New Jersey home. However, her case brings light to the persistence of slavery and the intense racial struggle with which New Jerseyans lived since gradual abolition began. Catherine represents the thousands of slaves and slaves for a term who functioned within an institution seemingly marked for death, yet which remained alive in New Jersey through the Civil War. Indeed, if slavery had been so marginal to New Jerseyans in the 1840s, the legislature would have simply abolished it and freed not only the remaining slaves but all the slaves for a term as well. Instead, they continued the state's gradual approach to abolition, but not because of an inherent need for slavery. Catherine and others like her were overall economically marginal by the 1840s. Slavery persisted because of the engrained association between race and slavery in the antebellum period. Most white New Jerseyans were comfortable with slavery's existence because they believed it had been marked for destruction and would die a natural death without violating the racial order. As blacks gradually gained freedom and pressed for more autonomy and power within the state, whites felt threatened and fell back on the racial status quo that had historically defined the relationship between the races. Most white New Jerseyans continued their gradual stance on black freedom even as late as 1865 to maintain that status quo.

Slavery's destruction in New Jersey then did not occur as an immediate by-product of the American Revolution, but of the Civil War, when the Thirteenth Amendment became part of the Constitution. Historians have always linked the gradual abolition movement to the Revolution and New Jersey's case is no different. The Revolution played a major role in the development of the conditions that led to gradual abolition's enactment in 1804. But as this book has shown, gradual abolition was not a quick harbinger of change but an elongated story of the Revolution's legacy that played out in early national and antebellum America. Therefore, gradual abolition's complicated and convoluted nature over six decades yields much more about how northerners understood the place of blacks in the new nation than what legislators thought in the statehouse in 1804. Even after their decision to begin gradual abolition, freedom remained a highly contested battleground.

If anything, slavery's slow death in the North suggests that the relationship between slave and free can never be easily delineated; the two ideals rarely existed as polar opposites in the United States or around the world. Freedom therefore was a process that spanned the Revolution to the Civil

War. Through this elongated and highly graduated lens, historians can see how white and black northerners struggled for decades to discover the true dimensions of their relationship to each other. Only by looking at the mechanics of this process can we fully understand how northerners understood their place in the larger American experience.

NOTES

Introduction

1. Bill of Sale, John Hagaman to Charles Sutphin, February 16, 1856, regarding "slave for life" Catherine, Hunterdon County Slave Births, Manumissions, and Miscellaneous Records, HCHS. For birth records of Catherine's two children, see Hunterdon County Birth Certificates of Children of Slaves, NJSA; Tax Ratables, Amwell Township, NJSA; Hodges, *Root and Branch*, , 6–33; U.S. Census Schedules, 1830–1860 for Amwell and Raritan, New Jersey, and Joshua, Illinois.

2. Ezell, ed., *The New Democracy in America*, 72–73. The term "Garden of America" or "Garden of North America" was a common term for New Jersey starting before the Revolution owing to New Jersey's key role in supplying food to New York, Philadelphia, and the Caribbean. See Fowler, "These were Troublesome Times Indeed," in Mitnick, ed, *New Jersey in the American Revolution*. The current nickname "Garden State" is credited to Abraham Browning of Camden, who called New Jersey the Garden State during the Philadelphia Centennial Exhibition on August 24, 1876, though the legislature did not officially adopt it until 1954, over the governor's veto.

3. 1790 Census Schedule, Historical Census Browser, University of Virginia, Geospatial and Statistical Data Center, http://mapserver.lib.vriginia.edu/collections. New Jersey had 11,423 slaves of a total population of 184,139 (6.20% enslaved). New England (Connecticut, Massachusetts [including Maine], New Hampshire, Rhode Island, and Vermont) had 3,763 slaves of a population of 1,009,206 (0.37% enslaved). New York had 21,193 slaves of a population of 340,241 (6.23% enslaved).

4. 1790 Census Schedule, Historical Census Browser, University of Virginia, Geospatial and Statistical Data Center, http://mapserver.lib.vriginia.edu/collections; White, *Somewhat More Independent*, 154; Hodges, *Root and Branch*, 162–86.

5. For examples of transatlantic approaches, see D. B. Davis, *The Problem of Slavery in Western Culture*; Davis, *The Problem of Slavery in the Age of Revolution*; Davis, *Slavery and Human Progress*; Eltis, *Economic Growth and the Ending of the Transatlantic Slave Trade*; Blackett, *Building an Antislavery Wall*; Rodgers, *Atlantic Crossings*; Drescher, *From Slavery to Freedom*; Linebaugh and Rediker, *The Many Headed Hydra*; Blackburn, *The Making of New World Slavery*; Bailyn, *Atlantic History*.

6. For revolutionary impact, see Lundin, *Cockpit of the Revolution* and Middlekauff, *The Glorious Cause*, 360–39.

7. New Jersey Amistad Commission, http://www.state.nj.us/education.amistad, accessed October 9, 2013; African Burial Ground Memorial, New York, http://www.nps.gov/afbg/index.htm.

8. Farrow, Lang, and Frank, *Complicity*, xxv. Also see Manegold, *Ten Hills Farm*, 239–56.

9. Jeremy Peters, "A Slavery Apology, But Debate Continues," *New York Times*, January 13, 2008.

10. For the comparative slavery model, see "AHR Forum: Crossing Slavery's Boundaries," 451–84.

11. Patterson, *Slavery and Social Death*; Kolchin, "Variations of Slavery in the Atlantic World," 551–54; Donoghue, "Out of the Land of Bondage"; Lovejoy and Hogendorn, *Slow Death for Slavery*, 234–60. For Lincoln, see Berlin, *Many Thousands Gone*, 23912. For prevailing views of northern slavery, see Berlin, *Many Thousands Gone*, 8; Berlin, *Generations of Captivity*, 102. For interposing New England on North, see Lepore, *The Name of War*.

13. For Massachusetts and Vermont, see Zilversmit, *The First Emancipation*, 114–16; Egerton, *Death or Liberty*, 93–121; McManus, *Black Bondage in the North*, 160, 164–67; Minardi, *Making Slavery History*, 18–19; Whitfield, *The Problem of Slavery in Early Vermont*, 3. For New Hampshire, see Zilversmit, *The First Emancipation*, 117; Melish, *Disowning Slavery*, 66.

14. Minardi, *Making Slavery History*, 7; Tomek, *Colonization and Its Discontents*, 3–4. Rhode Island's legislature titled its law "An Act authorizing the Manumission of Negroes, Mulattos and others and for the Gradual Abolition of Slavery," Connecticut had the "Gradual Abolition Act," Pennsylvania had its "Act for the Gradual Abolition of Slavery," and New Jersey passed the "Act for the Gradual Abolition of Slavery." New Yorkers agreed to the "Gradual Manumission Act." Of course, New York's "manumission law" enacted the same type of gradual program as New Jersey's or Pennsylvania's. For New York, see Hodges, *Root and Branch*, 168–73, and Harris, *In the Shadow of Slavery*, 70–71. For Pennsylvania, see Nash and Soderlund, *Freedom by Degrees*, 99–105, and D. Andrews, "Reconsidering the First Emancipation," 230–49. For Rhode Island and Connecticut, see Zilversmit, *The First Emancipation*, 119–24, Cottrol, *The Afro-Yankees*, 41–43, and Menschel, "Abolition Without Deliverance," 188. Menschel makes a similar argument about the use of "abolition" instead of "emancipation."

15. Richter, *Facing East from Indian Country*, 1–10; McTeigue, "The Conditions Under Which Slaves Lived in New Jersey," 5; Schermerhorn, *Money over Mastery, Family over Freedom*, 20; Ayers, *In the Presence of Mine Enemies*, 3.

16. Dorsey, *Hirelings*, 16–17.

17. An Act for the Gradual Abolition of Slavery, Feb.15, 1804, Acts 28th GA, 2nd sitting, chap. 103, 251–54; Dorsey, *Hirelings*, x–xi. Slave for a term births were recorded at the county level in "Black Birth Books" now held at the NJSA. Birth records are incomplete for most counties, with some not having any remaining records. For this study, I added all births of males born in 1805–1830 and females

born in 1809–1830. All of them would have been slaves for a term in 1830. The results are as follows by county: Bergen (792—records incomplete), Burlington (no records available), Cape May (no records available), Cumberland (no records available), Essex (227—records incomplete), Gloucester (8—records incomplete), Hunterdon (152—records incomplete), Middlesex (326—records incomplete), Monmouth (501), Morris (209), Salem (7—records incomplete), Somerset (672), and Sussex (172). This yielded a total of 3,066 slaves for a term. Adjusting for an estimated 25 percent mortality rate, I estimate that at least 2,300 slaves for a term were alive in 1830, though it could be more as records are incomplete. In 1830, the Federal Census recorded 20,557 African Americans in New Jersey, 6.4 percent of the total population of 320,823. Although I believe the census incorrectly recorded slaves and slaves for a term, I hold that about 10 percent of the black population remained slaves for life, the same as the census estimates, since some slaves would have been recorded as free and some freed people as slaves. The slave population would then be approximately 2,200. Adding the estimated 2,300 slaves for a term would yield 4,500 blacks in bound labor relationships. This would be 21.9 percent of the state's total black population, though it was probably more as slave for a term records are incredibly incomplete.

18. White, *Somewhat More Independent*, 47–48. For interstate slave trade, see Pingeon, "An Abominable Business," 14–35; A. P. Malone, *Sweet Chariot* ; Gigantino, "Trading in Jersey Souls," 281–302.

19. I borrow the term "slow death of slavery" and its variations throughout the manuscript from Lovejoy and Hogendorn, *Slow Death for Slavery*.

20. Melish, *Disowning Slavery*, 88–89; Conforti, *Imagining New England*; Minardi, *Making Slavery History*, 36–41; Menschel "Abolition Without Deliverance."

21. Nash and Soderlund, *Freedom by Degrees*, xv.

22. Hodges, *Root and Branch*; Hodges, *Slavery and Freedom in the Rural North*; White, *Somewhat More Independent*; Zilversmit, *The First Emancipation*. For a similar argument to Zilversmit, see McManus, *Black Bondage in the North*. For works specifically on slavery in New Jersey, see Cooley, "A Study of Slavery in New Jersey"; Marshall, *Manhood Enslaved*. Other works have placed African Americans at the center, though they focus more on the time after gradual abolition instead of the process of it. For examples, see Nash, *Forging Freedom*; Gellman, *Emancipating New York*; Harris, *In the Shadow of Slavery*; Dunbar, *A Fragile Freedom*; L. Alexander, *African or America?*.

23. Melish, *Disowning Slavery*, 84–118; Dorsey, *Hirelings*, x.

24. Berlin, *Many Thousands Gone*, 237, 239.

25. Ibid., 253.

26. Pomfret, *The Province of East New Jersey*, 3–17; Hodges, *Root and Branch*, 7–9; Berlin, *Many Thousands Gone*, 50–53; Clemens, *The Uses of Abundance*, 13–15.

27. Berlin, *Many Thousands Gone*, 53–55; Hodges, *Root and Branch*, 10–13, 18–19.

28. Berlin, *Many Thousands Gone*, 55–57; Hodges, *Root and Branch*, 25–32.

29. McConville, *These Daring Disturbers of the Public Peace*, 12–19; Clemens, *The Uses of Abundance*, 13–15; Pomfret, *The Province of West New Jersey*, 49–64; Pomfret, *The Province of East New Jersey*, 82–101, 182–98.

30. Hodges, *Root and Branch*, 36–39, 44–45; Tomlins, *Freedom Bound*, 489–91; East Jersey Laws, March 1682, chap. 8, "A Bill against Fugitive Servants and Entertainers of them," sec. 26, in Leaming and Spicer, *The Grants, Concessions, and Original Constitutions of the Province of New Jersey*, 239; East Jersey Laws, October 1694, chap. 2, "An Act Concerning Slaves . . . " in Leaming and Spicer, *The Grants . . .* , 340–42.

31. Hodges, *Root and Branch*, 40–47; Nash and Soderlund, *Freedom by Degrees*, 9–15.

32. Pomfret, *The Province of West Jersey*, 190–215; Pomfret, *The Province of East New Jersey*, 336–64; Hodges, *Root and Branch*, 63–68; Tomlins, *Freedom Bound*, 491–92; "An Act for Regulating Negro, Indian, and Mallatto Slaves within this Province of New Jersey," December 12, 1704, in Bush, *Laws of the Royal Colony of New Jersey*, 2: 28–30.

33. Tomlins, *Freedom Bound*, 491–93, 497; Hodges, *Root and Branch*, 68–70; Berlin, *Many Thousands Gone*, 177–78; Hoffer, *The Great New York Conspiracy of 1741*, 17–22; "An Act for Regulating of Slaves," March 11, 1713/14, in Bush, *Laws of the Royal Colony of New Jersey*, 2: 136–40.

34. Hodges, *Root and Branch*, 74–76, 80–82; Berlin, *Many Thousands Gone*, 178–83, 179, 181.

35. Hodges, *Root and Branch*, 88–97; Berlin, *Many Thousands Gone*, 183–87; Lepore, *New York Burning*, xi–xx; Hoffer, *The Great New York Conspiracy of 1741*, 67–77.

36. Hodges, *Root and Branch*, 101–9, 130; Berlin, *Many Thousands Gone*, 369.

Chapter 1. Debating Abolition in an Age of Revolution

1. Nash and Soderlund, *Freedom by Degrees*, 81–82, 89–90; Soderlund, *Quakers and Slaves*, 8–14, 169–72; Nash, *Forging Freedom*, 42; Zilversmit, *The First Emancipation*, 78–83.

2. Slaughter, *The Beautiful Soul of John Woolman*, 105–6, 132; Jackson, *Let This Voice Be Heard*, 35–37.

3. Jackson, *Let This Voice Be Heard*, 45, 52.

4. Slaughter, *The Beautiful Soul of John Woolman*, 103.

5. Ibid., 132–34.

6. Ibid., 163; *An Epistle of Caution*; Jackson, *Let This Voice Be Heard*, 52–55, 53.

7. *Friends' Weekly Intelligencer*, May 9, 1874.

8. Jackson, *Let This Voice Be Heard*, 54–56. For Benezet, see Sassi, "With a Little Help from the Friends," and Sassi "Africans in the Quaker Image."

9. Jackson, *Let This Voice Be Heard*, 78–79, 248.

10. Dillwyn, *Brief considerations on slavery and the expediency of its abolition*, 6.

11. Ibid., 8.

12. Granville Sharp to Samuel Allinson, July 28, 1774, and Samuel Allinson to Patrick Henry, October 17, 1774, Samuel Allinson Papers, RUASC; D.B. Davis, *Inhuman Bondage*, 144–45; D.B. Davis, *The Problem of Slavery in Western Culture*, 291–493.

13. Nash and Soderlund, *Freedom by Degrees*, 81–82, 89–90; Soderlund, *Quakers and Slaves*, 8–14, 169–172; Nash, *Forging Freedom*, 42; Zilversmit, *The First Emancipation*, 78–83; Jackson, *Let This Voice Be Heard*, 248–49.

14. Society of Friends Burlington Monthly Meeting Manumission Papers and Book of Manumissions, New Jersey Abolition Society and Burlington County Abolition Society Papers, BCHS; Burlington Society of Friends Quarterly Meeting, August 28, 1775, August 26, 1776, February 24, 1778, SFHL.

15. Ibid.; Zilversmit, *The First Emancipation*, 16–19; Nash and Soderlund, *Freedom by Degrees*, 8–14, 84–89; Samuel Allinson to Richard Hartshorne, December 26, 1772, Samuel Allinson Papers, RUASC; Zilversmit, *The First Emancipation*, 80; Philadelphia Society of Friends Yearly Meeting Minutes, October 4, 1777, and Burlington Society of Friends Quarterly Meeting Minutes, August 25, 1777, February 23, 1778, SFHL. For Fogg, see Salem Society of Friends Monthly Meeting Minutes, November 24, 1777, February 23, 1778, SFHL.

16. Indenture and Manumission of Negro Jane, Foster-Clement Collection, HSP. For another example, see Manumission Document of Slave Pompey, August 5, 1776, Item 1326, Sol Feinstone Collection and Manumission of Negro William, Unnumbered Slavery Collection Documents, David Library.

17. Nash and Soderlund, *Freedom by Degrees*, 8–14, 91; Zilversmit, *The First Emancipation*, 80; Philadelphia Society of Friends Yearly Meeting Minutes, September 27, 1775, October 4, 1777, SFHL.

18. Burlington Society of Friends Quarterly Meeting Minutes, August 30, 1779, SFHL.

19. Philadelphia Society of Friends Yearly Meeting Minutes, September 29, 1783, Burlington Society of Friends Quarterly Meeting Minutes, August 30, 1779, August 28, 1780, February 26, May 28, August 27, November 26, 1781, November 25, 1782, Salem and Gloucester Society of Friends Quarterly Meeting Minutes, September 22, 1780, September 20, 1782, Salem Society of Friends Monthly Meeting Minutes, May 25, August 31, 1778, October 26, 1778, SFHL.

20. Zilversmit, *The First Emancipation*, 91–93; Petition of Inhabitants of Chester Township, Burlington County to the General Assembly advocating the Gradual Abolition of Slavery, November 9, 1775, BAH Collection, Legislative Records, 1770–1781, NJSA; *Pennsylvania Gazette*, February 2, 1774; Petition of Inhabitants of Burlington County to the New Jersey State Legislature Advocating the Manumission of Slaves and Petition of Inhabitants of Cumberland County to the New Jersey State Legislature Advocating the Manumission of Slaves, BAH Collection, Legislative Records, no date, NJSA.

21. Copy of Letter to Pennsylvania General Assemblyman, 1774, Cox-Parrish-Wharton Papers, HSP.

22. Sharp, *Extract of a Letter*, 57–58; Sharp, *The Just Limitation of Slavery*.

23. Anthony Benezet to Samuel Allinson, October 30, 1772, Allinson Family Papers, HCQC.

24. Petition of the Citizens of Perth Amboy to the General Assembly Opposing Slave Manumissions, January 12, 1774, Petition of Inhabitants of Middletown, Monmouth County to the Assembly Opposing slave Manumissions, February 2, 1774, and Petition of Inhabitants of Monmouth County to the General Assembly opposing Slave Manumissions, February 2, 1774, BAH Collection, Legislative Records, 1770–1781, NJSA. For the introduction of more petitions to the legislature, see New Jersey GA Minutes, Votes, and Proceedings, September 19, 1776.

25. New Jersey General Assembly Minutes, Votes, and Proceedings, October 5, 1776, NJSA; Petition of Bergen County inhabitants to Council and General Assembly remonstrating against Articles 5 and 6 of the Treaty of Paris, May 3, 1783, State Library MSS Collection, NJSA; Paine, *Common Sense*. For general connections between slavery as a political issue in the Revolution, see Davis, *Inhuman Bondage*, 144–45; Okoye, "Chattel Slavery as the Nightmare of the American Revolutionaries," 1980; Helo and Onuf, "Jefferson, Morality and the Problem of Slavery."

26. Samuel Allinson to William Livingston, July 13, 1778, in Prince, Ryan, et al., eds., *The Papers of William Livingston*, 2: 387–88.

27. Nash, *Forging Freedom*, 40–42; *New York Journal*, April 4, 1776. For the original idea of the American paradox, see E. Morgan, "Slavery and Freedom."

28. Jacob Green to the Synod of New York and Philadelphia, October 18, 1779, Presbyteries of Morris County and Newark Papers, NJHS; Green, *A Sermon Delivered at Hanover, April 22, 1778*, as printed in Mitros, ed., *Jacob Green and the Slavery Debate*, 35–44. Also see 7–14.

29. *New Jersey Journal*, May 3, May 10, 1780.

30. *New Jersey Journal*, November 29, 1780. For passage of Pennsylvania Gradual Abolition Act, see Nash and Soderlund, *Freedom by Degrees*, 104–5. For spreading of abolitionist rhetoric, see Nash, *Forging Freedom*, 39.

31. *New Jersey Journal*, December 27, 1780.

32. *New Jersey Journal*, January 17, 24, 1781. For more debates in the *New Jersey Journal* between Green and others, see January 10, 24, 31, 1781.

33. Berlin, *Many Thousands Gone*, 193.

34. *New Jersey Gazette*, September 20, 1780; D. Cooper, *A Serious Address to the Rulers of America on the Inconsistency of their Conduct Respecting Slavery*.

35. Berlin, *Generations of Captivity*, 99–101.

Chapter 2. Sustaining Slavery in an Age of Freedom

1. Petition of Negro Prime to the Legislative Council and General Assembly, Trenton, November 6, 1786, BAH Collection, Legislative Records 1782–1787, NJSA.

2. Ibid.; Bainbridge Petition, Loyalist Claims Commission, British Public Records Office, AO 12/14/139–144, AO 12/101/255–56, AO13/108/31–46. For similar issues in New York, see Kruger, "Born to Run," 645–49.

3. Petition of Negro Prime to the Legislative Council and General Assembly, Trenton, November 6, 1786, BAH Collection, Legislative Records 1782–1787, NJSA.

4. Ibid.; Petition of Moore Furman to the Legislature Concerning the Custody of a Slave, May 19, 1785, BAH Collection, Legislative Records 1782–1787, NJSA, and Fishman, "Taking a Stand for Freedom in Revolutionary New Jersey," 353–56. Also see Nash, The Forgotten Fifth, 67. For Nash applied to New Jersey, see G. Wright, "Moving Toward Breaking the Chains," in Mitnick, ed., New Jersey in the American Revolution 115.

5. Lundin, Cockpit of the Revolution.

6. For Green's church, see Schama, Rough Crossings, 111–12; Hodges, Root and Branch, 143; New Jersey Gazette, October 4, 1780. For newspaper debates, see New Jersey Gazette, see November 8, 1780, January 10, February 14, March 21, April 1, June 27, 1781.

7. Samuel Allinson to William Livingston, August 12, 1778, in Prince, Ryan, et al., Papers of William Livingston, 2: 407–14.

8. William Livingston to Samuel Allinson, July 25, 1778, in ibid., 399–404; Zilversmit, The First Emancipation, 141–42.

9. Schama, Rough Crossings, 113–14; Hodges, Slavery, Freedom, and Culture Among Early American Workers, 67.

10. Middlekauff, The Glorious Cause, 360–69.

11. Abraham Clark to John Adams, August 23, 1776, in Gephart and Smith eds, Letters of Delegates to Congress, 5: 51.

12. Jedidiah Huntington to Jabez Huntington, September 28, 1776, in Sol Feinstone Collection, David Library of the American Revolution (hereafter David Library), Item 594.

13. Samuel Adams to Elizabeth Adams, December 19, 1776, in Gephart and Smith, eds, Letters of Delegates to Congress 5: 616–17 and Samuel Adams to John Adams, January 9, 1777, 6: 63–65.

14. William Whipple to Josiah Bartlett, December 23, 1776, in Gephart and Smith, eds, Letters of Delegates to Congress, 5: 652–53. For similar accounts, see William Ellery to Nicholas Cooke, December 24, 1776, 5: 653–56; Benjamin Rush to Richard Henry Lee, December 30, 1776, 5: 705–6; and William Whipple to Josiah Bartlett, January 9, 1777, 6: 77–78.

15. Nathanael Greene to Catharine Greene, December 4, 1776, in Showman, ed., The Papers of General Nathaniel Greene, 1: 365.

16. Thomas Nelson to Thomas Jefferson, January 2, 1777, in Gephart and Smith, eds, Letters of Delegates to Congress 6: 24–25.

17. Samuel Adams to James Warren, February 16, 1777, in Gephart and Smith, eds, Letters of Delegates to Congress 6: 297–99.

18. Richard Henry Lee to Arthur Lee, February 17, 1777, in Gephart and Smith, eds, *Letters of Delegates to Congress*, 6: 308–9. Also see John Adams to Abigail Adams, February 17, 1777, 6: 305–7 for more Jersey attacks.

19. Lobdell, ed., "The Revolutionary War Journal of Sergeant Thomas McCarty," 45 as cited in Middlekauff, *The Glorious Cause*, 512–13.

20. William Whipple to Joseph Whipple, February 2, 1777, in Gephart and Smith, eds, *Letters of Delegates to Congress* 6: 197–99.

21. Alexander Macwhorter and Elisha Boudinot to William Livingston, April 26, 1777, Edwin Ely Collection, NJHS.

22. Baron Friedrich Adam Julius von Wangenheim to brother, August 27, 1777, in Sol Feinstone Collection, Item 1501, David Library. Translation from German in Felcone, ed., *Abstracts of New Jersey Manuscripts in the Sol Feinstone Collection of the American Revolution*, 17–18.

23. Orderly Book, Alexander Scammell, Continental Army Adjutant General, NJHS. For more accounts of foraging, see New Jersey State Troops, Military Record Book, Captain John Craig's Company of the Essex County Militia, July and August 1781.

24. For General Orders, see First Continental Artillery Regiment Papers, NJHS, January 1780; Middlekauff, *The Glorious Cause*, 510–13; Quincy, *Basking Ridge in Revolutionary Days*, 7–8.

25. William Howe Orderly Book, December 19, 1776, April 27, June 14–15, 1777, CLUM.

26. Court Martial Records, War Office Records, WO 71/87/176–78 (September 2–25, 1778), WO 71/87/179–81 (September 5–25, 1778).

27. James Robertson to Lord George Germain, July 1, 1780, in K. G. Davis, ed., *Documents of the American Revolution, Colonial Office Series, 1770–1783*, 18: 107–10.

28. Benedict Arnold to Lord George Germain, October 28, 1780, Henry Clinton Papers, vol. 127, CLUM.

29. William Whipple to Josiah Bartlett, January 13, 1777, in Gephart and Smith, eds, *Letters of Delegates to Congress*, 6: 94–95.

30. Joseph Clark, Revolutionary War Officer Papers, June 1778, NJHS; Middlekauff, *The Glorious Cause*, 426–34.

31. Richard Varick to Philip Van Rensselaer, October 30, 1778 as cited in Hodges, *Slavery, Freedom, and Culture*, 43–44.

32. Nash, *The Forgotten Fifth*, 67; Holton, *Forced Founders*, 156–57.

33. For David Jones quote, see Egerton, *Death or Liberty*, 84. For Henry Clinton's proclamation, see "Proclamation of Sir Henry Clinton," *Royal Gazette*, July 3, 1779. For Dunmore's Proclamation, see Nash, *Forgotten Fifth*, 26–27; Gellman, *Emancipating New York*, 38; Nash, *Forging Freedom*, 45; Berlin, *Many Thousands Gone*, 257–58; G. Wright, "Moving Toward Breaking the Chains" in Mitnick, ed., *New Jersey in the American Revolution*, 127; Holton, *Forced Founders*, 156–63.

34. *The Journals of Henry Melchior Muhlenberg*, 3: 78, as cited in Nash, *The Forgotten Fifth*, 30.

35. Dunbar, *A Fragile Freedom*, 22; Egerton, *Death or Liberty*, 89.

36. B. Smith, "Runaway Slaves in the Mid-Atlantic Region During the Revolutionary Era," in Hoffman and Albert, eds, *The Transforming Hand of Revolution*, 199–230.

37. *New Jersey Gazette* information was gathered by a search of all issues of the *Gazette* between 1777 and 1783 with the keyword "negro, slave, or black." Additional statistical information from New York papers from Hodges and Brown, eds., *"Pretends to be Free."* For Phillis Sparrow, see Hodges, ed, *The Black Loyalist Directory*, 19. For Richard Stevens, see New Jersey Supreme Court Case File 34939, NJSA.

38. Dunbar, *A Fragile Freedom*, 21.

39. Testimony of Joseph Holmes, Jr, *Documents Relating to the Revolutionary History of the State of New Jersey*, 1: 380–81.

40. Inventories of Damages by the British and Americans in New Jersey, 1776–1782, Legislative Records, NJSA. For specific claims, see Middlesex County claims 1 and 214. For battleground between slavery and freedom, see Schama, *Rough Crossing*, 111–18. For the opposite interpretation, that British troops frightened slaves, see Marshall, *Manhood Enslaved*, 73.

41. *John Stockton v. William Cook*, New Jersey Supreme Court Case File 34416, NJSA; Inventories of Damages by the British and Americans in New Jersey, 1776–1782, Legislative Records, NJSA; Foy, "Seeking Freedom in the Atlantic World, 1714–1783," 75.

42. Extract of a letter from New Barbadoes, May 27, 1780, *Documents Relating to the Revolutionary History of the State of New Jersey*, 4: 445.

43. Samuel Hayes to William Livingston, July 16, 1777, in Prince, Ryan, et al., *Papers of William Livingston*, 2: 22; William Livingston to Richard Bache, May 22, 1777, 1: 338.

44. Hodges, *Root and Branch*, 146.

45. For slaves fleeing to British lines, see Harris, *In the Shadow of Slavery*, 55; Peter Vroom to Sir Guy Carleton, circa1782–1783, Revolutionary Era Papers, NJHS; Hodges, *Slavery and Freedom in the Rural North*, 95; G. Wright, "Moving Toward Breaking the Chains," in Mitnick, ed., *New Jersey in the American Revolution*, 115. For cases of imprisoned runaways, see New Jersey Council of Safety Minutes, May 12, May 22, 1777, NJSA.

46. Schama, *Rough Crossings*, 114. For reports of foraging, see Captain Jonathan Dayton's Report, December 9, 1781, Jonathan Dayton Papers, William Livingston to Jonathan Deare, March 1, 1779, William Livingston Papers, James Caldwell to William Alexander, October 25, 1778, James Caldwell Papers, all part of Edwin Ely Collection, NJHS. Also see Adelberg, "An Evenly Balanced County.".

47. Abraham Clark to James Caldwell, February 4, 1777, Louis Bamberger Collection, NJHS.

48. Lord Sterling to Quartermasters, December 27, 1778, in Sol Feinstone Collection, Item 54, David Library. For another example, see Hay and DeYoe, *New Barbadoes Neck in Revolutionary War Days*, 6–7. For failed federal compensation for damage claims, see A Bill to Compensate Citizens for Enemy Damage, May 19, 1779, in Rutland, ed, *The Papers of George Mason, 1725–1792*, 2: 502–4.

49. William Dow to the Council and Assembly, April 23, 1779, BAH Collection, Revolutionary War Documents, NJSA. For other damage claims, see List of Property Destroyed during the Revolution, Baldwin-Brown-Coe Family Papers, 1776–1893, NJHS, and Inventories of Damages by the British and Americans in New Jersey, 1776–1782, NJSA. For claims specifically mentioned, see Westfield, claims 6 and 41.

50. Zilversmit, *The First Emancipation*, 242; Essex County Wills, NJSA; Hodges, *Root and Branch*, 143.

51. Nash, *Forging Freedom*, 59.

52. General Sir Guy Carleton to General George Washington, May 12, 1783, Colonial Office Correspondence, 5/109/313.

53. Nash, *The Forgotten Fifth*, 42–46; Hodges, *Slavery and Freedom in the Rural North*, 105; Lord North to General Sir Guy Carleton, August 8, 1783, Colonial Office Correspondence 5/110/62. For evacuation and resettlement of ex-slaves, see Pybus, *Epic Journeys of Freedom*; Richard Oswald to Thomas Townshend, November 30, 1782 and Guy Carleton to George Washington, June 10, 1783, in K.G. Davis, ed., *Documents of the American Revolution, Colonial Office Series*, 354, 411; Kruger, "Born to Run," 654–65.

54. Egbert Benson, WS Smith, and Daniel Parker, Commissioners of the United States to Sir Guy Carleton, June 17, 1783, Colonial Office Correspondence CO5/110/60–61.

55. Extract of the Resolutions of a Meeting of a Number of Inhabitants of the County of Essex in the State of New Jersey at the County Courthouse in Newark on Monday the 19th day of May 1783, agreeably to invitations given in the two preceding New Jersey Journals and public notices put up in different parts of the county, Colonial Office Correspondence, CO5/8/421–23.

56. General Sir Guy Carleton to Lord North, June 6, 1783, in Davis, ed., *Documents of the American Revolution, Colonial Office Series*, 177–78.

57. Petition of Inhabitants of Essex County to the General Assembly Concerning War Damages, May 5, 1783, BAH Collection, Legislative Records 1782–1787, NJSA; Sarah Haviland to the American Commissioners at New York, June 23, 1783, in Guy Carleton Papers on microfilm, nos. 8123, 8132, David Library. For Haviland, see Kruger, "Born to Run," 649–50.

58. Hodges, *Root and Branch*, 156.

59. Dinah Archey to Sir Guy Carleton, August 8, 1783, African American History Collection, CLUM.

60. Court Martial Records, British War Office Records, WO 71/97/320–54.

61. Hodges, *Black Loyalist Directory*, 9–10, 25.

62. Anthony Smithers Petition, Loyalist Claims Commission, AO 12/99/358, 13/113A/156–62; John Baptist Petition, Loyalist Claims Commission, AO 12/99/358.

63. Ibid; Pybus, *Epic Journeys of Freedom*, 75–80.

64. George Mellick Notebook, 89, Andrew Mellick Papers, NJHS. For 1741 New York Conspiracy, see Lepore, *New York Burning*; Hoffer, *The Great New York Conspiracy of 1741*. For laws in the aftermath of 1712, see "An Act for Regulating of Slaves," March 11, 1713, Allinson, *Acts of the General Assembly of the Province of New Jersey*, chap. 39, 18–21. For those after 1741, see "An Act for regulating Taverns," March 15, 1739, Allinson, *Acts of the General Assembly of the Province of New Jersey*, chap. 158, 105; "An Act to restrain Tavernkeepers and others from selling strong liquors to Servants, Negroes, and Molatto Slaves and to prevent Negroes and Molatto Slaves from meeting in large companies, from running about at nights, and from hunting or carrying a gun on the Lord's Day," Allinson, *Acts of the General Assembly of the Province of New Jersey*, chap. 241, 191–92.

65. Hodges, *Slavery, Freedom, and Culture*, 72; Stratford, "Docket of Jacob Van Noorstrand," 58–67.

66. New Jersey Supreme Court Case Files 21064 and 37213, NJSA. For other cases, see files 37216 and 37232, NJSA.

67. Hodges, *Slavery and Freedom in the Rural North*, 94–95

68. Angelica Church to Alexander Hamilton, January 20, 1797, and *Claypoole's (Philadelphia) American Daily Advertiser*, December 19, 1776, as cited in Syrett, ed, *The Papers of Alexander Hamilton*, 20: 471–73.

69. Gellman, *Emancipating New York*, 36.

70. Marquis de Lafayette to George Clinton, March 3, 1778, in Idzerda, ed., *Lafayette in the Age of the American Revolution*, 1: 327–29.

71. Frey, *Water from the Rock*, 56–57.

72. Abstract of a Letter Received from Gervais Werch in Charleston, June 27, 1775, Henry Clinton Papers, vol. 11, CLUM. Also see John Stuart to Clinton, March 1776, Henry Clinton Papers, vol. 14.

73. Memoir of Chevalier Dubuysson, December 1776 to July 1777, in Idzerda, *Lafayette in the Age of the American Revolution*, 1: 73.

74. Jonathan Dickinson Sergeant to John Adams, August 13, 1776, in Taylor et al., *Papers of John Adams*, 4: 453–55.

75. Newspaper extract from *New York Packet and the American Advertisers*, July 1, 1779, in *Documents Relating to the Revolutionary History of the State of New Jersey*, 3: 490; Hatfield, *History of Elizabeth, New Jersey*, 476; Nash, *Forging Freedom*, 45; G. Wright, "Moving Toward Breaking the Chains," in Mitnick, ed, *New Jersey in the American Revolution*, 126.

76. Ege, *Pioneers of Old Hopewell*, 128–31.

77. Benjamin Franklin to Jonathan Shipley, July 7, 1775, in Gephart and Smith, *Letters of Delegates to Congress*, I, 1: 604–7.

78. Thomas Burke, Draft Address to the Inhabitants of the United States, May 29, 1777, in ibid., 7: 150; George Mason, "State Controls on Slavery Traffic Should Be Surrendered to the National Government," Speech at Continental Congress, August 22, 1787, in Rutland, ed, *The Papers of George Mason*, 3: 965–66.

79. Proclamation of Sir Henry Clinton, June 30, 1779, Henry Clinton Papers, vol. 62, CLUM; Alexander Innes to Lord Dartmouth, May 16, 1775, Earl of Dartmouth Papers, viewed at David Library; Proclamation of Sir Henry Clinton, June 30, 1779, and Robert Pigot to William Howe, April 10, 1778, in Guy Carleton Papers (Microfilm Item # 1083 and 2094); Thomas Gage to Lord Barrington, June 12, 1775, in Thomas Gage Papers, English Series, vol. 29, CLUM; Guy Carleton to Benjamin Thompson, March 21, 1783, in Secretary at War In-Letters, viewed at David Library; Nathanael Greene to George Washington, July 21, 1776, Microfilm Papers of Nathanael Greene, viewed at David Library. Also see Earl of Dunmore to Sir Henry Clinton, February 2, 1782, and Scheme for Raising Black Troops in South Carolina, January 5, 1782, Colonial Office Correspondence, CO 5/175/67–68 and 264–66.

80. Court Martial Transcripts, British War Office Records, WO 71/87/205–06 and 71/87/207–08.

81. Reverend Alexander MacWhorter's Letter in *Documents Relating to the Revolutionary History of the State of New Jersey*, 1: 350–53.

82. Patrick Ferguson, Proposed Plan for Bringing the Army Under Strict Discipline with Regard to Marauding, November 1779, vol. 78, Henry Clinton Papers, CLUM.

83. Court Martial Transcripts, British War Office Records, 71/96/126–37; "A State of the Militia, Refugees, and Other Loyal Inhabitants in New York and Long Island, August 1782," Colonial Office Records, CO5/1089/534.

84. Ibid.

85. Schama, *Rough Crossings*, 114–15; Egerton, *Death or Liberty*, 65–67; Extract of a letter from Monmouth County, June 12, 1780, in *Documents Relating to the Revolutionary History of the State of New Jersey*, 4: 434–35; David Forman to William Livingston, June 9, 1780, in Prince, Ryan et al., *Papers of William Livingston*, 3: 423. Also see *New Jersey Gazette*, April 12, 1780. For more on Sandy Hook and Tye, see *Old Times in Old Monmouth*, 70–115, esp. 72–75.

86. John Fell to Robert Morris, July 10, 1779, in Gephart and Smith, eds, *Letters of Delegates to Congress*, 12: 185–86.

87. Samuel Forman to William Livingston, August 6, 1780, in Prince, Ryan, et al. *Papers of William Livingston*, 4: 28–29.

88. William Livingston to Asher Holmes, March 21, 1780, in ibid., 3: 343–44; Hodges, *Slavery and Freedom in the Rural North*, 102.

89. A Letter from Freehold, April 15, 1782, in *Documents Relating to the Revolutionary History of the State of New Jersey*, V, 5: 424; Hodges, *Slavery and Freedom in the Rural North*, 105–6; Schama, *Rough Crossing*, 115–16.

90. *New Jersey Gazette*, June 5, 1782; Hodges, *Slavery and Freedom in the Rural North*, 104–5; Hodges, *Slavery, Freedom, and Culture*, 44.

91. Nash, *Forging Freedom*, 51–52; Nash, *The Forgotten Fifth*, 10–11; Dunbar, *A Fragile Freedom*, 22; Nash, *The Unknown Revolution*, 329; Wiencek, *An Imperfect God*, 227; "An Act for the better regulating the Militia," March 15, 1777, Acts GA, 1st session., chaps. 20, 26 ; "An Act for the Regulating, Training and Arraying of the Militia," April 14, 1778, Acts GA, 2nd sess., 2nd sitting, chap. 22, 44–45; Gough, "Black Men and the Early New Jersey Militia," 227–38.

92. Thomas Burke to John Laurens, December 26, 1780, in Burnett, ed, *Letters of Members of the Continental Congress*, 500–501.

93. James Madison to Joseph Jones, November 28, 1780, in Gephart and Smith, eds, *Letters of Delegates to Congress*, 16: 397–98; Nash, *The Unknown Revolution*, 329.

94. Nash, *The Forgotten Fifth*, 10–13; Nash, *Unknown Revolution*, 327–39; William Livingston to George Washington, February 22, 1777, in Prince, Ryan et al., *Papers of William Livingston*, 1: 250–51. For more on slaves serving in the military, see Egerton, *Death or Liberty*, 74–81; P. Foner, *Blacks in the American Revolution*; Greene, *Black Courage, 1775–1783*; Knoblock, *Strong and Brave Fellows*.

95. Anthony Wayne to John Martin, February 19, 1782, Anthony Wayne Papers, HSP.

96. Earl of Dunmore to Sir Henry Clinton, February 2, 1782, and Scheme for Raising Black Troops in South Carolina, January 5, 1782, Colonial Office Correspondence, CO 5/175/67–68 and 264–66.

97. Jonathan Dickinson Sergeant to John Adams, August 13, 1776, in Taylor et al., eds, *Papers of John Adams*, 4: 453–55.

98. John Adams to Jonathan Dickinson Sergeant, August 17, 1776, in Gephart and Smith, eds, *Letters of Delegates to Congress*, 5: 11–12.

99. Stone, ed, *Letters of Brunswick and Hessian Officers During the American Revolution*, 142. Data on New Jersey black soldiers from the Revolutionary War Index Files and New Jersey Revolutionary War Numbered Manuscripts, NJSA. Also see Quarles, *Negro in the American Revolution*, and Walling, *Men of Color at the Battle of Monmouth, June 28, 1778*.

100. Revolutionary War Index Files, NJSA; Samuel Sutphen Federal Pension Application, Series M805, Roll 783, File R10321, August 15, 1832; Honeyman, ed, "The Revolutionary War Record of Samuel Sutphen, Slave," 186–90, as reprinted in Gerlach, ed, *New Jersey in the American Revolution, 1763–1783*, 354–60. For more on Sutphen, also see Schleicher and Winter, "Patriot and Slave," 30–43. Casper Berger died in 1815, see Bergun Brokaw Account Book, 1812–1851, RUASC for his coffin purchase. For other cases of slaves who did not gain their freedom from service in the Revolution, see Quarles, *Negro in the American Revolution*, 183–84.

101. Samuel Sutphen Federal Pension Application, August 15, 1832. For another example of a rejected pension from a black soldier, see Minardi, "Freedom in the Archives," 128–40.

102. Revolutionary War Index Files, NJSA; Oliver Cromwell Federal Pension Application, Series M805, Roll 233, File S34613; Nell, *The Colored Patriots of the American Revolution*, 160–61. Nell uses a *Burlington Gazette* article from the 1830s to describe Cromwell's service (the article is an interview with Cromwell). The article claims that Cromwell crossed the Delaware with Washington and fought at Princeton and Trenton, but his pension application claims he did not enter service until 1777. For use of this information, see G. Wright, "Moving Toward Breaking the Chains" in Mitnick, ed, *New Jersey in the American Revolution*, 129. See Nell, *The Colored Patriots of the American Revolution*, 160–65, for other Jersey blacks in the Revolution. Additional information on Cromwell and Ceasar from New Jersey Revolutionary War Numbered Manuscripts #2237, 2380, 3774, 3775, 9902, NJSA.

103. New Jersey Revolutionary War Numbered Manuscripts, 5970–5975, NJSA.

104. Daniel and Henry Van Mater to Sir Henry Clinton, February 24, 1779, Microfilm Sir Guy Carleton Papers #1769; General Sir Guy Carleton to Lord North, June 6, 1783, in K.G. Davis, ed, *Documents of the American Revolution, Colonial Office Series*, 177–78.

105. M. Richards, "Patriots and Plunderers," 14–28; Hodges, *Root and Branch*, 154.

106. New Jersey Acts, chap. 5, "An Act to Punish Traitors and Disaffected Persons," October 4, 1776.

107. New Jersey Supreme Court Case Files 796, 33638, 36022, 38615, 37878, 36644, NJSA. Also see Somerset County summary accounts and miscellaneous, Department of Defense, Adjutant General's Office, Records of Commissioners of Forfeited Estates, 1777–1795, NJSA, and New Jersey Acts, chap. 34, "An Act of Free and general Pardon and for other purposes," June 5, 1777. For the largest county collection (120 inquests) see Essex County Inquisitions of Loyalists, Department of Defense, Adjutant General's Office, Records of Commissioners of Forfeited Estates, 1777–1795, NJSA.

108. Inhabitants of Morris County to the Council and Assembly, petition for a law to confiscate property of those who aid the enemy, May 28, 1781, in BAH Collection, Revolutionary War Documents, NJSA.

109. Inhabitants of Monmouth County to the Governor, Legislative Council and General Assembly, Petition requesting payment for enemy damage through forfeited estates, May 25, 1779, in BAH Collection, Revolutionary War Documents, NJSA.

110. Petition of Inhabitants of Sussex County to the General Assembly, concerning forfeited estates, March 17, 1779, Report of the Committee of the Legislative Council on the sale of forfeited Estates, May 1779, Petition of Inhabitants of Monmouth County to the Council and Assembly concerning the commissioner of Forfeited Estates, May 8, 1779, Petition of Monmouth County Commissioners of Forfeited Estates to the General Assembly concerning complaints against them, September 21, 1779, Petition of Monmouth County Commissioners of Forfeited Estates to the General Assembly concerning their previous petition, September 22, 1779, Petition of

Inhabitants of Sussex County to the General Assembly, concerning forfeited estates, March 17, 1779, in BAH Collection, Legislative Records, 1770–1781, NJSA.

111. Foy, "Seeking Freedom in the Atlantic World, 1713–1783," 64–65; Foy, "Eighteenth-Century Prize Negroes," 379–80, 385–86.

112. Foy, "Eighteenth-Century Prize Negroes," 379–81, 385–86, quotes 380, 386.

113. Ibid., 379; *New Jersey Gazette*, June 12, 1782.

114. John Bray to William Livingston, April 24, 1782, in Prince, Ryan et al., *Papers of William Livingston*, 4: 397–98; Sale Advertisement in *Documents Relating to the Revolutionary History of the State of New Jersey*, Second Series, 5: 446.

115. *New Jersey Gazette*, October 27, 1779.

116. Department of Defense, Adjutant General's Office, Records of Commissioners of Forfeited Estates, 1777–1795, NJSA. Most remaining inventories are from Essex, Monmouth, Sussex, and Somerset Counties.

117. Calculations of slaves come from loyalist claim records from Loyalist Records, American Revolution, Audit Office Records, Public Records Office, London (microfilm version in NJSA and David Library), Coldham, *American Loyalist Claims*, vol. 1; Coldham, *American Migrations, 1765–99*; Palmer, *Biological Sketches of Loyalists of the American Revolution*; E. A. Jones, *The Loyalists of New Jersey*.

118. For one example of a confiscated slave not listed, see William Livingston to Thomas Bradford, June 3, 1780, in Prince, Ryan et al. *Papers of William Livingston*, 413. Livingston claimed the slave, Andrew, is "legally the property of the state as his master's whole estate is confiscated to the public."

119. Absalom Bainbridge Petition, Loyalist Claims Commission, AO 12/101/255–56, 13/108/31–46; E. A. Jones, *Loyalists of New Jersey*, 15–16; Coldham, *American Migrations*, 378.

120. Richard Cochran Petition, Loyalist Claims Commission, AO 12/13/136–151, 12/85/5, 12/104/4, 12/109/102, 13/108/239–70; Jones, *Loyalists of New Jersey*, 45–46.

121. New Jersey Council of Safety Minutes, July 11, 1777, NJSA.

122. New Jersey GA Minutes, Votes, and Proceedings, February 19, 1778, NJSA.

123. Aptheker, ed., *A Documentary History of the Negro People in the United States*, 12–13; Nash, *The Unknown Revolution*, 321–22; P. Smith, *A New Age Now Begins*, 1343.

124. Quarles, *Negro in the American Revolution*, 106–10; Nash, *Unknown Revolution*, 333; Lambert, "The Confiscation of Loyalist Property in Georgia, 1782–1786," 80–94; Frey, *Water from the Rock*, 104–6; Maas, *The Return of the Massachusetts Loyalists*, 270–318.

125. Gellman, *Emancipating New York*, 65–66; Kruger, "Born to Run," 676–79; Yoshpe, *The Disposition of Loyalist Estates in the Southern District of the State of New York*, 91–93.

126. An Act for setting free Peter Williams, a Negro, late the Property of John Heard," Sept. 1, 1784, Acts 8th GA, 2nd sitting, chap. 53, 110.

127. "An Act for setting free Negro Prime," Nov. 21, 1786, Acts 11th GA, 1st sitting, chap. 176, 368; "An Act for setting Free Negro Cato," Nov. 25, 1789, Acts 14th GA, 1st sitting, chap. 269, 538.

128. Benjamin Quarles believes freeing the three slaves was a referendum on how whites felt about blacks in the new nation but ignores that the state sold the rest of them. See Quarles, *Negro in the American Revolution*, 184. For the state's lack of commitment to abolition, see William Livingston to James Pemberton, December 21, 1788 in Prince, Ryan et al., *Papers of William Livingston*, 5: 365–68.

Chapter 3. Abolishing Slavery in the New Nation

1. Julian Niemcewicz, *Under Their Vine and Fig Tree*, 23; Mercantini, "John and Susan Kean and the Culture of Slavery," 11–12.

2. Morgan, "Slavery and Freedom"; Berlin, *Many Thousands Gone*, 277–85; Mason, *Slavery and Politics*, 9–16; Melish, *Disowning Slavery*, 50; Gellman, *Emancipating New York*, 144–49.

3. Benjamin Rush to Unknown, May 29, 1788, Andrew De Coppet Collection, PUL. New York is similar to New Jersey; see S. White, *Somewhat More Independent*, 3–23.

4. Fischer, *The Revolution of American Conservatism*, 29–49, 164–66. See Zilversmit, *The First Emancipation* for summary of legislative battles for abolition.

5. Quotes from Wood, *The Horrible Gift of Freedom*, 2.

6. William Livingston to the New York Manumission Society, June 26, 1786, in Prince, Ryan et al., *Papers of William Livingston*, 5: 255–56.

7. Zilversmit, *The First Emancipation*, 152–53; Hodges, *Slavery and Freedom in the Rural North*, 115; Levine, "The Transformation of a Radical Whig," 213–15; Melish, *Disowning Slavery*, 50–64; Memorial of Inhabitants of Hunterdon County to the Legislative Council and General Assembly, no date, New Jersey Abolition Society and Burlington County Abolition Society Papers, BCHS; David Cooper, *A Serious Address to the Rulers of America on the Inconsistency of Their Conduct Respecting Slavery* as cited in Hack "Janus-Faced," 1.

8. William Rawle, Interrogatory on if slavery is consistent with the Pennsylvania Constitution, March 26, 1794, Rawle Family Papers, HSP.

9. William Livingston to James Pemberton, October 20, 1788 in Prince, Ryan et al., *Papers of William Livingston*, 5: 357–59; Zilversmit, *The First Emancipation*, 146, 152–53.

10. William Livingston to James Pemberton, December 21, 1788, in Prince, Ryan, et al., *Papers of William Livingston*, 5: 255, 365–68; Sedgwick, *A Memoir of the Life of William Livingston*; Prince, *William Livingston* , 20.

11. S. White, *Somewhat More Independent*, 27–36; Gellman, *Emancipating New York*, 46; Hodges, *Root and Branch*, 164–65; Hodges, *Slavery, Freedom, and Culture*, 50–52. For an opposite interpretation, see Dunbar, *A Fragile Freedom*, 23.

12. S. White, *Somewhat More Independent*, 27–28; William Livingston to James Pemberton, October 20, 1788, in Prince, Ryan et al., *Papers of William Livingston*, 5: 357–59; 1790 and 1800 Census Schedule, Historical Census Browser, University of Virginia, Geospatial and Statistical Data Center, http://mapserver.lib.virginia.edu/ collections; Minutes of the Proceedings of the New Jersey Abolition Society, 52, HCQC; Hack, "Janus-Faced," 4–6 (Paterson and Niemcewicz quotes on 6); Dorsey, *Hirelings*, 16–17.

13. New Jersey General Assembly Tax Ratables, Morris Township (1783, 1789, 1796, 1802, 1805) and Newark (1783, 1789, 1793, 1796, 1811), NJSA; S. White, *Somewhat More Independent*, 30–33. In Morris, the number of prime male slaves increased from 22 in 1783 to 35 in 1805 while they increased in Newark from 59 in 1783 to 64 in 1811.

14. Essex County Wills, NJSA; Supreme Court of New Jersey Case File 34077, NJSA; Supreme Court of New Jersey Case File 31316, NJSA; Hodges, *Root and Branch*, 167. Hodges states that 40 percent of wills statewide in the 1790s granted freedom for slaves but provides no citation; see Hodges, *Slavery and Freedom in the Rural North*, 126–27.

15. A survey of advertisements in the following newspapers between 1784 and 1804 (the number in parenthesis is the number of issues searched) was used: *Burlington Advertiser* (88), *New Jersey Gazette* (151), *New Jersey Journal* (936), *Jersey Chronicle* (52), *Political Intelligencer* (128), *Centinel of Freedom* (436), and *Federalist* (176). Also see S. White, *Somewhat More Independent*, 36; Harris, *In the Shadow of Slavery*, 62; Hodges, *Slavery and Freedom in the Rural North*, 118. These figures do not account for private sales. For examples, see Bill of Sale from John Smith to Caleb Crane, May 7, 1803, Louis Bamberger Collection, NJHS, and Bill of Sale from Nelly Ten Eyck to Joseph Clark, November 12, 1798, Clark Family Papers, RUASC.

16. Misc Ironworks documents, Chew Family Papers, Box 210, HSP; Disposition of R. Harris, February 1790, Pennsylvania Historical Society Misc. Collection, HSP.

17. S. White, "Impious Prayers," 263–65, 275–77; *The Devil or the New Jersey Dance*, 4–7.

18. John Nelson Abeel, undated 1780s sermon, John Nelson Abeel Papers, NJHS.

19. *New Jersey Journal*, February 4, 1792.

20. Gellman, *Emancipating New York*, 45–46; D. B. Davis, *Inhuman Bondage*, 153.

21. "An Act Respecting Slaves," March 14, 1798, Acts 22nd GA, 2nd sitting; 6 NJL 374, *State v. Van Waggoner*, April 1797, Supreme Court of New Jersey; Dowd, "Declarations of Dependence: War and Inequality in Revolutionary New Jersey, 1776–1815" in Lurie, ed. *A New Jersey Anthology*, 109–10; Soderlund, "The Delaware Indians and Poverty in Colonial New Jersey" in Smith, ed, *Down and Out in Early America*, 289–307. For additional cases on Indians, see Abolition Society for Burlington County to William Allinson, October 23, 1805, *State v. John Maxwell*, County of Sussex (On Habeas of Ruth, Samuel, Isaac, and Harry), *State v. Samuel Sherrerd*, County of Sussex

(On Habeas Corpus of Esther), New Jersey Abolition Society and Burlington County Abolition Society Papers, BCHS.

22. "An Act Respecting Slaves," March 14, 1798, Acts 22nd GA, 2nd sitting; "A Supplement to the Act entitled 'An Act for the Punishment of Crimes,'" March 7, 1801, Acts 25th GA, 2nd sitting.

23. 1800 Census Schedule, Historical Census Browser, University of Virginia, Geospatial and Statistical Data Center (http://mapserver.lib.vriginia.edu/collections); the best work on Quakers before and during the Revolution remains Soderlund, *Quakers and Slaves*. Also see Hodges, *Root and Branch*, 117; Wacker, *Land and People*, 194; Pernot, *After Freedom*, iv.

24. Harris, *In the Shadow of Slavery*, 51; *Memorial of Mount Holly Monthly Meeting of Friends concerning William Boen*.

25. Burlington Society of Friends Quarterly Meeting Minutes, 1781–1799, Salem Society of Friends Monthly Meeting Minutes, 1784–1791, April 25, 1785, and Pennsylvania Society of Friends Yearly Meeting Minutes, 1789, SFHL; Marshall, *Manhood Enslaved*, 17–19.

26. Petition of Quakers in New Jersey, Pennsylvania, Delaware, and Maryland to the Legislature Advocating the Abolition of Slavery, November 11, 1792, BAH Collection, Legislative Records, 1788–1796, NJSA.

27. Philadelphia Meeting for Sufferings of the Society of Friends Minutes, December 21, 1786, October 15, 1788, November 15, 1792, and December 20, 1792, SFHL; Philadelphia Yearly Meeting of the Religious Society of Friends, *To Our Fellow Citizens of the United States of North America and others Whom it May Concern*.

28. William Livingston to James Pemberton, October 20, 1788, in Prince, Ryan et al., *Papers of William Livingston*, 5: 357–59; Melish, *Disowning Slavery*, 52–53; Zilversmit, *The First Emancipation*, 152–60.

29. *New Jersey Journal*, March 31, 1790.

30. Zilversmit, *The First Emancipation*, 152–60; Berlin, *Many Thousands Gone*, 308–9; D. B. Davis, *Inhuman Bondage*, 153–54; Oakes, "The Compromising Expedient," 2028–29, 2042.

31. "An Act to prevent the importation of slaves into the State of New Jersey and to authorize the manumission of them under certain restrictions and to prevent the abuse of slaves," March 2, 1786, Acts 10th GA, 2nd sitting; Zilversmit, *The First Emancipation*, 159; Manumission Document of Tony, May 3, 1790, Minto-Skelton Papers, CLUM.

32. Zilversmit, *The First Emancipation*, 159; Burlington and Hunterdon Counties' petition to the Legislature for a law for the gradual abolition of slavery in New Jersey, May 1, 1792, State Library MSS Collection, NJSA.

33. Wansey, *Journal of an Excursion to the United States*, 100–101.

34. Hodges, *Root and Branch*, 172; New Jersey Supreme Court Case File 34201, NJSA.

35. "A supplement to an Act entitled 'An Act to prevent the importation of slaves . . . '" November 26, 1788, Acts 13th GA, 1st sitting; "An Act Respecting Slaves," March 14, 1798, Acts 22nd GA, 2nd sitting; Hodges, *Root and Branch*, 116; Marshall, *Manhood Enslaved*, 129; Quotes from Monaghan, "Reading for the Enslaved," 309–10.

36. S. White, *Somewhat More Independent*, 28–30; Hodges, *Root and Branch*, 172; Burlington County Deed Books A, B, C, D, F, H, NJSA; 1790 and 1800 Census Schedule, Historical Census Browser, University of Virginia, Geospatial and Statistical Data Center, http://mapserver.lib.virginia.edu/collections.

37. John Hunt Journal, esp. June 27, 15, July 24, July 25, August 24, 1787, May 5, 1788, John Hunt Papers, NJHS.

38. Ibid, esp. July 15, August 24, 1787, September 16, 1794.

39. William Allinson Journal, June 3, 1803, October 22, 1804, CLUM; Marshall, *Manhood Enslaved*, 17–19.

40. Ibid, esp. April 20, May 25, 1794, February 21, September 26, 1796, February 14, August 8, 24, 1797, CLUM.

41. Susana Emlen to William Dillwyn, February 28, 1790, Dillwyn Family Papers LCP. Also see John Cox to George Dillwyn, February 24, 1796, Cox-Parrish-Wharton Papers, HSP.

42. Burlington Society of Friends Quarterly Meeting Minutes, November 20, 1789, August 30, 1790, August 29, 1791; Salem Society of Friends Quarterly Meeting Minutes, May 17, 1790, September 21, 1792, September 20, 1793, September 26, 1794; Salem Society of Friends Monthly Meeting Minutes, July 25, 1791, June 29, 1795, June 25, 1810, all in SFHL; Minutes of the Proceedings of the New Jersey Abolition Society, 53–54, HCQC.

43. Association of Friends for the Free Instruction of Adult Colored Persons Papers, Appendix Letters, SFHL.

44. A. B. Smith, "The Bustill Family"; Samson Adams Papers, CLUM.

45. Newman, *The Transformation of American Abolitionism*, 4–6; Pennsylvania Abolition Society Preamble and Resolution, May 23, 1839, Cox-Parrish-Wharton Papers, HSP; PAS Acting Committee Minute Book, 1: 176 (September 24, 1788), 2: 114 (September 22, 1790), PAS Papers, HSP; Richard Waln to John Graunt and Friends of the Egg Harbor Monthly Meeting, November 14, 1788, and Richard Waln to Colin Camel, January 15, 1793, Richard Waln Papers, HSP; Richard Waln to Elias Boudinot, April 17, 1790, Elias Boudinot Papers, HSP; Kozel, "Digging on Behalf of the 'Natural Right to Liberty' " ; Kozel, "Testing 'Liberty' in New Jersey."

46. Pennsylvania Abolition Society Minute Book, 1: 185–89, PAS Papers, HSP; Joseph Bloomfield to Samuel Coates, March 13, 1793, Edwin Ely Collection, NJHS.

47. New Jersey Society for Promoting the Abolition of Slavery, *The Constitution of the New Jersey Society*; S. Miller, *Discourse Delivered April 12, 1797*, 9; Zilversmit, *The First Emancipation*, 173.

48. *Trenton Federalist*, January 24, 1803; *New Jersey Journal*, February 20, 1793. Data on membership for local abolition society chapters comes from database of Timothy Hack.

272 Notes to Pages 78–81

49. New Jersey Society for Promoting the Abolition of Slavery, *Cases Adjudged in the Supreme Court of New Jersey*; New Jersey Supreme Court Case File 33632, NJSA; Minutes of the Proceedings of the New Jersey Abolition Society, 7–10, HCQC; Hodges, *Root and Branch*, 167.

50. *State v. James Anderson*, New Jersey Society for Promoting the Abolition of Slavery, *Cases Adjudged in the Supreme Court of New Jersey*, 25–27.

51. New Jersey Supreme Court Case File 34984.

52. Elias Matthias to Rueban Pitcher, May 29, 1803, Elias Matthis to William Allinson, June 5, 1803, Account for Seizure of the Sloop Nancy, November 6, 1804, Statement of Sloop Nancy seized off Egg Harbor, May 1803, and William Allinson to John Moore, June 17, 1803, New Jersey Abolition Society and Burlington County Abolition Society Papers, BCHS; Minutes of the Proceedings of the New Jersey Abolition Society, 42, 82–83, and Burlington County Society for the Abolition of Slavery Papers, 42–46, HCQC; J. Cox to William Griffith, January 30, 1801, New Jersey Abolition Society and Burlington County Abolition Society Papers, BCHS; William Allinson Journal, June 3, 1803, CLUM.

53. American Convention for the Promoting the Abolition of Slavery and Improving the condition of the African Race, 11.

54. *Pennsylvania Gazette*, February 19, 1794; Joseph Bloomfield, Petition to the General Assembly of the State of Connecticut from the American Convention for the Promoting the Abolition of Slavery and Improving the condition of the African Race, MB Brainard Papers, Connecticut Historical Society; *New Jersey Journal*, February 5, 1794. For political activism, see Minutes of the Proceedings of the New Jersey Abolition Society, 11–24, 58–62, HCQC.

55. Petition of Inhabitants of Burlington County to the Legislature, advocating the gradual abolition of Slavery, October 10, 1796, BAH Collection, Legislative Records, 1788–1796, NJSA. Also see 1796 petitions from Windsor, Middlesex County, Monmouth County, Gloucester County in same collection and Griffith, *Address of the President of the New Jersey Society*. For examples of abolitionist print rhetoric, see *New Jersey Gazette*, November 7, 1785, March 13, 1786; *Jersey Chronicle*, July 11, 1795; *New Jersey Journal*, May 2, 1792, October 6, 1790; "An Oration delivered the evening prior to the commencement, 1786," Wells Family Papers, RUASC.

56. Joseph Bloomfield to Samuel Coats, August 30, 1795, Edwin Ely Collection, NJHS.

57. Gloucester County Society for Promoting the Abolition of Slavery Meeting Records, April 1796, Rowan University Library; New Jersey Abolition Society Papers, Minutes of the General Meeting, September 4, 1797, HCQC; for Society to Legislature, see Petition of Inhabitants of Burlington County to the Legislature, advocating the gradual abolition of Slavery, October 10, 1796, BAH Collection, Legislative Records, 1788–1796, NJSA; for Griffith quote, see New Jersey Society for the Abolition of Slavery, testimony to the Legislature in favor of the law for the gradual extinction of slavery, February 1, 1804, State Library MSS Collection, NJSA.

58. Minutes of the Proceedings of the New Jersey Abolition Society, 47–58, HCQC. For quotes, see Committee of Publication Report, 1798, New Jersey Abolition Society and Burlington County Abolition Society Papers, BCHS, and *Minutes of the Proceedings of the Seventh Convention of Delegates*, 8.

59. The Petition of the Free Blacks of the City of Philadelphia (1800?), Cox-Parrish-Wharton Family Papers, HSP.

60. Hillard, *Memory of Harry, Cuff, and Cato*, 2. For other slave petitions, see Cunningham, "'That the Name of Slave May not More Be Heard," in Benes, *Slavery and Antislavery in New England*, 71–81; Berlin, *Many Thousands Gone*, 231–32; Newman, *The Transformation of American Abolitionism*, 88–89.

61. Gellman, *Emancipating New York*, 160. Between 1784 and 1803, 110 runaway advertisements appeared in the following newspapers (the number in parenthesis is the number of issues searched): *Burlington Advertiser* (88), *New Jersey Gazette* (151), *New Jersey Journal* (936), *Jersey Chronicle* (52), *Political Intellegencer* (128), *Centinel of Freedom* (436), and *Federalist* (176). This was a decrease from the sixty found between 1778 and 1783. Revolutionary New York newspapers revealed no significant findings. For family formation and Bergen slaveholding, see Hack, "Janus-Faced," 15–21.

62. Account of James Alford (1769–1842), *Friends Weekly Intelligencer* 1 (1845), 246, 328, 340. Thanks to Christopher Densmore for this source.

63. G. Anderson to Robert Smith, February 22, 1798, New Jersey Abolition Society and Burlington County Abolition Society Papers, BCHS; Gersham Craft to Thomas Cope, January 4, 1804, Thomas Cope Family Papers, HCQC; Rugemer, *The Problem of Emancipation*, 42–43.

64. Susanna Emlen to William Dillwyn, June 8, 1792, Dillwyn Family Papers, LCP. For another example, see Humanitas, *Reflections on Slavery*, 13. For refugees in New York, see M. Jones, "Time, Space, and Jurisdiction in Atlantic World Slavery." For Philadelphia, see Susan Branson and Leslie Patrick, "Étrangers dans un pays étrange," in Geggus, ed, *The Impact of the Haitian Revolution in the Atlantic World*, 193–96.

65. S. White, "Impious Prayers," 276; Rugemer, *The Problem of Emancipation*, 43, 52–53; Harris, *In the Shadow of Slavery*, 49; Gellman, *Emancipating New York*, 45; D. B. Davis, *Inhuman Bondage*, 153; American Convention for the Promoting the Abolition of Slavery, 4.

66. *Centinel of Freedom*, January 6, 20, 1801; Fishman, *The African American Struggle for Freedom*, 129; Aptheker, *American Negro Slave Revolts*, 218; Atkinson, *The History of Newark, New Jersey*, 171; Hodges, *Slavery and Freedom in the Rural North*, 133.

67. Hodges, *Root and Branch*, 179–80; Hodges, *Slavery and Freedom in the Rural North*, 133; New Jersey Supreme Court Case files 37209, 37210, 37224, NJSA; *New Jersey Journal*, February 3, 1790.

68. Petitions of the Freeholders and Inhabitants of Bergen County to the Legislative Council and General Assembly Concerning the Crimes Committed by Slaves, January 30, 1801, Department of State, Secretary of State AM Papers, NJSA.

274 Notes to Pages 84–90

69. Hack, "Janus-Faced," 15–21.

70. Humanitas, *Reflections on Slavery*, 14.

71. Gellman, *Emancipating New York*, 130–31, 141; Melish, *Disowning Slavery*, xiv; Mason, *Slavery and Politics*, 7.

72. J. Davis, *Sectionalism in American Politics*, 7–22; Madison, *Debates of the Adoption of the Federal Constitution*, June 30, July 2, 1787.

73. Madison, *Debates of the Adoption of the Federal Constitution*, August 8, 1787; Waldstreicher, *Slavery's Constitution From Revolution to Ratification*, 70; Lemon, *The Best Poor Man's Country*; Melish, *Disowning Slavery*, 3–6.

74. Madison, *Debates of the Adoption of the Federal Constitution*, August 8, 22, 1787.

75. Ibid.

76. Ibid, July 8, 11, 1787; Einhorn, *American Taxation, American Slavery*, 172.

77. Mason, *Slavery and Politics*, 15; Joseph Bloomfield to Samuel Coates, June 30, 1794, Edwin Ely Collection, NJHS.

78. Fee, "The Transition from Aristocracy to Democracy," 100–103, 127; Prince, *New Jersey's Jeffersonian Republicans*, 7–18, 40–42; Murrin, "New Jersey and the Two Constitutions" in Conley and Kaminski, ed, *The Constitution and the States*, 55–76; Joseph Bloomfield to Jonathan Dayton, March 8, 1804, as cited in Fee, "The Transition from Aristocracy to Democracy," 127; Gavin Scott to Thomas Scott, October 23, 1800, Scott Family Papers, NJHS; Joseph Bloomfield to Ebenezer Elmer, December 28, 1800, Joseph Bloomfield Papers, NJHS. For examples of North-South dichotomy, see Johnstone, *The Address of Abraham Johnstone*; *Centinel of Freedom*, September 20, 1797. For Dayton quote, see Jonathan Dayton to Majors Ross and Cox, March 15, 1789, in Jonathan Dayton Papers, CLUM.

79. Wills, *Freedom's Triumph*, 7; Buel, *Securing the Revolution*, xi, 217, 230; J. R. Sharp, *American Politics in the Early Republic*, 9–10; Onuf, *Jefferson's Empire*, 80–83, 98–102; Purcell, *Sealed with Blood*, 92–132.

80. Onuf, *Jefferson's Empire*, 96.

81. Wills, *Freedom's Triumph*, 7; Joseph Bloomfield to Ebenezer Elmer, December 28, 1800, Joseph Bloomfield Papers, NJHS; Silas Dickerson to Mahlon Dickerson, Mahlon Dickerson and Philemon Dickerson Papers, NJHS; Buel, *Securing the Revolution*, xi, 217, 230; Pasley, "1800 as a Revolution in Political Culture," in Horn, Lewis, and Onuf, eds, *The Revolution of 1800*, 122–26; J. R. Sharp, *American Politics in the Early Republic*, 9–10.

82. Young, *The Democratic Republicans of New York*, 529–32; Wills, *Freedom's Triumph*, 7 (for final quote); Wilentz, *The Rise of American Democracy*, 72–94, 225–28.

83. *Newark Centinel of Freedom*, April 13, 1802. For links between Jefferson and slavery, see Fischer, *The Revolution of American Conservatism*, 165.

84. A Dialogue Between Quacko and Sambo, addressed to the New Jersey Federalists, particularly those of Burlington County (1801), Political Broadside Collection,

RUASC. "Assemblyman Parson" likely refers to William Pearson, a long-time Burlington County Federalist Assemblyman.

85. Wilentz, *The Rise of American Democracy*, 60–62, 225–27; Riordan, *Many Identities, One Nation*, 120–22.

86. *New Jersey Journal*, November 22, 1803 (for petitions); Wilentz, *The Rise of American Democracy*, 40–71.

87. Mason, *Slavery and Politics*, 15; Bergen County petition to the Legislature requesting repeal of the New Jersey Abolition Act of 1804, January 4, 1806, State Library MSS Collection, NJSA.

88. Tobias Lear to George Washington, April 5, 1791, George Washington to Tobias Lear, April 12, 1791, and Tobias Lear to George Washington, April 24, 1791, in Crackel, ed., *The Papers of George Washington, Digital Edition*. For Pennsylvania's law, see Finkelman, *An Imperfect Union*, 49–55.

89. *Political Intelligencer*, June 29, 1785; William Griffith to the Legislative Council and General Assembly of the State of New Jersey, February 1804, as reprinted in Price, *Freedom Not Far Distant*, 77–79.

90. Zilversmit, *The First Emancipation*, 194.

91. *New Jersey Journal*, October 10, 1792; Nash and Soderlund, *Freedom by Degrees*, 102; Gellman, *Emancipating New York*, 57; Harris, *In the Shadow of Slavery*, 57–58, 70–71; Mason, *Slavery and Politics*, 26; Griffith, *Eumenes*. Quotes from "To the Free Africans and other free People of Color in the United States from Convention of Deputies from the Abolition Societies in the United States, January 6, 1796" and "Plan for improving the condition of the Free Negroes," Broadside, 1789, Cox-Parrish-Wharton Papers, HSP.

92. Dwight, *An Oration*, 5; New Jersey General Assembly Minutes and Proceedings, 28th GA, 1803–1804, NJSA; Sweet, *Bodies Politic*, 250, 263; Wood, *The Horrible Gift of Freedom*, 2; Zilversmit, *The First Emancipation*, 192–200.

93. Pasler and Pasler, *The New Jersey Federalists*, 178–87. For politics in the Jeffersonian era, see Hodges, *Slavery and Freedom in the Rural North*, 135. For caucus system, see Prince, *New Jersey's Jeffersonian Republicans*, 107–16, 151; Joseph Bloomfield to Ebenezer Elmer, July 6, 1802, Edwin Ely Collection, NJHS; J. Freeman, "Corruption and Compromise in the Election of 1800," in Horn, Lewis, and Onuf, eds *The Election of 1800*, 100–105. For an opposing view, see Zilversmit, *The First Emancipation*, 194; Egerton, *Death or Liberty*, 119. Zilversmit argues abolition was not a party issue while Egerton claims Federalists instigated the law. Actually, more Federalists opposed the law than Republicans, the exact opposite of the legislative fight in New York. See *New Jersey Journal*, February 21, 1804, and Fischer, *Revolution of American Conservatism*, 54, for lack of a Federalist consensus on abolition.

94. Prince, *New Jersey's Jeffersonian Republicans*, 107–16, 151.

95. Harris, *In the Shadow of Slavery*, 63.

96. Joseph Bloomfield to Silas Dickerson, March 19, 1804, Edwin Ely Collection, NJHS.

97. Wood, *The Horrible Gift of Freedom*, 2; *Genius of Liberty*, February 17, 1804.

Chapter 4. Not Quite Free

1. Chandler, ed., *Peter Chandler* (for private circulation), 13; McTeigue, "The Conditions Under Which Slaves Lived in New Jersey," 4; Pingeon, *Blacks in the Revolutionary Era*, 5; Atkinson, *The History of Newark*, 171. Like Atkinson, other early histories repeated incorrect information. For one example, see Snell, *History of Hunterdon and Somerset Counties*, 105, which claims the legislature first discussed abolition in 1821.

2. Hodges, *Slavery and Freedom in the Rural North*, 148; Melish, *Disowning Slavery*, 84–87.

3. E. Foner, *The Story of American Freedom*, xvi.

4. Kolchin, "Variations of Slavery in the Atlantic World," 551–54; S. White, *Somewhat More Independent*, 47–48; L. Horton, "From Class to Race in Early America," 640; Nash and Soderlund, *Freedom by Degrees*, 175–78; Grivno, *Gleanings of Freedom*, 3.

5. *Laws of the United States, the State of New York, and New Jersey Relative to Slaves*. I agree with Joanne Pope Melish that slaves for a term (in her terminology *statutory* slaves) saw much the same treatment as their parents did, but disagree that whites were resistant to accepting them because they would be free during the actual service obligation. The creation of the multiple categories of race in New England comes from a determination to disown slavery rather than, as in New Jersey, to embrace its continuation. See Melish, *Disowning Slavery*, 88–89; Minardi, *Making Slavery History*, 36–41; Menschel, "Abolition Without Deliverance," 215–17; L. Horton, "From Class to Race in Early America," 640; Nash and Soderlund, *Freedom by Degrees*, 175–78.

6. Melish, "The Racial Vernacular," in Campbell, Guterl, and Lee, eds., *Race, Nation and Empire in American History*, 17–21; L. Horton, "From Class to Race in Early America," 630–31; B. Smith, *"The Lower Sort."* For an opposing viewpoint, see Sweet, *Bodies Politic*, 253.

7. GA Minutes, Votes, and Proceedings, 28th GA, 2nd sitting, 1803–4, NJSA.

8. "An Act for the Gradual Abolition of Slavery," Feb.15, 1804, Acts 28th GA, 2nd sitting, chap. 103, 251–54. For property rights effect on abolition in New Jersey, see Hodges, *Root and Branch*, 192; G. Wright, *Afro-Americans in New Jersey*, 25; Fogel and Engerman, "Philanthropy at Bargain Prices," 379.

9. Fogel and Engerman, "Philanthropy at Bargain Prices," 389–91. Fogel and Engerman computed the twenty-six year statistics from the 1850 South. For more on the value of female slaves' reproductive value and children, see D. G. White, *Ar'n't I a Woman?*, esp. chap. 2; J. Morgan, *Laboring Women*; Schwartz, *Born in Bondage*; T. Webber, *Deep Like the Rivers*; King, *Stolen Childhood*; Campbell, Miers, and Miller, eds, *Children in Slavery Through the Ages*.

10. New Jersey Supreme Court Case File 37221, NJSA.

11. Griffith, *Address of the President of the New Jersey Society*, esp. 8–9; Harris, *In the Shadow of Slavery*, 70–71; Schwartz, *Born in Bondage*, 1.

12. Sweet, *Bodies Politic*, 249.

13. *Minutes of the Seventeenth Session of the American Convention for Promoting the Abolition of Slavery*, 43.

14. S. Miller, *A Sermon preached at Newark*, 1–7.

15. 4 N.J.L 231, Supreme Court of Judicature of New Jersey, *State v. Aaron, slave of L. Solomon* (1818); John Hunt Journal, April 2, 1818, SFHL.

16. Ibid.; Birkner, *Samuel Southard*, 35–37. For Southard's slaveholding, see Bill of Sale, Nathan Price to Samuel Southard, April 23, 1814, and Samuel Parker to J. Story, August 2, 1818, Samuel Southard Papers, PUL.

17. 9 N.J. L. 167, Supreme Court of Judicature of New Jersey, *Oliver Ogden v. Robert Price and Joseph Price*, 1827.

18. Ibid.

19. New Jersey Supreme Court Case File 37221, NJSA; Mars, *Life of James Mars*, 24.

20. 15 N.J.L. 302, Supreme Court of Judicature of New Jersey, *Edward Stille v. William Jenkins*, May term, 1836.

21. For advertisement specifying exact birth date, see *Newark Centinel of Freedom*, April 30, 1805. For sale of the nine-month-old-child, see *New Jersey Journal*, May 21, 1816. For other sales see Mitros, ed, *Slave Records of Morris County*, 106–7; Holmes, *An Account of the United States of America*, 328; Schwartz, *Born in Bondage*, 1–5. For an alternate look at slave reproduction, see Klepp, *Revolutionary Conceptions*, 23–24.

22. A survey of all advertisements containing the words "negro, slave, and/or black" in the following newspapers between 1804 and 1824 (the number in parenthesis is the number of issues searched) yielded a total of 289 ads. Of the 289, 50 (17.3 percent) included a child born after July 4, 1804. *East Jersey Republican* (4), *Washington Whig* (283), *Rural Visitor* (62), *New Jersey Journal* (2083), *Centinel of Freedom* (1248), *New Jersey Telescope* (118), *Federalist* (468), and *Miscellany* (43).

23. Grivno, *Gleanings of Freedom*, 26.

24. *Newark Centinel of Freedom*, August 6, 1811. For manumission record, see Essex County Certificates of Deeds and Manumissions, Book A, NJSA. For registration of Mat, see Essex County Black Birth Book, NJSA. Morrell did not register Mat's birth until September 1811, when conceivably he found a buyer and needed to properly register the birth. For 1790 case, see 1 N.J.L. 36, *State v. Anderson* (September Term 1790).

25. 20 N.J.L. New Jersey Supreme Court, 1846, *Overseers of Franklin v. Overseers of Bridgewater*; New Jersey Supreme Court Case File 12912, NJSA; *Elizabeth Haines v. Henry Force*, 1836; 17 N.J.L. 385, Supreme Court of New Jersey, *Henry Force v. Elizabeth Haines*. The county court awarded Haines $300, but on appeal the court reversed the decision, citing that Haines should not have taken care of Force's slaves and instead surrendered them to the overseers of the poor.

26. *Middlesex Court of Common Pleas, vol. C, 1817*, NJSA. For other examples, see *New Jersey Supreme Court Case File 35040, NJSA, and Case of Job Dodd, Essex County Manumission Book A, NJSA.*

27. *New Jersey Gazette*, May 1, 1782, and April 25, 1785.

28. Mars, *Life of James Mars*, 24; Herndon and Murray, "A Proper and Instructive Education" in Herndon and Murray, eds., *Children Bound to Labor*, 1–11; L. Horton, "From Class to Race in Early America," 640, n. 21.

29. Herndon and Murray, "A Proper and Instructive Education" in Herndon and Murray, eds., *Children Bound to Labor*, 1–11; Herndon, "Proper Magistrates and Masters," in Herndon and Murray, eds, *Children Bound to Labor*, 43. For other works on indentured servants and apprenticeship in the Mid-Atlantic, see Salinger, *"To Serve Well and Faithfully"*; Grubb, "The Auction of Redemptioner Servants" and Grubb, "Immigrant Servant Labor," 249–76.

30. Sundue, *Industrious in Their Stations*, 163–65, 183–84. Also see case of *Respublica v. Keppele* (1793) as discussed by both Sundue and Steinfeld, *Invention of Free Labor*, 134–35. Also see H. Brewer, *By Birth or Consent*.

31. For Dillwyn, see Sarah Pcuper to Susannah Parrish, August 12, 1814, in Cox-Parrish-Wharton Papers, HSP; John Bodine Thompson, "Readington Negroes" Address at Readington, New Jersey Anniversary, October 17, 1894, RUASC; Melish, *Disowning Slavery*, 89.

32. Mars, *Life of James Mars*, 20.

33. *Address to the Legislature of New Jersey*, 4.

34. Hodges, *Slavery and Freedom in the Rural North*, 149.

35. Ibid.; Zilversmit, *The First Emancipation*, 196–99.

36. Zilversmit, *The First Emancipation*, 196–99. For abandoned children advertisements, see *Trenton Federalist*, May 22, 29, 1809, *Newark Centinel of Freedom*, May 9, 1809, April 24, 1810, and Piscataway Township Records, Certificates of Abandonment for Negro Children born of slave parents (1805–07), RUASC. For an example of a town's request for payment from the state, see Chester Overseers of the Poor Records, 41, NJHS.

37. Zilversmit, *The First Emancipation*, 192–95; L. Horton, "From Class to Race in Early America," 640.

38. Tobias Lear to George Washington, April 24, 1791, Item 776, Sol Feinstone Collection, David Library.

39. "An Additional Supplement to the Act entitled 'An Act for the Gradual Abolition of Slavery,'" November 26, 1808, Acts 33rd GA, 1st sitting, chap. 31, 112–13; Zilversmit, *The First Emancipation*, 199; Zilversmit, "Liberty and Property," 224; Upper Saddle River petition, New Jersey State Archives, State Library MSS Collection.

40. Zilversmit, *The First Emancipation*, 196–99; Zilversmit, "Liberty and Property," 224; Grigg, "'Ye relief of ye poor of sd towne'," 23–35; Percentages of expenditures from New Jersey Department of Treasury Day Books, Daybooks of Peter Gordon, Treasurer, Book Three, NJSA. Figures for 2012 are for the economy cost of the nineteenth-century expense using http://www.measuringworth.com/uscompare (accessed October 7, 2013).

41. "An Additional Supplement to the Act entitled 'An Act for the Gradual Aboli- tion of Slavery,' passed February 15th 1804," November 27, 1809, Acts 34th GA, 1st sitting, chap. 52, 200–201; *Trenton Federalist*, November 6, 1809. For suspending pay- ments, see *Centinel of Freedom*, November 14, 1809. For ending payments, see "An Act Concerning the Abolition of Slavery," February 22, 1811, Acts 35th GA, 2nd sit- ting, 313–14. For expenses from the state budget, see New Jersey Department of Trea- sury Day Books, Daybooks of Peter Gordon, Treasurer, Book Three, NJSA. Zilversmit gives a higher assessment of the budget being spent (40 percent), but a close analysis of the treasurer's records does not yield the same result. See Zilversmit, *The First Emancipation*, 196–99; Zilversmit, "Liberty and Property," 224.

42. Middlesex County Black Birth Book, 57 and 79, RUASC.

43. Morris County Petition to the Legislature Requesting Repeal of the New Jersey Abolition Act of 1804, January 1806, and Bergen County Petition to the Legislature Requesting Repeal of the New Jersey Abolition Act of 1804, January 4, 1806, State Library MSS Collection, NJSA. For toleration in northern abolition laws, see Fogel and Engerman, "Philanthropy at Bargain Prices," 381.

44. Middlesex County Black Birth Book, 57, RUASC; Schwartz, *Born in Bondage*, 14–16; Melish, *Disowning Slavery*, 91; R. Freeman, "The Free Negro in New York City," 66–67.

45. Finkelman, *The Law of Freedom and Bondage*, 49–53; Query of Registration by William Lewis, May 25, 1789, Legal Opinion by William Rawles on Registration, July 27, 1789, Petition of Frances Titus to Pennsylvania General Assembly, 1784, and Thomas Harrison to Samuel Benezet, September 20, 1795, in Historical Society of Pennsylvania Miscellaneous Collection, HSP.

46. 1830 Newark Census Schedules. 1830 is the first federal census that contains intact schedules for New Jersey. The white households that contained blacks made up 7.1 percent of the 1726 white households in Newark. Also see Hodges, *Root and Branch*, 193, 201; Harris, *In the Shadow of Slavery*, 76; Nash and Soderlund, *Freedom by Degrees*, 76–78; S. White, *Somewhat More Independent*, 47. For New England statis- tics, see Melish, *Disowning Slavery*, 129.

47. Manumission of Ann and Rufus Johnson, Johnson Family Records, Anderson Family Papers, NJHS; 1830 Census Schedule, Hardwick Township, Warren County, New Jersey.

48. Sayers Coe Daybook and Account Book, NJHS; 1830 Newark Census Sched- ule, 287; Essex County Black Birth Book, NJSA; Sarah Parkhurst, "A Sketch of the Life of Sarah Coe (1774–1853), wife of Sayers Coe" (1893) in Baldwin-Brown-Coe Family Papers, NJHS (for last quote).

49. Bergen County petition to the Legislature requesting repeal of the NJ Aboli- tion Act of 1804, January 4, 1806, State Library MSS Collection, NJSA.

50. *Report of the Committee Appointed in the Senate of Pennsylvania*, 5; *Minutes of the Seventeenth Session of the American Convention for Promoting the Abolition of Slav- ery*, 11; Charles Smith to Samuel Breck, March 27, 1833, in Breck Papers, LCP.

51. McMahon and Schriver, eds., *To Read My Heart*, 108.

52. Nancy Jackson to Estate of Colonel Robert Rutgers, December 2, 1824, Gerald Rutgers Papers, RUASC.

53. Herndon and Murray, "A Proper and Instructive Education," in Herndon and Murray, eds, *Children Bound to Labor*, 1–11; Hindle and Herndon, "Recreating Proper Families in England and North America," in Herndon and Murray, eds., *Children Bound to Labor*, 21–23; Berlin, *Many Thousands Gone*, 1–14; Schwartz, *Born in Bondage*, 1–17.

54. Somerset County Manumission Book, October or November (?) 18, 1805, NJSA.

55. Salem County Manumission Book, 95–97, NJSA; Sussex County Black Birth Book, July 4, 1822, NJSA; G. Moss, *Manumission Book of Monmouth County*, 44; Schwartz, *Born in Bondage*, 1–16, 155–76.

56. *Trenton Federalist*, June 30, 1823; *New Jersey Journal*, April 14, 1818; *Centinel of Freedom*, April 27, 1819.

57. Life expectancy statistics are for U.S. slaves c. 1830 from Fogel, Galantine, and Manning, eds., *Without Consent or Contract*, 285–86.

58. Melish, *Disowning Slavery*, 107; Fogel and Engerman, "Philanthropy at Bargain Prices," 379–91.

59. Berlin, *Many Thousands Gone*, 1–3.

Chapter 5. Slavery, Freedom, and Citizenship in the New Republic

1. Allinson, *Memoir of Quamino Baccau*, 13–14; Marshall, *Manhood Enslaved*, 3, 10, 15, 24, 28–29, 86–106.

2. Allinson, *Memoir of Quamino Baccau*, 15; Marshall, *Manhood Enslaved*, 10.

3. The 16 percent figure is from counties where manumission data are available (Bergen, Burlington, Essex, Middlesex, Monmouth, Morris, Salem, Somerset, and Sussex). New Jersey had 12,422 slaves and a total population of 211,149 in 1800. See 1800 Census Schedule, Historical Census Browser, University of Virginia, Geospatial and Statistical Data Center, http://mapserver.lib.vriginia.edu/collections.

4. Harris, *In the Shadow of Slavery*, 72–73. For manumission as an egalitarian reaction, see Berlin, *Slaves Without Masters*, 30; Berlin, *Many Thousands Gone*, 320; Nash, *Race and Revolution* , 18; Harris, *In the Shadow of Slavery*, 72–73; Kolchin, *American Slavery*, 77–78.

5. Sweet, *Bodies Politic*, 227; Wolf, *Race and Liberty in the New Nation*, xi, 39–44; Williams, *Slavery and Freedom in Delaware*; Fields, *Slavery and Freedom in the Middle Ground*; Whitman, *The Price of Freedom*, 93; Essah, *A House Divided*, 3, 37.

6. *An Address from the Pennsylvania Abolition Society*, 3–5 (for quote); Winch, *Philadelphia's Black Elite*, 71; J. Horton, *Free People of Color* , 57. Horton believes a generation separated free blacks from slavery. For similar issues in Boston, see Kantrowitz, *More Than Freedom*, 16, 24, 48.

7. Bethel, *The Roots of African American Identity*, 26–27; Waldstreicher, *In the Midst of Perpetual Fetes*; Norton, *Liberty's Daughters*; Kerber, *Women of the Republic*.

8. *Minutes of the Proceedings of the Eleventh American Convention* as cited in Zilversmit, *The First Emancipation*, 215. For the Society's end, see Zilversmit, *The First Emancipation*, 214–15, and Hodges, *Root and Branch*, 192. For quote from last meeting, see Minutes of the Proceedings of the New Jersey Abolition Society, HCQC, 111–13.

9. Minutes of the Proceedings of the New Jersey Abolition Society, HCQC, 7–10, 73–77, 99–113; John Griscom to Thomas Cope, January 14, 1805, Thomas Cope Family Papers, HCQC; *Minutes of the Proceedings of the Thirteenth American Convention*, 4–5, 12–13.

10. For Gloucester Society quote, see Minute Book and Miscellaneous Papers, Gloucester County Society for Promoting the Abolition of Slavery Papers, Rowan University Library. For Burlington County Society, see Burlington County Society for the Abolition of Slavery Minutes 1793–1809, HCQC, 57–59. Thank you to Tim Hack for the Gloucester auxiliary minutes.

11. Society of Friends, Philadelphia Meeting for Sufferings Meeting Minutes March 20, 1812, October 18, 1816, December 20, 1816; June 17, 1825, SFHL; Philadelphia Society of Friends, Minute on Slavery from Philadelphia Yearly Meeting Minutes, 1839, SFHL. For other examples of Quaker inactivity, see *Slavery and the Domestic Slave Trade* , and *Appeal of the Religious Society of Friends in Pennsylvania, New Jersey, and Delaware, etc* .

12. Society of Friends, Philadelphia Meeting for Sufferings Meeting Minutes, June 18, October 15, 1824, April 15, September 15, November 4, 1825, January 20, 1826, January 18, 1833, SFHL; Lovejoy, *Transformations in Slavery*, 140–64; Vincent, *Southern Seed, Northern Soil*, 32–34; Jordan, *Slavery and the Meetinghouse*, 19–21.

13. Curry, *The Free Black in Urban America*, 153–54; Hodges, *Root and Branch*, 192–93; Minute Book, June 30, 1817, Papers of the Pennsylvania Abolition Society (for quote), HSP; Newman, *Transformation of American Abolitionism*, 5–7.

14. Forbes, *The Missouri Compromise and Its Aftermath*, 38; Berlin, *Generations of Captivity*, 159–244; Rothman, *Slave Country*, ix–36.

15. Hillard, "To the Public," 8–9, 15–16, Miscellaneous Manuscripts, Connecticut Historical Society, as cited in Melish, *Disowning Slavery*, 104–6, 212.

16. Letters of an American Traveler, containing a brief sketch of the most remarkable places in various parts of the United States and the Canadas with some accounts of the character and manners of the People, written during an excursion in the year 1810, 1: 47, South Carolina Historical Society.

17. Harris, *In the Shadow of Slavery*, 72–74; S. White, *Somewhat More Independent*, 149.

18. *Centinel of Freedom*, October 6, 1807, June 14, 1814; Hodges, *Root and Branch*, 167.

19. *Centinel of Freedom*, March 12, October 22, November 19, 1811, October 22, 1816; *New Jersey Journal*, July 14, October 20, 1807; *Trenton Federalist*, March 4, 1811; John Williams and Jacob Sanders, Dispositions identifying Francis Cisco as an escaped slave from New Jersey, December 1845, African American History Collection, CLUM.

20. Nash and Soderlund, *Freedom by Degrees*, 140–42. Of 154 advertisements for New Jersey fugitives that appeared in New Jersey newspapers between 1804 and 1824, 32 advertised women. The following newspapers were used (number of issues searched in parentheses): *East Jersey Republican* (4), *Washington Whig* (283), *Rural Visitor* (62), *New Jersey Journal* (2083), *Centinel of Freedom* (1248), *New Jersey Telescope* (118), *Federalist* (468), *Miscellany* (43).

21. *Centinel of Freedom*, October 3, 1809, February 26, 1811; *New Jersey Telescope*, September 26, 1809.

22. *New Jersey Journal*, July 30, 1811; Gilje, *Rioting in America*, 63–81.

23. *Trenton Federalist*, April 6, 1812; *Raleigh North Carolina Star*, April 17, 1812; New Brunswick Common Council Minutes, July 7, 1815, NJHS; *To the Inhabitants of the Borough of York*.

24. Notebook Four, 749, Andrew Mellick Papers, NJHS; *Washington Whig*, January 22, 1816. Sam pleaded not guilty but Chloe pleaded guilty as she had indictments for arson and theft against her. For Hitchens's case, see Petition of several inhabitants of Hunterdon County to the Governor and Legislative Council, for mercy for Ann Hitchens, May 1817, BAH Collection, N.J. State Legislature, Petitions, Resolutions, Transactions, Accounts and Miscellaneous Papers, c. 1700–1845, NJSA.

25. *Confession of Rosan Keen*; Hearn, *Legal Executions in New Jersey*, 85–86. Baker, "Black Female Executions in Historical Context," 69, incorrectly lists Missouri as her place of execution.

26. Ann Cox to Joseph Parrish, September 12, 1811, Cox-Parris-Wharton Papers, HSP; Samuel Emlen to William Dillwyn, May 4, 1807, Dillwyn Family Papers, LCP.

27. Morris Court of Sessions, December Term 1808, *State v. Abraham Cooper*, as quoted in Mitros, *Slave Records of Morris County*, 108; Hodges, *Slavery and Freedom in the Rural North*, 148. For a similar case in New York, see *The Trial of Amos Broad and His Wife*.

28. Harris, *In the Shadow of Slavery*, 73; S. White, *Somewhat More Independent*, 48; Act to Prevent Importation of Slaves into N.J. and Authorize Manumission under certain restrictions, and prevent abuse of slaves, March 2, 1786; An Act Respecting Slaves, March 14, 1798; An Act Supplementary to the 1798 Act Respecting Slaves, December 3, 1804, NJSA; Essah, *A House Divided*, 37.

29. Certificate of Emancipation for Negro man Jack by John Runk, March 7, 1809, BAH Collection, Documents in Chronological Order, Department of State, NJSA; Sussex County Manumission Book, March 22, 1805, NJSA (for Youmans); D. B. Davis, *Inhuman Bondage*, 193–95.

30. Martin, *Divided Mastery*, 17–20. For Sam, see S. White, *Somewhat More Independent*, 152. For Simon, see Somerset County Manumission Book, September 17, 1831, NJSA.

31. McMahon and Schriver, eds., *To Read My Heart*, 44; Hodges, *Root and Branch*, 211–13; DeVoe, *The Market Book*, 344–45.

32. Rael, *Black Identity and Protest in the Antebellum North*, 57.

33. Larison, *Silvia Dubois*, 67–75. Quote on page 74. S. White, "African American Festivals and Parades," 18, 22–31; Harris, *In the Shadow of Slavery*, 88; Hodges, *Root and Branch*, 221–23.

34. African Association of New Brunswick (N.J.), Minute Book, 1817–1824, RUASC.

35. Mitros, *Slave Records of Morris County*, 77–81; Bergen Reformed Church Records and Bound Brook Presbyterian Church Records, RUASC; Daybook of Thomas Morrell, 1809–1838, Morrell Family Papers, NJSA.

36. McKinney, Philhower, and Kniffin, *Commemorative History of the Presbyterian Church*, 350–459; Daybook of Thomas Morrell, 1809–1838, Morrell Family Papers, NJSA; Trinity Cathedral Papers, NJHS. For more on Thomas Morrell, see Rowe and McKay, ed, *The Journals of the Rev. Thomas Morrell*. Also see Sobel, *The World They Made Together*, 192–200.

37. Somerset County Manumission Book, October 5, 1824, NJSA; 1830 Census Schedules, Newark, 291, 308, 325.

38. *Centinel of Freedom*, May 26, 1807, April 25, 1809; *New Jersey Journal*, September 27, 1814.

39. *Trenton Federalist*, October 30, 1809; *Centinel of Freedom*, December 11, 1810. For other examples of advertised sales, see *Trenton Federalist*, August 6, September 24, 1810, January 27, 1812, and *Centinel of Freedom*, November 11, 1806, December 15, 1812. For Jack's sale, see Bill of Sale, Jabez Canfield to Jacob Plum, November 2, 1807 with addenda dated April 22, August 7, 1813, May 15, August 10, 1816, Munn Family Papers, NJHS. See Burlington County Manumission Book B, NJSA for other purchases of slaves before manumission (John Romes, 1821, and Robert Taylor, 1822). Also see Rockman, *Scraping By*, 5–8, 57–67; Grivno, *Gleanings of Freedom*, 43, 47, 92–93, 116–19, 137–39, 143; Whitman, *The Price of Freedom*, 103–10; Berlin, *Many Thousands Gone*, 279; Cole, "Capitalism and Freedom," 1009–1110.

40. Middlesex County Manumission Book, May 7, 1811, NJSA; David Johnson Will, Essex County Wills #10839, NJSA. After the owner's death, 190 manumissions (10.8 percent of 1755 total) occurred.

41. Essex County Manumission Book, 55, NJSA.

42. Forty-six Newark and Morristown wills list slaves. See Will of Jeremiah Baldwin, Essex County Wills number 10326, NJSA, Inventory of Aaron Mellick and Will of Aaron Mellick, Estate of Aaron Mellick Papers and Andrew Mellick Papers, NJHS; Will of Lydia Williamson, Essex County Wills #10871, NJSA; Will of John Morris, Essex County Wills #11266, NJSA.

43. Life expectancy statistics are for U.S. slaves c.1830. See Fogel, Galantine, and Manning, eds., *Without Consent or Contract*, 285–86; Sweet, *Bodies Politic*, 232.

44. Wolf, *Race and Liberty in the New Nation*, xi, 28–29, 39–41 (first quote on 39); Nash and Soderlund, *Freedom by Degrees*, 164–65; Hodges, *Slavery and Freedom in the Rural North*, 150–58 (second quote 158); Hodges, *Root and Branch*, 177–78; Groth, "Slaveholders and Manumission," 33–50 (for similar ideas in New York); Essah, *A House Divided*, 3 (for similar ideas in Delaware).

45. Kulikoff, *The Agrarian Origins of American Capitalism*, 111–12, quote 111.

46. Essays Urging Development of American Industry, Papers of Peter Colt, Colt Family Papers, RUASC.

47. Lamoreaux, "Rethinking the Transition to Capitalism," 437–39; Merrill, "Cash Is Good to Eat," 42–71; Henretta, "Families and Farms," 3–32; Rothenberg, "The Market and Massachusetts Farmers," 283–314; Kulikoff, "The Transition to Capitalism," 120–144; *New Jersey Telescope*, March 17, 1809; Joseph Bloomfield to Ebenezer Elmer, January 29, 1800, Ebenezer Elmer Papers, RUASC; Aaron Kitchell to Joseph Bloomfield, December 20, 1808, New Jersey Letters Collection, 1800–1809, RUASC.

48. Johnson, "The Pedestal and the Veil," 299–308; Grivno, *Gleanings of Freedom*, 26–29, 116–19; Rockman, *Scraping By*, 5–8; Steinfeld, *The Invention of Free Labor*, 7–10, 130–39; Steinfeld, *Coercion, Contract, and Free Labor*, 3–8, 254–55; Grubb, "Immigrant Servant Labor," 249–76; Salafia, *Slavery's Borderland*, 118–19, 134–36. For the opposite argument, that free labor was more popular than coerced, see Nash, *The Urban Crucible*; Salinger, "*To Serve Well and Faithfully*," 3–10; Hodges, *Root and Branch*, 103–7; Dorsey, *Hirelings*, 16–17.

49. Steinfeld, *Coercion, Contract, and Free Labor*, 3–9, 254–55, 290–94; Grubb, "The Disappearance of Organized Markets," 1–30.

50. Kulikoff, *Agrarian Origins*, 111–12; Steinfeld, *Invention of Free Labor*, 130–39; Rockman, *Scraping By*, 5–8, 57–67.

51. McMahon and Schriver, eds., *To Read My Heart*, 44, 135, 176, 220. For the popularity of female slaves, see Hodges, *Slavery and Freedom in the Rural North*, 154–55; and S. White, *Somewhat More Independent*, 24–46.

52. Curry, *The Free Black in Urban America*, 8; Harris, *In the Shadow of Slavery*, 80; Dunbar, *A Fragile Freedom*, 28.

53. The advertisements come from a search of the following newspapers (number in parentheses is number of issues searched): *East Jersey Republican* (4), *Washington Whig* (283), *Rural Visitor* (62), *New Jersey Journal* (2083), *Centinel of Freedom* (1248), *New Jersey Telescope* (118), *Federalist* (468), and *Miscellany* (43).

54. Hodges, *Slavery and Freedom in the Rural North*, 161–63; 1804 Tax List, Hopewell Township, Cumberland County, RUASC.

55. Records of the Overseers of the Poor of Newark, Newark Town Records, 1807–1816, NJHS. For other examples, see Upper Freehold Town Books and Shrewsbury Overseer of the Poor Book, Monmouth County Archives and Woodbridge Township Overseer of the Poor Records, Woodbridge Township Records, RUASC. For

degraded condition of blacks in Philadelphia, see *The Present State and Condition of the Free People of Color*.

56. Habeas Corpus Petition against William Covenhoven, Middlesex County, 1816, New Jersey Supreme Court Case File 34538, NJSA.

57. Constitution of the Female Charitable Society and Society Meeting Minutes, Newark Female Charitable Society Papers, NJHS; Newark Female Charitable Society; MacWhorter, *A Charity Sermon Delivered for the Female Charitable Society, Instituted for the Relief of Poor and Distressed Widows and for the Instruction of Poor Children* (Newark, 1805) in Kinney Family Papers, NJHS; Petition of the Female Charitable Society of Newark to the General Assembly, requesting Incorporation, October 18, 1811, BAH Collection, Legislative Records, 1811–1934, NJSA; Stansell, *City of Women*, 30–36.

58. For the limiting public responsibility toward ex-slaves, see Wolf, *Race and Liberty in the New Nation*, 29–30 (Virginia); Reiss, *Blacks in Colonial America*, 76–77 (Rhode Island); Higginbotham, *In the Matter of Color*, 145–47 (New York). For ideas on citizenship, see Melish, "The Manumission of Nab," 36–41.

59. 8 N.J.L. 52, Supreme Court of New Jersey, *Township of Chatham v. Executors of Samuel Canfield*, September Term 1824.

60. 8 N.J.L. 64, Supreme Court of New Jersey, *Overseers of the Poor of South Brunswick v. Overseers of the Poor of East Windsor*, November Term, 1824; East Windsor Township Overseer of the Poor Records, 1824, NJHS. For another ex-slave's disputed care, see Theodorsus Bailey to Joseph Hornblower, January 15, 1822, Isaac Nichols and Lewis Thibou, Overseers of the Poor of Newark to Joseph Hornblower, March 28, 1822, and Joseph Hornblower to Theodorsus Bailey, January 12, 1822, Joseph Hornblower Papers, NJHS. For the opposite in South Carolina, see Minardi, *Making Slavery History*, 59–61.

61. Steiner, *History of Slavery in Connecticut*, 41–44, quote 42.

62. "An Act for the Gradual Abolition of Slavery, and for other Purposes Respecting Slaves," February 24, 1820, Acts 44th GA, 74–80.

63. 20 N.J.L. New Jersey Supreme Court, 1846, *Overseers of Franklin v. Overseers of Bridgewater*. For caring for a Connecticut slave for a term, see Samuel Wetmore to Norwich, Connecticut Selectmen, June 8, 1812, African American History Collection, CLUM.

64. E. Foner, "Free Labor and Political Ideology" in Stokes and Conway, eds., *The Market Revolution in America*, 99–123; L. Horton, "From Class to Race in Early America," 644–47; Litwack, *North of Slavery*, 29–33; Rael, *Black Identity and Protest in the Antebellum North*, 55; Waldstreicher, *In the Midst of Perpetual Fetes*, 2–3, 9, 85–86, quote 86.

65. Kantrowitz, *More than Freedom*, 6 (for first quotes).

66. Waldstricher, *In the Midst of Perpetual Fetes*, 313–25; S. White, "It Was a Proud Day," 15–16, 38–41; Rael, *Black Identity and Protest in the Antebellum North*, 55–62, quote 60; Bethel, *Roots of African American Identity*, 6, 81–91. Manisha Sinha

argues the opposite of this, claiming that blacks became far more radical in the early nineteenth century and created a link more to Haiti than to the American Revolution. However, I agree with Rael in that New Jersey blacks used the American Revolution as a starting place. See Sinha, "To 'cast just obliquy' on Oppressors," 149–60.

67. *Minutes of the Proceedings of the Twelfth American Convention*, 13.

68. Griffith, *Address of the President of the New Jersey Society*, 7–10, quotes 7, 8, 10.

69. Report of the Committee of Publication of the New Jersey Society for Promoting the Abolition of Slavery, 1804, reprinted in Pernot, *After Freedom*, 59–61.

70. M. T. Wright, *The Education of Negroes in New Jersey*, 63–64; *Minutes of the Proceedings of the Thirteenth American Convention*, 12–13.

71. M. T. Wright, *The Education of Negroes in New Jersey*, 70–73; *Freedom's Journal*, June 8, 1827; *Colored American*, June 19, 1841; Boylan, *Sunday School*, 22–25; Schmidt, *Slavery and Attitudes on Slavery*, 13.

72. *New Jersey Journal*, December 19, 1815.

73. *New Jersey Journal*, December 17, 1816; Boylan, *Sunday School*, 25–26.

74. Report of the Female Department of Colored School in the Newark Academy, September 2, 1821, Colored Sabbath School Reports Collection, 1819–1822, NJHS.

75. Ibid., December 2, 1821.

76. M. T. Wright, *Education of Negroes in New Jersey*, 72–74. Wright claims that a key lesson the Newark Sabbath School taught was "Servants, obey your masters." Samuel Emlen to Roberts Vaux, June 26, 1821, and November 21, 1821, Vaux Family Papers, HSP; Emlen Institution for the Benefit of Children of African and Indian Descent, 1765–1956, HCQC.

77. Waldstreicher, *In the Midst of Perpetual Fetes*, 333–37; Sweet, *Bodies Politic*, 379–92; Rael, *Black Identity and Protest in the Antebellum North*, 72–77; Melish, *Disowning Slavery*, 172–73. For minstrel shows, see L. Horton, "From Class to Race in Early America," 646; Roediger, *Wages of Whiteness*, 97–104; Lott, *Love and Theft*, 3–9, 38–42, quotes 3, 40.

78. Quotes from *Centinel of Freedom*, November 7, 1800; Klinghoffer and Elkis, "The Petticoat Electors," esp. 180–83; Lewis, "Rethinking Women's Suffrage." For earlier interpretations, see Fleming, *New Jersey*, 94; McCormick, *The History of Voting in New Jersey*, 68–70.

79. Klinghoffer and Elkis, "The Petticoat Electors," 178–185; Lewis, "Rethinking Women's Suffrage," 1025–1031; Atkinson, *The History of Newark*, 143; Moss, "The Persistence of Slavery," 307–8; Harris, *In the Shadow of Slavery*, 91–92. For Pennington's slaves, see Essex County Black Birth Book, April 6, 1809, and December 5, 1812, NJSA.

80. Lewis, "Rethinking Women's Suffrage,"1026–29.

81. *Centinel of Freedom*, December 9, 1800.

82. Quotes from Turner, "Women's Suffrage in New Jersey," 175, 179; Lewis, "Rethinking Women's Suffrage," 1030.

83. Turner, "Women's Suffrage in New Jersey,"180; Stansell, *City of Women*, 19–20.

84. Turner, "Women's Suffrage in New Jersey," 180.

85. *Trenton Federalist*, November 30, 1807.

86. Turner, "Women's Suffrage in New Jersey," 181–83; Notebooks Andrew Mellick, Jr., Papers, NJHS; Lewis, "Rethinking Women's Suffrage in New Jersey," 1031; Klinghoffer and Elkis, "'The Petticoat Electors,'" esp. 187–93. The rivalry between Elizabethtown and Newark continued until 1857 when Union County, with Elizabethtown as its county seat, separated from Essex.

87. Turner, "Women's Suffrage in New Jersey," 184; Klinghoffer and Elkis, "'The Petticoat Electors,'" 189.

88. Fischer, *Revolution of American Conservatism*, 329.

89. Klinghoffer and Elkis, "'The Petticoat Electors,'" 175.

90. Gellman and Quigley, eds, *Jim Crow New York*, 258. In New York, 73 percent of whites voted to restrict black voting.

91. Keyssar, *The Right to Vote*, 54–55.

92. Roth, "The Politics of the Page," 210–12, quote 210; C. Malone, "Rethinking the End of Black Voting Rights," 469–73, 493–95.

Chapter 6. Slavery in Motion

1. Pingeon, "An Abominable Business," 14–35; Zilversmit, *The First Emancipation*, 216–17; Hodges, *Root and Branch*, 191–93; Hodges, *Slavery and Freedom in the Rural North*, 150; E. L. Smith, "Rescuing African American Kidnapping Victims," 318–21; C. Wilson, *Freedom at Risk*, 2–4.

2. "An act for the gradual abolition of slavery and for other purposes respecting slaves," February 24, 1820, Acts 44th GA, 74–80; Votes and Proceedings, 43rd GA begun the 27th day of October 1818, 1st sitting and Votes and Proceedings, 44th GA begun the 26th day of October 1819, NJSA.

3. Mason, *Slavery and Politics in the Early American Republic*, 9–86, 130–57, quote 156; Riordan, *Many Identities, One Nation*, 224–29.

4. Ann Cox to Joseph Parrish, January 18, 1812, in Cox-Parrish-Wharton Papers, HSP (for quote); For slave sales, see Copy of Letter to Several Friends in Maryland respecting the sufferings of Black People, October 26, 1802, Cox-Parrish-Wharton Papers, HSP; An act supplemental to the Act entitled An act respecting slaves, Feb.1, 1812, Acts 36th GA, 2nd sitting. For parental consent, see Herdon and Murray, "A Proper and Instructive Education" in Herndon and Murray, eds., *Children Bound to Labor*, 9; "A Supplement to an Act, entitled 'An Act to prevent the Importation of Slaves into the State of New-Jersey," Nov. 26, 1788, Acts 13th GA, 1st sitting; Morris, *Free Men All*, 25–26. Other northern states passed similar laws that restricted sales of state, including Rhode Island (1779 and 1787), Vermont (1786), Connecticut (1788), and New York (1788, 1801, and 1828). Massachusetts provided the first antikidnapping statute in 1788. See Hurd, *The Law of Freedom and Bondage*, vol. 2.

5. *Centinel of Freedom*, September 29, 1812, March 26, 1816; A. Rothman, *Slave Country*, ix–25; For market impact on the South, see Deyle, *Carry Me Back*, and J. Rothman, "'The Hazards of the Flush Times,'" 651–77. For Jersey slave removals, see County Manumission Books of Bergen, Essex, Somerset, and Sussex as well as Department of State Records, Secretary of State's Letters, Deeds, and Misc., NJSA and Middlesex County Manumission Book, RUASC. A total of nineteen removals by masters survive.

6. Mars, *Life of James Mars*, 6–8, 19–21; Sweet, *Bodies Politic*, 248–50, 257–58.

7. Removal Document of George and Esther, slaves of Dr. James Gustin, September 18, 1817, Historical Society of Pennsylvania Miscellaneous Manuscript Collection, HSP; Johnson, *Soul by Soul*, 162–88; Deyle, *Carry Me Back*, 245–75.

8. Essex County Manumission Book B, 8, NJSA; Herdon and Murray, "A Proper and Instructive Education" in Herndon and Murray, *Children Bound to Labor*, 9–11.

9. Mars, *Life of James Mars*, 20–22.

10. Essex County Manumission Book B, 9, 31–33, NJSA; Harris, *In the Shadow of Slavery*, 73–74.

11. Sussex County Manumission Book, Box No. 1–5 1294–805, NJSA.

12. Morris, *Free Men All*, 27–28. For Nance and Jude, see Middlesex County Manumission Book, 134, RUASC; "An Act Relative to Slaves and Servants," Laws of the State of New York, Chapter 137, March 31, 1817; "An Act concerning Slaves and Servants," Laws of the State of New York, Chapter 88, April 9, 1813. Also see "Petition of John Boyd to the Legislature Requesting Permission and Transport his slaves to New York, October 27, 1829," BAH Collection, Legislative Records, 1811–1934, NJSA; Rael, "The Long Death of Slavery" in Berlin and Harris, eds., *Slavery in New York*, 111–46. For another case like Jude's, see Bacon, *Freedom's Journal*, 222.

13. Zilversmit, *The First Emancipation*, 113–15; Upham, *Narrative of Phebe Ann Jacobs*, 1–8 (first quote 1); Calhoun, *A Small College in Maine*, 162–63, 182 n28; Hovet, "Mrs. Thomas C. Upham's 'Happy Phebe,'" 267–70 (second quote 267); Berlin, *Slaves Without Masters*, 217–49.

14. Middlesex County Manumission Book, 127–30, RUASC; Middleton, *The Black Laws*, 20–21. For other Ohio removals, see G. Moss, *Manumission Book of Monmouth County*, 10.

15. Mason, *Slavery and Politics in the Early American Republic*, 149–50; Onuf, *Statehood and Union*, 114; Middleton, *The Black Laws*, 7–11, 21; Finkelman, *The Law of Freedom and Bondage*, 68–73; Finkelman, *Slavery and the Founders*, 37–80; Finkelman, "Slavery and the Northwest Ordinance,"; Finkelman, "Evading the Ordinance"; Finkelman, "Race, Slavery, and Law in Antebellum Ohio," in Benedict and Winkler, eds., *The History of Ohio Law*, 750.

16. Finkelman, *Slavery and the Founders*, 39 for quote. For the St. Clair connection, see Cayton, "Law and Authority in the Northwest Territory," in Benedict and Winkler, eds., *The History of Ohio Law*, 27; Arthur St. Clair to George Washington, May 1, 1790, in Carter, *Territorial Papers*, 7: 248.

17. Middleton, *The Black Laws*, 30.

18. Mason, *Slavery and Politics in the Early American Republic*, 150; Rockman, "The Unfree Origins of American Capitalism," in Matson, ed., *The Economy of Early America*, 335–62; Johnson, "The Pedestal and the Veil," 299–308; Rockman, *Scraping By*, 1–15. For other issues in Old Northwest freedom, see Elisha Wolcott to Salmon P. Chase, April 17, 1838, Salmon Chase Papers, HSP, and Gigantino, "The Flexibility of Freedom."

19. A. Rothman, *Slave Country*, 191–93; *New Orleans Chronicle*, July 14, 1818; *Charlestown, Virginia Farmer's Repository*, August 12, 1818; *Baltimore Patriot and Mercantile Advertiser*, August 7, 1818; *Charleston City Gazette and Daily Advertiser*, August 7, 1818.

20. Zilversmit, *The First Emancipation*, 216; Melish, *Disowning Slavery*, 101–3; Fogel and Engerman, "Philanthropy at Bargain Prices," 381; Kulikoff, *The Agrarian Origins of American Capitalism*, 226–63; Berlin, *Generations of Captivity*, 212–15.

21. *Centinel of Freedom*, January 30, 1810.

22. Urquhart, *A Short History of Newark*, 76–78, 87–88; G. Wright, *Afro-Americans in New Jersey*, 27–28; for trade connections, see Roediger and Blatt, eds., *The Meaning of Slavery in the North*, esp. xvii–44.

23. Cottrol, *The Afro-Yankees*, 32 for quote; Sweet, *Bodies Politic*, 260–61.

24. Joseph Shotwell to Elias Boudinot, January 15, 1792, vol. 3, 58, Elias Boudinot Papers, HSP. For an additional case, see Thomas Rogers to Jonathan Roberts, December 1, 1811, Jonathan Roberts Papers, HSP.

25. Henry Hunt to Samuel Hunt, September 17, 1809, William H. Tower Collection, PUL.

26. Daniel Clark to Jonathan Dayton, August 26, 1804, Jonathan Dayton Papers, NJHS.

27. Jonathan Dayton to Aaron Burr, May 18, 1804, in Kline and Ryan, eds., *Political Correspondence and Public Papers of Aaron Burr*, 2: 867.

28. A. Rothman, *Slave Country*, 27–29, 73–78, 92–93; Jonathan Dayton to Aaron Burr, May 18, 1804, in Kline and Ryan, eds., *Political Correspondence and Public Papers of Aaron Burr*, 2: 867–68.

29. A. Rothman, 19; David Eltis et al., *The Trans-Atlantic Slave Trade Voyages Database*, http://www.slavevoyages.org.

30. Pingeon, An Abominable Business," 16–18; *New Jersey Journal*, May 7, 1816; Holmes, *An Account of the United States of America*, 324; A. Rothman, *Slave Country*, 192–93 (for Steer quote).

31. Middlesex County Manumission Book, 217–95, RUASC; Pingeon, "An Abominable Business," 17–20; *Charleston City Gazette and Daily Advertiser*, August 7, 1818; *New Orleans Chronicle*, July 14, 1818.

32. Middlesex County Manumission Book, 217–95, RUASC; Pingeon, "An Abominable Business," 17–20, quote 20; Holmes, *An Account of the United States of America*, 324.

33. Pingeon, "An Abominable Business," 17–24.

34. Ibid., 17–26; Deposition of James M. Elain, concerning the exporting of slaves, May 22, 1818, in BAH Collection, Miscellaneous Depositions, 1743–1906, NJSA; Lightner, *Slavery and the Commerce Power*, 46.

35. Ibid.; "Flesh for Sale," 36–37.

36. Pingeon, "An Abominable Business," 24–26; *New Orleans Chronicle*, July 14, 1818.

37. Pingeon, "An Abominable Business," 22; quotes from *New Brunswick Fredonian*, August 6, 1818. Thanks to Jarrett Drake for this source.

38. Indictment of Charles Morgan, Subpoenas of Nicholas Van Winkle, Arrest Warrant for Lewis Compton and James Edgar (June 1818), Subpoenas in the *State v. Lewis Compton*, Warrant to Arrest Charles Morgan, all in BAH Collection, Oyer and Terminar Documents, Hunterdon and Middlesex Counties, NJSA; Indictment of James Edgar for Exporting a Slave, Indictment of Peter Hendry for exporting a slave, Indictments for exporting slaves, all in BAH Collection, Common Pleas (Bergen-Sussex Quarter Sessions), NJSA.

39. Petition of the Inhabitants of Middlesex County to the New Jersey Legislature opposing the transportation of slaves from New Jersey, October 28, 1818, BAH Collection, Legislative Records, 1811–1934, NJSA.

40. Ibid.; Sweet, *Bodies Politic*, 248–49, 260–61.

41. Harris, *In the Shadow of Slavery*, 96–133; Egerton, *Death or Liberty*, 169–72; quote from Sweet, *Bodies Politic*, 69; Melish, *Disowning Slavery*, 52–53; Newman, *Transformation of American Abolitionism*, esp. 60–85; Tomek, "Seeking 'An Immutable Pledge from the Slave Holding States.'"

42. An act to prohibit the exportation of slaves or servants of color out of this state, November 5, 1818, Acts 43rd GA, 3–6; Finkelman, *Imperfect Union*, 76; "An act for the gradual abolition of slavery and for other purposes respecting slaves," February 24, 1820, Acts 44th GA, 74–80.

43. *Washington Whig*, August 31, 1818; *Centinel of Freedom*, December 29, 1818 (for Wilson quote); Mason, *Slavery and Politics*, 138,163; quote from Annals of the Congress of the United States, 15th Cong., 2nd sess., 336–37, as cited in Mason, *Slavery and Politics*, 163.

44. E. Foner, *Free Soil, Free Labor, Free Men*, 9–11; Tomek, *Colonization and Its Discontents*, 241; Mason, *Slavery and Politics*, 4–5; Riordan, *Many Identities, One Nation*, 224–29. For private commentary on the Missouri Question, see Samuel Emlen to Roberts Vaux, December 14, 1819, Vaux Family Papers, HSP.

45. Forbes, *The Missouri Compromise and Its Aftermath*, 51–56 (Bateman quote 51–52); *National Recorder*, November 6, 1819; Fee, "The Transition from Aristocracy to Democracy in New Jersey," 240–42; Riordan, *Many Identities, One Nation*, 224–29; petition quote from *Niles' Weekly Register*, November 20, 1819, as cited in Kornblith, *Slavery and Sectional Strife*, 144–46.

46. Forbes, *The Missouri Compromise and Its Aftermath*, 51–56; *National Recorder*, November 6, 1819; Riordan, *Many Identities, One Nation*, 224–29; L. Richards, *Slave Power*, 75; Fee, "The Transition from Aristocracy to Democracy in New Jersey," 240–42; Mason, *Slavery and Politics*, 4–5, 48–54; Tomek, *Colonization and Its Discontents*, 241; "Votes and Proceedings 43rd GA," 59–61.

47. *Centinel of Freedom*, March 14, 1820.

48. "An act for the gradual abolition of slavery and for other purposes respecting slaves," February 24, 1820, Acts 44th GA, 74–80.

49. Forbes, *The Missouri Compromise and Its Aftermath*, 51–59; Riordan, *Many Identities, One Nation*, 228; Notes and Draft of Speech on Slavery, 1830–35, Samuel Southard Papers, PUL; *Short Statement of Facts*, 1–7.

50. A. P. Malone, *Sweet Chariot*, 92.

51. *Ibid.*, 101; for indentures, see Avery Papers, SHC.

52. *New Jersey Journal*, December 1, 1818; William Stone to John Marsh, December 10, 1818, Avery Papers, SHC.

53. Pennsylvania Society for Promoting the Abolition of Slavery to the American Convention for Promoting the Abolition of Slavery, December 10, 1818, Papers of the Pennsylvania Abolition Society, HSP; *Leesburg, Virginia, Genius of Liberty*, November 24, 1818; *Alexandria Gazette*, November 14, 1818; *Columbian*, August 3, December 12, 1818; Mason, *Slavery and Politics*, 82–83.

54. *Centinel of Freedom*, December 15, 1818; Minutes of the Pennsylvania Abolition Society, December 3, 1818, Papers of the Pennsylvania Abolition Society, HCP; *Genius of Liberty*, December 8, 1818; Pingeon, "An Abominable Business," 28; A. P. Malone, *Sweet Chariot*, 99–103; William Stone to John Marsh, December 10, 1818, Avery Papers, SHC.

55. There are several spellings for his last name, including Raburgh, Raborg, Raborgh, Rayboy, and Rayburgh. A. P. Malone, *Sweet Chariot*, 99–103; *Centinel of Freedom*, December 15, 1818; *New York City Hall Reporter*, vol. 4, 4, April 1819.

56. *Centinel of Freedom*, December 22, 1818.

57. A. P. Malone, *Sweet Chariot*, 99–103; *Centinel of Freedom*, December 15, 1818; *New York City Hall Reporter*, April 1819. For failed habeas corpus case, see Supreme Court Case File 37799 (*NJ v. William Raboy*, February 1819), NJSA.

58. *New York City Hall Reporter*, April 1819; "An Act Relative to Slaves and Servants," Laws of the State of New York, Chapter 137, March 31, 1817. The 1817 law prohibited the importation of slaves in New York. For 1793 Fugitive Slave law, see Lightner, *Slavery and the Commerce Power*, 40–41; New York Manumission Society Minutes, 11: 44–45, New York Historical Society.

59. *New York City Hall Reporter*, April 1819, quote 48; Wheeler, *Reports of Criminal Law Cases*, preface; New York Manumission Society Minutes, vol. 11, 44–45, New York Historical Society.

60. *New York City Hall Reporter*, April 1819, 50.

61. *Ibid.*; Morris, *Free Men All*, 35–40.

62. J. Parrish, "An Affection Address to the Inhabitants of the United States of America."

63. Morris, *Free Men All*, 35–40.

64. Nicholas Slabey to Thomas Shipley, October 22, 1819, Papers of the Pennsylvania Abolition Society, HSP.

65. *New York City Hall Reporter*, April 1819, 50; *Annals of Congress*, 17th Cong., 1st sess., March 17, 1822, 1379, as cited in Morris, *Free Men All*, 41 (for Colden quote).

66. *Trenton True American* article as reprinted in *Washington Whig*, August 31, 1818; Pingeon, "An Abominable Business," 27.

67. Joseph Watson to John Henderson and JW Hamilton, March 10, 1826, Joseph Watson Papers, HSP (for quote); *Freedom's Journal*, August 8, 1828, and June 8, 1827; E. L. Smith, "Rescuing African American Kidnapping Victims," 324–30; Newman, *Transformation of American Abolitionism*, 62–63. For previous kidnapping attempts, see Lightner, *Slavery and the Commerce Power*, 41–13; L. Alexander, *African or American?*, 34–35; and Wilson, *Freedom at Risk*.

68. James Bryan to Joseph Watson, March 18, 1826, Joseph Watson Papers, HSP.

69. Winch, "Philadelphia and the Other Underground Railroad," 3–4; E. L. Smith, "Rescuing African American Kidnapping Victims," 319–22.

70. E. L. Smith, "Rescuing African American Kidnapping Victims," 321–24, 330–35; John Henderson to Joseph Watson, January 2, 1826, Joseph Watson Papers, HSP. For a similar Jersey case, see Affidavit of Isaiah Sadler, September 13, 1824, Joseph Watson Papers, HSP.

71. E. L. Smith, "Rescuing African American Kidnapping Victims," 324–30, quote 340; Pickard, *The Kidnapped and the Ransomed*, 25–30, 219–36; Newman, *Transformation of American Abolitionism*, 62–63. For Garrigues, see *Centinel of Freedom*, December 22, 1818; *Freedom's Journal*, January 18, 1828; Wilson, *Freedom at Risk*, 30–31; Newspaper Clipping, May 7, 1828, in Joseph Watson Papers, HSP.

72. Joseph Watson to J. W. Hamilton and John Henderson, March 10, 1826, and Abstract of Documents directed to John Henderson, March 13, 1826, Joseph Watson Papers, HSP; E. L. Smith, "Rescuing African American Kidnapping Victims," 336.

73. E. L. Smith, "Rescuing African American Kidnapping Victims," 321–24, 330–35; Wilson, *Freedom at Risk*, 33–35; E. Lewis, ed., *Narrative of Samuel Scomp*, 39–41. Scomp's narrative is also reproduced in Blassingame, ed., *Slave Testimony*, 178–81.

74. Hodges, *David Ruggles*, 86–94, quote 89.

75. Fogel and Engerman, "Philanthropy at Bargain Prices," 392–93. For recent works on the internal trade, see Deyle, *Carry Me Back*; Johnson, *Soul by Soul*; Tadman, *Speculators and Slaves*.

76. Fogel and Engerman, "Philanthropy at Bargain Prices," 392–93; S. White, *Somewhat More Independent*, 152–55; Menschel, "Abolition Without Deliverance." Graham Hodges offers an alternative explanation of Fogel and Engerman's conclusions, *Slavery and Freedom in the Rural North*, 150, 160, 162, 212.

77. Fogel and Engerman, "Philanthropy at Bargain Prices," 392–33; 1820 Census Schedule, Historical Census Browser, University of Virginia, Geospatial and Statistical Data Center (http://mapserver.lib.virginia.edu/collections); Johnson Family Records, Anderson Family Papers, NJHS; 1830 Census Schedule, Hardwick Township, Warren County, New Jersey, 440; Data for slaves for a term population from Black Birth Books for each county.

78. *Report of the Committee Appointed in the Senate of Pennsylvania*, 3–7, quote 3; D. Smith, *On the Edge of Freedom*, 18.

79. Duncan, "'One negro, Sarah," 340–41. Thanks to Michael Pierce for bringing this article to my attention.

80. Deyle , *Carry Me Back*, 148; James F. Perry and Stephen S. Perry Papers, Dolph Briscoe Center for American History, University of Texas at Austin, accessed through Stampp, ed., *Records of Antebellum Southern Plantations*, Series G, Part 1, Reel 25, frame 1023–24 (hereafter cited as James and Stephen Perry Papers); Matrana, *Lost Plantations of the South*, 246–50. Thanks to Susan O'Donovan for this source.

81. Stephen Perry to J. H. Brower and Company, January 7, 1857, in James and Stephen Perry Papers, Series G, Part 1, Reel 25, frame 90–91.

82. Bill of Sale, Charles Sayre to Stephen Perry, February 23, 1857, and Stephen Perry to J. H. Brower and Company, February 1, 1858, in James and Stephen Perry Papers, Series G, Part 1, Reel 25, frames 136–37, 540–41; M. B. Jones, *Peach Point Plantation*, 134–57; "Charles D. Sayre," *The New Handbook of Texas* (http://www .tshaonline.org); U.S. Census, 1860, Brazoria County Slave Schedule, 1163.

83. Petition of Hendrick Smock to the Governor and Legislative Council, Requesting a Pardon for His Slave, Catharine Mervit and related Papers, May 1811, in Department of State, Secretary of State AM Papers, NJSA; Sommerville, *Rape and Race in the Nineteenth-Century South*, 19–101.

84. J. Parrish, *Remarks of the Slavery of the Black People*, 16.

85. A. Rothman, *Slave Country*, ix–25.

Chapter 7. Colonization and Gradualism's Persistence

1. Petition of Negro Prime to the Honorable Court in Trenton (no date) from Department of Education, NJSL, BAH Collection, NJSA (for quote); Berlin, *Slaves Without Masters*, 3–12. For blacks in the state militia, see Gough, "Black Men and the Early New Jersey Militia," 227–38. Also see E. Foner, *Free Soil, Free Labor, Free Men*, xxvii–xxviii, for the idea of blacks living in "halfway houses of semifree labor." For a link to slave past, see O'Donovan, *Becoming Free in the Cotton South*, 1–9, 264–71.

2. Melish, *Disowning Slavery*, 210–11, 215, 224–25; Minardi, *Making Slavery History*, 7, 13–15, 36–41.

3. Melish, *Disowning Slavery*, 119–20; Melish "The Racial Vernacular," 17–18, 23–26; Lepore, *The Name of War*, 182–90; Sweet, *Bodies Politic*, esp. 271–311.

4. *Extracts from an Article in the North American Review*, 7, first quote; Gellman and Quigley, eds., *Jim Crow New York*, 221, 218–20, second quote.

5. *Colored American*, April 8, 1837. Melish argues a similar idea that whites could not accept free blacks, but I contend that New Jerseyans did not need to broach this issue because they never abandoned slavery. See Melish, *Disowning Slavery*, 84–88. For a similar argument in Pennsylvania, see McCoy, "Forgetting Freedom: White Anxiety, Black Presence," 141–70. For similar argument in Boston, see Kantrowitz, *More Than Freedom*, 16, 24, 48.

6. *Gibbons v. Morse*, 7 N.J.L., Court of Errors and Appeals, 1821, NJSA; *Dred Scott v. Sandford*, 60 US 393. Also see Finkelman, "State Constitutional Protections of Liberty," 766. Finkelman notes that "unlike other northeastern states, New Jersey accepted the southern rule that all blacks were slaves until they proved otherwise."

7. *Boice v. Gibbons*, 8 N.J.L., Supreme Court of New Jersey, 1826, NJSA; Finkelman, "State Constitutional Protections of Liberty," 766.

8. Finley, *Thoughts on the Colonization of Free Blacks*; Robert Finley to John Mumford, February 1816, reprinted in I. Brown, *Biography of the Rev. Robert Finley*, 99, for quote; *Centinel of Freedom*, December 6, 1816; M. T. Wright, "New Jersey Laws and the Negro," 180.

9. Newark Colonization Society, 9–10 (for first and second quote); *African Repository and Colonial Journal*, July 18, 1838, 196.

10. *African Repository and Colonial Journal*, July 18, 1838, 191, third quote.

11. Ibid., October 1844, 305. For another example, see *The Eighth Annual Report of the American Society for Colonizing the Free People of Colour*.

12. *African Repository and Colonial Journal*, January 1, 1842, 8.

13. Finley, *Thoughts on the Colonization of Free Blacks*, 4–7 for quotes; Tomek, *Colonization and Its Discontents*, 3.

14. *Extracts from an Article in the North American Review*, 6 (last two quotes).

15. Ibid., 7–8 for quote; Tomek, *Colonization and its Discontents*, 3.

16. *Extracts from an Article in the North American Review*, 6, 10 for quotes; Tomek, *Colonization and Its Discontents*, 3–12.

17. *Proceedings of the Second Annual Meeting of the New Jersey Colonization Society*, 17.

18. Ibid., 10–11. National colonizationists used the same rhetoric, claiming that members needed to support the "condition of a very degraded portion of the human race." See American Colonization Society, *Memorial of the American Society for Colonizing the Free People of Color*, 5–6.

19. Petition of the Inhabitants of New Jersey to the New Jersey Legislature, advocating Colonization of Freedman in Africa, November 4, 1816, BAH Collection, Legislative Records, 1811–1934, NJSA.

20. *Freedom's Journal*, March 30, 1827.

21. Tomek, *Colonization and Its Discontents*, 1–4, 11, 18, 59, 95–100; Burin, "Rethinking Northern White Support," 200–205, quote 201.

22. *Proceedings of a Meeting Held at Princeton New Jersey*, 5, first quote; *Proceedings of the Second Annual Meeting of the New Jersey Colonization Society*, 17, 22, remaining quotes.

23. *African Repository and Colonial Journal*, November 1825, 9.

24. Ibid., May 1825, 88.

25. Ibid., November 1825, 282.

26. *Minutes of an Adjourned Session of the American Convention for Promoting the Abolition of Slavery*, 6.

27. *Seventh Annual Report of the American Society for Colonizing the Free People of Color*, 8, first quote; *African Repository and Colonial Journal*, November 1825, 280 second quote.

28. *African Repository and Colonial Journal*, March 1825.

29. Tomek, *Colonization and Its Discontents*, 22–25; *Extracts from an Article in the North American Review*, 12, for quote; *Proceedings of a Meeting Held at Princeton New Jersey*, 5; *Fifth Annual Report of the American Society for Colonizing the Free People of Color*.

30. *Fourteenth Annual Report of the American Society for Colonizing the Free People of Color*, xix.

31. *African Repository and Colonial Journal*, January 1845, 26, December 1846, 377. The claim of 18,000 slaves appears exaggerated as only 1,200 slaves arrived on American ships to Brazil in 1843 and 1844 combined. See Eltis et al., *The Trans-Atlantic Slave Trade Voyages Database*, http://www.slavevoyages.org.

32. Lyght, *Path of Freedom*, 25–26; Appleby, "Opinions on Slavery," 22. For slave trading and New Jersey Colonization, see reports from New Brunswick Colonization Society Minutes, New Brunswick Colonization Society Papers, RUASC.

33. Robert Finley to Rev. George Moodhull, March 22, 1817, Office of the President, University of Georgia Presidents File, 1801–1819, Hargrett Library, University of Georgia. Finley served as UGA president for six months.

34. Tomek, *Colonization and Its Discontents*, 101–2 (first quote 102); *Proceedings of a Meeting Held at Princeton* (1824); Newark Colonization Society, *A Sketch of the Colonization Enterprise*, 8 (second quote); Seventh Annual Meeting of the New Jersey State Colonization Society, reproduced in *African Repository and Colonial Journal*, January 1845, 26 (third quote). For other references to moral debts, see *African Repository and Colonial Journal*, March 1825, December 1846, January 1845, October 1844, August 1842.

35. Tomek, *Colonization and Its Discontents*, 7–8; *An Address to the Public on the Subject of the African School*, 3–8, quotes 3, 4, 7; *African Repository and Colonial Journal*, November 1825, 276. For linking school to ACS, see *Seventh Annual Report of the American Society for Colonizing the Free People of Color*. For final quote, see Joseph Hornblower to Rosana Stone, January 6, 1821, African American History Collection, CLUM.

36. Miller, *A Discourse Delivered April 12, 1797*.

37. Miller, *A Sermon preached at Newark, October 22, 1823*, 3–20, quotes 9, 10, 13, 15; *Tenth Annual Report of the American Society for Colonizing the Free People of Color*, for references to the importance of an African school in New Jersey.

38. *African Repository and Colonial Journal*, September 1826, 223; July 1826, 163 (for quotes). Also see Hodges and Nash, *Friends of Liberty*; Charles Goodrick to Benjamin Bussey, December 31, 1819, Benjamin Bussey Papers, CLUM.

39. Griffin, *A Plea for Africa*, 34, 70.

40. Minute Book, African Association of New Brunswick Papers, RUASC; M. T. Wright, *The Education of Negroes in New Jersey*, 78–83; Hodges, *Root and Branch*, 219–20; *Centinel of Freedom*, December 3, 1816.

41. Address Made to the Association on First of January 1820 by Jeremiah Gloucester of Philadelphia in Minute Book, African Association of New Brunswick Papers, RUASC.

42. *African Repository and Colonial Journal*, November 1825, 281.

43. Melish, *Disowning Slavery*, 192; Burin, "Rethinking Northern White Support," 199, 203; Tomek, *Colonization and Its Discontents*, 3, 9, 28–33, 43–45; *Freedom's Journal*, March 30, 1827 (for quote); *African Repository and Colonial Journal*, April 1841.

44. *Proceedings of a Meeting Held at Princeton*, 15.

45. *Proceedings of the Second Annual Meeting of the New Jersey Colonization Society*, 22.

46. *Report of the Board of Managers of the Pennsylvania Colonization Society*, 31.

47. *Minutes of an Adjourned Session of the American Convention for Promoting the Abolition of Slavery*, 20; *Address of the Board of Managers of the American Colonization Society*, 1820; Tomek, *Colonization and Its Discontents*, 50–51.

48. *Present State and Condition of the Free People of Color*, 21.

49. Malone, "Rethinking the End of Black Suffrage in Pennsylvania," 480–81; Tomek, *Colonization and Its Discontents*, 52–53.

50. *Essay on the Late Institution*, 36–37, 41.

51. Ibid.; Rugemer, *Problem of Emancipation*, 42–43; Hamilton, *A Word for the African*, 24–25; *Extracts from an Article in the North American Review*, 9; *Proceedings of the Third Annual Meeting of the New Jersey Colonization Society*, 18–19 (for Vroom).

52. Melish, *Disowning Slavery*, 210–11, 214–15, 224–25, quote 215; Minardi, *Making Slavery History*, 7, 13–15, 36–41. Melish does offer that colonization in the Mid-Atlantic worked differently from New England.

53. P. Hay, 8–10, 20–22, quote 22.

54. Ibid., 23–25.

55. *An Oration Delivered at Princeton*, 5–12, quotes 7, 9, 12; Caputo, "New Jersey's Role in the African Colonization Movement," 8–10.

56. *Thirteenth Annual Report of the American Society for Colonizing the Free People of Colour*, xii; *African Repository and Colonial Journal*, August 1829, 172; Newark Colonization Society, *A Sketch of the Colonization Enterprise*, 9–10; *Historical Notes on Slavery*, 15.

57. Newman, *Transformation of American Abolitionism*, 97–99, quote 97.

58. Bacon, *Freedom's Journal*, 78–80, 177–78; *Freedom's Journal*, June 8, March 30, 1827 for quote.

59. Bacon, *Freedom's Journal*, 180, 187–95; James, *The Struggles of John Brown Russwurm*, 108–26.

60. *Colored American*, September 1, 1838, for quotes; Seifman, "The United Colonization Societies of New York and Pennsylvania," 25; Bethel, *Roots of African American Identity*, 106–7; *The Colonization Scheme Considered*; *Centinel of Freedom*, December 7, 1819.

61. Gurley, Address at the Annual Meeting of the Pennsylvania Colonization Society, 7, 20, 37 for quotes. Also see Newark Colonization Society, *A Sketch of the Colonization Enterprise*, 9.

62. Garrison, *Thoughts on African Colonization*, 45–47.

63. D. P. Brown, *An Oration Delivered Before the Anti-Slavery Society*, quote 10; Roberts Vaux to Fredrick Tuckett, April 26, 1835, and Samuel Emlen to Roberts Vaux, September 19, 1837, Vaux Family Papers, HSP. For rejection of colonization within the abolition movement, see J. B. Stewart, *William Lloyd Garrison and the Challenge of Emancipation*, 56–74.

64. Tomek, *Colonization and Its Discontents*, 167–69; *Historical Notes on Slavery and Colonization*, 27–30, for Skinner; Seifman, "The United Colonization Societies of New York and Pennsylvania and the Establishment of the African Colony of Bassa Cove," 25–34.

65. *Colored American*, October 6, 13, July 21, 1838, January 9, 1839, in order by quote.

Chapter 8. Creating a Free Life

1. J. B. Stewart, "Modernizing Difference," 695–96; Bacon, *Freedom's Journal*, 107; Rael, *Black Identity and Protest in the Antebellum North*, 5–14, 158–60; Sweet, *Bodies Politic*, 209, 252–53, 313–15, 342.

2. See Introduction, note 17, for details on the enslaved population in 1830.

3. *Centinel of Freedom*, March 10, 1812; "An Act respecting Slaves," March 14, 1798, Acts 22nd GA, 2nd sitting, 364–73.

4. 1830 Newark Census Schedules; Hodges, *Root and Branch*, 193–94, 212; Nash, *Forging Freedom*, 72–73, 136–37; S. White, *Somewhat More Independent*, 152–55; Hodges, *Slavery, Freedom, and Culture Among Early American Workers*, 75; 1830 Newark Census Schedules; Melish, "White Workers, Black Neighborhoods."

5. Wacker, "Patterns and Problems in the Historical Geography . . . " in Ehrenberg, ed., *Pattern and Process*, 49–67; Wacker and Clemens, *Land Use in Early New Jersey*; S. White, *Somewhat More Independent*, 171–77; Nash, *Forging Freedom*, 169; Hodges, *Root and Branch*, 193; Harris, *In the Shadow of Slavery*, 74–75; *City Directory of Newark*. For housing elsewhere in the North, see Sweet, *Bodies Politic*, 359. For church in community life, see Peter Williams to New York Manumission Society, June 10, 1816, Grellet Papers, HSP.

6. Bartlett, *Robert Coe, Puritan*, 102–4; J. Cunningham, *Newark*, 91. For other black businessmen, see John Cox to Joseph Parrish, September 29, 1816, Cox-Parrish Papers, HSP; Susanna Emlen to William Dillwyn, December 8, 1809, Dillwyn Family Papers, LCP. For another example of master support, see Will of John Doughty as excerpted in Mitros, *Slave Records of Morris County New Jersey*, 96, 108–9.

7. New Jersey General Assembly Tax Ratables, Middle Township, Cape May County (1783, 1785–1786, 1789–1797, 1802, 1805–1810), NJSA; Will of Nero, Will Book A, Cape May County Surrogate Records, 99–100, NJSA. For tax classifications, see Wacker and Clemens, *Land Use in Early New Jersey*, 98, 242, 247.

8. Geismar, *The Archaeology of Social Disintegration in Skunk Hollow*, 3–32, quote 12. For other successful rural black settlements, see Doerflinger, "Rural Capitalism in Iron Country," 11, and Lyght, *Path of Freedom*, 38–39.

9. Proceedings under the Martin Act in the Nature of Foreclosure . . . , Edwin Corwin McKeag Papers, RUASC; Rael, *Black Identity and Protest in the North*, 23.

10. Stevens, *Outcast*, 49–51; *Hunterdon County Democrat*, June 15, 1870; Schmidt, *Slavery and Attitudes on Slavery*, 21. New York experienced the same type of free black living arrangements. In 1810, 69 percent of New York white households used free black labor. See S. White, *Somewhat More Independent*, 46–55.

11. 15 N.J.L. 266, *Stoutenborough v. Haviland*, Supreme Court of New Jersey, February Term, 1836, NJSA.

12. Thomas Booth to Samuel Allinson, Jr., January 19, 1840, New Jersey Abolition Society and Burlington County Abolition Society Papers, BCHS.

13. *Colored American*, April 8, 1837.

14. S. White, "African American Festivals and Parades," 18, 22–31; Harris, *In the Shadow of Slavery*, 88; Hodges, *Root and Branch*, 221–23, quote 221.

15. Vital Records of Hanover Presbyterian Church, NJHS; Stone House Plains Dutch Reformed Church Register, 1747–1901, NJHS; Cunningham, *Newark*, 131; Sobel, *The World They Made Together*, 178–213; Sweet, *Bodies Politic*, 111; Landers, *Pioneers, Pastors, and Patriots*, 69. Thanks to Bill and Doris Davis for this last source.

16. Stevens, *Outcast*, 151; Reformed Dutch Church of Middlebush, New Jersey Subscription List, October 6, 183?, Van Liew Family Papers, RUASC.

17. Baptist Church of Scotch Plains New Jersey Papers, 1747–1837, NJHS.

18. Sweet, *Bodies Politic*, 339 (first quote); *Colored American*, June 19, 1841 (remaining quotes).

19. Cunningham, *Newark*, 131; Curry, *The Free Black in Urban America*, 186–87; Harris, *In the Shadow of Slavery*, 82–84.

20. Ward, *Autobiography of a Fugitive Negro*, 11–12.

21. Kerr-Ritchie, *Rites of August First*, 136; Rugemer, *The Problem of Emancipation*, 222–57, esp. 232–35, 238–40, 243–46, 248, 252–57.

22. Cunningham, *Newark*, 131; Curry, *The Free Black in Urban America*, 186–87.

23. Newman, *Freedom's Prophet*, 63–73, 158–79; J. Lee, *Religious Experience and Journal of Mrs. Jarena Lee*; Winch, *Philadelphia's Black Elite*, 11–14; J. Horton and L.

Horton, *In Hope of Liberty*, 141–49; C. V. R. George, *Segregated Sabbaths*, 86–87; Payne, *History of the African Methodist Episcopal Church*, 13; *African Methodist Episcopal Church Magazine*, September and October 1841, 35–38.

24. *Colored American*, June 19, 1841.

25. M. T. Wright, *Education of Negroes in New Jersey*, 67–69; Newark Town Records, April 24, 1813, July 2, 1813, and October 13, 1813, NJHS; *Colored American*, May 18, 1839.

26. *Centinel of Freedom*, June 16, 1829.

27. M. T. Wright, *Education of Negroes in New Jersey*, 111 for 1830 quote; Curry, *The Free Black in Urban America*, 155.

28. M. T. Wright, *The Education of Negroes in New Jersey*, 116–17; G. Wright, *African Americans in New Jersey*, 31–32; Hodges, *Root and Branch*, 219–20.

29. M. T. Wright, *The Education of Negroes in New Jersey*, 116–17; G. Wright, *African Americans in New Jersey*, 31–32; Hodges, *Root and Branch*, 219–20; *Colored American*, December 12, 1840 for quotes.

30. Agricultural and Mechanic Association of Pennsylvania and New Jersey Papers, American Negro Historical Society Collection, HSP; Ballard, *One More Day's Journey*, 64.

31. United Sons of Salem Benevolent Society Minute Book, 2, 6, 9, 14, CLUM.

32. *Minutes and Proceedings of the First Annual Convention of the People of Colour*, 3, 5–9, 15, quotes 5, 15; J. Horton, *Free People of Color*, 60; Bethel, *The Roots of African American Identity*, 83, 127.

33. *To the Honorable The Senate and House of Representatives*, 8.

34. *Address to the Legislature of New Jersey*, 3–12, quotes 3, 5, 10.

35. *Colored American*, September 14, 1839.

36. Ibid., February 6, 1841.

37. Ibid., August 17, 1839.

38. Records of the New Jersey 1849 Convention in P. Foner and Walker, eds., *Proceedings of the Black State Conventions*, 3–5, quote 5.

39. *The North Star*, April 7, 1849 (for quotes); *Colored American*, February 6, 1841; *History and Proceedings Attending the Presentation of a Medal to Thomas Peterson-Mundy*, 2–3. Peterson Moody was further ensnared in slavery's legacy, marrying a former slave for a term.

40. Rael, *Black Identity and Protest in the Antebellum North*, 164–67; J. B. Stewart, "Modernizing Difference," 691–701; L. Horton, "From Class to Race in Early America," 630, 641–64; Gilje, *Rioting in America*, 87–115.

41. Melish, "The Racial Vernacular," 26; Winch, *Philadelphia's Black Elite*, 132–46; Melish, *Disowning Slavery*, 126–36; Laurie, *Beyond Garrison*, 21; Roediger, *Wages of Whiteness*, 13–14, 20, 31, 43–49; Arnesen, "Whiteness and the Historians' Imagination," 13–14.

42. *Philadelphia Album and Ladies' Literary Portfolio*, 8, 29 (July 19, 1834): 229.

43. Ibid.

44. Tomek, *Colonization and Its Discontents*, xvi; Bethel, *Roots of African American Identity*, 123.

45. Harry Horton to George Horton, August 14, 1834, Harry Horton Papers, CLUM.

46. James Creeson to Joseph Parrish, August 24, 1834, Cox-Parrish Papers, HSP (for Columbia); Winch, *Philadelphia's Black Elite*, 143–45; Tomek, *Colonization and Its Discontents*, xiii–xv.

Chapter 9. Debating Slavery's End

1. William Newbold to George Newbold, May 6, 1823, Misc. Collection, HCQC; *Genealogical and Memorial History of the State of New Jersey*, 4: 1300–1302.

2. Newman, *The Transformation of American Abolitionism*, 5–7.

3. Harrold, *Border War*, 15, 30–34; Wilson, *Freedom at Risk*, 90–109. The figure of 3,000 slaves and slaves for a term comes from *New Jersey Freeman*, June 1845. Two articles in the same issue conflict on the total of slaves and slaves for a term. One article estimates 3,700 while the other 3,000. I acknowledge the lower estimate as I believe 3,700 is too high since the 1840 census only lists 647 slaves, and many slaves for a term gained freedom in the 1830s. The February, 1846, edition estimates between three and four thousand "persons are held in slavery, a part of them are held under the name of apprentices but all of them in reality slaves."

4. See Introduction, note 17, for details on the enslaved population in 1830. Also see Melish, *Disowning Slavery*, 163; Minardi, *Making Slavery History*, 20–21; Wong, *Neither Fugitive nor Free*, 12–14.

5. Harrold, *Border War*, 10–22; Smith, *On the Edge of Freedom*, 8–9; Berlin, *Many Thousands Gone*, 228–29.

6. Harrold, *Border War*, 34–41, 44–52, 57; Wilson, *Freedom at Risk*, 2–8, 30–35; Morris, *Free Men All*, 17–28, 34–41, 44–52; "Supplement to an act concerning slaves" Acts 51st GA, 1st sitting, December 26, 1826, NJSA; Finkelman, "State Constitutional Protections of Liberty," 753–87, esp. 766–68; Cooley, "A Study of Slavery in New Jersey," 34; Melish, *Disowning Slavery*, 83–88.

7. *Speech of Mr. John Van Dyke, March 4, 1850*, 4; Deyle, *Carry Me Back*, 28–39; Johnson, *Soul by Soul*, 31–33; Harrold, *Border War*, 57; Wilson, *Freedom at Risk*, 2–8 and 30–35.

8. G. Wright, *African Americans in New Jersey*, 39–41; Rizzo, *Parallel Communities*, 55–58, 76–88, 99–109; C. V. R. George, *Segregated Sabbaths*, 135–59.

9. Ward, *Autobiography of a Fugitive Negro*, 11–12, 25–26, quote 11; Rizzo, *Parallel Communities*, 82; B. A. Andrews, *Reminiscences of Greenwich*, 31–32.

10. Matter of Negro Nancy and her three children, 1835, BAH Collection, Burlington County Court of Common Pleas, Unprocessed Loose Papers, Fugitive Slave Law Cases, NJSA; Finkelman, *An Imperfect Union*, 76, 144.

11. Hearing Minutes in Works Projects Administration, *Gloucester County Series Slave Documents*, 56–60.

12. *Pennsylvania and NJ Slave Trade, The Case of Severn Martin*, 1836, RUASC; Slave Case, *William Christian v. Negro Sam alias S. Martin*, copy of proceedings, August 12, 1836, Burlington County Court of Common Pleas, Unprocessed Loose Papers, Fugitive Slave Law Cases, NJSA.

13. Ibid.; Harrold, *Border War*, 108; "An Act for the Relief of Severn Martin, a coloured man, of the county of Burlington" March 6, 1837, Acts 61st GA, 2nd sitting, 337–38. For other accounts of fugitive trials in South Jersey like Martin's, see Minutes of Gloucester County Fugitive Slave Hearings, Gloucester County Clerk's Office Slave Records, NJSA and Supreme Court Case File 34339, NJSA.

14. Morris, *Free Men All*, 71–75, 79–80.

15. *National Inquirer*, December 24, 1836 as cited in Harrold, *Border War*, 60, also see 59–63.

16. Drew, *A North Side View of Slavery*, 32–36, quotes 33, 34; Proceedings in the case of Nathan, alias Alexander Helmsly, 1835, Burlington County Court of Common Pleas, Unprocessed Loose Papers, Fugitive Slave Law Cases, NJSA; For an accounting from the abolitionist perspective, see I. Parrish, *Brief Memoirs of Thomas Shipley and Edwin Atlee Read*; Finkelman, "State Constitutional Protections of Liberty," 759, 762–69.

17. Finkelman, "State Constitutional Protections of Liberty," 769–74, quote 772.

18. Ibid., 769–79, esp. 776, 779; *Colored American*, April 22, 1837; "A Further Supplement to an act entitled 'An Act concerning slaves,'" February 15, 1837, Acts 61st GA, 2nd sitting, 134–36.

19. Harrold, *Border War*, 61, 95, 98, 107; *Pennsylvania Freeman*, June 6, 1839, as cited in Harrold, *Border War*, 98.

20. Diary of John Mason Brown, December 29–31, 1834, RUASC. Donahower's name in various sources is also spelled Donahee or Donaho.

21. *Boston Recorder*, January 30, 1835 (reported story from *Freeman's Banner*). Some accounts have the altercation with the knife and gun taking place in the early morning hours while the group was traveling to the jail.

22. Harrold, *Border War*, 95, 109.

23. B. A. Andrews, *Reminiscences of Greenwich*, 33; Rizzo, *Parallel Communities*, 92.

24. Duryee, *The Duty of Pennsylvania Concerning Slavery*, 1–6; Wharton, *What has Pennsylvania to do with slavery?* 1, 4; Morris, *Free Men All*, 94–104, 114–118; *Friends' Weekly Intelligencer*, January 8, 1848; *The Liberator*, September 1, 1848. For another earlier Pennsylvania example dealing with the 1780 abolition law, see William Meredith to Roberts Vaux, February 12, 1815, Vaux Family Papers, HSP.

25. D. Smith, *On the Edge of Freedom*, 8–9, 39–45, 70–72; 115–19; Morris, *Free Men All*, 94–104, 114–18; *Friends' Weekly Intelligencer*, January 8, 1848; *The Liberator*, September 1, 1848 (for Anti-Slavery Society quote); Memorial Adopted by the New Jersey Anti-Slavery Society in Boonton, January 17, 1843, Department of State, Secretary of State AM Papers, NJSA (for Jersey Abolitionist quote); Cover, *Justice Accused*, 166–74; Finkelman, "State Constitutional Protections of Liberty," 776–79.

26. Petition of Inhabitants of New Jersey to the Legislature opposing the harboring of escaped slaves, January 30, 1837, and February 1, 1837, Legislative Records, 1811–1934, BAH Collection, NJSA.

27. Ibid.; D. Smith, *On the Edge of Freedom*, 115–19, 140–42; *Speech of Mr. John Van Dyke, March 4, 1850*, 4; *State of the Union, Speech of Hon. Garnett Adrain*, 4; *Speech of Mr. Miller of New Jersey, February 21, 1850*, 8.

28. *State of the Union, Speech of Hon. Garnett Adrain*, 4. This contrasts with Finkelman's interpretation of New Jersey as on the vanguard of northern personal liberty laws. Although I agree that from 1837 to 1842 it was incredibly progressive for the time, New Jersey politicians continued to position New Jersey as a strong supporter of interstate comity especially in contrast to other northern states after *Prigg*. See Finkelman, "State Constitutional Protections of Liberty," 754–59, 775–77.

29. *Speech of Mr. Miller of New Jersey, February 21, 1850*, 5–8; P. C. Davis, "The Persistence of Partisan Alignment," 157–74.

30. *Speech of Mr. Dayton of New Jersey, April 11, 1848*, 11–12.

31. *The Territorial Question, Speech of Honorable William Dayton, March 22, 1850*, 9, 11–12.

32. *Speech of Hon. John C. Ten Eyck, April 2, 1860*, 4; "Relative to the extension of slavery in any territory," Acts of the 71st New Jersey Legislature, February 16, 1847; "Against the extension of slavery into free territory . . . " Joint Resolution, Acts of the 73rd New Jersey Legislature, March 2, 1849; *Report of the Committee of the Anti-LeCompton Democratic Convention*, 2–3; *Kansas-The Lecompton Constitution: Speech of Hon. Jacob Wortendyke*, 6. See P. C. Davis, "The Persistence of Partisan Alignment," 157–174, for a rudimentary discussion of fugitives and the state's enslaved past that argues New Jersey feared federal intervention on any issue.

33. Record Book of the New Jersey Anti-Slavery Society, 1839–1841, New Jersey Anti-Slavery Society Papers, NJHS; for quote, see Christopher Breese to Theodore Dwight Weld, July 16, 1841, Weld-Grimke Papers, CLUM.

34. *The First Annual Report of the New York Committee of Vigilance*, 7–8, 13–16, 31–32, 55, 62–63, 71–72, 78–79, quote 79; Hodges, *David Ruggles*, 50–54, and 114–24. For other state's actions in New Jersey, see Vigilant Committee of Philadelphia Records, HSP. They routinely crossed the border to advocate for fugitive slaves, intending to "spread (the) antislavery truth."

35. Record Book of the New Jersey Anti-Slavery Society, New Jersey Anti-Slavery Society Papers, NJHS; *Colored American*, April 8, 1837, September 14, 1839, November 21, 1840, February 6, June 19, 1841.

36. *The Friend: A Religious and Literary Journal*, January 18, 25, 1840.

37. Harrold, *Border War*, 64–65.

38. *The Friend: A Religious and Literary Journal*, January 18, 25, 1840; Wong, *Neither Fugitive nor Free*, 2–3.

39. *The Friend: A Religious and Literary Journal*, February 15, 1840; Record Book of the New Jersey Anti-Slavery Society, January 13, 1841, New Jersey Anti-Slavery Society Papers, NJHS; Minute Book, Essex County Anti-Slavery Society, NJHS.

40. Record Book of the New Jersey Anti-Slavery Society, New Jersey Anti-Slavery Society Papers, NJHS; Petitions of the Anti-Slavery Society to the Legislature Opposing Slavery and Laws Against Blacks, January 13, 1840, January 17, 1843, Department of State, Secretary of State AM Papers, NJSA, for first and fourth quotes; State Convention of Abolitionists, *An Address to the People of New Jersey*, 2–3, for second and third quote; Zilversmit, *The First Emancipation*, 218–19; M. T. Wright, "New Jersey Laws and the Negro," 159–61; *Colored American*, August 8, 1840.

41. Samuel Dorrance to Theodore Dwight Weld, April 10, 1842, Weld-Grimke Papers, CLUM.

42. Memorial adopted by the New Jersey Anti-Slavery Society in Boonton, January 17, 1843, Department of State, Secretary of State AM Papers, NJSA.

43. *New Jersey Citizen*, October 1, 1842.

44. Switala, *Underground Railroad in New Jersey and New York*, 68; *New Jersey Freeman*, June 1844, for quotes; Cudd, "The Unity of Reform," 197–212; *Journal of the Senate of the United States, December 4, 1837*, 381.

45. Cunningham, *Newark*, 131–32; *The Liberator*, February 14, 1840 (which reprinted *Newark Daily Advertiser*).

46. Commentary from Marcus Ward, *Trenton American*, September 17, 1860, and *Newark Advertiser*, May 10, 1854, all cited in Gillette, *Jersey Blue*, 5; Hillstrom, "New Jersey and the Abolition Movement," 42.

47. *New Jersey Freeman*, July 1844, December 31, 1844, February 16, 1847; Cudd, "The Unity of Reform," 201 (despotism quote).

48. *New Jersey Freeman*, January 31, 1845.

49. *New Jersey Freeman*, October 26, 1844; *Colored American*, November 7, 1840 (for Pennington); Gillette, *Jersey Blue*, 5–7.

50. Thomas Booth to Samuel Allinson, Jr., January 19, 1840, New Jersey Abolition Society and Burlington County Abolition Society Papers, BCHS.

51. *New York Evangelist*, June 16, 1864; *Proceedings of the New Jersey State Constitutional Convention of 1844*, 163, 614–44; *New Jersey Freeman*, July 1844 for last quote.

52. *New Jersey Freeman*, September 1844 (first quote), January 31, 1845 (second and third quotes), and April 30, 1845 (fifth and sixth quotes); *New York Evangelist*, May 22, 1845, and August 20, 1846; *Friends' Weekly Intelligencer*, July 26, 1845 (fourth quote). Stewart was a long proponent of the idea that the U.S. Constitution's mandate of a republican form of government barred slavery's existence. He also argued this point in New Jersey. See A. Stewart, *A Legal Argument Before the Supreme Court*, 37.

53. Zilversmit, *The First Emancipation*, 218–19; Stewart, *A Legal Argument Before the Supreme Court of the State of New Jersey*, 5, 45 for quotes; *New Jersey Freeman*, June 1845, February 1846.

54. 20 N.J.L. 368, *State v. Post*, Supreme Court of New Jersey, May Term, 1845 (first quote); Zilversmit, *The First Emancipation*, 218–19; Hodges, *Slavery and Freedom*, 174–75; Cooley, "A Study of Slavery in New Jersey," 28; *The Constitution and Farmers' and Mechanics' Advertiser*, July 22, 29, 1845; *The Sentinel of Freedom*, July 22,

29, 1845; *New Jersey Freeman*, August 7, 1845, quotes 2, 3, 4, and January 10, 1846, last quote.

55. *New Jersey Freeman*, February 11, and March 12, 1846; *Report of the Revisers of the Statute Laws of New Jersey*, 3–5, 14, 20, 30, 38; *Jersey City Advertiser*, April 21, 1846; *The Constitution and Farmers' and Mechanics' Advertiser*, April 28, 1846.

56. Hodges, *Root and Branch*, 1–68; Bergen County Wills and Probates, NJSA (for Spear, see 3852).

57. Bergen County Wills and Probates Estate files 4373 (Merseles) and 4429 (Hopper), NJSA.

58. *Journal of the Proceedings of the Second Senate*, 721–25; Nelson, *History of Bergen and Passaic Counties*, 401; Bergen County Black Birth Book, December 26, 1816, November 15, 1818, March 8, 1831, August 15, 1835, NJSA.

59. *Journal of the Proceedings of the Second Senate*, 725–29.

60. Ibid., 730–32.

61. Zilversmit, *The First Emancipation*, 220–21; Act to Abolish Slavery, April 18, 1846, Title XI, chap. 6, 382–90.

62. Monmouth County Black Birth Book, Monmouth County Archives; 1850 Marlboro Census Schedule. For an alternative explanation of Alonzo, see Hodges, *Slavery and Freedom in the Rural North*, 175.

63. Bill of Sale for Catherine, February 16, 1856, and Hunterdon County Manumission Book, 426–27, HCHS; Bergen County Wills and Probates, Estate File 4936 (Berdan), 5295 (Ackerman), 5311 (Demorest), and 4966 (Van Buskirk), NJSA. Of course, historians have seen 1846 as the end of slavery in New Jersey in many cases. For one recent example, see Kantrowitz, *More Than Freedom*, 16.

64. Monmouth County Black Birth Book, Monmouth County Archives; 1870 Marlboro Township Census, 39; New Brunswick *Daily Fredonian*, April 1, 1868, as cited in Schmidt, *Slavery and Attitudes on Slavery in Hunterdon County*, 21.

65. *New Jersey Freeman*, May 15, September 4, 1847, April 27, 1848.

66. African Association of New Brunswick Minute Book, October 6 and December 1, 1821, and January 1, 1822, RUASC; Scott, "The African Association of New Brunswick," 12; Thomas Cuyler to Samuel How, June 16, 1855, Samuel Blanchard How Papers, RUASC; How, *Slaveholding Not Sinful*, 4–7, 50, 89–90, 93, quote 89. For an additional discussion of How, see P. C. Davis, "The Persistence of Partisan Alignment," 182–84. For thoughts on abolition, see Samuel How to HD Gause, August 27, 1856, and Samuel How to Albert G. Brown, March 18, 1857, Samuel Blanchard How Papers, RUASC.

67. Van Dyke, *Slaveholding Not Sinful*, 3–16, quotes 5, 16.

68. Samuel How to Albert G. Brown, March 18, 1857, Samuel Blanchard How Papers, RUASC.

69. *Slaveholding Not Sinful: An Answer*, 10–11; How, *Slaveholding Not Sinful*, 50.

70. Joseph Bradley, Opinion for Board of Chosen Freeholders of the County of Bergen at the instance of Mr. Knapp in answer to certain questions, December 15, 1857, Joseph Bradley Papers, NJHS.

Conclusion

1. Gillette, *Jersey Blue*, 4.
2. Fleming, *New Jersey: A History*, 116.
3. Gillette, *Jersey Blue*, 4; E. Foner, *Free Soil, Free Labor, Free Men*, ix–10.
4. *Governor's Message*, 15–18 (quote 18).
5. *Report of the Assembly Committee*, 347–415, quotes 358–59, 372.
6. Elliott, *Map of the United States showing by colors*.
7. Atkinson, *History of Newark*, 171. For another example, see Snell, *History of Hunterdon and Somerset Counties*, 105. It claims the legislature first discussed abolition in 1821.

8. Richardson, *The Messages and Papers of Jefferson Davis*, 1: 66 (for quote); Hattaway and Beringer, *Jefferson Davis, Confederate President* , 71–72; W. Davis, *Jefferson Davis*, 329; W. Cooper, 324–30.

9. *New York Evangelist*, July 4, 1861.

10. *Inaugural Address of Joel Parker*, 13–14; *First Annual Message of Joel Parker*, 26, 29–30; Stellhorn and Birkner, 132–35; Weber, *Copperheads*, 66–69; Gillette, *Jersey Blue*, 183–85.

11. Knapp, *New Jersey Politics During the Period of the Civil War,* , 92–93; Gillette, *Jersey Blue*, 185; "Act making appropriations to the New Jersey Colonization Society," March 24, 1852, Acts 76th Legislature, and "Act to encourage the emigration and settlement of the free people of color of New Jersey in Liberia," March 17, 1855, Acts 81st Legislature.

12. *Friends' Intelligencer*, April 16, 1864.

13. Ibid., March 19, 1864.

14. Gillette, *Jersey Blue*, 257–81, esp. 277–78, quotes 257, 281.

15. Weber, *Copperheads*, 8–11; Gillette, *Jersey Blue*, 257, 277, 281–82, 290–93; Knapp, *New Jersey Politics During the Period of the Civil War,* 63–64, 73–74, 95–105, 140–41.

16. *The Power of Amending the Constitution*, 1–8, quotes 2, 4, 6, 8.

17. *Camden Democratic Association, March 6, 1865.*

18. Debates, 89th GA, 26–27, 38–39, 50, 53, 84, 104; Gillette, *Jersey Blue*, 301–3.

19. Gillette, *Jersey Blue*, 301–3.

20. Charles Perrin Smith, Legislative Journal and Personal Reminiscences, 285, NJSA; Platt, *Charles Perrin Smith: New Jersey Political Reminiscences*, 4, 110, 139; Gillette, *Jersey Blue*, 304, 315, 323.

21. *Christian Advocate*, August 18, 1892; *New York Genealogical and Biographical Record*, October 1898.

22. Cooley, "A Study of Slavery in New Jersey," 28, 58.

23. *The Independent*, November 1, 1915.

24. Gellman and Quigley, eds., *Jim Crow New York*, 218–35; "An Act relative to slaves and servants," March 31, 1817, *Laws of New York*, chap. 137.

25. Kolchin, "Variations of Slavery in the Atlantic World," 551–54.

BIBLIOGRAPHY

Primary Sources

MANUSCRIPT COLLECTIONS

British Public Records Office, London
  Colonial Office Correspondence
  Court Martial Records, War Office
  Loyalist Claims Commission Records, Audit Office
  Secretary at War In-Letters, War Office
Burlington County, New Jersey Historical Society, Burlington (BCHS)
  New Jersey Abolition Society and Burlington County Abolition Society Papers
Campbell Library, Rowan University, Glassboro, New Jersey
  Gloucester County Society for Promoting the Abolition of Slavery Papers
Connecticut Historical Society, Hartford
  MB Brainard Papers
David Library of the American Revolution, Washington's Crossing, Pennsylvania
  Earl of Dartmouth Papers
  Guy Carleton Papers
  Nathanael Greene Papers
  Sol Feinstone Collection
  Unnumbered Slavery Collection
Haverford College Quaker Collection, Haverford, Pennsylvania (HCQC)
  Allinson Family Papers
  Burlington County Society for the Abolition of Slavery Papers
  Emlen Institution for the Benefit of Children of African and Indian Descent
  Minutes of the Proceedings of the New Jersey Abolition Society and Misc. Papers
  Miscellaneous Collection
  Thomas Cope Family Papers
Historical Society of Pennsylvania, Philadelphia (HSP)
  Agricultural and Mechanic Association of Pennsylvania and New Jersey Papers, American
  Negro Historical Society Collection
  Anthony Wayne Papers
  Chew Family Papers
  Cox-Parrish-Wharton Papers
  Elias Boudinot Papers
  Foster-Clement Collection

Grellet Papers
Jonathan Roberts Papers
Joseph Watson Papers
Papers of the Pennsylvania Abolition Society
Pennsylvania Historical Society Miscellaneous Collection
Rawle Family Papers
Richard Waln Papers
Salmon Chase Papers
Vaux Family Papers
Vigilant Committee of Philadelphia Records
Hunterdon County, New Jersey Historical Society, Flemington (HCHS)
Hunterdon County Slave Births, Manumissions, and Miscellaneous Records
Library Company of Philadelphia, Philadelphia (LCP)
Breck Papers
Dillwyn Family Papers
Library of Congress/National Archives and Records Administration, Washington, D.C.
Federal Revolutionary War Pension Applications, Series M805
Papers of the Continental Congress, Record Group 360
Monmouth County New Jersey Archives, Manalapan
Monmouth County Black Birth Book
Monmouth County Manumission Book
Shrewsbury Overseer of the Poor Book
Upper Freehold Town Books
New Jersey Historical Society, Newark (NJHS)
Anderson Family Papers
Andrew Mellick Papers
Baldwin-Brown-Coe Family Papers
Baptist Church of Scotch Plains New Jersey Papers
Chester Overseers of the Poor Records
Colored Sabbath School Reports, 1819–1822
East Windsor Township Overseer of the Poor Records
Edwin Ely Collection
Essex County Anti-Slavery Society Papers
Estate of Aaron Mellick Papers
First Continental Artillery Regiment Papers
John Hunt Papers
John Nelson Abeel Papers
Jonathan Dayton Papers
Joseph Bloomfield Papers
Joseph Bradley Papers
Joseph Clark, Revolutionary War Officers Papers
Joseph Hornblower Papers
Kinney Family Papers
Louis Bamberger Collection
Mahlon Dickerson and Philemon Dickerson Papers

Munn Family Papers
New Brunswick Common Council Minutes
New Jersey Anti-Slavery Society Papers
New Jersey State Troops, Military Record Book
Newark Female Charitable Society Papers
Newark Town Records
Orderly Book, Alexander Scammell, Continental Army Adjutant General
Presbyteries of Morris County and Newark Papers
Revolutionary Era Papers
Sayers Coe Daybook and Account Book
Scott Family Papers
Stone House Plains Dutch Reformed Church Register, 1747–1901
Trinity Cathedral Papers
Vital Records of Hanover Presbyterian Church
New Jersey State Archives, Trenton (NJSA)
Bergen County Black Birth Book
Bergen County Manumission Book
Bergen County Wills and Probate Records
Bureau of Archives and History Manuscript Collection (BAH Collection)
Burlington Court of Common Pleas, Unprocessed Loose Papers, Fugitive Slave Law Cases
Burlington County Deed Books A–H
Cape May County Surrogate Records
Charles Perrin Smith, Legislative Journal and Personal Reminiscences
Department of Defense, Adjutant General's Office, Records of Commissioners of Forfeited
Estates, 1777–1795
Department of Education, Bureau of Archives and History Papers
Department of State, Secretary of State AM Papers
Department of State Records, Secretary of State's Letters, Deeds, and Misc.
Essex County Black Birth Book
Essex County Certificates of Deeds and Manumissions
Essex County Manumission Books A-C
Essex County Wills
Gloucester County Clerk's Office Slave Records
Hunterdon County Birth Certificates of Children of Slaves
Inventories of Damages by the British and Americans in New Jersey, 1776–1782
Middlesex Court of Common Pleas Papers
Morrell Family Papers
Morris County Wills
New Jersey Council of Safety Minutes
New Jersey Department of Treasury Day Books, Daybooks of Peter Gordon, Treasurer
New Jersey General Assembly Minutes, Votes, and Proceedings, 1703–1996
New Jersey General Assembly Tax Ratables
New Jersey Supreme Court Case Files
New Jersey Revolutionary War Numbered Manuscripts
Revolutionary War Index Files

Salem County Manumission Book
Somerset County Black Birth Book
Somerset County Manumission Book
State Library MSS Collection
Sussex County Black Birth Book
Sussex County Manumission Book
New-York Historical Society, New York
New York Manumission Society Minutes
Princeton University Library Special Collections, Princeton, New Jersey (PUL)
Andrew De Coppet Collection
Samuel Southard Papers
William H. Tower Collection
Rutgers University Archives and Special Collections, New Brunswick, New Jersey (RUASC)
African Association of New Brunswick (N.J.), Minute Book, 1817–1824
Bergen Reformed Church Records
Bergun Brokaw Account Book
Bound Brook Presbyterian Church Records
Clark Family Papers
Colt Family Papers
Diary of John Mason Brown
Ebenezer Elmer Papers
Edwin Corwin McKeag Papers
Gerald Rutgers Papers
Hopewell Township, Cumberland County, Tax List (1804)
Middlesex County Black Birth Book
Middlesex County Manumission Book
New Brunswick Colonization Society Papers
New Jersey Letters Collection
Pennsylvania and New Jersey Slave Trade, The Case of Severn Martin
Political Broadside Collection
Piscataway Township Records, Certificates of Abandonment for Negro Children born of
    slave parents (1805–07)
Samuel Allinson Papers
Samuel Blanchard How Papers
Van Liew Family Papers
Wells Family Papers
Woodbridge Township Records
South Carolina Historical Society, Charleston
Manuscript Collection: Letters of an American Traveler, containing a brief sketch of the
    most remarkable places in various parts of the United States and the Canadas, with
    some accounts of the character and manners of the People, written during an excursion
    in the year 1810
Southern Historical Collection, University of North Carolina, Chapel Hill (SHC)
Avery Papers
Swarthmore Friends Historical Library, Swarthmore, Pennsylvania (SFHL)

Association of Friends for the Free Instruction of Adult Colored Persons Papers
Burlington Society of Friends Quarterly Meeting Minutes
John Hunt Journal
Philadelphia Meeting for Sufferings of the Society of Friends Minutes
Philadelphia Society of Friends Yearly Meeting Minutes
Salem and Gloucester Society of Friends Quarterly Meeting Minutes
Salem Society of Friends Monthly Meeting Minutes
Salem Society of Friends Quarterly Meeting Minutes
University of Georgia Hargrett Rare Book and Manuscript Library, Athens
  Office of the President, University of Georgia Presidents File, 1801–1819
William Clements Library, University of Michigan, Ann Arbor (CLUM)
  African American History Collection
  Benjamin Bussey Papers
  Harry Horton Papers
  Henry Clinton Papers
  Jonathan Dayton Papers
  Minto-Skelton Papers
  Samson Adams Papers
  Thomas Gage Papers
  United Sons of Salem Benevolent Society Minute Book
  Weld-Grimke Papers
  William Allinson Journal
  William Howe Orderly Book

PUBLISHED PRIMARY DOCUMENTS

An Address from the Pennsylvania Abolition Society to the Free Black People of the City of Philadelphia and its Vicinity. Philadelphia, 1800.
An Address to the People of New Jersey by the abolitionists of the state favorable to political action against American slavery in Convention at Paterson, January 12, 1841. New York, 1841.
An Address to the Public on the Subject of the African School Lately Established under the Care of the Synod of New York and New Jersey by the Directors of the Institution. New York, 1816.
Address of the Board of Managers of the American Colonization Society to the Auxiliary Societies and the People of the United States. Washington, D.C., 1820.
Address to the Legislature of New Jersey in Behalf of the Colored Population of the State by Citizens of Paterson. Paterson, 1841.
Allinson, William. *Memoir of Quamino Baccau: A Pious Methodist.* Philadelphia: Henry Longstreth, 1851.
American Colonization Society. *Memorial of the American Society for Colonizing the Free People of Color of the United States, January 28, 1828.* Washington, 1828.
American Convention for the Promoting the Abolition of Slavery and Improving the condition of the African Race. *Minutes of the Proceedings.* Philadelphia, 1794.
Andrews, Bessie Ayars. *Reminiscences of Greenwich.* Vinland, N.J., 1910.
Appeal of the Religious Society of Friends in Pennsylvania, New Jersey, and Delaware, etc to their Fellow-Citizens of the United States on Behalf of the Coloured Races. Philadelphia, 1858.
Aptheker, Herbert, ed. *A Documentary History of the Negro People in the United States.* New York: Citadel Press, 1951.

Blassingame, John, ed. *Slave Testimony: Two Centuries of Letters, Speeches, Interviews, and Autobi-
ographies*. Baton Rouge: Louisiana State University Press, 1977.

Brown, David Paul. *An Oration Delivered Before the Anti-Slavery Society of New York on the
Fourth Day of July, 1834*. Philadelphia, 1834.

Budka, Metchie, ed. Julian Niemcewicz, *Under their Vine and Fig Tree: Travels through America
in 1797–1799, 1805 with some further account of life in New Jersey*. Elizabeth, N.J.: Grassman,
1965.

Burnett, Edmund, ed. *Letters of Members of the Continental Congress*. Washington, D.C.: Carnegie
Institution, 1931.

Bush, Bernard. *Laws of the Royal Colony of New Jersey*. 5 vols. Trenton: New Jersey Archives, and
Records Management, 1977–1986.

*Camden Democratic Association, March 6, 1865: At a Meeting of the Association, the following
preamble and resolutions were unanimously adopted*. Camden, N.J., 1865.

Carter, Clarence Edwin. *Territorial Papers, VII, The Territory Northwest of the River Ohio, 1787–
1803*. Washington, D.C.: Government Printing Office, 1934.

Chandler, Henry, ed. *Peter Chandler: A Biographical Sketch and His Diary of a Business Trip in
New York, 1823–1824*. For Private Circulation.

City Directory of Newark for 1835–6. Newark, N.J.: Newark Daily Advertiser, 1835.

Coldham, Peter Wilson. *American Loyalist Claims*, Vol. 1. National Genealogical Society, Washington D.C., 1980.

———. *American Migrations, 1765–99*. Baltimore: Genealogical Publishing Corporation, 2000.

*Colonization Scheme Considered in its Rejection by the Colored People in its tendency to uphold
caste in its unfitness for Christianizing and Civilizing the Aborigines of Africa and for putting a
stop to the African Slave Trade: In a Letter to Theodore Frelinghuysen and Benjamin Butler
from Samuel Cornish and Theodore Wright, Pastors of the Colored Presbyterian Churches in
the Cities of Newark and New York*. Newark: Printed by Aaron Guest, 1840.

*Confession of Rosan Keen, A Black Girl of Sixteen Years of Age, who was tried and convicted for
Poisoning Enos Seeley, Esq of Cumberland County, N.J., at the September Term, 1843 and Hung
at Bridgeton on the 26th of April, 1844*. Philadelphia, 1844.

Cooper, David. *A Serious Address to the Rulers of America on the Inconsistency of their Conduct
Respecting Slavery*. Trenton, N.J., 1773.

Crackel, Theodore, ed. *The Papers of George Washington Digital Edition*. Charlottesville: University of Virginia Press, 2007.

Davis, K. G., ed. *Documents of the American Revolution, Colonial Office Series, 1770–1783*. Dublin:
Irish University Press, 1978, volumes 1–21.

Debates in the Eighty-Ninth General Assembly of the State of New Jersey on the Bill to Ratify an
Amendment to the Constitution of the United States. Trenton: State Gazette Office, 1865.

*The Devil or the New Jersey Dance: A Horrid Relation of facts which took place a few weeks ago in
New Jersey, published at the request of many people*. Boston, 1797.

DeVoe, Thomas. *The Market Book*. New York: Printed for the Author, 1860.

Dillwyn, William. *Brief considerations on slavery and the expediency of its abolition, with some hints
on the means whereby it may be gradually effected*. Burlington: Isaac Collins, 1773.

Documents Relating to the Revolutionary History of the State of New Jersey. 2nd ser., vols. 1–5.
Trenton: New Jersey State Archives, 1914.

Drew, Benjamin. *A North Side View of Slavery: The Refugee or the Narratives of Fugitive Slaves in
Canada*. New York: Negro University Press, 1868.

Duryee, William Rankin. *The Duty of Pennsylvania Concerning Slavery*. Philadelphia, 1840.

Dwight, Theodore. *An Oration Spoken Before the Connecticut Society for the Promotion of Freedom and the Relief of Persons Unlawfully Holden in Bondage*. Hartford, 1794.

Eighth Annual Report of the American Society for Colonizing the Free People of Colour of the United States with an Appendix. Washington, 1825.

Elliott, G. W. *Map of the United States showing by colors the area of freedom and slavery and the territories whose destiny is yet to be decided., exhibiting also the Missouri compromise line, and the routes of Colonel Fremont in his famous explorations*. 1856.

An Epistle of Caution and Advice concerning the Buying and Keeping of Slaves. Burlington, N.J., 1754.

Essay on the Late Institution of the American Society for Colonizing the Free People of Color of the United States. Washington, D.C., 1820.

Extracts from an Article in the North American Review for January 1824 on the Subject of the American Colonization Society, Printed for the New Jersey Colonization Society, 1824. Princeton, N.J., 1824.

Ezell, John, ed. *The New Democracy in America: Travels of Francisco de Miranda in the United States, 1783–84*. Norman: University of Oklahoma Press, 1963.

Felcone, Joseph, ed. *Abstracts of New Jersey Manuscripts in the Sol Feinstone Collection of the American Revolution*. Washington Crossing, Pa.: David Library of the American Revolution, 1976.

Fifth Annual Report of the American Society for Colonizing the Free People of Color of the United States. Washington, D.C., 1822.

Finley, Robert. *Thoughts on the Colonization of Free Blacks*. Washington, 1816.

First Annual Message of Joel Parker, Governor of New Jersey to the Senate and General Assembly, Read January 13, 1864 and Ordered to be Printed. Trenton, 1864.

First Annual Report of the New York Committee of Vigilance for the Year 1837, Together with Important Facts Relative to their Proceedings. New York, 1837.

"Flesh for Sale." Pamphlet series 1, *Addresses Before the Eastern Division of the New Jersey Board of Proprietors*. Perth Amboy, N.J., 1942.

Foner, Philip, and George Walker, ed. *Proceedings of the Black State Conventions, 1840–1865*, vol. 2. Philadelphia: Temple University Press, 1980.

Fourteenth Annual Report of the American Society for Colonizing the Free People of Color of the United States. Washington, 1831.

Garrison, William Lloyd. *Thoughts on African Colonization or An Impartial Exhibition of the Doctrines, Principles, and Purposes of the American Colonization Society Together with the Resolutions, Addresses, and Remonstrances of the Free People of Color*. Boston, 1832.

Gellman, David, and David Quigley, eds. *Jim Crow New York: A Documentary History of Race and Citizenship, 1777–1877*. New York: New York University Press, 2003.

Gephart, Ronald, and Paul Smith, eds. *Letters of Delegates to Congress, 1774–1789*. Washington, D.C.: Library of Congress, multiple years.

Gerlach, Larry, ed. *New Jersey in the American Revolution, 1763–1783: A Documentary History*. Trenton: New Jersey Historical Commission, 1975.

Governor's Message Concerning the resolution of Massachusetts, Connecticut, and Maine in regard to Missouri Compromise and slavery . . . January 8, 1856. Trenton, 1856.

Green, Jacob. *A Sermon Delivered at Hanover, April 22, 1778, Being the Day of Public Fasting and Prayer throughout the United States of America* (Chatham, 1779). In David Mitros, ed., *Jacob

Green and the Slavery Debate in Revolutionary Morris County, New Jersey, 35–44. Morris County Heritage Commission, 1993.

Griffin, Edward. *A Plea for Africa: A Sermon preached October 26, 1817 in the First Presbyterian Church in the City of New York before the Synod of New York and New Jersey at the Request of the Board of Directors of the African School Established by the Synod.* New York: Gould, 1817.

Griffith, William. *Address of the President of the New Jersey Society for Promoting the Abolition of Slavery to the General Meeting at Trenton on Wednesday the 26th of September, 1804.* Trenton: Sherman and Mershon, 1804.

———. *Eumenes: being a collection of papers written for the purpose of exhibiting some of the more prominent errors and omissions of the constitution of New Jersey as established on the second day of July, one thousand seven hundred and sixty six and to prove the necessity of calling a convention for revision and amendment.* Trenton, 1799.

Gurley, R. R. *Address at the Annual Meeting of the Pennsylvania Colonization Society, November 11, 1839.* Philadelphia, 1839.

Hamilton, William. *A Word for the African: A Sermon for the benefit of the American Colonization Society, Delivered in the Second Presbyterian Church, Newark, July 24, 1825.* Newark, 1825.

Hay, Philip. *Our Duty to our Colored Population: A Sermon for the Benefit of the American Colonization Society, Delivered in the Second Presbyterian Church, Newark, July 23, 1826.* Newark: W. Tuttle, 1826.

Hillard, Issac. *Memory of Harry, Cuff, and Cato, Black men now in slavery in Connecticut.* 1797.

Historical Notes on Slavery and Colonization with Particular Reference to the Efforts Which have Been Made in Favor of African Colonization in New Jersey. Elizabethtown, 1842.

History and Proceedings Attending the Presentation of a Medal to Thomas Peterson-Mundy in the City of Perth Amboy, New Jersey in Commemoration of his having been the first colored citizen in the United States to cast a vote under the fifteenth amendment. Perth Amboy, 1884.

Hodges, Graham, ed. *The Black Loyalist Directory: African Americans in Exile after the American Revolution.* New York: Garland, 1996.

Hodges, Graham, and Alan Edward Brown, eds. *"Pretends to be Free": Runaway Slave Advertisements from Colonial and Revolutionary New York and New Jersey.* New York: Garland, 1994.

Holmes, Isaac. *An Account of the United States of America, Derived from Actual Observations, During a Residence of Four Years in that Republic.* London: Caxton Press, 1832.

How, Samuel. *Slaveholding Not Sinful: Slavery, the Punishment of Man's Sin, Its Remedy, the Gospel of Christ. An Argument Before the General Synod of the Reformed Protestant Church, October 1855.* New Brunswick, 1856.

Humanitas, *Reflections on Slavery; with Recent Evidence of its Inhumanity Occasioned by the Melancholy Death of Romain, a French Negro.* Philadelphia, 1803.

Hurd, John Codman. *The Law of Freedom and Bondage in the United States*, vol. 2. Boston: Little, Brown, 1862.

Idzerda, Stanley, ed. *Lafayette in the Age of the American Revolution.* Ithaca, N.Y.: Cornell University Press, 1977, volumes 1–5.

Inaugural Address of Joel Parker Delivered at Trenton Upon Taking the Oath of Office as Governor of the State of New Jersey, January 20, 1863. Trenton, 1863.

Johnstone, Abraham. *The Address of Abraham Johnstone, a Black Man, who was hanged at Woodbury in the County of Gloucester and State of New Jersey on Saturday, the 8th day of July last, to the People of Color.* Philadelphia, 1797.

Journal of the Proceedings of the Second Senate of the State of New Jersey, 1846. New Brunswick, 1846.

Journal of the Senate of the United States of America being held at the City of Washington, December 4, 1837 and in the fifty-second year of the Independence of the United States. Washington, 1837.

Kansas-The Lecompton Constitution: Speech of Hon. Jacob Van Wortendyke of New Jersey in the House of Representatives, March 23, 1858. Washington, D.C., 1858.

Kornblith, Gary. *Slavery and Sectional Strife in the Early American Republic, 1776–1821.* Laham, Md.: Rowman and Littlefield, 2010.

Kline, Mary-Jo, and Joanne Wood Ryan, eds. *Political Correspondence and Public Papers of Aaron Burr.* Princeton, N.J.: Princeton University Press, 1983.

Laws of the United States, the State of New York, and New Jersey Relative to Slaves. New York, 1811.

Leaming, Aaron and Jacob Spicer. *The Grants, Concessions, and Original Constitutions of the Province of New Jersey, The Acts Passed During the Proprietary Governments.* Philadelphia, 1758.

Lee, Jarena. *Religious Experience and Journal of Mrs. Jarena Lee, Giving Account of Her Call to Preach the Gospel.* Philadelphia, 1849.

Lewis, Enoch, ed. *Narrative of Samuel Scomp, African Observer, A Monthly Journal containing Essays and Documents Illustrative of the General Character and Moral and Political Effects of Negro Slavery.* Philadelphia, 1827.

Larison, C. W. *Silvia Dubois, a Biography of the Slave Who Whipt Her Mistres and Gand Her Fredom.* Ed. Jared Lobdell. New York: Oxford University Press, 1988.

Madison, James. *Debates of the Adoption of the Federal Constitution in the Convention Held at Philadelphia in 1787; with a Diary of the Debates of the Congress of the Confederation.* Philadelphia: Lippincott, 1881.

McKinney, William, Charles Philhower, and Harry Kniffin, *Commemorative History of the Presbyterian Church in Westfield, New Jersey, 1728–1928.* Westfield, N.J.: Westfield Presbyterian Church, 1929.

McMahon, Lucia, and Deborah Schriver, eds. *To Read My Heart: The Journal of Rachel Van Dyke, 1810–1811.* Philadelphia: University of Pennsylvania Press, 2000.

Mars, James. *Life of James Mars, A Slave Born and Sold in Connecticut. Written by Himself.* Hartford, Conn.: Press of Case, Lockwood, 1864.

Memorial of Mount Holly Monthly Meeting of Friends concerning William Boen, a Colored Man, read in the Yearly Meeting of Friends, Held in Philadelphia, 1829. Philadelphia, 1831.

Miller, Samuel. *Discourse Delivered April 12, 1797 at the Request of and Before the New York Society for Promoting the Manumission of Slaves and Protecting such of them as have been or may be liberated.* New York, 1797.

———. *A Sermon preached at Newark, October 22, 1823 before the Synod of New Jersey for the Benefit of the African School, under the Care of the Synod.* Trenton, 1823.

Minutes and Proceedings of the First Annual Convention of the People of Colour Held by adjournments in the City of Philadelphia from the sixth to the eleventh of June, 1831. Philadelphia, 1831.

Minutes of an Adjourned Session of the American Convention for Promoting the Abolition of Slavery and Improving the Condition of the African Race convened at Baltimore, on the twenty-fifth of October, 1826. Baltimore, 1826.

Minutes of the Proceedings of the Eleventh American Convention for Promoting the Abolition of Slavery. Philadelphia, 1806.

Minutes of the Proceedings of the Seventh Convention of Delegates From the Abolition Societies Established in Different Parts of the United States Assembled at Philadelphia. Philadelphia, 1801.

Minutes of the Proceedings of the Thirteenth American Convention for Promoting the Abolition of Slavery and Improving the Condition of the African Race Assembled at Philadelphia. Hamilton-Ville, 1812.

Minutes of the Proceedings of the Twelfth American Convention for Promoting the Abolition of Slavery and Improving the Condition of the African Race. Philadelphia, 1809.

Minutes of the Seventeenth Session of the American Convention for Promoting the Abolition of Slavery and Improving the Condition of the African Race Convened at Philadelphia, on the third day of October 1821. Philadelphia, 1821.

Mitros, David, ed. *Jacob Green and the Slavery Debate in Revolutionary Morris County, New Jersey.* Morristown, N.J.: Morris County Heritage Commission, 1993.

———. *Slave Records of Morris County, New Jersey: 1756–1841.* Morristown, N.J.: Morris County Heritage Commission, 2002.

Moss, George, ed. *Black Birth Book of Monmouth County, New Jersey.* Freehold, N.J.: Office of the County Clerk, 1989.

———. *Manumission Book of Monmouth County, New Jersey.* Freehold, N.J.: Office of the Monmouth County Clerk, 1992.

Newark Colonization Society, *A Sketch of the Colonization Enterprise and of the Soil, Climate, and Production of Liberia.* Newark, 1838.

Newark Female Charitable Society, *The Record of the Newark Female Charitable Society for a Hundred Years, 1803–1903.* Newark: Newark Female Charitable Society, 1903.

New Jersey Society for Promoting the Abolition of Slavery. *The Constitution of the New Jersey Society for Promoting the Abolition of Slavery.* Burlington, 1792.

———. Cases Adjudged in the Supreme Court of New Jersey Relative to the Manumission of Negroes. Burlington, 1794.

New York City Hall Reporter 4, 4, April 1819.

Old Times in Old Monmouth: Historical Reminiscences of Old Monmouth County, New Jersey. Freehold, N.J.: Monmouth Democrat, 1887.

Oration Delivered at Princeton, New Jersey November 16, 1824 Before the New Jersey Colonization Society by the Honorable Theodore Frelinghuysen. Princeton, 1824.

Paine, Thomas. *Common Sense: Address to the Inhabitants of America on the Following Interesting Subjects . . .* Philadelphia, 1776.

Parrish, Isaac. *Brief Memoirs of Thomas Shipley and Edwin Atlee Read Before the Pennsylvania Society for the Abolition of Slavery, October 1837.* Philadelphia, 1838.

Parrish, John. Unpublished pamphlet, "An Affection Address to the Inhabitants of the United States of America more especially the Rulers and such as hold slaves." Philadelphia, 1805.

———. *Remarks of the Slavery of the Black People Addressed to the Citizens of the United States Particularly to those who are in legislative or executive stations in General or State Governments and also to such individuals as hold them in bondage.* Philadelphia, 1806.

Pernot, M. M., ed. *After Freedom.* Burlington, N.J.: Burlington County Historical Society, 1987.

Philadelphia Yearly Meeting of the Religious Society of Friends. *To Our Fellow Citizens of the United States of North America and others Whom it May Concern.* Philadelphia, 1799.

Pickard, Kate E. R. *The Kidnapped and the Ransomed. Being the Personal Recollections of Peter Still and his Wife "Vina" after Forty Years of Slavery.* New York, 1856.

Platt, Hermann. *Charles Perrin Smith: New Jersey Political Reminiscences, 1828–1882.* New Brunswick, N.J.: Rutgers University Press, 1965.

The Power of Amending the Constitution: Speech of Hon. Andrew J. Rogers of New Jersey, Delivered in the House of Representatives of the United States, January 9, 1865. Washington, 1865.

Present State and Condition of the Free People of Color of the City of Philadelphia and Adjoining Districts as Exhibited by the Report of a Committee of the Pennsylvania Society for Promoting the Abolition of Slavery. Philadelphia, 1838.

Price, Clement. *Freedom Not Far Distant: A Documentary History of Afro-Americans in New Jersey.* Newark: New Jersey Historical Society, 1980.

Prince, Carl, Dennis Ryan, et al., eds. *The Papers of William Livingston.* Vols. 1–5. Trenton: New Jersey Historical Commission, 1979.

Proceedings of a Meeting Held at Princeton New Jersey July 14, 1824 to form a society in the State of New Jersey to Cooperate with the American Colonization Society. Princeton, 1824.

Proceedings of the New Jersey State Constitutional Convention of 1844. Works Progress Administration, 1942.

Proceedings of the Second Annual Meeting of the New Jersey Colonization Society Held at Princeton, July 10, 1826. Princeton, 1826.

Proceedings of the Third Annual Meeting of the New Jersey Colonization Society, Held at Princeton, August 15, 1827. Princeton, 1827.

Report of the Board of Managers of the Pennsylvania Colonization Society with an Appendix. Philadelphia, 1830.

Report of the Committee Appointed in the Senate of Pennsylvania to Investigate the Cause of an Increased Number of Slaves Being Returned for that Commonwealth by the Census of 1830, over that of 1820. Harrisburg, 1833.

Report of the Committee of the Anti-LeCompton Democratic Convention, Held at Somerville, September 30, 1858 Appointed to Draft An Address to the Voters of the Third Congressional District of the State of New Jersey. New Brunswick, 1858.

Report of the Assembly Committee on Slavery, Appendix to Senate Journal. Trenton, 1858.

Report of the Revisers of the Statute Laws of New Jersey, Read January 19, 1846 and ordered to be printed for the Senate. Trenton, 1846.

Rowe, Kenneth, and Michael McKay, eds. *The Journals of the Rev. Thomas Morrell: Dissent and Reform in the United Methodist Tradition.* Historical Society, Northern New Jersey Conference, The United Methodist Church, 1984.

Rutland, Robert ed. *The Papers of George Mason, 1725–1792.* Chapel Hill: University of North Carolina Press, 1970.

Sedgwick, Theodore. *A Memoir of the Life of William Livingston with Extracts from his Correspondence and Notices of Various Members of His Family.* New York: J&J Harper, 1833.

Seventh Annual Report of the American Society for Colonizing the Free People of Color of the United States with an Appendix. Washington, 1824.

Sharp, Granville. *Extract of a Letter from the Author to a Gentleman at Philadelphia,* July 18, 1775, contained in *The Just Limitation of Slavery in the Laws of God Compared with the Unbounded Claims of the African Traders and British American Slaveholders by Granville Sharp with a copious Appendix.* London, 1776.

————. *The Just Limitation of Slavery in the Laws of God*. London, 1776.

Short Statement of Facts Connected with the Conduct of Mr. Southard on what is usually called the Missouri Question. Washington, 1821.

Showman, Richard, ed. *The Papers of General Nathaniel Greene*. Chapel Hill: University of North Carolina Press, 1976.

Slaveholding Not Sinful: An Answer by Henry K How to John Van Dyke, Esq's Reply to the Argument of Rev. Dr. How. New Brunswick, 1856.

Slavery and the Domestic Slave Trade in the United States by the Committee Appointed by the Late Yearly Meeting of Friends Held in Philadelphia, in 1839. Philadelphia, 1841.

Speech of Hon. John C. Ten Eyck of New Jersey Delivered in the United States Senate, April 2, 1860. Washington, 1860.

Speech of Mr. Dayton of New Jersey on the War with Mexico and in Defense of his vote in favor of the treaty, delivered in the Senate of the United States, April 11, 1848. Washington, 1848.

Speech of Mr. John Van Dyke of New Jersey, Delivered in the House of Representatives of the United States, March 4, 1850 on the Subject of Slavery and in Vindication of the North from Charges Brought Against it by the South. Washington, 1850.

Speech of Mr. Miller of New Jersey on the Propositions to Compromise the Slavery Question and the Admission of California into the Union, Delivered into the Senate of the United States, February 21, 1850. Washington, 1850.

Stampp, Kenneth, ed. *Records of Antebellum Southern Plantations from the Revolution Through the Civil War*. Frederick, Md.: University Publications of America, 1985.

State of the Union, Speech of Hon. Garnett Adrain of New Jersey in the House of Representatives, January 15, 1861. Washington, 1861.

Stellhorn, Paul, and Michael Birkner, *The Governors of New Jersey, 1664–1974*. Trenton: New Jersey Historical Commission, 1982.

Stewart, Alvan. *A Legal Argument Before the Supreme Court of the State of New Jersey*. New York: Finch and Weed, 1845.

Stone, William, ed. *Letters of Brunswick and Hessian Officers During the American Revolution*. New York: Da Capo, 1970.

Syrett, Harold, ed. *The Papers of Alexander Hamilton*. New York: Columbia University Press, 1961, volumes 1–26.

Taylor, Robert et al., eds. *Papers of John Adams*. Cambridge, Mass.: Harvard University Press, 1979, volumes 1–6.

Tenth Annual Report of the American Society for Colonizing the Free People of Color of the United States. Washington, 1827.

The Territorial Question, Speech of Honorable William Dayton of New Jersey in the Senate of the United States, March 22, 1850. Washington, 1850.

Thirteenth Annual Report of the American Society for Colonizing the Free People of Colour of the United States with an Appendix, Second Edition. Washington, 1830.

The Trial of Amos Broad and His Wife on Three Several indictments for assaulting and beating Betty, A slave, and her little female child, Sarah, aged three years. New York, 1809.

To the Abolition and Manumission Societies in the United States, American Convention for Promoting the Abolition of Slavery. Philadelphia, 1817.

To the Honorable The Senate and House of Representatives of the Commonwealth of Pennsylvania in General Assembly met: The Memorial of the Subscribers, free people of color in the County of Philadelphia. Harrisburg, 1832.

To the Inhabitants of the Borough of York and Its Vicinity to the Distance of 10 Miles. York, Pa., 1803.

Upham, Mrs. T. C. *Narrative of Phebe Ann Jacobs.* American Tract Society, no listed publication date.

Van Dyke, John. *Slaveholding Not Sinful: A Reply to the Argument of Rev. Dr. How.* New Brunswick, 1856.

Wansey, Henry. *Journal of an Excursion to the United States of North America in the Summer of 1794.* New York: Johnson Reprint Collection, 1969.

Ward, Samuel Ringgold. *Autobiography of a Fugitive Negro: His Anti-slavery Labours in the United States, Canada, and England.* London, 1855.

Wharton, Samuel. *What has Pennsylvania to do with slavery?* Philadelphia, 1840.

Wheeler, Jacob. *Reports of Criminal Law Cases with Notes and References Containing also a View of the Criminal Laws of the United States.* Albany, N.Y.: Banks and Gould, 1851.

Wills, Thomas. *Freedom's Triumph: An Oration Delivered Before the Republican Citizens of Jersey on the Fourth of March 1809: Being the Inauguration of James Madison as President of the United States.* New York, 1809.

Works Projects Administration. *Gloucester County Series Slave Documents.* Newark, N.J.: Historical Records Survey, 1940.

NEWSPAPERS AND PERIODICALS

African Methodist Episcopal Church Magazine
African Repository and Colonial Journal
Alexandria Gazette
Baltimore Patriot and Mercantile Advertiser
Boston Recorder
Burlington Advertiser
Centinel of Freedom
Christian Advocate
Colored American
Columbian
Charlestown, Va. *Farmer's Repository*
City Gazette and Daily Advertiser (Charleston ,SC)
Constitution and Farmers' and Mechanics Advertiser
East Jersey Republican
Fredonian (New Brunswick, N.J.)
Freedom's Journal
The Friend: A Religious and Literary Journal
Friends' Weekly Intelligencer
Genius of Liberty (Leesburg, Va.)
Genius of Liberty (Morristown, N.J.)
Hunterdon County Democrat
Hunterdon County Gazette
The Independent
Jersey Chronicle
Jersey City Advertiser
The Liberator

Miscellany
National Recorder
Newark Advertiser
New Jersey Citizen
New Jersey Freeman
New Jersey Gazette
New Jersey Journal
New Jersey Mirror
New Jersey Telescope
New Orleans Chronicle
New York Evangelist
New York Journal
New York Genealogical and Biographical Record
New York Times
North Star
Pennsylvania Gazette
Philadelphia Album and Ladies' Literary Portfolio
Political Intelligencer
Raleigh North Carolina Star
Royal Gazette
Rural Visitor
Sentinel of Freedom
Trenton American
Trenton Federalist
Washington Whig

Secondary Sources

BOOKS

Alexander, Leslie. *African or American? Black Identity and Political Activism in New York City, 1784–1861.* Chicago: University of Chicago Press, 2008.

Atkinson, Joseph. *The History of Newark, New Jersey Being a Narrative of Its Rise and Progress.* Newark: William Guild, 1878.

Aptheker, Herbert. *American Negro Slave Revolts.* New York: Columbia University Press, 1943.

Ayers, Edward. *In the Presence of Mine Enemies: War in the Heart of America, 1859–1863.* New York: Norton, 2003.

Bacon, Jacqueline. *Freedom's Journal: The First African American Newspaper.* Lanham, Md.: Lexington Books, 2007.

Bailyn, Bernard. *Atlantic History: Concept and Contours.* Cambridge, Mass.: Harvard University Press, 2005.

Ballard, Allen. *One More Day's Journey: The Story of a Family and a People.* Lincoln, Neb.: Universe, 2004.

Bartlett, J. Gardner. *Robert Coe, Puritan: His Ancestors and Descendants, 1340–1910.* Boston: Private Publication, 1911.

Berlin, Ira. *Generations of Captivity: A History of African American Slaves.* Cambridge, Mass.: Harvard University Press, 2003.

———. *Many Thousands Gone: The First Two Centuries of Slavery in North America.* Cambridge, Mass.: Harvard University Press, 1998.

———. *Slaves Without Masters: The Free Negro in the Antebellum South.* New York: Vintage, 1974.

Bethel, Elizabeth. *The Roots of African-American Identity: Memory and History in Free Antebellum Communities.* New York: Saint Martin's, 1997.

Birkner, Michael. *Samuel Southard: Jeffersonian Whig.* Madison, N.J.: Farleigh Dickinson University Press, 1984.

Blackburn, Robin. *The Making of New World Slavery: From the Baroque to the Modern, 1492–1800.* New York: Verso, 1998.

Blackett, R. H. M. *Building an Antislavery Wall: Black Americans in the Atlantic Abolitionist Movement, 1830–1860.* Baton Rouge: Louisiana State University Press, 1983.

Boylan, Anne. *Sunday School: The Formation of an American Institution, 1790–1880.* New Haven, Conn.: Yale University Press, 1988.

Brewer, Holly. *By Birth or Consent: Children, Law, and the Anglo American Revolution in Authority.* Chapel Hill: University of North Carolina Press, 2005.

Brown, Isaac. *Biography of the Rev. Robert Finley, D.D. of Basking Ridge, New Jersey.* Philadelphia: J.W. Moore, 1857.

Buel, Richard. *Securing the Revolution: Ideology in American Politics, 1789–1815.* Ithaca, N.Y.: Cornell University Press, 1972.

Calhoun, Charles. *A Small College in Maine: Two Hundred Years of Bowdoin.* Brunswick, Maine: Bowdoin College, 1993.

Campbell, Gwyn, and Suzanne Miers, and Joseph Miller, eds. *Children in Slavery Through the Ages.* Athens: Ohio University Press, 2009.

Clemens, Paul. *The Uses of Abundance: A History of New Jersey's Economy.* Trenton: New Jersey Historical Commission, 1992.

Conforti, Joseph. *Imagining New England: Explorations of Regional Identity From the Pilgrims to the Mid-Twentieth Century.* Chapel Hill: University of North Carolina Press, 2001.

Cooper, William. *Jefferson Davis, American.* New York: Knopf, 2000.

Cottrol, Robert. *The Afro-Yankees: Providence's Black Community in the Antebellum Era.* New York: Greenwood, 1982.

Cover, Robert. *Justice Accused: Antislavery and the Judicial Process.* New Haven, Conn.: Yale University Press, 1975.

Cunningham, John. *Newark.* Newark: New Jersey Historical Society Press, 1988.

Curry, Leonard. *The Free Black in Urban America, 1800–1850.* Chicago: University of Chicago Press, 1981.

Davis, David Brion. *Inhuman Bondage: The Rise and Fall of Slavery in the New World.* New York: Oxford University Press, 2006.

———. *The Problem of Slavery in the Age of Revolution, 1770–1823.* New York: Oxford University Press, 1975.

———. *The Problem of Slavery in Western Culture.* New York: Oxford University Press, 1965.

———. *Slavery and Human Progress.* New York: Oxford University Press, 1984.

Davis, Joseph. *Sectionalism in American Politics, 1774–1787.* Madison: University of Wisconsin Press, 1977.

Davis, William. *Jefferson Davis: The Man and His Hour.* New York: HarperCollins, 1996.

Deyle, Stephen. *Carry Me Back: The Domestic Slave Trade in American Life*. New York: Oxford University Press, 2005.

Dorsey, Jennifer, *Hirelings: African American Workers and Free Labor in Early Maryland*. Ithaca, N.Y.: Cornell University Press, 2011.

Drescher, Seymour. *From Slavery to Freedom: Comparative Studies in the Rise and Fall of Atlantic Slavery*. New York: New York University Press, 1999.

Dunbar, Erica. *A Fragile Freedom: African American Women and Emancipation in the Antebellum City*. New Haven, Conn.: Yale University Press, 2008.

Ege, Ralph. *Pioneers of Old Hopewell: With Sketches of her Revolutionary Heroes*. Hopewell, N.J.: Race and Savidge, 1908.

Egerton, Douglas. *Death or Liberty: African Americans and Revolutionary America*. New York: Oxford University Press, 2009.

Einhorn, Robin. *American Taxation, American Slavery*. Chicago: University of Chicago Press, 2006.

Eltis, David. *Economic Growth and the Ending of the Transatlantic Slave Trade*. New York: Oxford University Press, 1987.

Essah, Patience. *A House Divided: Slavery and Emancipation in Delaware, 1638–1865*. Charlottesville: University of Virginia Press, 1996.

Farrow, Anne, Joel Lang, and Jenifer Frank. *Complicity: How the North Promoted, Prolonged, and Profited from Slavery*. New York: Ballantine, 2005.

Fields, Barbara. *Slavery and Freedom on the Middle Ground: Maryland during the Nineteenth Century*. New Haven, Conn.: Yale University Press, 1985.

Finkelman, Paul. *An Imperfect Union: Slavery, Federalism, and Comity*. Chapel Hill: University of North Carolina Press, 1981.

———. *The Law of Freedom and Bondage: A Casebook*. New York: Oceana Publications, 1986.

———. *Slavery and the Founders: Race and Liberty in the Age of Jefferson*. 2nd ed. New York: Sharpe, 2001.

Fischer, David Hackett. *The Revolution of American Conservatism: The Federalist Party in the Era of Jeffersonian Democracy*. New York: Harper & Row, 1965.

Fishman, George. *The African American Struggle for Freedom and Equality*. New York: Routledge, 1997.

Fleming, Thomas. *New Jersey: A History*. New York: Norton, 1984.

Fogel, Robert, Ralph Galantine, and Richard Manning, eds. *Without Consent or Contract: Evidence and Methods*. New York: Norton, 1992.

Foner, Eric. *Free Soil, Free Labor, Free Men: The Ideology of the Republican Party Before the Civil War*. New York: Oxford University Press, 1970.

———. *The Story of American Freedom*. New York: Norton, 1999.

Foner, Philip. *Blacks in the American Revolution*. Westport, Conn.: Greenwood Press, 1975.

Forbes, Robert. *The Missouri Compromise and Its Aftermath: Slavery and the Meaning of America*. Chapel Hill: University of North Carolina Press, 2007.

Frey, Sylvia. *Water from the Rock: Black Resistance in a Revolutionary Age*. Princeton: Princeton University Press, 1991.

Geismar, Joan. *The Archaeology of Social Disintegration in Skunk Hollow: A Nineteenth-Century Rural Black Community*. New York: Academic Press, 1982.

Gellman, David. *Emancipating New York: The Politics of Slavery and Freedom*. Baton Rouge: Louisiana State University Press, 2006.

George, Carol V. R. *Segregated Sabbaths: Richard Allen and the Emergence of Independent Black Churches, 1760–1840*. New York: Oxford, 1973.

Gilje, Paul. *Rioting in America*. Bloomington: Indiana University Press, 1999.

Gillette, William. *Jersey Blue: Civil War Politics in New Jersey, 1854–1865*. New Brunswick, N.J.: Rutgers University Press, 1995.

Greene, Robert. *Black Courage, 1775–1783: Documentation of Black Participation in the American Revolution*. Washington, D.C.: National DAR, 1984.

Grivno, Max. *Gleanings of Freedom: Freed and Slave Labor along the Mason-Dixon Line, 1790–1860*. Urbana: University of Illinois Press, 2011.

Harris, Leslie. *In the Shadow of Slavery: African Americans in New York City, 1626–1863*. Chicago: University of Chicago Press, 2003.

Harrold, Stanley. *Border War: Fighting over Slavery before the Civil War*. Chapel Hill: University of North Carolina Press, 2010.

Hatfield, Edwin. *History of Elizabeth, New Jersey*. New York: Carlton and Lanahan, 1868.

Hattaway, Herman, and Richard Beringer. *Jefferson Davis, Confederate President*. Lawrence: University Press of Kansas, 2002.

Hay, Clyde, and Willard DeYoe, *New Barbadoes Neck in Revolutionary War Days*. Madison, N.J.: Fairleigh Dickinson University Press, 1964.

Hearn, Daniel. *Legal Executions in New Jersey: A Comprehensive Registry, 1691–1963*. New York: McFarland, 2005.

Higginbotham, A. Leon. *In the Matter of Color: Race and the American Legal Process: The Colonial Period*. New York: Oxford University Press, 1978.

Hodges, Graham. *David Ruggles: A Radical Black Abolitionist and the Underground Railroad in New York City*. Chapel Hill: University of North Carolina Press, 2010.

———. *Root and Branch: African Americans in New York and East Jersey*. Chapel Hill: University of North Carolina Press, 1999.

———. *Slavery and Freedom in the Rural North: African Americans in Monmouth County, New Jersey 1665–1865*. Madison, N.J.: Madison House, 1997.

———. *Slavery, Freedom, and Culture Among Early American Workers*. Armonk, N.Y.: Sharpe, 1998.

Hodges, Graham, and Gary Nash. *Friends of Liberty: A Tale of Three Patriots, Two Revolutions, and the Betrayal That Divided a Nation: Thomas Jefferson, Thaddeus Kosciuszko, and Agrippa Hull*. New York: Basic, 2008.

Hoffer, Peter Charles. *The Great New York Conspiracy of 1741*. Lawrence: University Press of Kansas, 2003.

Holton, Woody. *Forced Founders: Indians, Debtors, Slaves, and the Making of the American Revolution in Virginia*. Chapel Hill: University of North Carolina Press, 1999.

Horton, James. *Free People of Color: Inside the African American Community*. Washington, D.C.: Smithsonian Institution Press, 1993.

Horton, James, and Lois Horton, *In Hope of Liberty: Culture, Community, and Protest among Northern Free Blacks, 1700–1860*. New York: Oxford University Press, 1998.

Jackson, Maurice. *Let This Voice Be Heard: Anthony Benezet, Father of Atlantic Abolitionism*. Philadelphia: University of Pennsylvania Press, 2009.

James, Winston. *The Struggles of John Brown Russwurm: The Life and Writings of A Pan-Africanist Pioneer, 1799–1851*. New York: New York University Press, 2010.

Johnson, Walter. *Soul by Soul: Life Inside the Antebellum Slave Market*. Cambridge, Mass.: Harvard University Press, 1999.

Jones, Edward Alfred. *The Loyalists of New Jersey: Their Memorials, Petitions, Claims, Etc. from English Records*. Boston: Gregg Press, 1972.

Jones, Marie Beth. *Peach Point Plantation: The First 150 Years*. Waco, Tex.: Texian Press, 1982.

Jordan, Ryan. *Slavery and the Meetinghouse: The Quakers and the Abolitionist Dilemma*. Bloomington: Indiana University Press, 2007.

Kerber, Linda. *Women of the Republic: Intellect and Ideology in Revolutionary America*. Chapel Hill: University of North Carolina Press, 1997.

Kerr-Ritchie, J. R. *Rites of August First: Emancipation Day in the Black Atlantic World*. Baton Rouge: Louisiana University Press, 2007.

Laurie, Bruce. *Beyond Garrison: Antislavery and Social Reform*. New York: Cambridge University Press, 2005.

Kantrowitz, Stephen. *More than Freedom: Fighting for Black Citizenship in a White Republic, 1829–1889*. New York: Penguin, 2012.

Keyssar, Alexander. *The Right to Vote: The Contested History of Democracy in the United States*. New York: Basic Books, 2000.

King, Wilma. *Stolen Childhood: Slave Youth in Nineteenth Century America*. Bloomington: Indiana University Press, 1998.

Klepp, Susan. *Revolutionary Conceptions: Women, Fertility, and Family Limitation in America, 1760–1820*. Chapel Hill: University of North Carolina Press, 2009.

Knapp, Charles. *New Jersey Politics During the Period of the Civil War and Reconstruction*. Geneva, N.Y.: W.F. Humphrey, 1924.

Knoblock, Glenn. *Strong and Brave Fellows: New Hampshire's Black Soldiers and Sailors of the American Revolution, 1775–1784*. Jefferson, N.C.: McFarland, 2003.

Kolchin, Peter. *American Slavery, 1619–1877*. New York: Hill and Wang, 1994.

Kulikoff, Allan. *The Agrarian Origins of American Capitalism*. Charlottesville: University of Virginia Press, 1992.

Landers, R. Gloria. *Pioneers, Pastors, and Patriots: The 250-Year History of Lamington Presbyterian Church*. Bedminster, N.J.: Lamington Presbyterian Church, 1990.

Lemon, James. *The Best Poor Man's Country: Early Southeastern Pennsylvania*. Baltimore: Johns Hopkins University Press, 1972.

Lepore, Jill. *The Name of War: King Philip's War and the Origins of American Identity*. New York: Vintage, 1998.

———. *New York Burning: Liberty, Slavery, and Conspiracy in Eighteenth Century Manhattan*. New York: Knopf, 2005.

Lightner, David. *Slavery and the Commerce Power: How the Struggle Against the Interstate Slave Trade Led to the Civil War*. New Haven, Conn.: Yale University Press, 2006.

Linebaugh, Peter, and Marcus Rediker. *The Many Headed Hydra: Sailors, Slaves, and Commoners, and the Hidden History of the Revolutionary Atlantic*. Boston: Beacon, 2000.

Litwack, Leon. *North of Slavery: The Negro in the Free States*. Chicago: University of Chicago Press, 1961.

Lott, Eric. *Love and Theft: Blackface Minstrelsy and the American Working Class*. New York: Oxford, 1995.

Lovejoy, Paul. *Transformations in Slavery: A History of Slavery in Africa*. 2nd ed. Cambridge, Mass.: Harvard University Press, 2000.

Lovejoy, Paul, and Jan Hogendorn. *Slow Death for Slavery: The Course of Abolition in Northern Nigeria, 1897–1936.* Cambridge: Cambridge University Press, 1993.

Lundin, Charles. *Cockpit of the Revolution: The War for Independence in New Jersey.* Princeton: Princeton University Press, 1940.

Lyght, Ernest. *Path of Freedom: The Black Presence in New Jersey's Burlington County.* Cherry Hill, N.J.: E&E Publishing, 1978.

Maas, David. *The Return of the Massachusetts Loyalists.* New York: Garland, 1989.

Malone, Ann Patton. *Sweet Chariot: Slave Family and House Old Structure in Nineteenth-Century Louisiana.* Chapel Hill: University of North Carolina Press, 1992.

Manegold, C. S. *Ten Hills Farm: The Forgotten History of Slavery in the North.* Princeton: Princeton University Press, 2010.

Martin, Jonathan. *Divided Mastery: Slave Hiring in the American South.* Cambridge, Mass.: Harvard University Press, 2004.

Marshall, Kenneth. *Manhood Enslaved: Bondmen in Eighteenth and Early Nineteenth Century New Jersey.* Rochester: University of Rochester Press, 2011.

Mason, Matthew. *Slavery and Politics in the Early Republic.* Chapel Hill: University of North Carolina Press, 2006.

Matrana, Marc. *Lost Plantations of the South.* Jackson: University Press of Mississippi, 2009.

McConville, Brendan. *These Daring Disturbers of the Public Peace: The Struggle for Property and Power in Early New Jersey.* Ithaca, N.Y.: Cornell University Press, 1999.

McCormick, Richard. *The History of Voting in New Jersey: A Study of the Development of Election Machinery, 1664–1911.* New Brunswick, N.J.: Rutgers University Press, 1953.

McManus, Edgar. *Black Bondage in the North.* Syracuse: Syracuse University Press, 1973.

Melish, Joanne Pope. *Disowning Slavery: Gradual Emancipation and "Race" in New England, 1780–1860.* Ithaca, N.Y.: Cornell University Press, 1998.

Middlekauff, Robert. *The Glorious Cause: The American Revolution, 1763–1789.* New York: Oxford University Press, 2005.

Middleton, Stephen. *The Black Laws: Race and the Legal Process in Early Ohio.* Athens: Ohio University Press, 2005.

Minardi, Margot. *Making Slavery History: Abolitionism and the Politics of Memory in Massachusetts.* New York: Oxford University Press, 2010.

Mitchell, Mary Niall. *Raising Freedom's Children: Black Children and Visions of the Future After Slavery.* New York: New York University Press, 2008.

Mitnick, Barbara, ed. *New Jersey in the American Revolution.* New Brunswick, N.J.: Rutgers University Press, 2005.

Morgan, Jennifer. *Laboring Women: Reproduction and Gender in New World Slavery.* Philadelphia: University of Pennsylvania Press, 2004.

Morris, Thomas. *Free Men All: The Personal Liberty Laws of the North.* Baltimore: Johns Hopkins University Press, 1974.

Muhlenberg, Henry Melchior. *The Journals of Henry Melchior Muhlenberg,* translated by Theodore G. Tappert and Johan W. Doberstein, 3 vols. Philadelphia: German Society of Pennsylvania, 1942–58.

Nash, Gary. *Forging Freedom: The Formation of Philadelphia's Black Community, 1720–1840.* Cambridge, Mass.: Harvard University Press, 1988.

———. *The Forgotten Fifth: African Americans in the Age of Revolution.* Cambridge, Mass.: Harvard University Press, 2006.

————. *Race and Revolution.* Madison, N.J.: Madison House, 1990.

————. *The Unknown Revolution: The Unruly Birth of Democracy and the Struggle to Create America.* New York: Viking, 2005.

————. *The Urban Crucible: Social Change, Political Consciousness, and the Origins of the American Revolution.* Cambridge, Mass.: Harvard University Press, 1979.Nash, Gary, and Jean Soderlund. *Freedom by Degrees: Emancipation in Pennsylvania and its Aftermath.* New York: Oxford University Press, 1991.

Nell, William. *The Colored Patriots of the American Revolution.* New York: Arno Press, 1968.

Nelson, William. *History of Bergen and Passaic Counties, New Jersey.* Philadelphia: Everts and Peck, 1882.

Norton, Mary Beth. *Liberty's Daughters: The Revolutionary Experience of American Women, 1750–1800.* Ithaca, N.Y.: Cornell University Press, 1980.

O'Donovan, Susan. *Becoming Free in the Cotton South.* Cambridge, Mass.: Harvard University Press, 2010.

Onuf, Peter. *Jefferson's Empire: The Language of American Nationhood.* Charlottesville: University of Virginia Press, 2000.

————. *Statehood and Union: A History of the Northwest Ordinance.* Bloomington: Indiana University Press, 1987.

Palmer, Gregory. *Biological Sketches of Loyalists of the American Revolution.* Westport, Conn.: Meckler, 1984.

Pasler, Rudolph, and Margaret Pasler. *The New Jersey Federalists.* Madison, N.J.: Farleigh Dickinson University Press, 1975.

Patterson, Orlando. *Slavery and Social Death: A Comparative Study.* Cambridge, Mass.: Harvard University Press, 1982.

Payne, Daniel. *History of the African Methodist Episcopal Church.* Nashville: AME Sunday School Union, 1891.

Pingeon, Francis. *Blacks in the Revolutionary Era.* Trenton: New Jersey Historical Commission, 1976.

Pomfret, John. *The Province of East New Jersey: The Rebellious Proprietary.* Princeton: Princeton University Press, 1962.

————. *The Province of West New Jersey, 1609–1702: A History of the Origins of an American Colony.* New York: Octagon Books, 1976.

Prince, Carl. *New Jersey's Jeffersonian Republicans: The Genesis of an Early Party Machine, 1789–1817.* Chapel Hill: University of North Carolina Press, 1964.

————. *William Livingston: New Jersey's First Governor.* Trenton: New Jersey Historical Commission, 1975.

Purcell, Sarah. *Sealed with Blood: War, Sacrifice, and Memory in Revolutionary America.* Philadelphia: University of Pennsylvania Press, 2011.

Pybus, Cassandra. *Epic Journeys of Freedom: Runaway Slaves of the American Revolution and Their Global Quest for Liberty.* Boston: Beacon, 2006.

Quarles, Benjamin. *Negro in the American Revolution.* Chapel Hill: University of North Carolina Press, 1961.

Rael, Patrick. *Black Identity and Protest in the Antebellum North.* Chapel Hill: University of North Carolina Press, 2002.

Reiss, Oscar. *Blacks in Colonial America.* Jefferson, N.C.: McFarland, 1997.

Richards, Leonard. *Slave Power: The Free North and Southern Domination, 1780–1860.* Baton Rouge: Louisiana State University Press, 2000.

Richardson, James, ed. *The Messages and Papers of Jefferson Davis and the Confederacy Including Diplomatic Correspondence, 1861–65.*Vol. 1. New York: Chelsea House, 1983.

Richter, Daniel. *Facing East from Indian Country: A Native History of Early America.* Cambridge, Mass.: Harvard University Press, 2001.

Riordan, Liam. *Many Identities, One Nation: The Revolution and Its Legacy in the Mid-Atlantic.* Philadelphia: University of Pennsylvania Press, 2007.

Rizzo, Dennis. *Parallel Communities: The Underground Railroad in South Jersey.* Charleston, S.C.: History Press, 2008.

Rockman, Seth. *Scraping By: Wage Labor, Slavery, and Survival in Early Baltimore.* Baltimore: Johns Hopkins University Press, 2009.

Rodgers, Daniel. *Atlantic Crossing: Social Politics in a Progressive Age.* Cambridge, Mass.: Harvard University Press, 1998.

Roediger, David. *Wages of Whiteness: Race and the Making of the American Working Class.* New York: Verso, 1991.

Roediger, David, and Martin Blatt, eds. *The Meaning of Slavery in the North.* New York: Garland, 1998.

Rothman, Adam. *Slave Country: American Expansion and the Origins of the Deep South.* Cambridge, Mass.: Harvard University Press, 2005.

Rugemer, Edward. *The Problem of Emancipation: The Caribbean Roots of the American Civil War.* Baton Rouge: Louisiana State University Press, 2008.

Salafia, Matthew. *Slavery's Borderland: Freedom and Bondage Along the Ohio River.* Philadelphia: University of Pennsylvania Press, 2013.

Salinger, Sharon. *"To Serve Well and Faithfully" Labor and Indentured Servants in Pennsylvania.* New York: Cambridge University Press, 1987.

Schama, Simon. *Rough Crossings: Britain, the Slaves, and the American Revolution.* New York: HarperCollins, 2006.

Schermerhorn, Calvin. *Money over Mastery, Family over Freedom: Slavery in the Antebellum Upper South.* Baltimore: Johns Hopkins University Press, 2011.

Schmidt, Hubert. *Slavery and Attitudes on Slavery in Hunterdon County, New Jersey.* Flemington, N.J.: Hunterdon County Historical Society, 1941.

Schwartz, Marie Jenkins. *Born in Bondage: Growing Up Enslaved in the Antebellum South.* Cambridge, Mass.: Harvard University Press, 2000.

Sharp, James Rogers. *American Politics in the Early Republic: The New Nation in Crisis.* New Haven, Conn.: Yale University Press, 1993.

Slaughter, Thomas. *The Beautiful Soul of John Woolman, Apostle of Abolition.* New York: Hill and Wang, 2008.

Smith, Billy, ed. *Down and Out in Early America.* University Park: Pennsylvania State University Press, 2004.

———. *The "Lower Sort": Philadelphia's Laboring People, 1750–1800.* Ithaca, N.Y.: Cornell University Press, 1990.

Smith, David. *On the Edge of Freedom: The Fugitive Slave Issue in South Central Pennsylvania, 1820–1870.* New York: Fordham University Press, 2013.

Smith, Page. *A New Age Now Begins: A People's History of the American Revolution,* vol. 2. New York: McGraw Hill, 1976.

Snell, James. *History of Hunterdon and Somerset Counties, New Jersey with Illustrations and Biographical Sketches of the Prominent Men and Pioneers.* Philadelphia: Everts and Peck, 1881.

Sobel, Mechal. *The World They Made Together.* Princeton, N.J.: Princeton University Press, 1987.

Stansell, Christine. *City of Women: Sex and Class in New York, 1789–1860.* Urbana: University of Illinois Press, 1987.

Steiner, Bernard. *History of Slavery in Connecticut.* Baltimore: Johns Hopkins University Press, 1893.

Steinfeld, Robert. *Coercion, Contract, and Free Labor in the Nineteenth Century.* New York: Cambridge University Press, 2001.

———. *The Invention of Free Labor: The Employment Relation in English and American Law and Culture 1350–1870.* Chapel Hill: University of North Carolina Press, 1991.

Stevens, Stephanie. *Outcast: A Story of Slavery in Readington Township, Hunterdon County New Jersey.* Whitehouse Station, N.J.: Merck, 2003.

Stewart, James Brewer. *William Lloyd Garrison and the Challenge of Emancipation.* New York: Harlan Davidson, 1992.

Soderlund, Jean. *Quakers and Slaves: A Divided Spirit.* Princeton, N.J.: Princeton University Press, 1985.

Sommerville, Diane. *Rape and Race in the Nineteenth Century South.* Chapel Hill: University of North Carolina Press, 2003.

Sundue, Sharon. *Industrious in their Stations: Young People at Work in Urban America, 1720–1810.* Charlottesville: University of Virginia Press, 2009.

Sweet, John Wood. *Bodies Politic: Negotiating Race in the American North, 1730–1830.* Philadelphia: University of Pennsylvania Press, 2003.

Switala, William. *Underground Railroad in New Jersey and New York.* Mechanicsburg, Pa.: Stackpole, 2006.

Tadman, Michael. *Speculators and Slaves: Masters, Traders, and Slaves in the Old South.* Madison: University of Wisconsin Press, 1989.

Tomek, Beverly. *Colonization and Its Discontents: Emancipation, Emigration, and Antislavery in Antebellum Pennsylvania.* New York: New York University Press, 2011.

Tomlins, Christopher. *Freedom Bound: Law, Labor, and Civic Identity in Colonizing English America, 1580–1865.* Cambridge: Cambridge University Press, 2010.

Urquhart, Frank. *A Short History of Newark.* Newark: Baker Printing, 1916.

Vincent, Stephen. *Southern Seed: Northern Soil: African-American Farm Communities in the Midwest, 1765–1900.* Bloomington: Indiana University Press, 1999.

Wacker, Peter. *Land and People: A Cultural Geography of Preindustrial New Jersey.* New Brunswick, N.J.: Rutgers University Press, 1975.

Wacker, Peter, and Paul Clemons. *Land Use in Early New Jersey.* Newark: New Jersey Historical Society, 1995.

Waldstreicher, David. *In the Midst of Perpetual Fetes: The Making of American Nationalism, 1776–1820.* Chapel Hill: University of North Carolina Press, 1997.

———. *Slavery's Constitution from Revolution to Ratification.* New York: Hill and Wang, 2009.

Walling, Richard. *Men of Color at the Battle of Monmouth, June 28, 1778: The Role of African Americans and Native Americans at Monmouth.* Hightstown, N.J.: Longstreet House, 1994.

Weber, Jennifer. *Copperheads: The Rise and Fall of Lincoln's Opponents in the North.* New York: Oxford, 2006.

Webber, Thomas. *Deep Like the Rivers: Education in the Slave Quarter Community, 1831–1865.* New York: Norton, 1978.

White, Deborah Gray. *Ar'n't I a Woman? Female Slaves in the Plantation South.* New York: Norton, 1987.

White, Shane. *Somewhat More Independent: The End of Slavery in New York City, 1770–1810.* Athens: University of Georgia Press, 1991.

Whitfield, Harvey Amani. *The Problem of Slavery in Early Vermont, 1777–1810.* Barre: Vermont Historical Society, 2014.

Whitman, T. Stephen. *The Price of Freedom: Slavery and Manumission in Baltimore and Early National Maryland.* Lexington: University of Kentucky Press, 1997.

Wiencek, Henry. *An Imperfect God: George Washington, His Slaves, and the Creation of America.* New York: Farrar, Straus, and Giroux, 2003.

Wilentz, Sean. *The Rise of American Democracy: Jefferson to Lincoln.* New York: Norton, 2005.

Williams, William. *Slavery and Freedom in Delaware, 1639–1865.* Wilmington, Del.: SR Books, 1996.

Wilson, Carol. *Freedom at Risk: The Kidnapping of Free Blacks in America, 1780–1865.* Lexington: University Press of Kentucky, 1994.

Winch, Julie. *Philadelphia's Black Elite: Activism, Accommodation, and the Struggle for Autonomy.* Philadelphia: Temple University Press, 1993.

Wolf, Eva Sheppard. *Race and Liberty in the New Nation: Emancipation in Virginia from the Revolution to Nat Turner's Rebellion.* Baton Rouge: Louisiana State University Press, 2006.

Wong, Edlie. *Neither Fugitive nor Free: Atlantic Slavery, Freedom Suits, and the Legal Culture of Travel.* New York: New York University Press, 2009.

Wood, Marcus. *The Horrible Gift of Freedom: Atlantic Slavery and the Representation of Emancipation.* Athens: University of Georgia Press, 2010.

Wright, Giles. *Afro-Americans in New Jersey: A Short History.* Trenton: New Jersey Historical Commission, 1988.

Wright, Marion Thompson. *The Education of Negroes in New Jersey.* New York: Arno Press and New York Times, 1971.

Yoshpe, Harry. *The Disposition of Loyalist Estates in the Southern District of the State of New York.* New York: AMS Press, 1967.

Young, Alfred. *The Democratic Republicans of New York.* Chapel Hill: University of North Carolina Press, 1967.

Zilversmit, Arthur. *The First Emancipation: The Abolition of Slavery in the North.* Chicago: University of Chicago Press, 1967.

ARTICLES AND BOOK CHAPTERS

Adelberg, Michael. "An Evenly Balanced County: The Scope and Severity of Civil Warfare in Revolutionary Monmouth County, New Jersey." *Journal of Military History* 73, 1 (January 2009): 9–47.

AHR Forum. "Crossing Slavery's Boundaries," *American Historical Review* 105, 2 (April 2000): 451–84.

Andrews, Dee. "Reconsidering the First Emancipation: Evidence from the Pennsylvania Abolition Society Correspondence, 1785–1810." *Pennsylvania History* 64 (Summer 1997): 230–49.

Arnesen, Eric. "Whiteness and the Historians' Imagination." *Historically Speaking* 3, 3 (February 2002): 19–22.

Baker, David. "Black Female Executions in Historical Context." *Criminal Justice Review* 33, 1 (2008): 64–88.

Branson, Susan, and Leslie Patrick. "Étrangers dans un pays étrange: Saint-Domingan Refugees of Color in Philadelphia." In David Geggus, ed., *The Impact of the Haitian Revolution in the Atlantic World*. Columbia: University of South Carolina Press, 2001.

Burin, Eric. "Rethinking Northern White Support for the African Colonization Movement: The Pennsylvania Colonization Society as an Agent of Emancipation." *Pennsylvania Magazine of History and Biography* 127, 2 (April 2003): 197–229.

Cayton, Andrew R. L. "Law and Authority in the Northwest Territory." In Michael Les Benedict and John Winkler, eds., *The History of Ohio Law*. Athens: Ohio University Press, 2004.

Cole, Shawn. "Capitalism and Freedom: Manumissions and the Slave Market in Louisiana, 1725–1820." *Journal of Economic History* 65, 4 (December 2005): 1008–1027.

Cudd, John. "The Unity of Reform: John Grimes and the New Jersey Freeman." *New Jersey History* 97, 4 (Winter 1979): 197–212.

Cunningham, Valerie. " 'That the Name of Slave May Not More Be Heard': The New Hampshire Petition for Freedom, 1779." In Peter Benes, ed., *Slavery and Antislavery in New England*. Boston: Dublin Seminar for New England Folklife, 2003.

Doerflinger, Thomas. "Rural Capitalism in Iron Country: Staffing a Forest Factory." *William and Mary Quarterly* 59, 1 (January 2002): 3–38.

Donoghue, John. "Out of the Land of Bondage: The English Revolution and the Atlantic Origins of Abolition." *American Historical Review* 115, 4 (October 2010): 943–74.

Dowd, Gregory Evans. "Declarations of Dependence: War and Inequality in Revolutionary New Jersey, 1776–1815." In Maxine Lurie, ed., *A New Jersey Anthology*. New Brunswick, N.J.: Rutgers University Press, 2002.

Duncan, Georgena. "One negro, Sarah . . . one horse named Collier, one cow and calf named Pink': Slave Records from the Arkansas River Valley." *Arkansas Historical Quarterly* 69, 4 (Winter 2010): 325–45.

Finkelman, Paul. "Evading the Ordinance: The Persistence of Bondage in Indiana and Illinois," *Journal of the Early Republic* 9, 2 (Spring 1989): 21–51.

———."Race, Slavery, and Law in Antebellum Ohio." In Michael Les Benedict and John Winkler, ed., *The History of Ohio Law*. Athens: Ohio University Press, 2004.

———. "Slavery and the Northwest Ordinance: A Study in Ambiguity." *Journal of the Early Republic* 6, 4 (Winter 1986): 343–70.

———. "State Constitutional Protections of Liberty and the Antebellum New Jersey Supreme Court: Chief Justice Hornblower and the Fugitive Slave Law." *Rutgers Law Journal* 23, 4 (1992): 753–87.

Fishman, George. "Taking a Stand for Freedom in Revolutionary New Jersey: Prime's Petition of 1786." *Science and Society* 56, 3 (Fall 1992): 353–56.

Fogel, Robert, and Stanley Engerman. "Philanthropy at Bargain Prices: Notes on the Economics of Gradual Emancipation." *Journal of Legal Studies* 3, 2 (June 1974): 377–401.

Foner, Eric. "Free Labor and Political Ideology." In Melvyn Stokes and Stephen Conway, eds., *The Market Revolution in America: Social, Political, and Religious Expressions, 1800–1880*. Charlottesville: University of Virginia Press, 1996, 99–123.

Fowler, David. "These Were Troublesome Times Indeed": Social and Economic Conditions in Revolutionary New Jersey." In Barbara Mitnick, ed., *New Jersey in the American Revolution*. New Brunswick, N.J.: Rutgers University Press, 2005.

Foy, Charles. "Eighteenth-Century Prize Negroes: From Britain to America." *Slavery and Abolition* 31, 3 (September 2010): 379–93.

———. "Seeking Freedom in the Atlantic World, 1714–1783." *Early American Studies: An Interdisciplinary Journal* 4, 1 (Spring 2006): 46–77.

Freeman, Joanne. "Corruption and Compromise in the Election of 1800: The Process of Politics on the National Stage." In James Horn, Jan Lewis, and Peter Onuf, eds., *The Revolution of 1800: Democracy, Race, and the New Republic*. Charlottesville: University of Virginia Press, 2002.

Genealogical and Memorial History of the State of New Jersey. Vol. 4. New York, 1919.

Gigantino, James, II. "The Flexibility of Freedom: Slavery and Servitude in Early Ohio." *Ohio History* 119 (2012): 89–100.

———. "Trading in Jersey Souls: New Jersey and the Interstate Slave Trade." *Pennsylvania History: A Journal of Mid-Atlantic Studies* 77, 3 (Summer 2010): 281–302.

Gough, Robert. "Black Men and the Early New Jersey Militia." *New Jersey History* 88, 4 (December 1970): 227–38.

Grigg, John. "'Ye relief of ye poor of sd towne': Poverty and Localism in Eighteenth-Century New Jersey." *New Jersey History* 125, 2 (2010): 23–35.

Groth, Michael. "Slaveholders and Manumission in Dutchess County, New York." *New York History* 78, 1 (January 1997): 33–50.

Grubb, Farley. "The Auction of Redemptioner Servants, Philadelphia, 1771–1804: An Economic Analysis." *Journal of Economic History* 48, 3 (September 1988): 583–603.

———. "The Disappearance of Organized Markets for European Immigrant Servants in the United States: Five Popular Explanations Reexamined." *Social Science History* 18, 1 (Spring 1994): 1–30.

———. "Immigrant Servant Labor: Their Occupational and Geographic Distribution in the Late Eighteenth Century Mid-Atlantic Economy." *Social Science History* 9. 3 (Fall 1985): 249–76.

Hack, Timothy. "Janus-Faced: Post-Revolutionary Slavery in East and West Jersey, 1784–1804." *New Jersey History* 127, 1 (2012).

Helo, Ari, and Peter Onuf. "Jefferson, Morality and the Problem of Slavery." *William and Mary Quarterly* 60, 3 (July 2003): 583–614.

Henretta, James. "Families and Farms: Mentalite in Pre-Industrial America." *William and Mary Quarterly* 35, 1 (January 1978): 3–32.

Herndon, Ruth Wallis. "'Proper Magistrates and Masters': Binding Out Poor Children in Southern New England, 1720–1820." In Ruth Wallis Herndon and John Murray, eds., *Children Bound to Labor: The Pauper Apprentice System in Early America*. Ithaca, N.Y.: Cornell University Press, 2009.

Herndon, Ruth Wallis, and John Murray. "A Proper and Instructive Education: Raising Children in Pauper Apprenticeship." In Ruth Wallis Herndon and John Murray, eds., *Children Bound to Labor: The Pauper Apprentice System in Early America*. Ithaca, N.Y.: Cornell University Press, 2009.

Hindle, Steve, and Ruth Wallis Herndon. "Recreating Proper Families in England and North America: Pauper Apprenticeship in Transatlantic Context." In Ruth Wallis Herndon and John Murray, eds., *Children Bound to Labor: The Pauper Apprentice System in Early America*. Ithaca, N.Y.: Cornell University Press, 2009.

Honeyman, A. Van Doren, ed., "The Revolutionary War Record of Samuel Sutphen, Slave." *Somerset County Historical Quarterly* 3 (1914): 186–90.

Horton, Lois. "From Class to Race in Early America: Northern Post-Emancipation Racial Recon-struction." *Journal of the Early Republic* 19, 4 (Winter 1999): 629–50.

Hovet, Theodore. "Mrs. Thomas C. Upham's 'Happy Phebe': A Feminine Source of Uncle Tom." *American Literature* 51, 2 (May 1979): 267–70.

Johnson, Walter. "The Pedestal and the Veil: Rethinking the Capitalism/Slavery Question." *Journal of the Early Republic* 24, 2 (Summer 2004): 299–308.

Jones, Martha. "Time, Space, and Jurisdiction in Atlantic World Slavery: The Volunbrun House-hold in Gradual Emancipation New York." *Law and History Review* 29, 4 (November 2011): 1031–1060.

Klinghoffer, Judith Apter, and Lois Elkis. "The Petticoat Electors:" Women's Suffrage in New Jersey, 1776–1807." *Journal of the Early Republic* 12, 2 (Summer 1992): 159–93.

Kolchin, Peter. "Variations of Slavery in the Atlantic World." *William and Mary Quarterly* 59, 3 (July 2002): 551–54.

Kozel, Susan. "Testing 'Liberty' in New Jersey, 1775–1793: The Intersection of Slavery and Select Manumission Supreme Court Cases." *New Jersey History* 127, 1 (2012).

Kulikoff, Allan. "The Transition to Capitalism in Rural America." *William and Mary Quarterly* 46, 1 (January 1989): 120–44.

Lambert, Robert. "The Confiscation of Loyalist Property in Georgia, 1782–1786." *William and Mary Quarterly* 20, 1 (January 1963): 80–94.

Lamoreaux, Naomi. "Rethinking the Transition to Capitalism in the Early American Northeast." *Journal of American History* 90, 2 (September 2003): 437–61.

Lewis, Jan. "Rethinking Women's Suffrage in New Jersey, 1776–1807." *Rutgers Law Review* 63, 3 (Spring 2011): 1017–35.

Lobdell, Jared C., ed. "The Revolutionary War Journal of Sergeant Thomas McCarty." *Proceedings of the New Jersey Historical Society* 82 (1964).

Malone, Christopher. "Rethinking the End of Black Voting Rights in Antebellum Pennsylvania." *Pennsylvania History* 72, 4 (October 2005): 466–504.

McCoy, Michael. "Forgetting Freedom: White Anxiety, Black Presence, and Gradual Abolition in Cumberland County, Pennsylvania, 1780–1838." *Pennsylvania Magazine of History and Biography* 136, 2 (April 2012): 141–70.

Melish, Joanne Pope. "The Manumission of Nab." *Rhode Island History* 68, 1 (Winter/Spring 2010): 36–41.

———. "The Racial Vernacular: Contesting the Black/White Binary in Nineteenth Century Rhode Island." In James Campbell, Matthew Pratt Guterl, and Robert Lee, eds., *Race, Nation and Empire in American History*. Chapel Hill: University of North Carolina Press, 2007.

Menschel, David. "Abolition Without Deliverance: The Law of Connecticut Slavery 1784–1848." *Yale Law Journal* 111, 1 (September 2001): 183–222.

Mercantini, Jonathan. "John and Susan Kean and the Culture of Slavery in the New Nation." *New Jersey History* 127, 1 (2012).

Merrill, Michael. "Cash Is Good to Eat: Self-Sufficiency and Exchange in the Rural Economy of the United States." *Radical History Review* 3 (Fall 1976): 42–71.

Minardi, Margot. "Freedom in the Archives: The Pension Case of Primus Hall." In Peter Benes, ed., *Slavery and Antislavery in New England*. Boston: Dublin Seminar for New England Folk-life, 2003.

Monaghan, E. Jennifer. "Reading for the Enslaved, Writing for the Free: Reflections on Liberty and Literacy." *Proceedings of the American Antiquarian Society* 108, 2 (October 1998): 309–41.

Morgan, Edmund. "Slavery and Freedom: The American Paradox." *Journal of American History* 59, 1 (June 1972): 5–29.

Moss, Simon. "The Persistence of Slavery and Involuntary Servitude in a Free State." *Journal of Negro History* 35, 3 (1950): 289–314.

Murrin, Mary. "New Jersey and the Two Constitutions." In Patrick Conley and John Kaminski, eds., *The Constitution and the States: The Role of the Original Thirteen in the Framing and Adoption of the Federal Constitution*. Madison, Wis.: Madison House, 1988.

Oakes, James. "The Compromising Expedient: Justifying a Proslavery Constitution." *Cardozo Law Review* 17 (1995–96): 2023–56.

Okoye, F. Nwabueze. "Chattel Slavery as the Nightmare of the American Revolutionaries." *William and Mary Quarterly* 37, 1 (January 1980): 5–28.

Pasley, Jeffrey. "1800 as a Revolution in Political Culture: Newspapers, Celebrations, Voting, and Democratization in the Early Republic." In James Horn, Jan Lewis, and Peter Onuf, eds., *The Revolution of 1800: Democracy, Race, and the New Republic*. Charlottesville: University of Virginia Press, 2002.

Pingeon, Francis. "An Abominable Business: The New Jersey Slave Trade, 1818." *New Jersey History* 109, 3–4 (February 1991): 14–35.

Quincy, Eliza Susan. *Basking Ridge in Revolutionary Days*. Excerpt. *Somerset County Historical Quarterly* (1960): 7–8.

Rael, Patrick. "The Long Death of Slavery." In Ira Berlin and Leslie Harris, eds., *Slavery in New York*. New York: New Press, 2005.

Richards, Michael. "Patriots and Plunderers: Confiscation of Loyalist Lands in New Jersey." *New Jersey History* 86, 1 (February 1968): 14–28.

Rockman, Seth. "The Unfree Origins of American Capitalism." In Cathy Matson, ed., *The Economy of Early America: Historical Perspectives and New Directions*. University Park: Pennsylvania State University Press, 2006.

Roth, Sarah. "The Politics of the Page: Black Disfranchisement and the Image of the Savage Slave." *Pennsylvania Magazine of History and Biography* 134, 3 (July 2010): 209–33.

Rothenberg, Winifred B. "The Market and Massachusetts Farmers, 1750–1855." *Journal of Economic History* 41, 2 (June 1981): 283–314.

Rothman, Josh. "The Hazards of the Flush Times: Gambling, Mob Violence, and the Anxieties of the Market Revolution." *Journal of American History* 95, 3 (December 2008): 651–77.

Sassi, Jonathan. "Africans in the Quaker Image: Anthony Benezet, African Travel Narratives, and Revolutionary-Era Antislavery." *Journal of Early Modern History* 10, 1–2 (2006): 95–130.

———. "With a Little Help from the Friends: The Quaker and Tactical Contexts of Anthony Benezet's Abolitionist Publishing." *Pennsylvania Magazine of History & Biography* 135, 1 (January 2011): 33–71.

Schleicher, William, and Susan Winter. "Patriot and Slave: The Samuel Sutphen Story." *New Jersey Heritage* 1, 1 (2002): 30–43.

Seifman, Eli. "The United Colonization Societies of New York and Pennsylvania and the Establishment of the African Colony of Bassa Cove." *Pennsylvania History: A Journal of Mid-Atlantic Studies* 35, 1 (January 1968): 23–44.

Sinha, Manisha. "To 'cast just obliquy' on Oppressors: Black Radicalism in the Age of Revolution." *William and Mary Quarterly* 64, 1 (January 2007): 149–60.

Smith, Anne Bustill. "The Bustill Family." *Journal of Negro History* 10, 4 (October 1925): 638–44.

Smith, Billy. "Runaway Slaves in the Mid-Atlantic Region during the Revolutionary Era." In Ronald Hoffman and Peter Albert, eds., *The Transforming Hand of Revolution: Reconsidering the American Revolution as a Social Movement.* Charlottesville: University of Virginia Press, 1995.

Smith, Eric Ledell. "Rescuing African American Kidnapping Victims in Philadelphia as Documented in the Joseph Watson Papers at the Historical Society of Pennsylvania." *Pennsylvania Magazine of History and Biography* 129, 3 (July 2005): 317–45.

Soderlund, Jean. "The Delaware Indians and Poverty in Colonial New Jersey." In Billy Smith, ed., *Down and Out in Early America.* University Park: Pennsylvania State University Press, 2004.

Stewart, James Brewer. "Modernizing Difference: The Political Meaning of Color in the Free States, 1776–1840." *Journal of the Early Republic* 19, 4 (Winter 1999): 691–712.

Stratford, Dorothy. "Docket of Jacob Van Noorstrand." *Genealogical Magazine of New Jersey* 43 (1968): 58–67.

Tomek, Beverly. "Seeking 'An Immutable Pledge from the Slave Holding States': The Pennsylvania Abolition Society and Black Resettlement." *Pennsylvania History* 75, 1 (Winter 2008): 26–53.

Turner, Edmund Raymond. "Women's Suffrage in New Jersey, 1790–1807." *Smith College Studies in History* 1, 4 (1916).

Wacker, Peter. "Patterns and Problems in the Historical Geography of the Afro-American Population of New Jersey, 1726–1860." In Ralph Ehrenberg, ed., *Pattern and Process: Research in Historical Geography.* Washington, D.C.: Howard University Press, 1975.

White, Shane. "Impious Prayers: Elite and Popular Attitudes Towards Blacks and Slavery in the Middle-Atlantic States, 1783–1810." *New York History* 67, 3 (July 1986): 260–83.

———. "It Was a Proud Day: African American Festivals and Parades in the North, 1741–1834." *Journal of American History* 81, 1 (June 1994): 13–50.

———. *Somewhat More Independent: The End of Slavery in New York City, 1770–1810.* Athens: University of Georgia Press, 1991.

Winch, Julie. "Philadelphia and the other Underground Railroad." *Pennsylvania Magazine of History and Biography* 111, 1 (January 1987): 3–25.

Wright, Giles. "Moving Toward Breaking the Chains: Black New Jerseyans and the American Revolution." In Barbara Mitnick, ed., *New Jersey in the American Revolution.* New Brunswick, N.J.: Rutgers University Press, 2005.

Wright, Marion Thompson. "New Jersey Laws and the Negro." *Journal of Negro History* 28, 2 (April 1943): 156–99.

Zilversmit, Arthur. "Liberty and Property: New Jersey and the Abolition of Slavery." *New Jersey History* 88, 4 (December 1970): 215–26.

THESES, DISSERTATIONS, AND CONFERENCE PAPERS

Appleby, Theodore. "Opinions on Slavery in Burlington County as Reflected in the New Jersey Mirror and Burlington County Advertiser, 1830–1861." MA Thesis, Rutgers University, 1940.

Caputo, Michael. "New Jersey's Role in the African Colonization Movement." MA Thesis, Montclair State College, 1965.

Cooley, Henry. "A Study of Slavery in New Jersey." PhD Dissertation, Johns Hopkins University, 1896.

Davis, Philip Curtis. "The Persistence of Partisan Alignment: Issues, Leaders, and Votes in New Jersey, 1840–1860." PhD Dissertation, Washington University, 1978.

Fee, Walter. "The Transition from Aristocracy to Democracy in New Jersey, 1789–1829." PhD Dissertation, Columbia University, 1933.

Freeman, Rhonda. "The Free Negro in New York City in the Era Before the Civil War." PhD Dissertation, Columbia University, 1966.

Hillstrom, David. "New Jersey and the Abolition Movement." BA Thesis, Princeton University, 1965.

Kozel, Susan. "Digging on Behalf of the 'Natural Right to Liberty': One Quaker's Persistent Actions to Support Manumissions in New Jersey, 1790–1799." Conference Paper, Society of Historians of the Early American Republic, July 15, 2011.

Kruger, Vivienne. "Born to Run: The Slave Family in Early New York, 1627–1827." PhD Dissertation, Columbia University, 1985.

Levine, Michael. "The Transformation of a Radical Whig Under Republican Government: William Livingston, Governor of New Jersey, 1776–1790." PhD Dissertation, Rutgers University, 1975.

Melish, Joanne Pope. "White Workers, Black Neighborhoods: Reconsidering Early America." Conference Paper, Society of Historians of the Early American Republic, July 14, 2011.

McTeigue, Francis. "The Conditions Under Which Slaves Lived in New Jersey." MA Thesis, Seton Hall University, 1965.

Scott, Austin. "The African Association of New Brunswick." Paper read before New Brunswick Historical Society, 1906.

INDEX

Note: Page numbers in italics represent images.

abandonment clause (1804 gradual abolition law), 91, 106–10
Abbett, Leon, 247
Abeel, David, 102
Abeel, John Nelson, 70
abolition movement: black abolitionists, 225–26; eighteenth-century Quakers, 13–14, 18–26, 29–30, 33–34, 65, 71–78; Revolutionary age, 18–63, 250. *See also* gradual abolition and gradualist philosophy; Quakers (Society of Friends); radical abolition movement
abolition/abolitionists, definitions of, 5
Ackerman, Abraham, 235
Ackerman, John, 61
Act for the Gradual Abolition of Slavery (Jersey's 1804 gradual abolition law), 3, 5, 63, 65, 92–94, 97, 106–10, 254n14; abandonment clause, 91, 106–10; compensation for property rights, 91–92, 97–98; and Jeffersonian Republicans, 92–94; and slaves for a term, 7, 94, 254–55n17
Adams, John, 37, 48, 54–55
Adams, Samson, 76–77
Adams, Samuel, 36–37
Adrain, Garnett, 222–23, 224
African Association of New Brunswick, 127–28, 184–85, 236
African Burial Ground (New York City), 3
African Methodist Church (Newark), 196
African Methodist Episcopal (AME) Churches, 202, 203, 207, 216
African Presbyterian Church (Newark), 202–3, 204
African Repository and Colonial Journal, 177, 189

African School at Parsippany, 128, 183–85
African Society of Newark, 184
African Zion Church (New York), 175–76
agency, African American, 10–11. *See also* negotiated freedoms
Agricultural and Mechanic Association of Pennsylvania and New Jersey, 205
Alexander, Elizabeth, *127*
Alexandria Gazette, 164
Alford, James, 83
Alien and Sedition Acts, 87
Allen, Richard, 203
Allen, William, 153
Allinson, Samuel, 21–25, 27, 34, 75, 116
Allinson, William, 75, 116
American Colonization Society (ACS), 5, 174–93, 205. *See also* colonization movement in New Jersey
American Convention for Promoting the Abolition of Slavery, 119, 181
Amistad Commissions, 3
Amosen, Nero, 197
Anderson, Benjamin, 113
Anderson, Isaac, 78
Anderson, James, 80
Andover Iron Works (Amwell), 69
Andrews, Bessie Ayres, 216, 221
antebellum New Jersey (1830s–1840s), 213–39; alignment with southern understandings of slavery, 214–15, 222–25, 237, 238–39, 302n28; anti-abolition sentiment, 228–30; "apprentices for life," 9, 215, 234–36, 237–38; Boonton abolitionists, 228, 229; debates over sinfulness of slavery, 236–37; the 1836 ruling ending prima facie slavery, 8, 195, 199–200, 214, 220; the 1844 state Constitution, 230, 231;

Brown, David Paul, 191
Brown, Jacob, 75
Brown, James, 158
Brown, Moses, 156
Browning, Abraham, 253n2
Bryant, Louisa, 221
Burgin, Enoch, 135
Burke, Thomas, 49
Burlington County, New Jersey: abolitionism, 71, 74, 76, 119–20, 140; free blacks in, 71; and Jersey role in Missouri Crisis, 162; manumissions, 74, *131*, *134*; Quakers, 19–24, 75–76, 78, 90, 120
Burlington County Society for Promoting the Abolition of Slavery, 119–20, 140
Burlington School Society for the Free Instruction of the Black People, 76
Burros, Hannah, 76
businesses, black-owned, 76–77, 196–97, 210
Bustill, Cyrus, 76–77, 118
Butler, Andrew, 224

Calhoun, John C., 163
Camden Democratic Association, 246
Campbell, William, 48
Canfield, Jabez, 129–30
Canfield, Samuel, 137
Cannon, Patty, 168, 169
Cannon-Johnson kidnapping syndicate, 168–69
capitalism and bound labor/slavery, 132–33
Carleton, Guy, 43–44, 57–58
Carolina Quakers, 120
Carr, Jane, 153
Carteret, George, 13
Case, Thomas, 56
Cater, Edward, 59–60
Catherine (slave of John Hagaman), 1, 11, 235, 249–50
Catherine Market (New York City), 126
Ceasar, John, 56
Centinel of Freedom (Newark newspaper), 123, 163, 165, 204
Chamberlain, Joshua Lawrence, 153
Chandler, Peter, 95, 114–15
Chatham Township Overseers of the Poor, 137
Chester Pennsylvania Monthly Meeting, 20
Chesterfield Quakers, 22–23, 24, 25

children: of apprentices for life, 235–36; child labor and slaves for a term, 104; kidnappings and interstate movement, 149, 168; of slaves for a term, 112; slaves for a term separated from their manumitted parents, 102–3, 112–14, 152. *See also* slaves for a term
Christian Advocate, 248
Church, Angelica, 47
churches, black, 201–3, 204–5
churches, white, 200–203; baptisms in, 128; early abolition period, 128–29; marriages between free blacks and slaves, 128–29; segregated/integrated, 201, 203; slaveholding members after 1846, 236–37. *See also* Presbyterian churches of New Jersey; religious commitments to abolition
Cisco, Francis, 122
Civil War and the end of slavery in New Jersey, 241–48, 250; misperceptions of the state's slave past, 240–41, *242*, 248; postwar, 248; Thirteenth Amendment debates, 246–48, 250; wartime partisan politics and legislative debates, 243–48
Clark, Abraham, 34–36, 42
Clark, Daniel, 156–57
Clark, Joseph, 39
Clay, Henry, 186
Clinton, Henry, 49
Clinton Memorial African Methodist Episcopal Zion Church (Newark), 202
Coates, Samuel, 81
Cochran, Richard, 60
Coe, Benjamin, 197
Coe, Sayers and Sarah, 111
Colden, Cadwalader David, 166–67
Coleman, Samuel, 119
Collins, Elizabeth, 75
Collins, Isaac, 77
colonial New Jersey, 11–17; and African slave trade, 16; Caribbean Barbadian planters and their slaves, 13–15; Dutch New Netherland, 11–13; East and West Jersey, 13–14, 26; first African slaves, 11–12; free black neighborhoods, 12; overlapping land grants and land riots, 13; plantation generation, 14–17; proprietary period (charter generation), 13–14; slave codes and restrictions, 14–17; slave revolts, 16; slaves' negotiated freedoms, 16. *See also* Quakers (Society of Friends)

222–25, 240, 243; Thirteenth Amendment
debates, 246–48
Denman family of Elizabethtown, 105
The Devil or the New Jersey Dance (1797
pamphlet), 69–70
Dickerson, Silas, 88, 93
Dill, Isaiah, 217
Dillwyn, William, 21, 24, 76, 83, 104, 125
domestic servants, 69, 153, 198–99, 232, 236
Donahower (slave catcher), 221
Dorrance, Samuel, 228
Doughty, Samuel, 179, 186
Douglass, Frederick, 202
Dow, William, 42
Drake, Jinlay, 40
Draper, William, 49
Dred Scott decision (1857), 176
Dubois, Silvia, 126–27, 127, 200
Dunmore, Lord: on black enlistment, 53, 54;
Proclamation (1775), 31, 40, 41, 49, 51, 53
Dunn, Seth, 108–9
Duryea, John, 56
Duryee, William Rankin, 222
Dutch New Netherland, 11–13
Dutch Reformed Churches, 12, 201
Dutch West India Company, 12
Duyree, Jacob, 45
Dwight, Theodore, 92

early abolition period New Jersey (1804–
1830), 6–8, 95–115, 116–48, 149–73,
174–93; abandonment of the cause by
abolitionists and Quakers, 117–22; bobalition broadsides, 142–43, 144, 175; bound
laborers' roles in capitalist economy/labor
market, 132–33; citizenship and dependency in the new nation, 139–48;
colonization movement, 174–93; cottager
system, 135; criminal assaults on individual masters and property, 124–25; the
1804 gradual abolition law, 3, 5, 63, 65,
92–94, 97, 106–10, 254n14; the 1820 slave
code, 150, 163, 173, 241; free black
communities, 110–11, 118, 122–25,
126–29; fugitive slave runaways, 122–23,
129; gradations of slavery and new racial
categories, 96, 110–12, 118, 138–39,
276n5; gradualist rhetoric and paternalism, 97–98, 103–4, 118, 136, 140–42;
interstate movement of slaves, 7, 149–73;

manumission negotiations, 117, 125–26,
129–32, 133–35, 148; manumission
records, 117, 131, 131–35, 134, 280n3;
Missouri Controversy and Jersey anti-
expansionism, 7, 150, 161–63, 173, 224;
negotiations between slaves and masters,
116–17, 122–32, 148; new flexibility of the
slavery institution, 117, 125–29, 148; poor
laws and poor relief for ex-slaves, 135–39;
racial tensions and white fears of violence,
123–25; rhetoric of black inferiority,
142–43, 175–76, 190–91, 193; slaves for a
term, 96–115, 105, 151–52, 158, 160–61,
167, 169, 170–71, 173, 276n5; voting rights
and citizenship, 143–48. *See also* colonization movement in New Jersey; interstate
movement of Jersey slaves
Earnest, Jack, 197
East Jersey: ages of slaves at manumission,
131; and the 1846 legislative debate over
abolition, 232; growth of slave communities (1790s), 84; immigration of
Caribbean Barbadian planters and their
slaves, 13–14; and Jersey Jeffersonian
Republicans' efforts to end slavery, 90–91;
proprietary period (charter generation),
13–14, 26; and radical abolition
movement, 226; Revolutionary War and
economic damage, 43; slavery's strength
in, 26, 30, 65, 67–68, 71, 74–75, 82. See
also *names of individual counties*
economic interests of slaveowners: and early
American capitalism, 132–33; economic
competition from free blacks, 208, 209;
Quaker slaveholders, 22–23; Revolutionary War, 33, 34, 38–46, 49–51, 66–67.
See also interstate movement of Jersey
slaves; property rights; slaves for a term
Edgar, Thomas, 41
Edmundson, William, 19–20
education, black: and abolitionist pater-
nalism/racism, 81, 92, 98, 103–4, 140–42;
antebellum period (1830s), 203–5; black-
controlled schools, 203–5; and colonization movement, 180–81, 183–85;
integrated/segregated schools, 141; lack of
state support/funding, 203–4; New Jersey
Abolition Society, 81, 92, 98, 103; private
benevolent association schools, 141–42;
Quakers, 23–24, 74, 75–76, 140–41;

ACKNOWLEDGMENTS

The completion of this volume has been years in the making and owes thanks to dozens upon dozens of people who have helped it and me along the way. Allan Kulikoff has been attached (some would probably say saddled) with this project for as long as I have. He read each chapter far too many times than he probably needed to and has served as a gracious and wise guide to me for almost a decade now. I can never begin to repay the debt I owe him. Likewise, my thanks to John Inscoe, Tim Cleaveland, Stephen Mihm, Kathleen Clark, Jim Cobb, and Bill Stueck who all helped this project (and me) along in its early stages in countless and important ways. My colleagues both in History and African & African American Studies at Arkansas have similarly provided needed encouragement and support, especially Beth Schweiger, my fellow early American historian, who critically read drafts of several chapters, and Calvin White, Jr. who has served as colleague, advisor, and I am proud to say, friend.

Like all historians, I am indebted to my sources and those who have been invaluable in helping me find them. The staffs at the New Jersey State Archives, Historical Society of Pennsylvania, Library Company of Philadelphia, New Jersey Historical Society (especially Maureen O'Rourke and James Amemasor), Swarthmore Friends Historical Library (especially Chris Densmore), and the William Clements Library were always ready and willing to answer questions, point me in new directions, and offer a smile after a hard day at the microfilm reader; my thanks to all of them.

Getting to the twenty-odd archives I worked at for this project was, of course, not cheap. I could not have completed this book without the many organizations that believed in it enough to fund me. Research grants and fellowships from the University of Georgia help me get this project started, while research and travel grants and a summer research stipend from the University of Arkansas History Department and the J. William Fulbright

College of Arts & Sciences made final research and revisions possible. Likewise, a one course teaching release and a flexible teaching schedule from the History Department provided time to digest those sources. Three grants from the New Jersey Historical Commission, a division of the Department of State, also tremendously helped fund this project. The Commission has been an early and active supporter of my work, offering a Samuel Smith Fellowship, a research grant to help me complete the final phase of research, and a book subvention grant that helped make this final version possible. I thank the people of New Jersey for this support.

In addition, fellowships from the David Library of the American Revolution, the Library Company of Philadelphia and Historical Society of Pennsylvania, the William Clements Library at the University of Michigan, and an Albert Beveridge Grant for Research in the History of the Western Hemisphere from the American Historical Association greatly assisted the book's completion. Finally, a fair amount of my early research was self-supported either with generous in-kind housing and food during research trips from my parents or through my own work as a mystery shopper. By mystery shopping everything from McDonalds' to Ruth's Chris to Verizon, I scraped together enough money to pay my train fare each morning to the archives in the days when grants were not plentiful. To those who were adversely affected by one of my reports, my sincere apologies.

Dozens have read all or parts of this manuscript and many more have heard me discuss slavery in New Jersey at various academic conferences. My thanks to everyone who has offered valuable insights and comments on my work. They truly made it stronger. I would be remiss if I did not thank Bob Lockhart at the University of Pennsylvania Press who took an early interest in this project and offered excellent suggestions on how to craft this final version. Likewise, Susan O'Donovan and the other anonymous reviewer for the Press gave meaty criticisms that zeroed in on exactly how I needed to refine and reorganize. Perhaps my most critical critics were those who surrounded me at Georgia. Jason Manthorne, Rhiannon Evangelista, Sam Crowie, Steve Nash, Min Song, La Shonda Mims, Jenny Schwartzberg, Kathi Nehls, John Paul Hill, Zac Smith, and Jennifer & Dori Wunn all made my time in Athens more rewarding. I also thank Caree Banton, Liang Cai, Bill and Doris Davis, Jarrett Drake, Justin Fanslau, Ben Fagan, Robert Finley, Timothy Hack, Louise Hancox, Colin Holloway, Kelly Kennington, Sarah Levine-Gronningsater, Kelly Ann Mahon, Lucia McMahon, Barton Myers, Michael Pierce, Paul Polgar, Charles Robinson,

Claudio Saunt, Mitchell Smith, Steve Smith, Dan Sutherland, Jeannie Whayne, and Randall Woods who all offered advice, friendship, or research assistance during the completion of this project. I also thank Penn State University Press and Kent State University Press who allowed me to reproduce parts of chapters that I previously published with them as articles.

Finally, the debt I owe my family goes beyond what I can describe here. My sister, Diane, has been with me literally from day one and has provided support, advice, and love through these past thirty-one years. She, along with my brother-in-law Joseph, gave me more than my fair share of home-cooked meals and free lodging, while my three nephews, John, Anthony, and Dominic continue to give me numerous opportunities to be the fun uncle and offer never ending love. Diane read and commented on this entire manuscript, which not only challenged me to be a better writer and historian each time she used her red pen, but showed me beyond a shadow of a doubt that she is the smarter sibling.

I never thought that by the time I finished this book I would find a partner that I would want to share everything with; I am glad I was wrong. Stephanie Heath survived her introduction to life with a historian by constantly teaching me about the joys of life outside of the office. She has challenged me to be a better person and helped me grow in ways I never thought were possible a short time ago. I cannot but help looking forward to every day we will spend together. As we embark on our new life I know I am both a better historian and better man for being with her.

Above all, my parents, Lois and Jim Gigantino, have made me who I am today. They are without a doubt the best set of cheerleaders, mentors, and friends anyone could have ever asked for. They have encouraged my intellectual curiosity, challenged me to think about the world around me, and taught me the importance of family. They have shown me endless encouragement, devotion, generosity, and love. It is to them that I dedicate this book, for without them, nothing in my life would have been possible.